MEDIAMERICA

Form, Content, and Consequence
of Mass Communication

Edward Jay Whetmore
University of San Francisco

Wadsworth Publishing Company, Inc.
Belmont, California

Communications Editor: Rebecca Hayden
Production Editor: Anne Kelly
Designer: Nancy Benedict
Copy Editor: Carol Reitz
Cover Illustration: Catherine Bleck
Part Opening Illustrations: Catherine Bleck
Time Line Illustrations: Jim M'Guinness

Printed in the United States of America
1 2 3 4 5 6 7 8 9 10—83 82 81 80 79

Library of Congress Cataloging in Publication Data

Whetmore, Edward Jay.
    Mediamerica: form, content, and consequence of mass communication.

    Includes bibliographical references and index.
    1. Mass media—United States—History. 2. Mass media—Social aspects—United States. I. Title.
HN90.M3W48   301.16'1   78-21590
ISBN 0-534-00604-3

This book is for Phyllis JoAnn Armstrong (1923–1970), who was an amazing lady and continues to be a guiding spirit in my life.

Preface

A trip to the library will show you that there have been thousands of books written about media. Each medium has been covered in depth, so why another mass media book?

Mediamerica has grown out of some frustrations I've had as a teacher. I have looked for a text that communicates to students some of the excitement I've experienced in my involvement with mass media—a text that goes beyond facts and figures to the heart and soul of the mass communication process.

You will find names, places, and statistics here, but I think history is most relevant when it relates to what is happening now. In short, my emphasis in this text is on what *is* happening as well as what *has* happened. We will explore the *whys* as well as the *whats*. Why did rock music rise to dominate popular music? Why has the Super Bowl come to be the most popular sporting event? All *mediated* phenomena offer clues about ourselves and our culture.

Mediamerica concentrates on what *is* and not what *should be*. Look at all the books behind me in the picture on the next page. Every one of them is about mass media, yet when I started to write about the country's largest-selling weekly tabloid, I could not find one word about it in any of them! Admittedly, the *National Enquirer* is not exactly the *New York Times*, but it does sell more than four million copies every week. Nor could I find anything on *Roots*, the TV show viewed by 125 million Americans; or Don

Imus, formerly New York's most popular deejay; or *Jaws*, one of the most popular films ever made. Perhaps some of these things are too recent to appear in most books, but many media textbook authors have made it clear they prefer not to acknowledge the existence of the *National Enquirer*, TV commercials, and Top-40 radio. But they *do* exist, and for most of us, they are a large part of what mass media are all about.

So we'll deal with *Star Trek*, rock music, and *Mad* magazine along with more traditional topics, because they all play an important part in our mass communication system. You may not be completely happy with the content of mass media; none of us is. But if you're going to try to change it, first you must examine *what* it is and *why* it is.

When I was in college, my teachers seemed to have largely negative opinions about mass media. We read texts and listened to lectures about how bad newspapers, magazines, radio, and especially television were. There are many problems with mass media, but I just cannot accept this antimedia perspective. Perhaps I'm too optimistic. I find the form and content of mass media fascinating, but fascination need not mean bias. I don't think I am handicapped in helping you to develop your critical perspective as a media consumer.

During the last ten years, I have worked professionally as a disc jockey, and also in advertising, public relations, and television.

I've included a few of these personal media experiences here. This is a textbook, not a biography, but I hope my own experiences as a producer and consumer of mass information will help you understand your own experiences. So overwhelming are the forces of mass communication that we are all involved, whether we like it or not.

I hope to hear from you and your instructors about your reactions to the book. I'll be glad to respond to any questions or comments you may have.

Acknowledgments

In a project of this size it is virtually impossible to thank everyone who has helped, but there are several I especially want to acknowledge. More than anyone else *Mediamerica* owes its existence to Rebecca Hayden, Communications Editor at Wadsworth. She was always there to offer gentle, thoughtful, and constructive criticism when it was needed, and I appreciate it. Jack Rochester of Wadsworth was especially helpful in getting the book started. Thanks also to Autumn Stanley and John Daniel for editorial input above and beyond the call of duty.

About two dozen reviewers have been involved at various stages. I especially want to single out five whose tough criticism or encouragement, or both, made me go extra miles in trying to make this the best book it could be: John Jay Black, Utah State University; Ben Cunningham, California State University, Long Beach; Marshall Fishwick, Virginia Polytechnic Institute and State University; William R. Payden, Los Angeles Valley College; and John L. Wright, Education Department, Greenfield Village and Henry Ford Museum.

Without secretarial help I would still be typing chapter one. My thanks to Laura Yangangahara, Ruth Ann Suzuki, and Mara Lane. Finally, a special thanks to the dozens of students who have read chapters and offered their input. I am continually and pleasantly surprised by their enthusiasm for what I have tried to do with *Mediamerica.*

Edd Whetmore

Contents

PART THREE
The Phenomena of Mass Communication   227

MEDIAMERICA

PART ONE
Print: The Gutenberg Gallery

From the Holy Bible to the *Playboy* interview, print media have supplied us with billions of words in the last 600 years. Print media are covered first here because they came first and are still the most revered of all media.

Media analysts often speculate about what might have happened had Gutenberg invented television instead of movable type. Would there still have been wars, famines, kings and queens, and Elvis Presley? No one really knows, but most agree that the print media have exerted a tremendous influence on our social and cultural development.

In this part, I have devoted one chapter each to books and magazines and two chapters to newspapers. This is not to say that any one medium is more important than another. But, for many, newspapers seem to be a source of comparison, the "yardstick"

for all mass media. Even defining what constitutes a newspaper can be troublesome. Is *Rolling Stone* a newspaper or a magazine? Actually *Rolling Stone*, the *National Enquirer*, and others like them are *tabloids*, which do not necessarily belong to either camp. I have included tabloids with newspapers for reasons of *form* rather than *content*. Their format is borrowed from successful daily newspapers like the *New York Daily News*.

The most frustrating thing about writing a general text is space limitation. I would like to have devoted a dozen chapters to each medium, but of course that is not practical. I hope that the queries, concepts, and source material at the end of each chapter will lead you to the further exploration so necessary to developing a real understanding of each medium.

1
Welcome to Mediamerica

**There's something happening here
What it is ain't exactly clear . . .
I think it's time to stop/Hey what's that sound
Everybody look what's going down . . . —Stephen Stills**

The Birth of Mass Communication

In 1436, Johann Gutenberg was broke, but the inventor was not used to asking for handouts. He had moved from his native Mainz to Strasbourg with servants and plenty of capital. His sudden need for funds had sprung from a desire to develop what he called a "secret art."

Before long, he was able to find several partners who were interested in this mysterious new art. Among them was Andreas Dritzehen, who mortgaged his property and borrowed on his inheritance to invest in Gutenberg's idea. He had boasted to a friend that the project "will not fail us, before a year is passed we shall have our capital again." Such candor was rare among the investors in Gutenberg's project. When asked about their investment, they avoided mentioning printing specifically, instead speaking vaguely of "the work" or "the adventure and art."

Historians now know that the art involved a set of "molds" that could be arranged and rearranged to print virtually any message. Gutenberg's secret was a new kind of printing press using movable type, which would greatly expand the dissemination of the printed word (see 1.1). No longer would printers have to carve a new set of molds for each page.

The invention of the Gutenberg press with its movable type gave rise to mass literacy and the birth of what we call "mass communication." The term *mass* is of critical importance. In earlier days, the masses could communicate only by using the oral or story form, since most books were handwritten and very expensive. Gutenberg's press changed all that. Culture, history, and religion, preserved on the pages of books, could now conceivably be made available to everyone. It was the beginning of mass culture.

During its first 200 years, the publishing business was usually the tool of the church and state. Early books and pamphlets encouraged readers to accept the doctrine of the ruling elite. But mass literacy brought with it a more sophisticated and questioning media consumer. Eventually, many people, encouraged by their new literacy, began to question the right of divine rule and authority. It is no accident that the rise of printed literature coincided with the Renaissance and the reformation.

Defining Communication

What we know about the form and content of mass media is part of a larger body of knowledge we call "communication." Communication researcher Frank E. X. Dance offers fifteen separate definitions of communication. One says:

The connecting thread appears to be the idea of something being transferred from one person to another. We use the word communication sometimes to refer to what is so transferred, sometimes to the means by which it is transferred, and sometimes to the whole process.

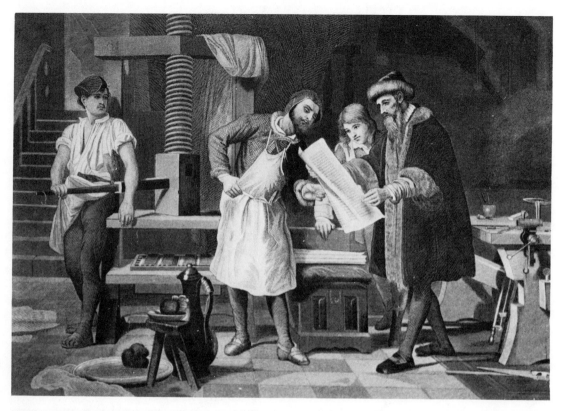

Gutenberg demonstrates his new movable type to investors.

We refer to what is being transferred as the "content." For example, so far the content of this chapter may be summarized as:

1. A brief historical sketch of how the Gutenberg press came into being.

2. A brief discussion of the significance of Gutenberg's invention.

3. A definition of *communication*.

So the message of this book is the *content* of its communication. *Form* involves how a message is being transferred. There are many ways to send a message. We can whisper, shout, write, dance, or paint. We might choose to use any number of technological devices.

The model in 1.2 by Shannon and Weaver is a simple representation of how communication works. It can be used for both interpersonal and mass communication. In interpersonal communication, Romeo could be a source. He uses words and gestures to *encode* the message, "I love you." The destination, of course, is Juliet. She sees and hears the message, decoding it. She then offers some feedback to the source, becoming a source herself, and starting the process all over again.

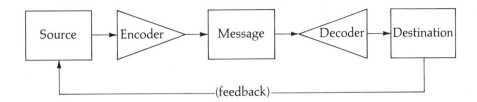

Shannon/Weaver model of the communication process (from Wilbur Schramm and Donald F. Roberts, eds., *The Process and Effects of Mass Communication.* Copyright 1972, University of Illinois Press. Used by permission.).

In mass communication, the source may be one person, but more often it is a group of people. In print, there are writers, editors, typesetters, distributors, and many more. In electronic media, there are script writers, actors, directors, and others. Each group becomes a source. The encoding process involves a media form like a book, radio, or television set. The message is decoded by the media consumer, who may or may not offer feedback.

Encoding and decoding are very important links in the communication processes. The advertising campaign that uses the wrong medium is unsuccessful. The government agency that sends health care books to a remote South American village and then realizes the people there can't read has not successfully communicated.

Communication researcher Harold Lasswell feels that the basic components of the communication process are identified in one question: *Who* says *what* through what *channel* to *whom?*

Consequences, or effects, involve every step of the process. Form involves *how* the message is communicated; content involves *what* is communicated. A consequence can result from either or from both. But to understand effects fully, we need to examine all components of the communication process.

Form: Mass Media

We call a medium a "mass medium" if it meets two requirements:

1. *It must reach many people.* Gutenberg's press made books a mass medium. Later came other media: newspapers, magazines, radio, and television, to name a few. All are mass media because they can reach many people simultaneously.

2. *It requires the use of some technological device, located between source and destination.*

Mass media can be illustrated in much the same way as interpersonal communication. Let me use this book as an example of how mass media fit the Shannon/Weaver model. The thoughts you're reading now come from me, the source. I encode them using the English language and my typewriter. From here, they go air mail to my publisher in California, arriving (I hope) on time. They are edited, changes are made, and finally they go to the printer. The technological device used by these modern-day Gutenbergs represents the medium. It comes after encoding and before decoding. That technological device is *the book.*

Now you go to the bookstore, wait in line, buy the book, and open it to the first page. There you begin *decoding* my message by reading it. Finally my thoughts have reached you, their destination.

So this book qualifies as a mass medium because it is designed to reach many people and it uses a technological device between source and receiver.

Content: Mass Message

Controversial communication researcher Marshall McLuhan's favorite slogan is: "The medium is the message." He stresses that, since all mass messages pass through a technological device, they are no longer the same message at all but have been radically changed. His slogan is an exaggerated plea for examining the *form* of mass messages as well as their *content* (see 1.3).

From the very beginning of the process, mass messages are different from interpersonal ones. A source who designs a mass message realizes it will be altered by media. Try to imagine John Lennon and Paul McCartney, gathered with their wives, suddenly blurting out "I want to hold your hand" in harmony. It makes a very strange interpersonal message. Yet the thought, "I want to hold your hand," which came from the source to the receiver through radio and records, was one of the most successful messages in the history of mass communication! It was a message designed for and delivered to the mass audience.

Consequence: Mass Culture

A lot of mass communication research involves mass culture. We use the term *mass culture* to identify the *effects* of mass media. In the Lennon/McCartney example, the media were radio and records. Of course, films, newspapers, magazines, and television all played a part in the Beatles' success. But you would not be familiar with "I Want to Hold Your Hand," or even with Lennon and McCartney, unless you were participants in mass culture. Mass culture involves a body of knowledge you *share* with others in your environment.

Communication researcher Alex Gode points out that all communication "makes common to two or several what was the monopoly of one or some." Mass culture, made possible by mass communication, is shared by virtually everyone. This sharing process opens up many possibilities, and not all of them are pleasant. Critics worry about the possible effects of TV violence on the nation's children. Will children's beliefs and attitudes about violence be affected by their endless diet of cops and robbers? Are we becoming so mesmerized by the *mediated* world of commercial products that we forget that material things are not everything in life?

Have we forgotten "quality art" and its importance in a world filled with the popular art found on mass media?

Other critics worry that the mass audience is too easily swayed and influenced, that the era of the individual is over. We may be trading our individualism for a more collective, tribal identity we don't yet completely understand. On the other hand, we may simply be on the verge of a new kind of individualism. Futurist Alvin Toffler contends that products like home video and audio recorders will bring about more diverse media content that will "un-mass" the mass media. In either case, there can be no doubt that this is a time of transition. The mass message is one of tremendous flux in the way we see ourselves in relation to others. No person or nation can afford to be self-oriented as in the past. In the world of instantaneous communication, everything we do affects everyone else all the time. And that is what mass culture is all about.

The Technological Embrace

Can you imagine a world without mass communication? There would be no newspapers, radios, televisions, or McDonald's golden arches. Before Gutenberg, myths, proverbs, and fairy tales used to pass wisdom from one generation to the next were limited by their channel capacity. *Channel capacity* is

the term communication researcher Wilbur Schramm and others use to describe the ability of a particular medium to transfer a message successfully.

Remember the parlor game where each person whispers a story to the next? The end version is usually entirely different from the original. Obviously, verbal exchange is not necessarily the best way to transfer a story. We cannot remember long messages exactly, and we tend to embellish or exaggerate some details and omit others. Naturally, the ability to remember exact words differs for every individual. Gutenberg's printing offered everyone a *precise* method of exchanging information. You can still go back and read the original Gutenberg Bibles if you can read Latin. They haven't changed. Nor have the handwritten books from before Gutenberg's time, but those books could reach only one reader at a time.

Chaucer's *Canterbury Tales* offers an example of a series of folk tales that became part of the mass culture thanks to the printing press. Though they were written some 80 years before Gutenberg's invention, once they were set in type, they became standard literature for the information-hungry mass audience. The tales remain intact and are still literary standards in our mass society.

Archie Bunker, Elvis Presley, the Flintstones, Richard Nixon, Shangri La, Volkswagen, Amos 'n' Andy, F. Scott Fitzgerald, the hula hoop—all were brought to us in whole

Who Is Marshall McLuhan?

Herbert Marshall McLuhan is the director of the University of Toronto's Center for Culture and Technology. Although he received his Ph.D. in English, he has become associated with a group of theories about the impact of electronic media.

McLuhan is the most controversial figure in mass communication. Shunning traditional research methods, he is fond of telling his critics, "I don't pretend to understand all my stuff—after all, I'm very difficult!"

Empirical researchers seem most upset by his complete lack of "proof" to back countless assertions. McLuhan offers a theory, gives one or two brief examples, and then goes on to the next theory. He seldom cites serious academic research or gives footnotes. To whose who criticize this technique, McLuhan responds, "I don't explain, I explore."

His argument that it is how, not what, a medium communicates that matters seems to defy common sense. He maintains that watching television actually requires more involvement than reading a book and that it is the amateur, not the professional, who can best solve complex technical problems in everything from physics to marketing.

In person, he delivers lectures in an offhand and matter-of-fact way, as if everyone should see the obvious logic of his argument. (If you saw Woody Allen's film *Annie Hall,* then you caught a glimpse of

McLuhan in action.) His books are hard to read since he jumps from one thought to another with very little connection. When criticized for his writing style, he simply maintains that it's an example of an "interface," or two things that seem unrelated, until you look more closely.

Though he has been accused of favoring electronic media over print, McLuhan spends most of his time reading and says he watches very little television. He's been called everything from the "electronic guru" to "that nutty professor from Canada." A synopsis of The Gospel According to McLuhan:

HISTORY: 600 Years of Linear Thought

Since Gutenberg, humans have been trained to believe that all "real" truth and knowledge are in books and printed material. This has perpetrated the fallacy of linear thought. We live our lives the way we read, knowing this is the "correct way." We discuss one topic at a time, take things and teach things in "logical" sequence. YOU HAVE TO WALK BEFORE YOU RUN, YOU HAVE TO CRAWL BEFORE YOU WALK! McLuhan says walking may come first, running may come first. "There is absolutely no inevitability as long as there is a willingness to contemplate what is happening."

WHAT: The Medium Is the Message/Massage

The medium is the *message* because our technological and social progress has always been affected

more by the nature of what we communicate *with* than by individual messages contained in the communication.

The medium is the *massage* because it massages us thousands of times each day. We are virtual prisoners in an infinite collection of unrelenting media. These media have a profound effect on the way we think and behave toward one another.

The Media and Technologies: Human Extensions

The media, like other technological innovations, have been designed by us to extend the functions of the body and brain. The radio is an extension of the ear, just as the wheel is an extension of the foot, and the computer an extension of the central nervous system. Radio and television have catapulted music to a mass emotional experience unprecedented in the history of art.

WHERE: The Global Village

Early people clustered in small villages for convenience and self-protection. Enter industrial progress and the population explosion. Tribes grew bigger and bigger, jobs became more specialized, and a change in identity developed. Rivalries became more acute. People were now grouped in cities, towns, and *nations.* Print encouraged factions to develop because it failed to perceive *the whole!* Now air travel and the electronic media are "shrinking" the world back to tribal size, and tribalization is encouraged by the demise of print. Hence we are becoming once again a "village," but this time a "global village." Such upheavals do not always come easily. According to Alfred North Whitehead, "The major advances in civilization are processes that all but wreck the societies in which they occur."

HOW: Collide-o-Scope/ Breaking Down the Walls

The electronic media tend to break down the social and ethnic barriers between people by familiarizing everyone with everyone. Information is instantaneous. The poor see the rich, blacks see whites, and with an increased awareness comes increasing unrest. The electronic media are both the enemy of ignorance and factors in social havoc. Then they *amplify* that same havoc through instant news coverage. They bring together divergent ideas, views, and ethics in a Collide-o-Scope of change.

WHEN: Speed/Instantaneous Communication and Information

The electronic media make possible instant communication worldwide with radio, TV, telephone, and other devices. Technology provides instant access to all but a few forms of private communication. Their privacy violated and their most cherished patterns threatened, generations raised without these electronic media are bombarded with them in later stages of life when they are less able to accept rapid change. This fact (plus the H-bomb, a technological extension of the club) has created a unique fissure between the postwar generation and its elders.

Photo by Harry Benson, *People Weekly,* © Time, Inc.

WHO: We Are Them!

It becomes increasingly absurd to talk about protecting "us" from "them." The global village is running out of elbow room. Pollution, radiation, and other related problems are of concern to all of us. We are "them." We are the children of the global village. We are the tribal members of humanity.

or in part via mass communication. They all involve habits that have touched our lives, stories, myths, and culture in one way or another. How have we changed as a result of these mass communication experiences?

McLuhan contends that we now live in a "global village" where we share our hopes, dreams, and fears in a "worldpool" of information. He says that in the global village, the old social, racial, and ethnic barriers of the past will break down, so media will eventually help us achieve world peace and harmony. Others disagree, citing the social unrest of the 1960s, the Vietnam War, and Watergate as examples of problems created and nurtured, at least in part, by mass media. Just about everyone agrees that mass media have altered the evolution and destiny of spaceship earth and its crew, but no one is quite sure how.

Competing Technologies in Mass Communication

One of the most intriguing theories about how mass media affect our lives involves the clash of communication technologies. In certain time periods, one particular medium seems to dominate. Thus we speak of the pre-Gutenberg oral or folk period, the rise of print, the golden age of radio, and so on.

Most of us spend more time watching television than reading. This shift of our attention away from books has disturbed many people.

What effect might it have on our attitudes and beliefs? To cite one example, our decisions in the voting booth are probably influenced heavily by the 30-second campaign commercials we see on TV. Do these give candidates enough time to discuss the complex issues and forces at work in our society, or do they reduce the political arena to a world of meaningless slogans and redundant clichés? In the 1960s, David Brinkley gave this reaction to surveys showing that most Americans relied almost solely on television news: "Then they're getting damn little news."

One thing is certain: In many ways, print and electronic media are at war with one another. Their form and content represent different approaches to delivering entertainment, reporting the news, and distributing vital information.

They are at war because we experience the two media in different ways. A book is something we experience alone, often in a quiet, isolated environment. Remember the last time you sat next to someone who was whispering in the library? It probably distracted you. Yet loud audience reaction is common in most movie theaters. Even when the audience is silent, the film is a shared experience. We can experience radio and television equally well alone or with others. Rivalry between different media, then, is a rivalry of different *forms*. The form of a mass medium directly affects what the message will be, how we perceive and understand the message, and how that message affects us.

"And now the news at eleven. To begin with, everything I said on the six-o'clock news was wrong."

Drawing by Levin; © 1976, The New Yorker Magazine, Inc.

Media Education and Research

Relationships between media form, content, and consequence are often difficult to understand. So much is happening so fast that traditional approaches to problem-solving are often obsolete. Many college and university departments have begun to erase established boundaries and experiment with multidisciplinary approaches to understanding communications. A new word, *communicology*, is appearing more often. Communicology is the study of both interpersonal and mass communication processes under what is called the "communication umbrella." The umbrella has many supportive ribs including journalism, theater arts, speech and rhetoric, technical writing, advertising, broadcasting, public relations, and popular culture.

The basis for most communication research techniques is found in psychology and sociology. Many researchers in communication, like Albert Bandura and Melvin L. DeFleur, are not even members of communication departments. Most educators now agree that technology is reshaping our environment so fast that teaching specific vocational skills to communication students is only part of the job.

The study of communication involves a second and perhaps more important task: to help students learn to land on their feet in unforeseen communication situations. We can train students to operate today's television cameras, but tomorrow's cameras will be different. Cable TV may revolutionize the commercial broadcast system we now study. Satellites could provide daily programs from foreign countries.

Many of you will never become involved in the production of mass media messages, but all of you will continue to be message consumers. Directly or indirectly, you will have a hand in deciding the future of mass media and the way they shape your life. This book is part historical and part exploratory. It offers historical information, not as an indicator of things to come, but as a backdrop to how we got here. We'll explore what is happening now and speculate on what is to come. This is not an encyclopedia of mass communication trying to give you all the relevant information about mass media, nor could it be. But I hope it will be a catalyst to start you thinking about mass media. You don't have to think very hard to come up with ways media *directly* affect our lives. Examples are everywhere.

Part One includes chapters on the print media. These media have a rich history and you will meet some of the more important contributors in their 500 years. Of course, print media started with books, the "permanent press," and books are still the most revered of all mass media.

Separate chapters deal with the two worlds of the newspaper: "hard" and "soft" news. In recent years, the function of the newspaper has changed. Readers' needs have been affected by the appearance of other mass media. There are serious questions about the newspaper and its relationships with government and the public. America's concept of freedom of the press has changed.

Magazines are the most rapidly changing of all print media. Their trends often provide early clues to changes in the characteristics of the mass audience. Dozens of new magazines appear each year and dozens of others disappear. Magazines are a prime example of the "curious collective": the paradox of the single author and the mass audience.

Part Two, "Electronic Media: Edison Came to Stay," is about all the media that rely on electric power to get their message to you. No one invented electricity, of course, and several people had a hand in harnessing it, but Edison's contribution in coupling it with message delivery was unsurpassed.

First came the record players and films, but in the beginning these were regarded as mere amusement. Radio became the first mass medium to link the source and the destination together simultaneously; it played an important part in the social and political development of its day. A separate chapter deals with the recording industry (now a by-product of radio) and music itself. Contemporary music enjoys a unique relationship with the youth culture and dominates radio's entertainment programming. It is important to explore that music and understand what it may mean.

Television, like newspapers, really operates in two worlds. There is prime time—the hours when most of us watch TV—and the "other side" of television—daytime and syndicated programs. Our look at TV's other side includes the study of cable TV, public TV, UHF, satellites, and other factors that could have an impact on prime time's dominance. Often when we think of television, we think of the programs that former Federal Communications Commission (FCC) Chairman Newton Minow called "the vast wasteland." Writer Horace Newcomb, among others, has a different perspective. He feels that television is an art form, the nation's most popular art, and that our choice of TV programs says important things about our society.

Film, like television, is an audiovisual medium, but it delivers larger-than-life-size people and has been described as the "American dream machine." Since it has been around longer than any other electronic medium, we have developed a more serious attitude about its effects.

In the final part, "The Phenomena of Mass Communication," we cover some issues related to the growing power of the mass media. Many feel that the most important function of mass media is to deliver the news. Do media really keep us up to date with what's happening in our rapidly shrinking world? We explore how that job gets done and learn about some important issues facing those who do it and the rest of us as well.

Advertising and public relations are media-related industries, completely dependent on mass media for their existence. People working in these industries are media specialists who design the pretty packages for information consumers.

Popular culture is not an industry but a social by-product of mass media. Virtually everything we see, touch, smell, hear, and taste has something to do with mass media. These *mass-mediated* experiences make up our life-syles and our culture.

In Chapter 14, "Media, Message, and Social Change," we examine several current controversies in mass communications. Some may already be familiar to you. They involve sex role stereotyping, racism, and violence.

Finally, we look into the mediated future. How will new technologies change society? In the world of mass communication, some of yesterday's dreams included:

1. A wire service that would give the small-town newspaper a reporter in every news capital on the globe.

2. A radio news network that would let all Americans hear a speech by their President at the same time it was being given.

3. A communication device that could bring sound and pictures simultaneously into every American home.

These dreams are now realities. New predictions for mass communication, its form, content, and consequence, challenge the imagination.

Queries and Concepts

1. If you had to give up all mass media, which one would you miss the *most?* Which would you miss the *least?* Why?

2. Pick a topical news story aired on tomorrow's TV newscast. Then listen for the same story on radio and also clip it out of the newspaper. Which facts are

common to all stories? Which are missing from at least one story?

3. List five questions about a mass medium you would like to have answered. Which involve form? Content? Consequence?

Readings and References

The Birth of Mass Communication

Elizabeth Geck
Johannes Gutenberg: From Lead Letter to the Computer. Bad Godesberg, Germany: Inter Natione Books, 1968.
An interesting account of Gutenberg's life and his influence on the rise of mass communication. Easy to read and comprehensive enough for everyone.

Defining Communication

Frank E. X. Dance
"The 'Concept' of Communication." *Journal of Communication,* June 1970, pp. 201–10.
Every definition of communication you ever wanted, along with a bibliography of original sources. The article is tough to read, but the definitions will make you stop and think.

Mass Media

Donald Pember
Mass Media in America, 2d ed. Chicago: Science Research Associates, 1977.
I am indebted to this book for the two-pronged approach to defining mass media.

Mass Message; The Technological Embrace

Gerald E. Stearn, ed.
McLuhan: Hot and Cool. New York: New American Library, 1967.
An anthology of essays laudatory and critical of McLuhan's theories, with responses from McLuhan himself. One critic calls him "a belated Whitman" while another says his writings are "a viscous fog through which loom stumbling metaphors."

Mass Culture

See Chapter 13, "Popular Culture and Mass Communication," and the readings and references at the end of that chapter.

Media Education and Research

See Chapter 14, "Media, Message, and Social Change," and the readings and references at the end of that chapter.

2

Books: The Permanent Press

**He had grown up to a thousand books, a thousand lies;
he had listened eagerly to people who pretended to know,
who knew nothing. . . .—F. Scott Fitzgerald**

The Power and the Glory

John-Boy Walton has just graduated from Walton's Mountain School and won a scholarship to Boatwright University. The university has everything a mythical Virginia college from the 1930s should have: red brick, ivy-covered walls, and serious professors smoking pipes and talking quietly with their students. John-Boy and his father wander into the library and suddenly the strings come up; the music is inspirational—this is a holy place!

Students cluster around, talking softly about an important lesson. Everything is a whisper. John-Boy stares, his mouth agape. There are thousands of books. Books everywhere. Books lining the soft, old, almost yellow walls. Books in the corners. Books on shelves. Books on tables. Books about religion, astronomy, physics, botany, literature, and, most important to John-Boy, poetry.

"Daddy," he murmurs as if hypnotized, "I'm going to read them all, every one of them."

"I know you are, son," the father replies softly. "I know you are."

You might consider this scene, as remembered from *The Waltons*, an overdramatization, and I won't argue with you. Still, television, books, radio, and all media messages are like mirrors holding up some facet of our culture so we can dissect it and learn about ourselves. This episode reminds us of our fascination with print and our total reliance on it. Sometimes it takes on a holy and ritualistic flavor.

McLuhan says phonetic writing "has the power to translate man from the tribal to the civilized sphere." There can be no civilized society without reading and writing.

Print governs our culture. It is the keeper of records, great literature, and all accomplishments. It is the medium that, more than all others, daily dictates the fortunes and failures of men and women. Teachers who publish flourish; those who don't perish. Students who read the right books go to the head of the class, meet the right people, and go on to the right colleges. Those who don't drop out and wind up on street corners, hanging around with the wrong crowd and getting into all sorts of trouble.

Casey Stengel's knowledge of English grammar may have been limited, but his baseball managerial skills were legendary, as was his reverence for the printed word. When anyone dared question his baseball knowledge, he would answer: "You could look it up." "Looking it up" means consulting books.

Print is the Supreme Court, the ultimate arbiter of our culture. If we want to know who is the *best* at a particular activity, we consult a copy of the Guinness *Book of World Records*. From the pages of books flows truth, the answer to any conceivable question. When we say we are doing it "by the book," we mean we are doing it in a civilized, correct, coherent, logical manner (see 2.1).

Bookbinding is also powerful. It adds an additional touch of respectability to print. The hardback book is considered the ultimate

Doing it by the book: Americans look for know-how from the book. We do it by the book because the book offers us a blueprint for action and a way to achieve success. This selection of *Esquire* books offers the young man the *Esquire* point of view on everything from good grooming to good drinking. (P.S. Don't clip the coupon, I'm afraid this limited offer has expired!)

credible source, followed in order by the paperback book, the magazine, and finally the newspaper. The better the binding, the greater the credibility! All of these are preferable to the electronic media, which seem somehow fleeting and unstable. *Print is for keeps!* (See 2.2.)

The power of the *form* of the book goes beyond cultural cliché. We do not only *what* books tell us, but *how* they tell us. We perform most activities the same way we read, in a *linear* fashion. Linear (from *line*) means one thing at a time, one job at a time, one spouse at a time. This seems quite normal; in fact, we are so conditioned to doing things one at a time that any other way seems absurd. Yet in preliterate cultures, people tend to do many things simultaneously. Their life-styles have a kind of all-at-once-ness. Hawaiians never

Print is for keeps.

If your product needs a reflective audience, a selective audience PRINT IT!

If the purchase requires deliberation— or liberation from the accepted way of doing things, nothing performs like print.

Print it. Print is for keeps.

Shirley Polykoff
Copywriter
and President

Shirley Polykoff
Advertising, Inc.

Magazine Publishers Association, Inc. 575 Lexington Avenue, New York, N.Y. 10022

had a written language until the missionaries came in the 19th century. Perhaps that is why things on the Islands are still done according to what they call "Hawaiian time," and that means hours of delay. If you are to meet some people at one o'clock, it may be two or later before they show up.

McLuhan has predicted that as literate societies spend less time with books and more time with electronic media, they will return to this preliterate state. He says, "Ours is a brand new world of all-at-once-ness, time has ceased, space has vanished." Our concepts of time and space are influenced by the *form* of our dominant media. The real message of the book medium may not be *what* it says, but *how* it says it. That media message has had important consequences in our mass culture.

The Gutenberg Legacy

When Gutenberg's movable type ushered in the new era of mass communication, Gutenberg was totally unaware of it. He was more interested in deriving some creative pleasure from the experience and turning a profit for his investors. What happened was of considerably greater consequence. Often inventors and other technological pioneers receive little recognition in their lifetimes. We are "numb" to our changing environment, much too preoccupied with day-to-day problems to get "the big picture."

Look around the room where you are right now. Take a good look. You are at home, in a classroom, in a library. No doubt you've been here many times before. Yet have you ever noticed the pattern on the ceiling? The small holes in the wall? The plaster chips on the floor? The linoleum pattern? The trademark on the desk in front of you? By stopping and looking at these things, you are really seeing them for the first time, getting a glimpse of the "invisible environment" that always surrounds you. Our information environment, created by books and other mass media, is very much like that. It surrounds us constantly, leaving no part of us unaltered or untouched. Yet we are completely oblivious of it. We think if we're not reading at the moment, books have no influence on us.

We human beings have always had the urge to keep records of ourselves, our friends, our dreams. Inside each of us is a secret archivist; we like to collect things that prove our accomplishments are of lasting value. Books provide the opportunity for a permanent record. They perform a different function than the newspapers and magazines we chew up and recycle daily. No one really knows how long books have been around, but the earliest records show there were clay tablets in Babylonia about 4,500 years ago.

Chinese scholars may have invented the first books, a series of bamboo strips tied together. But bamboo, clay, and stone were impractical and not easily transported. According to most accounts, the Chinese were the first to invent paper, but the earliest inexpensive writing materials were made by Egyptians from the papyrus plants growing along the Nile River.

The Romans invented codex, a kind of binding that allowed them to organize laws and other important materials into easily transportable form. Some early forms of paper appeared in Italy and Spain in the 12th century. At that time, books were handwritten primarily on vellum or parchment, and that practice continued into the 15th century. In fact, in some parts of Europe, vellum and parchment are still used today. At the end of the 15th century, Gutenberg used paper along with movable type and an old wine press to print his first book, a Bible.

It is estimated that more than 30,000 titles were printed in the first 50 years of mass-produced books (1450–1500). Early works were usually law books, Bibles, or other religious publications. Later came folklore, stories, and verse like Chaucer's *Canterbury Tales.* The costly hand-copied manuscripts that had been the exclusive property of the ruling elite gave way to mass-produced works that encouraged literacy among the masses.

The mechanical procedures of printing changed very little during the first 350 years. All type had to be set by hand and each page pressed separately. About 1800, the French invented a machine that made paper in one continuous roll. In England, the first successful iron press replaced the old wooden ones. In 1810, a steam-powered press replaced earlier hand-operated models. In 1884, Ottmar Mergenthaler, a German-born American, invented the linotype. Now type could be set by machine, greatly speeding production.

In recent years, a number of technological developments have sped up the printing process, including computer typesetting and offset, or cold-type, printing. Both of these techniques may eventually have a much greater impact than linotype did on the distribution of the printed word.

The Permanent Press in America

In 1620, books landed at Plymouth Rock with the Pilgrims. Twenty years later, Stephen Day was commissioned to print one of the first books published in the New World, *The Whole Booke of Psalms.* Just as in Europe, most early books in America were about law or religion. The Bible was the most popular of all.

Benjamin Franklin's *Poor Richard's Almanack* was the rage from 1733 to 1758. It was a collection of tide tables, harvest suggestions, and proverbs like "Early to bed and early to rise makes a man healthy, wealthy, and wise." Franklin also started the first subscription library in the colonies. In many ways, his was the first American mass communication success story.

Until 1800, the price of books kept them out of the hands of many U.S. citizens. Books were priced at a dollar or more, which amounted to a week's pay for the average wage earner. During the next 50 years many cities started compulsory public schools, and a new generation grew up hungry for the printed word. Heavy demand for books plus technological innovation helped lower the price. It is important to remember that in America reading was considered the right of everyone. Though many successful publishers were upper-class Americans, printing was not controlled by the ruling elite because the new nation had established freedom of the press in its Bill of Rights. Education of the masses posed no threat to a nation that had already rejected a king.

By the 1840s, the price of some books was down to ten cents. Horatio Alger and other authors of this era stressed action, romance, adventure, and the puritan ethic of honesty and hard work (see 2.3). The message of these inexpensive novels became part of the Ameri-

Horatio Alger and the American Dream

Perhaps the most successful of all the 19th-century novelists was Horatio Alger (1834–1899). Though the literary merit of his work was subject to criticism, his writings were both prolific and widely read. His 120 titles sold around 30 million copies. The name Horatio Alger became synonymous with the American struggle for upward social mobility. Here's the philosophy of the Alger novel in a nutshell, taken from his first book, *Ragged Dick:* "I hope, my lad," Mr. Whitney said, "you will prosper and rise in this world. You know in this free country poverty is no bar to a man's advancement."

Alger's belief in piety, purity, frugality, and hard work was a legacy from his conservative father, a Unitarian minister in Revere, Massachusetts. For a time Horatio thought he too would have a career as a minister and he graduated from Harvard Divinity School before his success with *Ragged Dick.*

Alger eventually moved to New York and became somewhat of a celebrity, lending his name to a number of reform and antivice crusades, including the New York Society for the Suppression of Vice.

All the Alger novels idolized the self-made man. The hero was "a bright-looking boy with brown hair, a ruddy complexion, and dark blue eyes, who looked, and was, frank and manly. . . ." The villain was often another boy, son of a rich but corrupt family. He often had a "slender form and sallow complexion, and dressed with more pretension than taste. . . ." Inevitably, the hero triumphed.

Alger's own life story mirrored the success of his heroes, but though his books brought him fame and fortune beyond his wildest dreams, he did know sorrow. At 17, Alger's father talked him out of marrying his "one true love" because he was too young. And Alger longed to write "one great book," to be applauded by the critics who scoffed at his "boys' stories." That book was never written, though he once chose a title: *Tomorrow.*

The important cultural contribution of the Alger novel had nothing to do with literary quality. Popular media reflect the emotions and ideologies of their times. Alger's ideas were already in the thoughts and feelings of Americans. Though his medium and message may no longer dominate the social landscape, the implications of Alger's work have formed our cultural legacy. His millions of readers have grown up and passed that legacy along to succeeding generations.

can culture. People across the country shared the same romantic notions, agonies, and ecstasies through the pages of the books they read.

By 1900, nine out of every ten Americans could read, and read they did. Naturally, not all of the social and political events of that day can be explained by books, but the medium's influence was great. Just as *Uncle Tom's Cabin* had spurred the cause of freedom for slaves before the Civil War, Upton Sinclair's *The Jungle* exposed the wretched condi-

tions of Chicago's meat-packing plants. During the 1930s, John Steinbeck's *The Grapes of Wrath* sensitized many to the plight of those who fled the Dust Bowl during the Depression. All of these had a lasting impact on the consciousness of the nation.

In the 1940s, paperbacks changed the role of books in America. First popular more than 100 years ago, paperbacks have had escalated sales since World War II. With gross sales at $500 million, paperbacks now account for about a sixth of all book sales, and they no longer deal only with "lighter" material. Almost all of the world's literature, from Shakespeare to Saul Bellow, now appears in paperback. Even that once stalwart hardback, the textbook, has yielded. The evidence is in your hands.

Even more so than hardbounds, paperbacks are often read and then passed on to others. Used-book stores have given over shelf after shelf to paperbacks. The average paperback now costs about two dollars, up from 50 cents during the 1950s. Still, most magazines cost one dollar or more and paperbacks have a much longer life. Many are word-for-word replicas of hardbound books that originally cost five times more. Other titles appear only in paperback.

Speedy production of paperbacks has made possible the *instant book*. Often based on a timely political event, the instant book appears within a few weeks. In 1976, the Israeli Army assault on the airport at Entebbe spawned three books within one month.

Gross book sales topped $3 billion for the first time in the early 1970s. Of these books, nearly half were textbooks or legal, medical, and other professional works. Millions of copies of popular paperbacks, like *All the President's Men*, were also sold as required reading in courses. Book clubs accounted for another 10 percent of the total, offering highly touted selections to members at discount prices. Authors know that selection as a "Book-of-the-Month" can mean instant success. Of course, book reviews also influence sales.

Meanwhile, commercial publishers try their best to get their titles on the influential "best-seller" lists, particularly the one published in the *New York Times*. Yet, sources inside the industry reveal that such lists are inaccurate at best. One bookseller said, "If George Gallup conducted his political polls the same way, we'd have Harold Stassen, Mary Tyler Moore, Al Capone, and Rin Tin Tin as America's favorite candidates for the presidency." Best-seller lists never include books like *The Living Bible*, for example, despite the fact that it sold more copies than any other book in a recent year. Also missing are dictionaries, cookbooks, and titles that sell well in rural locations, which are seldom polled. Most of the confusion could be cleared up if commercial publishing houses were willing to disclose sales figures, but most don't want the competition to know exactly how they are doing.

Some writers are now receiving more royalties from the sale of film rights than from the books themselves. Sometimes the film is even made first and a book is then based on the film. *Love Story*, written by Eric Segal, a Yale professor, was originally a screenplay that was later marketed as a novel. Both versions enjoyed tremendous success. Peter Benchley's *Jaws*, another best-seller, was an even greater success as a movie; it became one of the biggest box-office blockbusters in the history of American film. The book based on *Close Encounters of the Third Kind* provides another example.

Drawing by Modell; © 1976, The New Yorker Magazine, Inc.

We seem to have an increasing reliance on media other than books for entertainment. Despite the paperback boom and increasing total book sales, America's love affair with books may have gone sour. According to *Library Trends*, although 78 percent of Americans 18 years and older read a newspaper every day, fewer than one in five could answer yes to the question, "Do you happen to be reading any books or novels at the present?" A Gallup survey reveals that about one in four adults constitutes the hard-core book reader. A little less than half of the adults in the survey reported that they "read occasionally—perhaps at the rate of one book a year." Only one in four possesses a library card.

Critics are disturbed by this, particularly those in the academic community whose business it is to assess the impact of mass media. Many decry the time Americans spend with electronic media. "If we spent more time reading," they say, "we would be much improved." Usually the argument stops there, for it is always assumed that information derived from books is far more valuable than that derived from other mass media. Perhaps it's because we hold books in such high regard.

The more we learn about all mass media, the more we know that each medium has a different impact and delivers certain kinds of information more effectively than others. Media forms may be at war with one another, but there's also a potential symbiosis. Eventually we may discover which medium performs which information tasks most effectively. This would greatly extend our communication abilities and avoid confusing and harmful duplication. Considerably more empirical research needs to be done before we can "assume" that any single medium will enable us to be "much improved."

The Business of Books

The business of making books is of great cultural significance. Media analyst Charles Madison lists four major "eras" in American book publishing. *The colonial era* lasted from the 17th century until about 1865. Early colonial publishers in Philadelphia, New York, and Boston tended to come from the upper classes. Men like Matthew Carey, Charles Wiley, and James Monroe were well-educated aristocrats who thought the books they published should offer something of lasting value. Periodicals, they felt, catered to the kind of

instant gratification that might be harmful to the masses. In those days, publishing was something of a private club and there were so few publishers that most knew each other by their first names.

The gilded age (1865–1900) brought an abrupt change. The number of publishers mushroomed and, with the arrival of the dime novel, publishing became big business. George P. Munro was a six-dollar-a-week clerk when he convinced his employer's brother to publish cheap reprints of "pirated" editions of popular fiction. Thirty years later he left an estate valued at more than $10 million. The Munro story was typical of this era, when publishing experienced its most rapid growth.

The commercialization of literature (1900–1945) was a period of great technological advance. The antiquated printing practices of the 17th and 18th centuries were set aside for streamlined commercial procedures more in keeping with the Industrial Revolution. Bookselling, as well as publishing, had become big business.

Famous authors found publishers less willing to meet their financial demands as competition increased and publishing costs skyrocketed. The new, unknown author was having an increasingly difficult time breaking into print. A new, untested book required substantial financial commitment. Most publishing companies were cutting back and trying to ensure success with the books they did publish.

The era of *publishing goes public* (1945–present) represents the biggest business practice

"*Seventh floor, Books: 'Don't Say Yes When You Want to Say No,' 'Freedom from Fear,' 'Winning Through Intimidation,' and 'Power! How to Get It, How to Use It.'*"

Drawing by Stan Hunt; © 1976, The New Yorker Magazine, Inc.

changes in publishing's history. The postwar era brought another boom in the demand for books as former GIs flocked into American classrooms. The textbook business flourished. Older family-type publishing houses sold stock and became corporations.

Ultimately, book publishing is both a business and a cultural enterprise. It is important to remember that *cultural* means all culture and not only what some would call "high" or "elite" culture. Dr. Spock's *Baby and Child Care, Star Wars,* and Shakespeare are all part of the cultural "stew." The book medium is used to convey messages of every imaginable description. Each makes some contribution to the American experience. Examination of each can yield interesting and worthwhile data about the complex nature of American society.

Issues and Answers

Purity in Print

As long as there have been books, there has been censorship. English King Henry VIII issued a list of prohibited books in 1529, and for the next 170 years, each English monarch issued a similar list. Those caught reading or circulating prohibited works were subject to fines and imprisonment. Printers were also publishers, distributors, and retailers. They were held liable for anything that came off their presses. In Europe, thousands of titles were in print by 1600. As literacy and information spread, the threat of revolution swept Europe. The book medium fed increasing demands for social, religious, and political freedom. The ruling elite were losing the battle for control of the press.

Many people feel that the days of book banning have passed. Science fiction author Ray Bradbury wrote *Fahrenheit 451* (from the temperature at which paper catches fire) about a society where all books were burned and destroyed. It shocked and dismayed many readers. Was it science fiction, or wasn't it?

The banning and burning of books have been commonplace in America. Historian Paul Boyer has speculated on the reasons behind this. His theory is that while America developed a unified identity after the Civil War, it also developed a unified conscience.

In 1873, Anthony Comstock (see 2.4) founded a nonprofit social organization known as the New York Society for the Suppression of Vice. He headed that controversial society for 40 years. According to Boyer, the vice society movement:

. . . was in response to the deep seated fears about the drift of urban life in the post Civil War years. The origin of Comstock's society, the first of its kind in America, is illustrative. Throughout the nineteenth century, as today, New York City possessed a magnetic attraction for ambitious and restless young men from other parts of the country. The metropolis which held so much promise for these youths, however, was also somehow threatening. The familiar sources of guidance and support: family, church, close-knit community had been left behind, and often it seemed that the city offered nothing in their place.

Book censorship was a paternal approach. The reader was to be protected from falling to the depths of depravity. The problem then, as now, was figuring out exactly what constitutes the "depths," or even "depravity." The Supreme Court has never successfully defined obscenity.

During the 1920s, the term *banned in Boston* described literature of "questionable taste." A partial list of authors whose works were banned in Boston included H. G. Wells, John Dos Passos, Theodore Dreiser, Sinclair Lewis, Upton Sinclair, Ernest Hemingway, and Robert W. Service. Upton Sinclair didn't seem to mind; he mused, "We authors are using

Anthony Comstock and the Suppression of Vice

Anthony Comstock arrived in New York, "the wickedest city in the world," shortly after the Civil War in 1867. He had been born in 1844 to devout Connecticut parents.

According to his biographers, he worked in a dry-goods store until 1872, when he noticed that "shocking" literature was being passed around by other employees. Until then there was little or no enforcement of the antismut laws in New York City, but Comstock brought suit and had a fellow employee arrested for distributing such material. As it turned out, that was only the beginning. His Society for the Suppression of Vice was backed by most of the New York aristocracy, and Comstock became legendary in his self-appointed task of "cleaning the filth out of this town."

Sporting thick muttonchop sideburns, a pot belly, thick neck, and jutting jaw, he railed against what he called the "base villains" of pornography and their "pathetic and awful" cases. In 1893 he greeted a roomful of reporters with an impromptu belly dance to illustrate graphically the evils of the Chicago World's Fair. It must have been quite a sight!

America as our sales territory and Boston as our advertising department." The mass audience has always expressed a pronounced curiosity about banned literature, and this curiosity can lead to increased sales.

The Nazi book burnings of the 1930s and the Soviet suppression of books today may seem far removed from American society. Yet in 1953, more than 100 titles were banished from the worldwide libraries of the United States Information Service after "exposure" by Senator Joe McCarthy's congressional subcommittee. Among them were the works of American patriot Thomas Paine. McCarthy contended the books were "procommunist" and several public book burnings were held. *Saturday Review* editor Norman Cousins moaned, "What do we do about the charge that a nation that became great because of a free flow of ideas has itself become frightened of ideas?"

There are still stories of a school board prohibiting certain books in its library, or a teacher being fired for requiring reading of a controversial text. In a poetry class I took as a community college student, the instructor assigned Allen Ginsberg's *Howl and Other Poems.* The bookstore refused to carry it, so the instructor supplied the copies himself. When we read it out loud in class, he closed all the doors and urged us not to report it to the local chapter of the John Birch Society, which had been placing students with tape recorders in some controversial classes.

In March of 1976, several members of the Island Trees School District Board of Education in New York entered a high school library and confiscated 60 books they later said were "anti-American, anti-Semitic, anti-Christian, and just plain filthy." Removed were Pulitzer Prize winners *The Fixer* and *The Laughing Boy.* Also banned were Kurt Vonnegut's *Slaughterhouse Five,* Desmond Morris's *The Naked Ape,* and *Go Ask Alice,* which makes a strong statement against the use of drugs by teenagers.

The board's action stirred quite a controversy in the small Long Island town. Eventually New York City's WCBS aired an editorial condemning such actions as "prejudgments of the worst kind." In their opinion: "The idea of students getting off on this forbidden literature suits us just fine!"

The president of the school board went on the air to reply, contending that "what is taught in schools should reflect local values" and "one of the purposes of a board of education is to see that local control is maintained and that the will of the majority prevails." He also emphasized, "Education is supposed to be an uplifting experience, but if you have to get down into the gutter to do it, then it is just not worth it. For as the twig is bent, so grows the tree." The New York Civil Liberties Union filed a class action suit demanding that the books be returned to the library and contending that no board of education had the right to go over the heads of administrators to blacklist certain works.

Pornography is often a big part of the censorship question. Community and national standards change from day to day. *Ulysses,* the famous novel by James Joyce, was once banned in this country. There was some banning of *Lolita, Tropic of Cancer, Fanny Hill, Candy,* and others that seem tame by today's standards.

During the 1950s, the liberal Warren Court struck down most state obscenity laws as being too vague and subjective. The more conservative Burger Court of the 1970s reversed the Warren rulings and in *Miller* v. *California,* it struck down all national standards, reestablishing the right of local juries to apply local community standards in judging obscenity. Now local governments are again arresting editors and publishers, and there have been some convictions by local juries. Some of these cases are on appeal, and it will be many years before all the results are in. In fact, the results will probably never be "all in." The war between government and "obscene" publishers seems to be a never-ending one.

Queries and Concepts

1. What would our culture be like if we weren't doing it by the book? What if we were doing it by the TV or by the radio? What would happen to our relationships with government? With each other?

2. A survey project: Poll your ten favorite adults by posing the age-old cliché: "Read any good books lately?" How many have they read in the last six months? How many are of the "pop" variety?

3. What is the single book that has had the greatest influence on *your* life? Why?

4. The things that make America unique are embodied in American myths and stories like those of Horatio Alger. Make a list of other stories and myths that seem to be a vital part of the American character. How many are closely related to a mass medium?

5. Can you think of any sentences, words, or phrases that should not be allowed in print? Should there be an age limit involved in the freedom to read any kind of information? If so, draw up some guidelines. If not, what about books on how to make bombs and set them off by remote control? Do you want your local terrorist to have that information?

Readings and References

The Gutenberg Legacy

S. H. Steinberg
Five Hundred Years of Printing. New York: Criterion Books, 1959.
Though old, this brief book is really not out of date since it concentrates on the visual aspects of print and how they developed. Technical advances in the press are also treated.

The Permanent Press in America

John C. Oswald
Benjamin Franklin, Printer. Detroit: Gale Research, 1974.
Of all of the Franklin biographies, this is perhaps the most reverent. Originally pub-

lished in 1917, it is still easy to read. The author often uses language from the colonial era to describe his subject.

Lawrence C. Wroth
The Colonial Printer. Charlottesville: University Press of Virginia, 1964.
This book describes printing in the pre–Revolutionary War period, including discussions of Franklin, Day, and others. A very thorough and in-depth look at the colonial printer.

The Business of Books

David Shaw
"Book Business Best Sellers: Are They Really?" *Los Angeles Times* News Service, October 24, 1976.

Charles A. Madison
Book Publishing in American Culture. New York: McGraw-Hill, 1966.
There is ample material on book publishing in America in just about any library, and I reviewed a dozen books or so until I found

Madison's. It has a good index of all publishers, with a couple of paragraphs on each if you are curious about any specific company. The best material is on the earlier eras of publishing and I recommend that you go to a more recent source for current data, sales figures, and other information. *Writer's Market* (see Chapter 5) lists the kinds of books each major house publishes and the number of titles each produces yearly.

Issues and Answers:
Purity in Print

Paul S. Boyer
Purity in Print: The Vice Society Movement and Book Censorship in America. New York: Scribner's, 1968.
This is probably the liveliest and most thorough book in the area. Boyer is a scholar with a sense of humor who delivers the problems of book censorship with gusto. Recommended reading if you're interested. The author brings out details about historical characters that make them come alive.

3

Newspapers, Part One:
The Greening of American Journalism

**Fairly soon the press began to sense that news was not
only to be reported but also gathered, and indeed,
to be made. What went into the press was news.
The rest was not news.—Marshall McLuhan**

Hard and Soft News

A 1977 issue of the *Honolulu Advertiser* carried
five stories on the front page (see 3.1): a gas
explosion in Louisiana, a local story about
some native Hawaiians who want to take an
island back from the government, an interview
with former President Ford and his wife, a
story about the preacher at Jimmy Carter's
church, and a very short story about the arms
race. Only the gas explosion and arms race
stories were *hard news.*

Hard news is factual accounting; soft news
is the background information. It's hard news
when a public figure has a heart attack, but
soft news when his wife is interviewed in the
next room. Hard news is fact and statistics:
time, temperature, tide tables, box scores, and
the number of votes cast for a candidate. Soft
news is opinion and color: columns, comics,
editorials, and "Dear Abby."

Hard news, in theory, is the "facts" in the
story. Soft news is nice if there is time, but
nonessential. Many stories contain both soft
and hard news. The shotgun murderer who
kills six people is hard news. His neighbors
describing him as one who worshiped Hitler
is soft news. Hard news events are serious
matters of importance to everyone. Soft news
events are *human interest* and *feature* stories.

There were three photographs on the front
page in 3.1: Ford and his wife, the Carter
preacher, and a silhouette against the sky.
None was essential to understanding the
corresponding story. None really added any

vital information or helped the reader understand the facts. The total space taken by
photographs was roughly equal to the space
left for the stories. So there wasn't much room
for hard news on the front page. Looking
through the rest of the paper, I began to separate the soft news from the hard. About 80
percent of the news was soft. There were very
few facts; there was a lot of interpretation and
opinion, feature material, syndicated columns,
and comics.

The *New York Times* carries a lot of hard
news, the *New York Daily News* offers very
little. Each has developed an audience that
expects the balance between fact and feature
found there. Although every newspaper is different, each has readers who depend on it to
deliver a particular blend of hard and soft
news about the world around us. In doing so,
newspapers help us develop a sense of participation in the Global Village. They are an important part of our social and cultural identity.

Mass and Special-Interest Audiences

Newspapers are our "cultural bath." We bathe
in massive amounts of information. Few
people read the newspaper from cover to
cover; it would take most of the day. Instead,
most of us read the newspaper selectively.

All media deal with two audiences: the *mass*
audience and the *special-interest* audience.
Media consumers are members of both.

Front page:
February 21, 1977.

Gas explosions rock Louisiana and Dallas

United Press International

Three gas explosions rocked areas of Louisiana and Dallas yesterday.

The first forced the evacuation of a wide area of Louisiana and the other two shot fireballs into the night sky of Dallas, shaking residential areas on the city's northeast side several miles away.

In Plaquemine, La., a deadly cloud of chlorine gas, leaking from an explosion at a chemical plant, spread across a section of southeast Louisiana near Baton Rouge, forcing evacuation of a large area.

In Dallas, two freight train tank cars loaded with liquified propane exploded and threatened at least two other propane-filled tankers on a northbound train. Firemen were prevented from fighting the blaze because of the possibility of further explosions.

There were no deaths of injuries reported.

State police in Louisiana said officers were fanning out in St. Gabriel and north of Plaquemine, on the west bank of the Mississippi River, urging residents to leave their homes.

Dallas fire officials said there were five men aboaro the Santa Fe freight train, which was bound for Gainesville, Tex., when the first explosion occurred. The men abandoned the train and Santa Fe officials said all workers "more or less" had been accounted for.

Fire officials estimated they would have to let the blaze burn itself out.

"A fire like this can't be fought with water," a fire department spokesman said. "It may take two days for this thing to get burned out."

The Dallas explosions rocked buildings several miles away and the fireballs could be seen across town.

Police said there were some reports of looting as persons in the area fled their houses and apartments, but it was brought under control by a police tactical unit.

The explosions occurred about 7:35 p.m., the fire department said.

"We were driving along and were about three miles away when we saw this huge fireball," said one witness. "The whole sky just lit up."

Persons living near the scene said the blasts occurred about four minutes apart.

Mr. and Mrs. Louis Basser, driving near the site, said the explosion blew out the front windshield of their automobile and peppered them with glass. They were treated for superficial cuts.

Flames engulfed the car for about 40 or 50 feet as he drove along, Basser said. "I thought for a moment there Carter had caught it from the Russians," he said.

The Louisiana accident occurred at a Dow Chemical Co. plant. A cloud of the poisonous green gas, which can cause lung burns, spread south and east of the plant under five to 10 m.p.h. winds.

A state police spokesman said he was unsure whether the leak was sealed immediately.

"I'm not sure whether they got that closed off or not," he said. "We're not worrying about that yet. We're just trying to get the people evacuated.

A state police helicopter was sent to the area to determine the measurements of the cloud and its direction.

In a similar accident last December, a 42-mile cloud of gas spread from an Allied Chemical Co. plant in the same general area. It dissipated in a light rain, but 10,000 persons were evacuated including 6,000 students at Southern University. No major injuries were reported.

"From what I understand, this one is larger than the Allied Chemical Company one," said the police spokesman.

A spokesman for Dow, Roland Carson, said the leak continued more than an hour after it originally began.

"We're talking about several hundred pounds," he said, though he did not have an exact amount of gas released. Another company spokesman said there was one minor case of "inhalation" at the plant.

The Honolulu Advertiser

Hawaii's Prizewinning Newspaper

home edition
20c on Oahu – Beyond Oahu 25c

Aloha!

Today is Monday,
Feb. 21, 1977

Hawaii

Ricardo Verdadero: mule skinner for the last team of mules left on an Oahu sugar plantation
Page A-3

The Nation

Rain falls in parts of the drought-stricken Pacific coast
Page C-1

Washington

President Carter and open government: it's too early to tell
Page A-12

The World

Undisclosed number of persons die in crash of a Soviet airliner
Page C-1

Editorial

The realities of Hawaii's geographical situation must be considered in planning emergency oil storage
Page A-11

People

It may not be spring but here's some advice on spring cleaning from one of the most fastidious cleaning men in town
Page B-1

Sports

Hilo's Vulcans top seeded in NAIA District 8 playoffs and host yet unnamed opponent Friday in Hilo
Page D-1

The Index

4 sections, 40 pages

Ann Landers	B3
Bridge	D7
Classified ads	C4-12
Comics	D7
Crossword puzzle	D7
Editorials	A10
Entertainment	B4-5
George Daacon	A3
Horoscope	D7
Letters to the editor	A11
Ms. Fixit	A4
Obituaries	B6
Sports	D1-5
Tides	A4
TV log	B2
Wayne Harada	B4
Weather	A4

The Family Circus
By Bil Keane

"I dropped the tooth.

15 more on target isle?

Advertiser photo by Vickie Ong

Mrs. Frenchy DeSoto ponders a beckoning Kahoolawe from aboard a boat which approached the island.

'Mass invasion' plans thwarted

By VICKIE ONG and SANDRA S. OSHIRO
Advertiser Staff Writers

Fifteen or more persons are believed to have taken up residence on Kahoolawe yesterday, after a grander plan to place more than 100 protesters on the target island was thwarted.

A Coast Guard spokesman said footprints were found yesterday morning along the northern shoreline, where Marines camping on the restricted island had sighted a fire burning the night before. But a search of the immediate area produced no one, the spokesman said.

However, the Protect Kahoolawe Ohana reported yesterday that it was successful in dispatching at least 14 persons to the island in the group's continuing protest against military bombing practice there.

The 14 persons and an additional supporter of the Ohana who reportedly had paddled to the island aboard a surfboard are believed to have escaped detection by Coast Guard patrols.

The landed group would bring the total number of protesters on the restricted island to at least 17. Ohana members Walter Ritte and Richard Sawyer are said to have remained hidden on the island since their Jan. 30 "invasion."

There were unconfirmed reports last night that as many as 50 persons in four boats had landed on the island yesterday, including one from Lanai carrying 32 persons.

Early yesterday, the Coast Guard cutter Cape Newagen intercepted a boat and six persons aboard who apparently were bound for Kahoolawe also. The boat — carrying sleeping bags, surfboards and food supplies — was turned back to Maui's Makena Beach.

Persons aboard the craft reportedly refused to allow the Coast Guard to board the boat and were cited for that refusal, Navy spokesman Scott Stone said. The boat also was cited for overloading.

It was not immediately known whether this boat that was turned back was part of the Ohana's landing group or a decoy sent out by leaders of the main operation.

According to Stone, the Navy will proceed with its routine training

See POPULATION on Page A-4

Fords talk about sin and Jimmy

By HELEN THOMAS
UPI White House Reporter

PALM SPRINGS—They're enjoying themselves but he misses the White House. She thinks Jimmy Carter has no business telling people to quit living in sin. He thinks Carter could make big strides promoting peace.

He just grins and says "maybe" when asked if he'll run for president again. She doesn't want that decision made until closer to election time.

These, from the perspective of this desert golf resort, are some of the thoughts and feelings private citizen Jerry Ford and wife Betty expressed in an interview.

The former president was on the golf course at the outset, when Betty was asked how she feels about President Carter advising government employes "living in sin" to get married.

"He sounds like a very good evangelist," she said, but "I don't think that's (his) business. I guess he can set an example, which he does . . .

"Not that I approve of living in sin. He equates looking at a lady with lust as sinful. He obviously interprets the Bible literally. I believe in the Bible. I study it every day. But I think the Bible is made up of stories and examples set to inspire us to lead a good life."

Then Ford joined the interview in the living room of the spacious home, rented for a year at the Thunderbird Country Club while they await construction of their own house on the club's 13th fairway, with a magnificent view of mountains and desert.

It was difficult to tell how serious Ford was in saying he might try again for the White House.

Asked the same question, Betty said: "I would like to make that decision closer to the time (of the election). I know he'll always be involved in politics. Actually, I can't imagine him not being active. He feels very strongly that we've got to revive the Republican party."

Mrs. Ford, tanned from the desert sun wore a bright green T shirt and light plaid slacks. Ford wore a white golf outfit and looked younger and trimmer than during his 2½ years in the White House.

Both looked rested and happy, and appeared to be adjusting well te their new life. But there was no question they miss living in the White House.

Asked his feelings toward the presidency, Ford said, "You can't help but miss it. I just can't understand those who didn't like it. I miss the opportunity to make decisions. I have been busy making decisions on a personal basis but it's quieter."

On the other hand, he was asked, "How do you like this hardship post?"

"I really enjoy it," he said. "It makes a lot of sense for Betty, too, and it's helping me to improve my golf game."

Ford said he has not been in personal contact with Carter, but said top aide Bob Barnett is in touch with the White House and we have good communication."

He said Carter has the opportunity to make decisions that could be "helpful in the long run to peace in the world," such as in the Middle

See FORDS on Page A-4

UPI photo

Jerry and Betty Ford: Relaxed and tanned.

Russians: Carter in danger zone

Washington Post Service

MOSCOW—The Soviet Union has advised the Carter Administration with notable firmness in recent days that continued strong support for Russian dissidents is bound to have a negative effect on relations between the two countries.

The message has been formally conveyed in Washington by Soviet Ambassador Anatoly Dobrynin, according to the official Soviet news agency Tass, and has been stressed in authoritative press commentaries.

The implication of these warnings is that Moscow considers U.S. support for human-rights activists a potentially major obstacle to progress in areas of mutual interest, especially in strategic arms control.

"Relations of peaceful coexistence and constructive cooperation between the U.S.S.R. and the U.S.," the Communist party newspaper Pravda said yesterday, ". . . can fruitfully develop only when they are based on mutual respect for the principles of sovereignty and noninterference in internal affairs."

Pravda contrasted American "words expressing reasonable intentions" on such matters as a Strate-

See RUSS on Page A-4

Plains preacher resigns under fire

PLAINS, Ga. (UPI) — The Rev. Bruce Edwards, pastor of President Carter's hometown Baptist church, resigned under fire yesterday, saying a segment of the church hasn't accepted his support of a move to integrate the church.

Edwards' resignation came at a church meeting following the morning worship service.

"I had no intention of resigning going into the meeting," said Edwards. "It was a special conference called to pay an outstanding debt the church has."

Edwards said church member Dale Gay moved that he be fired immediately. He said a lengthy discussion followed as to whether the motion could be made during a special meeting called to discuss another topic.

"After a long discussion and bitter words being said back and forth, I finally just hung it up and gave my resignation," said Edwards. "A motion was made that my resignation not be accepted but I said whether they accepted it or not, I would still leave and asked that that motion be withdrawn and it was."

Edwards said he did not feel the action represented the feelings of most of the congregation. He said many church members were absent and others who had moved out of town had come back for the meeting.

"It was definitely a calculated move on the part of a certain section of the church," he said. "In November, when 200 members were present, I was sustained and the 1965 resolution (barring blacks) was overturned. Today, with just over 100 members present, the motion was made to fire me."

President Carter transferred his membership from the Plains church to a Baptist church near the White House after taking office last month.

Edwards said there were no charges brought against him at the meeting. "The only thing that resembled a charge was that I had lost my effectiveness," he said. "No one would say anything that I had done or not done to lose my effectiveness."

He said the opposition stemmed from his "effort to integrate the church."

Edwards said he felt that had he not resigned, the motion to fire him would have passed. "There was a lot of hostility and bitter feelings," he said. "I felt by resigning that maybe I could help the church heal its wounds and all this bickering back and forth would stop. I had as much as I felt I could take."

In Washington, a White House spokesman said Carter would have no comment on Edwards' resignation.

The Rev. Bruce Edwards
"It was a calculated move

Newspapers run stories of general interest for everyone; they run sports, stocks, and features for various special-interest audiences. The wide variety of their articles gives newspapers what communication authors John Merrill and Ralph Lowenstein call "internal specialization," allowing the newspapers to appeal to a large diverse audience. In this way, newspapers are like some magazines—*Reader's Digest*, for example—which draw a large readership of people with different age, educational, and social backgrounds.

The newspaper format sets an information *agenda* by grading events according to how important or interesting they may be to the reader. Just as on radio or TV, the lead story is supposed to be the day's most significant event; in newspapers, general-interest and important stories are displayed prominently on or near the front page. Inside the newspaper, the special-interest reader finds information in neatly divided sections: sports, editorial, family, and business. This helps readers set their own agendas. Some may read "Dear Abby" first, then work the crossword puzzle, and never get around to the front page. Sports fans start with the sports page or a favorite sports columnist. A stockbroker may go straight to the business section.

Of course, sometimes special-interest news makes it to the front page. So many people have become fans that sports news often appears on the front page. If Wall Street has its worst day in 20 years, most of us will read about it. But on a normal day, only the spe-

cial-interest audience will pore over the day's stock quotations.

The more successfully a newspaper meets the mass and special-interest needs, the higher its circulation. The higher the circulation, the greater the revenues. Advertising revenues make it possible for you to buy the paper at a fraction of its production cost. Advertising also makes daily delivery possible. A newspaper is a *mass* medium that depends on mass circulation, and a large *audience* to make a profit.

What You See Is What You Get

Americans have an insatiable appetite for printed news. There is a need to know what's happening and a feeling that it hasn't happened unless it has appeared in the paper. Why read the full newspaper account of the baseball or football game you saw last night? You want to verify your own perceptions with those of a trained reporter, a professional observer who was on the scene. Seeing it in print makes it real.

In many ways, the event described in a newspaper story is not the original event at all, but an approximation that suits both the medium and the reader. Newspaper stories are abbreviated, condensed versions of the real thing. A quote standing alone, for example, with no explanation of events preceding or following it, may appear absurd or sensational. Politicians are often irritated when they see their words in the morning paper. Their immediate response is that they were misquoted or the words were "taken out of context."

In a sense, all speeches are taken out of context, since they have been taken from one medium (interpersonal speech) and put into another (print). Take your pocket tape recorder and tape a conversation at random. Then transcribe the first several sentences. What you write on paper will seem very different from what you overheard. If it were printed, the difference would be still greater. We don't *talk* the way we *read*. Talk, as they say, is cheap. But print has a *finality*, a permanence about it that can change the meaning of events and messages, making them appear different from the original.

Those who have written for a school or local paper know that the typed, double-spaced story seems different from the one that appears in lines of neat type on the page of a newspaper. Even if your editor lets every word stay as is (and that's rare), there is something almost *magic* about the power of print. The words look so official when they finally appear.

In addition, reporters bring their own perspectives to a story. No matter how hard they try to remain objective, they inevitably develop opinions about a newsmaker based on personal judgments and past behaviors. Whether the reporters are aware of it or not,

personal bias can play a major role in how they "see" a news event.

Nor is the reporter the only person who influences the news. A story must pass through many hands before it appears in print. There are copy editors who correct errors and edit for easier reader comprehension. Perhaps a photographer assigned to a story turns in a picture that tells a "different story" from the reporters. Very few reporters write their own headlines, and headlines can reflect still another point of view.

Media consumers need to be aware of these variables before making important decisions based on information received from the newspaper.

Business Trends in Newspaper Publishing

According to *Editor and Publisher*, there are more than 1,750 daily newspapers and almost 8,000 nondailies published in the United States today. Of these, about 150 are metropolitan dailies or "metros," big-city papers that come out every day. In many major cities, the number of metros has been decreasing. For example, in New York in 1900 there were 14 English language dailies. In 1978 there were only four left. Why the decrease?

For one reason, the metros have been particularly hard hit by rising labor costs. Unionized plant personnel may take home more pay than reporters do. Printing plant workers have joined truck drivers and construction workers as among the most highly paid blue-collar workers in America. Another problem is the skyrocketing cost of newsprint. In 1940, newsprint cost about 50 dollars per short ton. By 1977 it cost over 300 dollars per short ton and was still climbing.

One way the metros have dealt with rising production costs has been to raise the selling price of the paper. In the last ten years, street prices of most papers rose from 10 to 15 or even 20 cents per copy. The cost of advertising has also risen. (One reason the *Los Angeles Times* was able to hold its selling price down to 10 cents longer than most was that it has the highest ad revenues—much of them from classified ads—in the country.) Most newspapers get about 75 percent of their income from advertising, which means the paper you buy for 15 cents probably costs about 75 cents to make. Advertising also makes daily delivery possible for about five dollars a month. This reliance on income from advertising also means that more than half of the space in most newspapers is devoted to ads.

Another problem facing metros is circulation. Although the total circulation of most metros continues to rise, it is not keeping up with the rise in population. Metro owners have paid for exhaustive marketing studies to find out why there is less interest in their product. They found that some age (20–29

years) and special-interest groups feel there is nothing for them in the paper.

Metros are also threatened by the suburban dailies, whose numbers have increased during the past ten years. As city dwellers move to the suburbs, they often prefer the suburban dailies that are particularly important in their communities. The smaller local newspaper is one of the few forums where citizens can exchange information with one another on a *community-wide* basis. Classified and local advertisers reach the entire local market. Suburban dailies can deal directly with community issues that metros cannot or will not cover.

Any discussion of the decline of the metros is incomplete without mentioning the impact of electronic media. In the early 1970s, a Roper poll reported that 49 percent of the population felt that television was the most believable news source, whereas 20 percent cited newspapers. Most preferred television as their main news source. Electronic media deliver the up-to-the-minute kind of news once covered by the extra newspaper edition. Are we giving up newspapers in favor of electronic media? Many blame television for the plight of the metros and for what they feel is a poorly informed citizenry.

It is often assumed that any decrease in the number of newspapers or in their circulation translates into a less-informed public. But there may be a *symbiosis* at work here, too: Newspapers provide a wide range of news

Time Line: Five Eras of American Newspaper Journalism

The Early Years

1690 *Publick Occurrences both Forreign and Domestick* is the first U.S. newspaper; it folds after one issue.

1721 James and Benjamin Franklin are early colonial printers. James starts the *New England Courant.*

1735 John Peter Zenger is acquitted of charges of seditious libel, thus setting precedence for truth as defense in libel cases.

1767 John Dickinson writes his series of ''Letters from a Farmer in Pennsylvania'' in the *Pennsylvania Chronicle,* characterizing the political nature of early papers.

1783 *The Pennsylvania Evening Post and Daily Advertiser* is the first American daily newspaper.

1798 The Sedition Act marks the effort to suppress the young nation's free press.

1808 First on-the-spot correspondents in Washington report political news for the papers back home.

1820s A colorful era for an information-starved public. Sea-coast city papers hire boats to meet incoming ships carrying news. Pony express riders race each other from Washington to Boston and New York to carry congressional news.

The Penny Press

1833 Benjamin Day begins the *New York Sun.* Now everyone can afford a daily paper. His success is soon imitated by dozens of others.

1835 James Gordon Bennett launches the *New York Herald.*

1841 Horace Greeley starts the *New York Tribune.* Nine years later it is the first major newspaper to come out for the abolition of slavery. It is the first to develop the editorial page as we know it today.

1844 Samuel Morse invents the telegraph, wires are strung between major cities, and news now travels instantaneously.

1848 The Associated Press is founded. It serves papers of many political persuasions, so encourages reporters to write stories more objectively.

1865 After the Civil War, industrialization invades the press room and newspapers become increasingly mechanized.

Yellow Journalism

1878 Joseph Pulitzer founds the *St. Louis Post-Dispatch.*

1883 Pulitzer's *New York World* brings what was eventually called yellow journalism to America's largest city.

1886 *World* circulation tops 250,000 and surpasses the *Daily News* as New York's most widely read newspaper.

1887 William Randolph Hearst is put in charge of the *San Francisco Examiner.* Long an admirer of Pulitzer, he imitates *World* style and the *Examiner* prospers.

1895 Hearst comes to New York, buys the *New York Journal,* and hires away many *World* personnel.

1896 "Circulation war" between the *Journal* and *World*. Within 12 months, the *Journal* has the top circulation.

1896–98 Stories in the yellow press whip up public sympathy for a war with Spain.

1900 One-third of all metropolitan dailies practice yellow journalism.

1900 President McKinley is assassinated. The Hearst papers are blamed for inspiring the murderer.

1901–10 Circulation of most yellow papers falls and yellow journalism rapidly disappears.

Objective Journalism

1896 Adolph Ochs takes over the *New York Times.*

1900 Associated Press moves to New York and expands.

1914 *New York Times* begins a policy of publishing important documents in their entirety, further justifying its slogan, "All the news that's fit to print."

1923 The Canons of Journalism adopted by the American Society of Newpaper Editors stress the social responsibility of newspapers and reporters to report the news "fairly."

1933 The American Newspaper Guild is founded as the first union for news people.

1941 *The Wall Street Journal* is taken over by Bernard Kilgore. Circulation soars as the *Journal* practices detached reporting with emphasis on financial news and detailed analyses of economic events.

1942 Voluntary "Code of Wartime Practices for the American Press" is issued by government; the press is willing to cooperate.

1947 Hutchin's Commission report is critical of press practices. It argues for tighter regulation of print journalism.

1958 United Press and International News Service combine to form United Press International.

New Journalism

1958 Both major wire services begin running more "interpretative" articles and columns.

1960 The *New York Herald Tribune* begins using a magazine-style layout—more pictures and a lighter writing style.

1960s American metros lose circulation in many cities. Many combine to save press and circulation expenses. Many dailies in business for 60 years or more fold.

1962 Tom Wolfe, the father of new journalism, joins the staff of the *New York Herald Tribune.*

1963 Sportswriter Jimmy Breslin begins column for the *Herald Tribune,* using writing techniques borrowed from fiction.

1968 Some Democratic convention reporters find they need more than objectivity to tell the story. Domestic violence and increasing hostility over the Vietnam War make "objective" reporting difficult.

1968–69 *Underground* newspapers like the *Los Angeles Free Press* and the *Village Voice* experience rapid circulation increases.

1971 President Nixon temporarily blocks *New York Times, Washington Post,* and *Boston Globe* publication of the Pentagon Papers.

1972 Hunter Thompson's *Fear and Loathing: On the Campaign Trail 1972* appears as a series of articles in *Rolling Stone.*

1972 Bob Woodward and Carl Bernstein's *Washington Post* articles help expose Watergate scandals. President Nixon resigns.

1978 Over 60 percent of U.S. dailies are owned by large chains. Daily circulation rises to over 60 million and ad revenues top $10 billion.

opinion and interpretation, radio a quick summary of the headlines, and television a brief eyewitness account of the day's events. All perform different sorts of news-related functions while covering the same events. The consumer receiving information from all media is probably better informed than the one who insists that a single medium is the "best" way to get the news. For that matter, researcher Leo Bogart determined that most people who watched TV news found it increased their desire to read the newspaper. Newspapers can provide details missing from 30-minute TV newscasts.

Despite all of the changes of the last 300 years, the newspaper continues to exert a tremendous influence on our daily lives. We still visit the information pond to take our daily plunge in the cultural bath of newspapers. This ritual is likely to continue.

Five Eras of American Newspaper Journalism

Historians differ as to the best way to divide the history of newspaper journalism. The five-way division in 3.2 appears here for the first time (as far as I know) and merits some explanation. The key involves objective or factual reporting versus subjective or advocacy reporting. The early, yellow, and new journalism eras are dominated by the subjective opinions of reporters, editors, and owners. The penny press and objective eras are characterized by more dispassionate attempts to report the news. Any division suffers from some degree of oversimplification, but this one does point out a continuing historical cycle that I believe is significant.

The Early Years   During the first years of American newspapers, opinions of the owner-editors were paramount in deciding how a story was to be "played." There were several small papers in each metropolitan area, and each reflected a particular point of view. Owner-editors usually printed stories to appeal to the faithful and bring new subscribers into the fold. Newspapers crusaded for political causes and decried political injustice. Editorial opinion did not appear on a special page, but came within a story, often in the lead paragraph, sometimes in italics. Since editors and reporters were advocates for a point of view, we refer to this period as the beginning of "advocacy journalism."

The most heated debate appeared in the letters to the editor column. Historian Frank Luther Mott notes that letters were often contributed by editors as well as readers. After the Revolution, debate centered on the adoption of a federal constitution, taxes, the treaty with England, and problems with the French.

Did newspapers in the new nation really have freedom of the press? Massachusetts adopted a tax on newspapers, and later on newspaper advertising, that smacked of state control. New printers were often poor and susceptible to promises of lucrative government printing contracts or post office appointments. In 1798 Congress passed the Sedition Act. It provided that "any person . . . writing, printing or uttering any false, scandalous or malicious statement against the Government of the United States . . . should be imprisoned not over two years and pay a fine not exceeding $2,000." This was interpreted by most editors as direct censorship, since those likely to be punished were those who disagreed with the then-powerful Federalist Party.

There were several trials under the act and a few prominent printers were fined and sent to prison. But when Thomas Jefferson was elected president in 1800 he pardoned the prisoners, and the House Judiciary Committee denounced the Sedition Act as unconstitutional. All fines collected were returned with interest.

The last 30 years of the early period have been called the "dark ages" of partisan journalism. The profession was rife with corruption, and attacks on political leaders grew increasingly vicious. The personal lives of prominent figures were considered fair game, and Jefferson probably suffered the most. Andrew Jackson was never a favorite of journalists either, but he knew how to use the press to his own advantage. In 1830 he endowed the *Washington Globe* with a federal printing contract and it became the official organ of the Jackson administration.

The Penny Press Until this time, newspapers had been sold by yearly subscription, although several publishers (including Horace Greeley) tried unsuccessfully to publish a cheap daily paper that could be sold issue by issue on the streets for as little as two cents per copy. But the going price for most papers was still six cents a day. At last, in 1833, thanks to technical improvements that sped production and distribution, Benjamin Day was able to bring the price of the *New York Sun* down to a penny a copy.

Advocacy journalism did not magically disappear in 1833, but the "penny press" did help develop a different kind of newspaper. The *New York Sun* offered to "lay before the public, at a price well within the means of everyone, all the news of the day. . . ." In contrast to the advocacy journals, the *Sun* was really apolitical. It offered very little political news, but reported short breezy items about local people and domestic events. One of the most popular features was the police office report, which carried a long list of local people who had been arrested for drunkenness and rowdy behavior (see 3.3).

Within a few months the *Sun*'s circulation surpassed all others in New York. Since the *Sun* did not depend on any one political constituency, it appeared to present the news impartially to all. Its overnight success prompted a number of imitators, including the *New York Herald* and the *New York Tribune*. All sold for a penny and all were successful. Soon the penny press appeared in Philadelphia and Baltimore. Penny press owners seldom had a personal ax to grind; their pur-

Independence Day at the New York Sun

"Police Office" was one of the most popular columns in the *Sun*. This sample is from the July 4, 1834, issue as reproduced in Frank Luther Mott's *American Journalism*. Note the occasional editorial quip.

Police Office

Margaret Thomas was drunk in the street—said she never would get drunk again "upon her honor." Committed, "upon honor."

William Luvoy got drunk because yesterday was so devilish warm. Drank 9 glasses of brandy and water and said he would be cursed if he wouldn't drink 9 more as quick as he could raise the money to buy it with. He would like to know what right the magistrate had to interfere with his private affairs. Fined $1—

forgot his pocketbook, and was sent over to bridewell.

Bridget McMunn got drunk and threw a pitcher at Mr. Ellis, of 53 Ludlow st. Bridget said she was the mother of 3 little orphans—God bless their dear souls—and if she went to prison they would choke to death for the want of something to eat. Committed.

Catharine McBride was brought in for stealing a frock. Catharine said she had just served out 6 months on Blackwell's Island, and she wouldn't be sent back again for the best glass of punch that ever was made. Her husband, when she last left the penitentiary, took her to a boarding house in Essex st., but the rascal got mad at her, pulled her hair, pinched her arm, and kicked her out of bed. She was determined not to bear such treatment as this, and so got drunk and stole the frock out of pure spite. Committed.

Bill Doty got drunk because he had the horrors so bad he couldn't keep sober. Committed.

Patrick Ludwick was sent up by his wife, who testified that she had supported him for several years in idleness and drunkenness. Abandoning all hopes of a reformation in her husband, she bought him a suit of clothes a fortnight since and told him to go about his business, for she would not live with him any longer. Last night he came home in a state of intoxication, broke into his wife's bedroom, pulled her out of bed, pulled her hair, and stamped on her. She called a watchman and sent him up. Pat exerted all his powers of eloquence in endeavoring to excite his wife's sympathy, but to no purpose. As every sensible woman ought to do who is cursed with a drunken husband, she refused to have anything to do with him hereafter—and he was sent to the penitentiary.

From Frank Luther Mott, *American Journalism, a History.* Copyright 1962 Macmillan Publishing Company, Inc. Used by permission.

---

pose was to provide the public with the news at the cheapest possible price and, of course, to show a profit.

This is not to say the penny press papers did not take positions. Horace Greeley's *New York Tribune* printed his famous writings on the suffering in the New York slums in 1837–1838; and Greeley called his paper "the great moral organ," claiming it was on a much higher ethical plane than competing penny papers. The *Tribune* did much to convince religious and community leaders that the cheap newspaper could be an instrument for good, and that journalism was not the exclusive bailiwick of sensation-seeking commercial publishers. But none of Greeley's opinion articles appeared on the news pages. In fact, the *New York Tribune* was the first paper to develop an editorial page as we know it today.

Mott credits the penny press with changing the concept of news. Newspapers of the early era had emphasized politics and events in Europe. The penny press shifted attention to hometown events, particularly those involving crime and sex. There was also the *human interest* story—forerunner of today's feature or soft news.

Another blow to advocacy journalism came with the invention of the telegraph in 1844 and the founding of the Associated Press (AP) four years later. The AP was to provide all news stories for a fee, but what about a political slant? It was decided that events would be reported as dispassionately as possible, so

Personal Profile: Joseph Pulitzer

Every year on his birthday Joseph Pulitzer gave each of his friends a little gift and passed out cigars to his top executives. This reverse of the usual order made sure that no one forgot his birthday, but it also said something about the paradoxical nature of one of history's most influential journalists.

His was an Horatio Alger story. He started out penniless, worked hard, and saved his money. He turned the *St. Louis Post-Dispatch* into one of the finest newspapers in America in less than five years. Then he moved on to New York, where he boosted the *New York World*'s circulation from 20,000 to more than 250,000.

Though what he did was amazing, the way he did it was even more notable. Both his papers were examples of yellow journalism. The "yellows" had a lively and uncompromising style that included the world of emotion as well as that cf fact. No political party or candidate felt safe from the sting of the *World*.

Pulitzer was careful to distinguish his brand of advocacy journalism from Hearst's. The Hearst papers, he explained, were simply "malicious and hateful." In all fairness, Hearst's own political ambi-

tions may have sparked his most vicious attacks, while Pulitzer's worst ulterior motive was to increase circulation. But contemporary critics see very little difference between the practices of the two yellow journalism giants.

A colorful character in his own right, Pulitzer was often cantankerous and arbitrary, demanding superhuman performance from his workers, who often put in 16-hour days. Ironically, the originally penniless trustbuster became part of the capitalistic establishment he criticized with such vehemence, and his profits from the *World* helped buy a yacht and hire personal servants. But his paper never wavered from the original editorial

commitments that had been made when Pulitzer took command in 1883. It continued to crusade for social and economic equality. It is this spirit that is embodied in the most coveted award in American journalism, the Pulitzer Prize.

During the final 20 years of his life, Pulitzer was virtually blind and seldom came to the *World* offices, gaining a reputation as an eccentric recluse. The reputation was well deserved. During the summer of 1911 he mused, "From the day on which I first consulted the occulist up to the present time I have only been three times in the *World* building. Most people think I'm dead. . . ." Before the end of the year, he was.

---

as not to offend any subscriber. AP offered its service to newspapers of every political persuasion.

Yellow Journalism The slavery issue and the threat of civil war heated up the political

debate in the late 1850s. More and more penny press space was given over to political news. Later, battles between the Yankee and rebel armies were reported in detail. After the war, a young ex-soldier named Joseph Pulitzer (see 3.4) arrived in St. Louis to seek his fortune. Almost immediately he became involved in local politics and to everyone's surprise was elected to the state legislature. There he became an ardent spokesman for the common people, fighting graft and corruption.

In 1878 Pulitzer bought the *St. Louis Dispatch* at a sheriff's auction and combined it with the *Post*. The new *Post-Dispatch* enlivened its columns with crusades against lotteries, tax evasion, and the city administration.

Buoyed by his success, Pulitzer moved east and acquired the *New York World*, which had been losing $40,000 a year. Pulitzer promptly announced that the *World*, under his leadership, would "expose all fraud and sham, fight all public evils and abuses . . . and battle for the people in earnest sincerity."

The phenomenal success of this formula changed journalism forever. The news reporter searched for an "unusual" slant to the story; there were stunts and "people's crusades." One reporter pretended insanity to be admitted to a state asylum, and then exposed conditions there. *World* crusades against telephone and railroad monopolies were incessant. Most articles used diagrams, illustrations, and later, photographs. The *World* made daring use of the editorial cartoon.

Pulitzer's fiercest rival was William Randolph Hearst. He bought New York's competing *Journal* in 1895, and in two years the *Journal* surpassed Pulitzer's *World* circulation. Money was no object and Hearst hired the best writers and illustrators away from his competition. Like Pulitzer, his paper em-

barked on giant crusades, but none more extravagant than the publicity he bought for the *Journal* itself. There were full-page ads in other publications and giant billboards and notices plastered everywhere. Through it all, Hearst maintained that profits were secondary. His was a mission to defend "the average person" (see 3.5).

Like Pulitzer, Hearst was not above using stunts in the pursuit of circulation and even of news itself. According to legend, Hearst sent an illustrator named Remington to Havana to document atrocities and cover the "war" that was soon to break out there. Remington cabled:

HEARST, JOURNAL, NEW YORK
EVERYTHING IS QUIET. THERE IS NO TROUBLE HERE. THERE WILL BE NO WAR. WISH TO RETURN. REMINGTON.

To which Hearst replied:

REMINGTON, HAVANA
PLEASE REMAIN. YOU FURNISH THE PICTURES AND I'LL FURNISH THE WAR. HEARST.

No one knows whether the story is actually true. But it is true the Hearst papers helped convince Americans that their pride and freedom were threatened; before long, America was at war with Spain.

In 1895 the Hearst-Pulitzer battle centered on the Sunday newspaper editions. The *World* was the undisputed leader in that area.

Sunday supplements were costly to produce but very profitable. They featured large sensationalized articles and drawings about science or pseudo-science along with crime, sports, society news, and colored comics.

Most renowned of all *World* cartoonists was Richard Outcault and his *Yellow Kid.* The comic strip depicted local scenes and situations and soon became the city's favorite. This prompted Hearst to hire Outcault away from Pulitzer and feature the strip in his competing Sunday *Journal.* Pulitzer claimed he had sole rights and hired another artist to draw his own version of the strip. For a while New York had two *Yellow Kid's.* So famous was the character, the strip, and the story of the competing journalists that critics began to call both "yellow papers." Eventually the term *yellow journalism* was used to describe this era of American journalism.

Objective Journalism Not everyone was happy with yellow journalism. Some readers boycotted the *Journal* and *World,* and some libraries and clergymen canceled their subscriptions. They believed that the exploitation of sex and crime news was a public menace. Critics cited Hearst's involvement in the Spanish-American War as one of the dangers of yellow journalism.

But other things were also happening in New York—in 1896, Adolph Ochs rescued the *New York Times* from bankruptcy. Within a few years, he made it one of the country's most successful newspapers without the help

of yellow journalism, ushering in the whole new era of objective journalism. By 1914, the *Times* had a policy of printing speeches, treaties, and government documents *in full,* the ultimate expression of objectivity.

Reporters were professional observers whose role was limited to reporting "just the facts." The period after 1900 saw journalism move from a vocation to a profession. Dozens of journalism schools began springing up across the country. Perhaps the approach that most schools taught as "proper reporting" is summarized best in George Fox Mott's *New Survey of Journalism.* According to Mott, the beginning reporter should realize at the outset that

. . . there is little or no opportunity in the reporting of news for the writer to give rein to his innermost thoughts, however high, or his deepest feelings, however subtle . . . reporting the news, even the hot news, is a coldly impersonal job. The Editor wants to find the facts in the story and not the writer's personal impressions or emotions. He has learned from long experience that effective newswriting must be objective.

In 1923, the American Society of Newspaper Editors stated rather concretely what was already the practice in most major American newspapers: "A journalist who uses his power for any selfish or otherwise unworthy purpose is faithless to a high trust." This "selfishness" included slanting front-page stories to a particular political perspective.

Citizen Kane and His Declaration of Principles

The office is dark except for the dim light from a gas lamp. Charles Foster Kane has taken over the *New York Inquirer* and moved into the office, bag and baggage, reminding a befuddled editor that "the news goes on 24 hours a day and I want to be here for all of it." In his first 24 hours he has fired that editor, dropped the price of the *Inquirer* from three cents to two, and remade the front page four times. He is joined by his business manager, Mr. Bernstein, and his best friend, Jed Leland:

Bernstein: You just made the paper over four times tonight, Mr. Kane—that's all.

Kane: I've changed the front page a little, Mr. Bernstein. That's not enough—there's something I've got to get into this paper besides pictures and print—I've got to make the *New York Inquirer* as important to New York as the gas in that light.

Leland: What're you going to do, Charlie?

Kane: My Declaration of Principles—don't smile, Jed. (Getting the idea) Take dictation, Mr. Bernstein.

Bernstein: I can't write shorthand, Mr. Kane.

Kane: I'll write it myself. (Kane grabs a piece of rough paper and a grease crayon. Sitting down on the bed next to Bernstein, he starts to write.)

Bernstein: (Looking over his shoulder) You don't wanta make any promises, Mr. Kane, you don't wanta keep.

Kane: (As he writes) These'll be kept. (Stops and reads what he has written) I'll provide the people of this city with a daily paper that will tell all the news honestly. (Starts to write again, reading as he writes) I will also provide them . . .

Leland: That's the second sentence you've started with "I."

Kane: (Looking up) People are going to know who's responsible. And they're going to get the news—the true news—quickly and simply and entertainingly. (With real conviction) And no special interests will be allowed to interfere with the truth of that news. (Writes again, reading as he writes) I will also provide them with a fighting and tireless champion of their rights as citizens and human beings—Signed—Charles Foster Kane.

Leland: Charlie . . . (Kane looks up)

Leland (continuing): Can I have that?

Kane: I'm going to print it. (Calls) Mike!

Mike: Yes, Mr. Kane.

Kane: Here's an editorial. I want to run it in a box on the front page.

Mike: (Very wearily) Today's front page, Mr. Kane?

Kane: That's right. We'll have to remake again—better go down and let them know.

Mike: All right, Mr. Kane. (He starts away)

Leland: Just a minute, Mike. (Mike turns)

Leland (continuing): When you're done with that, I'd like to have it back. (Mike registers that this, in his opinion, is another screwball and leaves. Kane looks at Leland.)

Leland (continuing): I'd just like to keep that particular piece of paper myself. I've got a hunch it might turn out to be one of the important papers—of our time. (A little ashamed of his ardor) A document—like the Declaration of Independence—and the Constitution—and my first report card at school. (Kane smiles back at him, but they are both serious. The voices of the newsboys fill the air.)

That scene, from perhaps the greatest American film ever made, *Citizen Kane,* is fantasy, of course. But it captures precisely the image of the crusading editor that we all carry around in our heads. The editor who fights for the public's rights "as citizens and human beings" is part of the folklore of American journalism and is based on the real-life stories of men like

---

Not all journalists would agree that slanted reporting had disappeared entirely. World War II stories, for example, certainly had their biases. (Headlines routinely referred to the Japanese as "Japs.") And many smaller publications like *I. F. Stone's Weekly* followed earlier traditions of advocacy journalism. Still, most editors insisted on objectivity and got it. Objectivity became synonymous with good journalism, and few challenged it. Papers still conducted crusades, of course, but journalists were careful to print both sides of an issue

Hearst (who served as the obvious model for *Citizen Kane*) and Pulitzer.

Though journalism has changed in many ways since the beginning of the century, most of us still think of newspaper work as romantic, glamorous, and socially vital. Films like *Citizen Kane* (the crusading publisher) and *All the President's Men* (the crusading reporters) reinforce that image.

wherever possible, and they generally bent over backwards to double-check facts and figures before printing them.

Modern journalistic business methods reinforce the practice of objective reporting. Local ownership of the metropolitan daily has rapidly become a thing of the past. Large chains like the Newhouse and Gannett groups have bought up dozens of major newspapers. Often this means that one chain owns both major newspapers in a city. (Newhouse, for example, owns both the *Oregonian* and the

Oregon Journal of Portland, Oregon; the Gannett group owns both the *Advertiser* and the *Star Bulletin* of Honolulu.) These large corporations are seldom overtly concerned with national political matters and are primarily interested in making a profit. As for local political issues, top management is often thousands of miles away and does not wish to get involved. Of course, most papers do take sides on local and national issues on the editorial pages, and local editors and reporters do have a stake in the community. But there is not the kind of all-out pressure that comes from an owner-editor on the scene.

New Journalism Not all would agree that objective journalism is a blessing. Some feel, for example, that an insistence on two sides to every story may have prevented journalists from doing what print does best, describing the complexities of an issue or event. According to Marshall McLuhan:

The old (objective) journalism tried to give an objective picture of the situation by giving the pro and the con. It was strangely assumed that there were two sides to every case. It never occurred to them that there might be 40 sides, 1,000 sides . . . no, only two sides.

During the McCarthy hearings of the early 1950s, the press was careful to maintain its objectivity. Senator Joseph McCarthy from Wisconsin was making serious allegations about Communists in the United States. Most journalists disagreed with McCarthy and his

methods but maintained objectivity in their stories; however, a few did not. The *New York Times* editorialized against McCarthy. Columnist Drew Pearson and broadcast journalist Edward R. Murrow were among those who vehemently denounced McCarthy's tactics. Murrow's famous *See It Now* broadcast, using clips from the Senator's own speeches, seemed to help turn the public tide against McCarthy.

At this point, the press began to seriously reexamine the role of the reporter (see 3.6). Perhaps facts alone weren't enough. The public had a right to get *more* than the facts. Veteran reporters were in a position to make value judgments about the facts as well as report them.

In 1958, both the Associated Press and the new United Press International (UPI) began running more interpretative articles and columns on their wires. The use of large pictures and more visually attractive magazine-style layouts became common practice in most metros. A band of renegade journalists began experimenting with *new journalism*, the new nonfiction. Theirs was a subjective, no-holds-barred writing style. Objectivity, they said, had been a sacred cow for long enough. They said truth was best reported by those who let their emotions become *part* of the story.

In the 1960s, dozens of *underground* newspapers like the *East Village Other, Los Angeles Free Press,* and *Berkeley Barb* appeared. These had a definite left-of-center political viewpoint and their bias showed in almost every article. The underground press was irreverent, funny,

Army Counsel Joseph Welch (left) and Wisconsin's Senator McCarthy during the 1954 hearings that were McCarthy's final turn in the spotlight. McCarthy had been close to a number of reporters, and later the press began to reexamine its role in reporting the news.

frank, and often outrageous. It was also very popular. Apparently, there was an audience for subjective journalism.

New journalism is still more at home in underground newspapers and magazines than on the front pages of metros. But the underground press left its mark on those "above ground." Newspapers now devote more space to soft news and new journalism stories than ever before, and reporters are not as timid about expressing their points of view. Today, every *Los Angeles Times* carries a soft news analysis story on the front page. The reporter's point of view is often part of the story.

Each of the five eras of American journalism has had its own distinct flavor, famous names, dates, and places. All contributed to and reflected the social order of their day.

Early newspapers were formed in a new society, still seeking a political and social direction. They were chaotic and sometimes bitter, and so were their readers. The penny press resulted from increasing technology and

mechanization. Penny papers may have served the first real popular desire for equality and honest government. Their zeal in this pursuit reflects the zeal of the times. The objective years may have been a necessary consequence of yellow journalism. The more sophisticated reader was entitled to something less sensational. It is probably too early to pass judgment on new journalism, but it was born of the social and political chaos of the 1960s and is changing modern news practices. Critics worry that readers spotting a bias in a story may grow to distrust newspapers and reporters as much as they now distrust the politicians the stories are often about.

Newspaper messages are vital links to the social norms and behaviors of their times. The newspaper, like all mass media, contributes to and amplifies those behaviors. In every case, an important part of this contribution involves *how* as well as *what* was presented, *form* as well as *content, medium* as well as *message.*

Issues and Answers

Public, Press, and Government

Like all freedoms, the freedom to print information must ultimately be tempered by a certain responsibility. Most of us think of freedom as absolute, yet freedom of speech does not include the right to yell "fire" in a crowded theater. Originally, freedom of the press involved only books, but as newspapers, magazines, and other media appeared, each brought its unique problems.

The entire problem of freedom of the press involves relationships between three entities: press, public, and government.

The Press   Early Gutenbergs could not imagine press freedom. They produced only those manuscripts authorized by the ruling elite. Today's American printers cannot imagine such a system. Freedom of the press was guaranteed in the Bill of Rights and tested with the Sedition Act.

Occasionally newspapers feel pressure from the public. During the excesses of yellow journalism, many people threatened to boycott newspapers or put pressure on publishers to practice their trade more responsibly. And newspapers also from time to time have felt pressured by the government. President

Nixon used *prior restraint* to block newspaper publication of the Pentagon Papers, which he claimed were classified information. When this happened, the press was livid.

Most journalists are civil libertarians who feel that the press has the right to publish anything it likes (see 3.7). They contend that the public's "right to know" takes precedence over other considerations. They reason that if the public has access to diverse information and many points of view, it will make the right decisions.

The Government   Government is, at least in theory, the agent of the public. But government has grown so large that some think of it as a separate entity that has gotten away from the people. When Jimmy Carter successfully campaigned for the presidency in 1976, he promised to "return government to the people."

In press matters, the government often plays a paternal role as the public protector. This was the rationale used by President Nixon during the Pentagon Papers affair. He said general knowledge of such information was a threat to the people. He didn't get away with it; the Supreme Court decided Nixon had overstepped his bounds. Nevertheless, most people agree there is a need for *some* government regulation of the press. Without it, people would be free to publish and distribute anything, no matter how libelous or obscene. The result would be a kind of anarchy of print.

A Michigan newspaper "takes on" the judges. This is the reverse of the usual situation, in which judges restrain reporters during controversial trials.

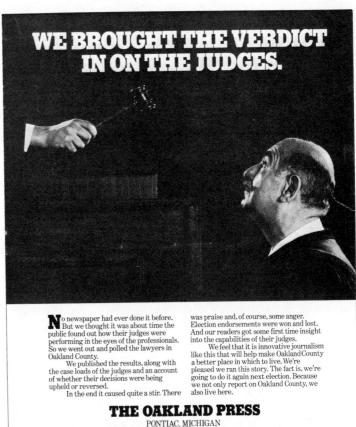

WE BROUGHT THE VERDICT IN ON THE JUDGES.

No newspaper had ever done it before. But we thought it was about time the public found out how their judges were performing in the eyes of the professionals. So we went out and polled the lawyers in Oakland County.

We published the results, along with the case loads of the judges and an account of whether their decisions were being upheld or reversed.

In the end it caused quite a stir. There was praise and, of course, some anger. Election endorsements were won and lost. And our readers got some first time insight into the capabilities of their judges.

We feel that it is innovative journalism like this that will help make Oakland County a better place in which to live. We're pleased we ran this story. The fact is, we're going to do it again next election. Because we not only report on Oakland County, we also live here.

THE OAKLAND PRESS

PONTIAC, MICHIGAN

A CAPITAL CITIES COMMUNICATIONS, INC. NEWSPAPER.
WE TALK TO PEOPLE.

THE OAKLAND PRESS (Pontiac, Michigan) • CITIZEN-JOURNAL (Arlington, Texas) • NEWS-DEMOCRAT (Belleville, Illinois) • FORT WORTH STAR-TELEGRAM • THE KANSAS CITY STAR TIMES • Women's Wear Daily • Home Furnishings Daily • Daily News Record • Footwear News • Supermarket News • Electronic News • American Metal Market • W • Energy User News • Men's Wear • Metal/Center News

The Public The public may exert no direct power, but it has a tremendous role to play in this "tug of war." Direct public feedback to the media comes from letters and replies to editorials, but the consumer's main influence on the press is economic: the power of the purse—if they don't like it, they refuse to buy. Loss of circulation will eventually kill any commercial publication. Likewise advertisers can withhold their support if they don't like the content of a publication, with or without regard for the reading public's position.

The public also puts pressure on government if it feels a publication is getting out of hand. New laws can be passed or sanctions used to limit the ability of a publisher to disseminate information.

Public consumer advocates watch over the media. Pressure groups representing ethnic and social minorities are ever alert to media treatment of their members. During the 1970s, blacks, women, Mexican-Americans, and others won significant concessions from the newspapers. Their primary demands were for more equitable hiring practices and fairer media images of their groups.

A Question of Balance Over the years the balance of power between press, public, and government has shifted. During the colonial years, the King of England determined what colonists could read. The new nation established freedom of the press as a cornerstone of its democracy, but unrestricted press freedom posed some problems. The balance of power has shifted to reflect current social and political trends.

The excesses of the early years and yellow journalism prompted reform movements within newspapers themselves. Competing publishers stepped in and reformed news practices in response to public demand. The government has, for the most part, stayed out of the business of reforming the press. But as mass media have grown in power and status, there have been calls for the government to "do something."

The 1947 Hutchin's Commission on Freedom of the Press concluded: "It becomes an imperative question whether the performance of the press can any longer be left to the unregulated initiative of the few who manage it." Committee skepticism reflects the growing power of mass media to determine our political and social attitudes and beliefs. Press

coverage of a political candidate may mean the difference between victory and defeat. Most agree that the presidential candidate debates in 1960 and 1976 played a significant role in determining the winner. It was up to the press, through analysis, to determine the winners and losers long before election day.

Most observers agree that today's balance is weighted heavily in favor of the press. Prepublication censorship is unknown and obscenity remains the only area in which there is systematic government intervention. Though cries of censorship are heard whenever anyone suggests government regulation, the growing power of mass media seems to demand some shift in the balance.

If we are to limit the freedom of the press for the benefit of all, should we also limit who may practice journalism? Since reporters and editors determine the content of information we must have to make important decisions, should we require some credentials from them to make sure they operate in our best interests? Doctors and lawyers must pass rigorous government exams to be admitted to practice. Medical and bar associations police their own ranks, weeding out the occasional incompetent or unethical member. Of course this doesn't guarantee that all incompetents will be dismissed, but it helps.

The beginning reporter can be a high school dropout or a Ph.D., a highly ethical person or one willing to exploit the media for personal or political purposes. There are journalism associations, fraternal codes, ethics committees, and the like, but none has the power to purge its ranks of incompetent or unethical members.

Since journalists have not acted to regulate themselves, some contend that it is the business of government to do so. They envision a regulatory agency similar to those that police the legal and medical professions.

Most journalists abhor the thought of any government regulation, maintaining it would violate freedom of the press. How can the government have such power over media when media are supposed to act as watchdogs? It might be easy for government to blunt press criticism by punishing it through a regulatory agency. Yet will any private business regulate itself in the public interest without the threat of external control?

Many books have been written about these press/public/government relationships; this has been a very simple overview. I hope that it will start you thinking about these problems and encourage you to do additional reading. A good starting point is the references at the end of this chapter.

Queries and Concepts

1. Delve into your own local newspaper, sifting the hard news from the soft. What is the balance of the front section in terms of numbers of stories? How many total column inches are devoted to each?

2. How many people in your class read at least one story from a newspaper every day? Which section do they prefer and why?

3. Pick your favorite character from the history of American journalism and find a biography. Write a brief portrait along the lines of the story on Pulitzer in this chapter.

4. Citizen Kane's crusade and the Watergate reporters represent two of the images we have about journalism as a career. Can you think of others? Where did they come from?

5. Does the same company control all print news outlets in your nearest big city? Does it have any interests in the broadcast media?

6. Contact a local reporter, a government official, and a consumer advocate. Do they think the government should license or regulate reporters?

Readings and References

Hard and Soft News

William L. Rivers
The Mass Media: Reporting, Writing, Editing, 2d ed. New York: Harper & Row, 1975.

This is a complete *reporter's* handbook that covers all media. See especially "The World of the Journalist" and "Writing." The latter offers a "straight news" formula for carefully separating fact from opinion.

Paul V. Sheehan
Reportorial Writing. Radnor, Pa.: Chilton Books, 1972.
This book will give you an idea of what the hard news reporter's goals are. Sheehan's approach is based on the assumption that most news is hard news, though he does allow for the "human interest story" and the "interesting angle."

Mass and Special-Interest Audiences

Allen Kirschner and Linda Kirschner, eds.
Journalism: Readings in the Mass Media. Indianapolis, Ind.: Odyssey Press, 1971.
This anthology is full of useful articles about the role of the press in society and its audiences. See especially "Audience and Effect."

What You See Is What You Get

Marshall McLuhan
Understanding Media, 2d ed. New York: McGraw-Hill, 1964.
Much of McLuhan's work deals with the permanence of print and the unique characteristics of the newspaper form. See especially

chapters: 9 (The Written Word: An Eye for an Ear), 16 (The Print: How to Dig It), 18 (The Printed Word: Architect of Nationalism), and 21 (The Press: Government by News Leak).

Business Trends in Newspaper Publishing

Editor and Publisher. New York: Editor and Publisher, annual.
As far as facts and figures are concerned, this is the bible of newspaper and magazine publishing. Available in most libraries.

Five Eras of American Newspaper Journalism

Journalists are preoccupied with their history. There have been hundreds, maybe thousands of books published on the subject. Those selected here are included for their comprehensiveness and/or readability. Use the bibliographies to pursue specific historical eras or personalities if you wish. None of these really covers the fifth era: new journalism. See also the readings and references in Chapter 4.

Frank Luther Mott
American Journalism. Riverside, N.J.: Macmillan, 1962.
This has the most complete treatment of American journalism of any text I know. Very popular among journalists and journalism

history teachers. The excellent index enables you to go to your area of interest.

Robert A. Rutland
The Newsmongers: Journalism in the Life of the Nation, 1690–1972. New York: Dial Press, 1973.
A breezier and more up-to-date version of journalism history than Mott. More lively and readable, though less comprehensive.

W. A. Swanberg
Citizen Hearst. New York: Scribner's, 1961.
Pulitzer. New York: Scribner's, 1972.
Swanberg is a biographer who makes his characters come alive, and both volumes illuminate the subject matter in a way few others do. Hearst and Pulitzer are so revered by most journalists that their darker sides are seldom revealed. As interesting as any biographies you will find, each of these books has a useful bibliography and index.

Issues and Answers: Public, Press, and Government

When journalism writers are not busy writing about history, they are writing about government and the press. Again there are dozens of books available and the criteria for inclusion here involve comprehensiveness and readability.

Georgetown Law Journal
Media and the First Amendment in a Free Society. Amherst: University of Massachusetts Press, 1973.
An anthology with contributions by Walter Cronkite and former Senator Sam Ervin, among others. Use the table of contents to go right to the area that interests you. This is a potpourri designed to have something for just about everybody.

Jerome A. Barron
Freedom of the Press for Whom? The Right of Access to Mass Media. Bloomington: Indiana University Press, 1973.
Includes sections on campus press, underground press, crime, citizens' groups, and television. Media access as a prime issue in media control.

William L Rivers and Michael J. Nyhan, eds.
Aspen Notebook on Government and the Media. New York: Praeger, 1973.
This book comes out of the collective minds of 50 top people in government and communications who gathered at Aspen, Colorado, for a seminar in 1972. It includes sections on the public's right to know, government's role, and citizen access to the media. The final section offers a summary of the principal issues in the area and is one of the most succinct (20 pages) overviews available.

4

Newspapers, Part Two:
Soft News and the New Journalism

The New York Times slogan, "all the news that's
fit to print," advertises the fact that news
is actually fiction. —Marshall McLuhan

What Is New Journalism?

New journalism is perhaps the most overworked
and misunderstood term used in media today.
At one time or another, "new j" has been used
to describe every newspaper trend of the last
two decades. This preoccupation, and the
confusion, are understandable: The debate that
revolves around new journalism involves the
very purpose of reporting and the role of journalism in society.

This does not mean that new j has drastically altered the front page of American
newspapers—it has not. Newspapers cover
most news events in the same fashion they
did in the 1950s. Many stories come directly
from the AP or UPI wire, and wire service
reporters still do their best to report world
events as objectively as possible.

New journalism was originally called the
new nonfiction because it had its own particular
style. New j stories tend to be colorful,
dramatic, and highly personal. Most agree that
they are considerably more "fun" to write and
read than traditional newspaper stories. New
journalism differs from traditional reporting
in several ways—it is subjective, personal, passionate, bizarre, and heavily stylized.

Subjective New journalism is based on the
conviction that objectivity in reporting is an
impossible, and perhaps undesirable, goal.
New journalism writer Hunter S. Thompson
(see 4.1) put it this way:

Objective Journalism is a hard thing to come by
these days. We all yearn for it—but who can point
the way? Most journalists only *talk* about objectivity. . . . As for my objectivity well my doctor
says it swole up and busted about ten years ago.
The only thing I ever saw that came close to objective journalism was a closed-circuit TV setup that
watched shoplifters in the General Store at Woody
Creek, Colorado.

So much for Objective Journalism. Don't bother
to look for it here—not under any byline of mine;
or anyone else I can think of. With the possible
exception of box scores, race results and stock
market tabulations, there is no such thing as objective, journalism. The phrase itself is a pompous
contradiction in terms.

This is a complete turnaround from the
view of the traditional journalist, who
"covered" the event but expressed no particular point of view. New journalists seem to be
saying, "Since objectivity is impossible, let the
reader beware—I'm going to tell it as I see it
and *feel* it."

Personal In many newspapers, bylines are
rare. Traditionally, many stories come from
wire services or local reporters who remain
nameless. The assumption is that if two good
reporters are assigned to an event, they will
bring back pretty much the same story. New
journalism writers, by contrast, *have* to have
bylines, since they leave a personal stamp on
every story. Often new j stories are written
in the first person, and the story is seen

Hunter S. Thompson— New Journalist

Perhaps the best known of the original new journalists is Hunter S. Thompson, who heads the national affairs desk at *Rolling Stone.* He has ridden on a motorcycle with a Hell's Angel and in a limousine with Richard Nixon to "get the story." His unorthodox methods and writing style, plus a heavy reliance on what he calls "recreational drugs," have made him one of the most controversial figures in journalism.

He seldom leaves the reader in doubt about his personal feelings. In *Fear and Loathing: On the Campaign Trail '72,* he made it quite clear which presidential candidate he liked ("George McGovern is too decent a man to become President") and disliked ("It is Nixon himself who represents that dark, venal, and incurably violent side of the American character").

Thompson's antics are followed closely by millions of *Doonesbury* readers, where he is known as Uncle Duke.

Copyright 1974, G.B. Trudeau. Distributed by Universal Press Syndicate.

through the eyes of the reporters. Their own feelings, emotions, and other intimate life details are as much a part of the story as is the subject itself.

Passionate New journalists are seldom calm about their subjects. They have often formed a point of view before investigating the "facts." In this way they are similar to the yellow journalists.

Bizarre Another thing that distinguishes new j stories is their content. Though new j stories often deal with ordinary subject material, quite often they are about things reporters have never studied before. New journalism writers attempt to strip away the usual to find the unusual. No subject is too bizarre and there are no taboos.

Stylized   New journalism differs from traditional reporting in *form* as well as in *content*. New journalists use dialogue extensively (verbatim where possible), as well as flashbacks, long strings of adjectives, and colorful phrases usually reserved for fiction. According to writer Tom Wolfe, new j form allows reporters to use all the "tools" of the fiction writer. The difference, of course, is that new j writers create characters and plots not from their imagination, but from real people and events. (Actually, there is little new in this. Over the years, many fiction writers have based plots on personal experience. Interesting people they met became fictional characters in their books. F. Scott Fitzgerald once remarked, "Sometimes I wonder whether Zelda [his wife] and I are real people, or simply characters in one of my novels.") It has become even harder to separate new journalism from fiction because writers like Hunter S. Thompson rely heavily on their fantasies while reporting real-life events. These fantasies become so interwoven with the facts that we often don't know which is which.

New Journalism Sampler

Not everyone agrees on one definition of new journalism. Perhaps the most effective way to explain it is to present excerpts from three publications that "covered" the same story (see 4.2). The *Washington Post* Service's article comes closest to the traditional straight news story; next, the more stylized prose of *Newsweek*; and finally, Hunter Thompson's new j piece, "The Kentucky Derby is Decadent and Depraved." Note Thompson's descriptive detail and heavy use of dialogue.

We witness events of the Kentucky Derby from Thompson's subjective view. He is obviously relishing his fantasy role as a photographer for *Playboy* magazine. His fantasies comprise a large part of the story. For Thompson, it is the fantasies that count; he doesn't even bother to cover the race itself until well into the story.

New Journalism in the 1970s

Journalism researcher Everette Dennis claims that "new journalism" has become a label for several distinctly different kinds of reporting; the *new nonfiction* of Thompson, Wolfe, and others is only one new j form. Another is *alternative journalism* or modern muckraking and appears in publications as diverse as the *Village Voice* and the *Columbia Journalism Review*. Then there is *advocacy journalism*, which appears in "point of view" papers such as those sponsored by feminists, Black Panthers, and labor unions. *Underground journalism* features stories on the drug culture and radical politics and is found in the *Berkeley Barb* and the *Los Angeles*

Free Press. Precision journalism is the reporting of "social indicators and matters of public concern" but in "highly readable prose." The Knight newspapers and others like the *San Francisco Chronicle* have featured many such articles. This is perhaps the most objective form of new j.

Most daily newspapers have been influenced, though hardly revolutionized, by one or more of these forms. The *Los Angeles Times* began the practice of carrying a soft news or feature story each day on the left side of its front page (see 4.3). These stories often deal with investigation of local politics or personal observations of one reporter who has been assigned to a story for a long time. Stories often run 2,000 words or longer, a length that was unheard of in the 1950s.

In 1968, the *Washington Post* began a section called "Style." Editor Thomas Kendrick explains that "Style" subscribes to the "literary" and new "advocacy" strain of new j.

Style's focus is squarely on the human dimension. Style writers are striving to gather facts without excising their human context, freeze drying their emotional impact . . . and in the same vein they try to cut through the reality behind institutional stereotypes of a Mardi Gras or Republican convention.

Kendrick freely admits that, although "personal journalism" (as he calls it) tries to "extend the range and impact of daily journalism," it also involves "serious risks, even for

talented writers and experienced reporters." These include inaccuracies, tired or strained adjectives, and erroneous biases.

Criticism of New Journalism

For some critics and many working journalists, new journalism is heresy. Critic Dwight Macdonald contends, "It's a bastard form, having it both ways, exploiting the factual authority of journalism and the atmospheric license of fiction." Michael Arlen, a writer for *The New Yorker*, says the "real failure of new journalism . . . is in the new journalist's determination and insistence that we see life largely on *his* terms." *Saturday Review* writer John Tebbel argues that new j is really "the old new journalism," since "from the time newspapers began in this country until the nineteenth century was half completed, the press was utterly subjective, irresponsible, and unabashedly activist."

Style too can be a problem. New j writers spend much time and effort developing an individual style that they feel helps them communicate their personal perspective. Critics contend that if more effort were spent checking content and less worrying about style, new j might become more widely accepted, particularly in newspaper writing. They feel that the flashy stylized new j prose gets in the way of reporting the facts. Critic Edward Hoagland says, "First person journalism is fashionable now though the excesses

Three Versions of the Kentucky Derby

Washington Post:
"Dust Commander Derby Winner"

Dust Commander, the smallest and least expensive colt in a field of 17, yesterday captured the 96th and richest running of the Kentucky Derby, returning $32.60.

Owner Robert Lehmann, who last week shot two tigers and a leopard in India, arrived at Churchill Downs yesterday morning in ample time to see his 15.2 hands (62 inches), 900-lb. son of the young sire Bolt Commander bag $128,800 of the $171,300 purse. Lehmann bought Dust Commander for $6,500 at the Keeneland fall yearling sale.

The 100,000 fans at Churchill Downs dismissed Dust Commander at 15-to-1 although he had scored in the Blue Grass stakes at Keeneland last week at 35-to-1. Eight recent Blue Grass winners now have taken the Derby.

Dust Commander, closing briskly along the inside under jockey Mike Manganello, took command at the eighth pole and drew out smartly, completing the 1¼ miles in 2:03 2/5 over a good track. My Dad

George, the $2.80-to-1 favorite, also got through on the rail at the top of the stretch, finishing second by a half length over High Echelon.

Newsweek:
"Dust Commander's Dust"

Sonny Werblin, the flamboyant former owner of the New York Jets, came to Kentucky with last year's brilliant two-year-old champion, Silent Screen, and a partying entourage of Broadway racing fans. John Jacobs brought Personality, a compact son of Hail to Reason and Affectionately, probably the two best horses ever bred by his father, the late Hirsch Jacobs. Bud McManus and Arnold Winick came north with My Dad George and Corn Off the Cob, the two top campaigners of the Florida season. A logical case could have been made for any of them—and for half a dozen other invaders—before Saturday's Kentucky Derby. But it has been a rough year for logic among those who have followed the wildly unpredictable crop of three-year-olds, and things didn't become any simpler in the Derby.

The rich and famous favorites were convincingly trounced by a small, unimpressive-looking 15-to-1 shot named Dust Commander, whose owner, trainer, and jockey have spent most of their careers in racing at minor-league way stations in Ohio and Kentucky.

Hunter S. Thompson:
"The Kentucky Derby Is Decadent and Depraved"

Welcome to Derbytown
I got off the plane around midnight and no one spoke as I crossed the dark runway to the terminal. The air was thick and hot, like wandering into a steam bath. Inside, people hugged each other and shook hands . . . big grins and a whoop here and there. "By God! You old bastard! Good to see you, boy! Damn good . . . and I mean it."

In the air-conditioned lounge I met a man from Houston who said his name was something or other—"but just call me Jimbo"—and he was here to get it on. "I'm ready for anything, by God! Anything at all. Yeah, what are you drinkin?" I ordered a Margarita with ice, but he

of its practitioners are going to kill off its fashionability soon."

Whether we agree with these critics or not, we have to agree that American journalism is changing, and new j has a lot to do with the change. The most important reason for new j's appearance now may be our increasing

dependence on other mass media. If we want up-to-the-minute news, we can get it from television and radio. The newspaper is something else, an experience to be enjoyed at our leisure. It moves more slowly and must deliver something television and radio cannot. New j gives us the personal perspective of the wouldn't hear of it: "Naw, naw . . . what the hell kind of drink is that for Kentucky Derby time? What's wrong with you, boy?" He grinned and winked at the bartender. "Goddam, we gotta educate this boy. Get him some good whiskey. . . ."

I shrugged. "Okay, a double Old Fitz on ice." Jimbo nodded his approval.

"Look." He tapped me on the arm to make sure I was listening. "I know this Derby crowd, I come here every year, and let me tell you one thing I've learned—this is no town to be giving people the impression you're some kind of faggot. Not in public, anyway. Shit, they'll roll you in a minute, knock you in the head and take every goddam cent you have."

I thanked him and fitted a Marlboro into my cigarette holder. "Say," he said, "you look like you might be in the horse business . . . am I right?"

"No," I said. "I'm a photographer."

"Oh yeah?" He eyed my ragged leather bag with new interest. "Is that what you got there—cameras? Who you work for?"

"*Playboy*," I said.

He laughed. "Well goddam! What are you gonna take pictures of—

nekkid horses? Haw! I guess you'll be workin' pretty hard when they run the Kentucky Oaks. That's a race just for fillies." He was laughing wildly. "Hell yes! And they'll all be nekkid too!"

I shook my head and said nothing; just stared at him for a moment, trying to look grim. "There's going to be trouble," I said. "My assignment is to take pictures of the riot."

"What riot?"

I hesitated, twirling the ice in my drink. "At the track. On Derby Day. The Black Panthers." I stared at him again. "Don't you read the newspapers?"

The grin on his face had collapsed. "What the hell are you talkin' about?"

"Well . . . maybe I shouldn't be telling you . . ." I shrugged. "But hell, everybody else seems to know. The cops and the National Guard have been getting ready for six weeks. They have 20,000 troops on alert at Fort Knox. They've warned us—all the press and photographers—to wear helmets and special vests like flak jackets. We were told to expect shooting. . . ."

"No!" he shouted; his hands flew up and hovered momentarily between us, as if to ward off the

words he was hearing. Then he whacked his fist on the bar. "Those sons of bitches! God Almighty! The Kentucky Derby!" He kept shaking his head. "No! Jesus! That's almost too bad to believe!" Now he seemed to be jagging on the stool, and when he looked up his eyes were misty. "Why? Why here? Don't they respect anything?"

I shrugged again. "It's not just the Panthers. The FBI says busloads of white crazies are coming in from all over the country—to mix with the crowd and attack all at once, from every direction. They'll be dressed like everybody else. You know—coats and ties and all that. But when the trouble starts . . . well, that's why the cops are so worried."

He sat for a moment, looking hurt and confused and not quite able to digest all this terrible news. Then he cried out "Oh . . . Jesus! What in the name of God is happening in this country? Where can you get away from it?"

"Not here," I said, picking up my bag. "Thanks for the drink . . . and good luck."

writer who "captures" the event, for better or worse, in a way no TV, radio, or traditional print reporter can.

Marshall Fishwick, who edited an anthology entitled *New Journalism,* feels new j is a natural outgrowth of our changing culture. We are simply more casual about everything, less apt

to follow the rules, and more apt to bend or break them. At the same time, we feel a renewed need to move closer to one another. We want more intimate information about the people in the news as well as the family next door. Our world is now a Global Village and new journalism is global gossip. *Washington*

The *Los Angeles Times* offers a candid view of Ike's love life as well as the normal front-page news.

Los Angeles Times

LARGEST CIRCULATION IN THE WEST, 1,020,987 DAILY, 1,309,677 SUNDAY

VOL. XCVI FIVE PARTS—PART ONE 96 PAGES WEDNESDAY MORNING, JUNE 22, 1977 CC Copyright © 1977 Los Angeles Times DAILY 15c

FAMILY DENIES DIVORCE PLAN

Love for Wife Fills Eisenhower Letters

BY ROBERT J. DONOVAN
Times Associate Editor

VALLEY FORGE, Pa.—The family of the late Dwight D. Eisenhower, disturbed over a book and an upcoming television program that deals in part with his relationship with Lt. Kay Summersby, has made available to The Times his loving wartime letters to his wife, Mamie.

Lt. Summersby was Eisenhower's driver and secretary in Europe and North Africa.

The Eisenhower family is particularly outraged by the two-part television program about the hero of Normandy being prepared by ABC for showing several months hence.

The first draft of the screenplay from which the program will be filmed is in possession of the family, and many of the scenes are clearly based on Lt. Summersby's 1976 book,

Excerpts from Eisenhower's letters to his wife. Part 1, Page 12.

"Past Forgetting: My Love Affair with Dwight D. Eisenhower." She died of cancer shortly after writing it.

The 319 Eisenhower letters to his wife will be published early next year by Doubleday in a book titled "Letters to Mamie," edited by their son, Brig. Gen. John S. D. Eisenhower, who lives in Valley Forge with his wife, Barbara.

As will be seen, the Eisenhower letters definitely cast doubt on a story, given currency by former President Harry S. Truman before his death in 1972, that the general was planning to divorce his wife after the war and marry Kay Summersby. This story is the curtain-raiser in the ABC show in its initial form.

Although indicating a poignant attachment of Eisenhower to his wife, the letters do not, on the other hand, clarify his months-long overseas relationship with Lt. Summersby.

His letters to his wife are filled with expressions of love, closeness and yearning for a shared peacetime life. Time and again, over months of separation, he poured out laments of loneliness and of nostalgia for the prewar years of their marriage. He acknowledged that in the past he had been beguiled by other women but said he had never been in love with anyone but Mamie—and never would be. "You suit me to a T," he wrote from Algiers on Feb. 11, 1943.

He characteristically addressed his wife as "darling," "my darling," "sweetheart" or "my sweetheart." The letters were signed "Ike" or "Your Ike." "You're the only woman I could ever live with," he wrote in one 1943 letter. He subsequently remarked that Mamie filled his "thoughts and hopes for the future."

Like many couples long separated by the war, the two of them, Mrs. Eisenhower particularly, seem to have had periods of depression and irritation when mutual understanding through hurried letters was difficulty. They recognized that times had changed them. But Eisenhower insisted that no "problem" separated them—only distance, and that would be overcome.

The letters told how the general wanted to bring Mrs. Eisenhower to Europe to live with him as soon as Germany had surrendered. However, his letters indicated that he kept encountering the problem of favoritism. How could a five-star general fairly bring his wife over when the soldiers in the ranks could not bring theirs?

Lt. Summersby's name appears here and there in Eisenhower's letters, but off-handedly. Obviously, Army wives in Washington read stories about attractive members of the Women's Army Auxiliary Corps on duty at field headquarters. Evidently, Mrs. Eisenhower raised her eyebrows about it, so to speak, in some of her letters.

From Algiers, on Feb. 25, 1943, Eisenhower replied to her: "I love you—don't go bothering your pretty head about WAACS, etc., etc."

The Eisenhower-Summersby companionship in the field, in the headquarters and on the wartime social

Please Turn to Page 12, Col. 1

SECOND DAY'S TALKS—French President Valery Giscard d'Estaing, left, sits opposite Soviet President Leonid I. Brezhnev at start of Tuesday's session at which the Soviet leader took a hard line. AP Wirephoto

Brezhnev Sees Perils in U.S. Rights Stand

New Cold War Possible, Aide Asserts, as Giscard Hears Kremlin's Hard Line

BY DON COOK
Times Staff Writer

PARIS—Soviet President Leonid I. Brezhnev took an all-around hard line Tuesday in lengthy political discussions with French President Valery Giscard d'Estaing.

On U.S.-Soviet matters, Brezhnev's spokesman said the Kremlin feels that the Carter Administration, by pursuing its human rights policies, "is no longer waging ideological conflict but an ideological war which may lead to a new cold war."

The Kremlin leader, according to spokesman Leonid Zamyatin, told President Giscard d'Estaing on their second day of talks that there has been no progress in strategic arms negotiations with the United States. Brezhnev also bluntly warned France against edging back into military cooperation with the North Atlantic Treaty Organization, the spokesman said.

As Brezhnev's hard-line positions on practically every topic became known, it was clear he was seeking to blame the United States for any new arms race or cold war.

In a toast Tuesday night at a formal dinner at the Elysee Palace—his only speech of the three-day visit—Brezhnev warned that "Peace in Europe and even more in the rest of our planet is far from being as stable as one would like—it is threatened by countless dangers, both obvious and hidden, and the most important of these is that the arms race is not only not being halted but is being stepped up."

Without naming the United States, he spoke of "poisonous propaganda from war-mongering circles and enemies of detente" whom he accused of seeking "to sow mistrust and hostility between states and peoples."

Brezhnev said earlier that nothing of significance had yet developed in the arms talks held with Secretary of State Cyrus R. Vance, and reiterated that any agreement had to be based on the 1974 accord reached in Vladivostok with President Gerald R. Ford.

Brezhnev's totally negative reading of the strategic arms situation contrasted sharply with comments by the chief American arms negotiator, Paul C. Warnke, on his arrival in Moscow Tuesday for a new round of talks with the Russians. Warnke talked about "significant progress," said he was approaching his meetings with "guarded optimism, and added that the United States was "quite encouraged" by how things are going.

Brezhnev's new efforts to enlist the French in any arms control or disarmament discussions—now under way or proposed for the future—got a polite but firm brushoff from Giscard d'Estaing. So, also, did Brezhnev's criticism of French defense policies.

As for arms negotiations, Giscard d'Estaing laid down a familiar and probably unfulfillable French precondition: He said that France was ready to take part in real disarmament negotiations "as long as the final aim is general disarmament under effective international control," which is certainly not what the Kremlin has in mind.

On French defense policy, for the first time since Gen. Charles De Gaulle withdrew French forces from NATO more then 10 years ago, the Russians are turning critical. Brezhnev, according to his spokesman, told Giscard d'Estaing that the Russians had noted recent statements by French military leaders and others about a "forward defense policy" and readiness to a fight longside the NATO allies in a battle to the east, in Germany.

But a battle against whom?, Brezhnev asked rhetorically.

The French official spokesman said that Giscard d'Estaing simply replied

Please Turn to Page 8, Col. 1

New U.S.-British Air Pact Chances Called Very Good

Optimistic View by American Negotiator Comes Only Hours After Warning That Flights Might Halt

LONDON (AP)—The chief U.S. negotiator at the U.S.-British air transportation talks said Tuesday night that chances were extremely good for a new agreement.

He made the optimistic prediction only hours after U.S. Transportation Secretary Brock Adams said in Washington that most scheduled airline service between the United States and Britain probably would end this morning.

Failure of the two nations to reach a new commercial air agreement could disrupt vacation and business plans of thousands of air travelers.

Ambassador Alan Boyd, who heads the U.S. negotiating team in London, told reporters:

"While a few important issues remain, there is the strongest possibility the deadline will be met and air services will continue without disruption." He gave no details.

Boyd made his statement during last-ditch talks to try to beat the deadline of 12:01 a.m. EDT today, when the 31-year-old Bermuda pact would expire.

A shutdown would affect the scheduled flights of Pan American World Airways, Trans World Airlines, National Airlines and British Airways. It would not involve chartered airline flights or the scheduled flights of other airlines that fly between the two countries, such as Air India, Iranair and El Al.

The supersonic Concorde flights operated by British Airways between London and Washington under a U.S.-approved test program also would be affected.

The four affected airlines had announced that if there was a shutdown, they would reroute their U.S.-London flights to airports outside the two countries. Under that plan, passengers would be taken to their destinations on other airlines or by charter shuttle flights—a situation that would add hours to flight times.

Before Boyd made his announcement, Adams told reporters in Washington, "Despite more than nine months of negotiations,it appears more likely each hour that scheduled air service between the United States and Great Britain will end at midnight tonight.

"The responsibility for this unfortunate action, if it occurs, rests with the British government."

Adams noted that the British a year ago renounced the Bermuda air agreement of 1946.

He said it was his "responsibility to advise American travelers of the possible interruption of scheduled air service to London and Hong Kong (a British colony)."

Adams said that without an agreement, "we are planning on the cessation of service because there has been ample time to reach a conclusion if Great Britain intended to do so."

In contrast to the stand taken by the United States, British officials have said the deadline could be extended. And British Prime Minister James Callaghan told the House of Commons, "It would be almost un-

Please Turn to Page 7, Col. 1

Billboard Firm Gave Gifts, Vacations to 20 Officials

A wide range of public officials in California and Nevada were given gifts and expense-free vacations in Las Vegas and Palm Springs by a billboard company which needed their support, The Times has learned.

Ryan Outdoor Advertising Co., La Mirada, provided officials with free hotel rooms, hotel credit cards, meals, shows and scrip usable as cash at the resorts—often with no limit.

Bookkeeping records and other documents obtained by The Times disclosed that at least 20 public officials from seven cities and four counties were listed as receiving gifts for "public relations" and other purposes.

Notations on the ledgers included: "help in getting permits," "new business," "possible future favors."

Most of the officials were in key positions to influence governmental decisions involving billboards. Among them were city councilmen, transit district official, billboard and building inspectors, tax assessors, a planning commissioner and two planning directors.

These officials represented such jurisdictions as Los Angeles, Orange and Clark (Nev.) counties, and the cities of Las Vegas, El Monte, Sierra Madre, Artesia, Banning, Bell and La Mirada.

The Times' documentation covered a period between 1970 and 1976 when the billboard industry was under intense pressure after passage of the

Times Staff Writers George Reasons, Mike Goodman and William C. Rempel compiled this report.

federal Highway Beautification Act.

Throughout Southern California and Nevada local government agencies began developing ordinances to comply with the federal act. In some cases, billboard construction was severely limited and in other areas was outlawed.

The stakes were high. A modern steel billboard costs about $12,000 to build and rents for about $1,700 a

Please Turn to Page 27, Col. 1

House Opposes Ban on Saccharin

Votes for 15-Month Delay, Test by FDA

From Times Wire Services

WASHINGTON—The House voted Tuesday to block any government ban on the use of saccharin during the next 15 months.

The bill would also require the Food and Drug Administration to spend $1 million for its own study of the artificial sweetener's possible cancer-causing effects.

The vote was 45 to 35, under a rule that counted only those members on the floor at the time of the vote.

The saccharin measure was an amendment to an agriculture appropriations bill that was later approved, 380 to 35.

The FDA had announced earlier this year that it planned to ban saccharin as an additive in food and beverages but would allow it to be sold as a nonprescription drug. The agency had said Monday that its proposed ban would be delayed until this fall

Please Turn to Page 18, Col. 1

Councilmen Vote Selves 2-Stage, 10% Pay Raise

BY ERWIN BAKER
Times City Bureau Chief

Without a word of comment, the Los Angeles City Council gave preliminary approval Tuesday to a two-stage, 10% salary increase for 18 elected officials, including the 15 council members.

The vote was 11 to 2 for adoption of a Personnel Committee recommendation, which provides for payment of the first 5% on July 1 and another 5% on July 1, 1978.

The council's action—and its swiftness—was certain to draw the attention of about 16,000 civilian employes under council control.

They would receive an average 1.7% increase under instructions given by the council in a secret session to its negotiating team which is currently bargaining with employe groups on wage adjustments for next year.

The lawmakers delayed a final vote on the raises until next Tuesday because of a parliamentary technicality.

After the 11-2 roll call, Councilman Marvin Braude, who had been recorded as aye, asked for reconsideration to change his vote to no. He said he thought the roll call had been on another matter.

But the council refused, 5 to 9.

Ten votes will be required for approval of the ordinance next Tuesday.

If the measure wins final approval from the council and Mayor Bradley, the raises will range from $5,000 for the mayor to $3,300 for council members and the controller.

This is what the salaries would be, with present compensation listed first:

—Mayor, $55,000; July 1, $57,750; July 1, 1978, $60,500.

City attorney, $46,750; July 1, $49,087.50; July 1, 1978, $51,425.

—Controller and council members, $33,000; July 1, $34,650; July 1, 1978, $36,300.

The roll call:

For—Louis R. Nowell, Don Lorenzen, John Ferraro, Zev Yaroslavsky, Pat Russell, Gilbert W. Lindsay, Dave

Please Turn to Page 24, Col. 1

FINANCE CHIEF URGES CAUTION

State Warned of Possible '79 Deficit

BY ROBERT FAIRBANKS
Times Staff Writer

SACRAMENTO—Finance Director Roy M. Bell said Tuesday that state government will face a deficit in 1979 if lawmakers follow through on plans to create school aid and property tax relief programs bigger than those envisioned by Gov. Brown.

Since the state cannot legally operate with a deficit, the only alternatives two years from now would be heavy cuts in state spending, which are never likely, or a tax increase.

Legislative Analyst A. Alan Post echoed Bell's prediction and said taxes would rise. Earlier, he had predicted that even Gov. Brown's programs for school aid and property tax relief would force a tax increase, though in four years, not two.

Bell and Post spoke shortly after Assembly Speaker Leo T. McCarthy (D-San Francisco) blocked plans for enactment of a school aid bill before the Legislature begins its summer recess on Friday.

McCarthy said he wanted to assure that school aid and property tax relief are considered together because of their impact on state taxes during the years ahead.

However, since it seemed unlikely that the Legislature could deal with both before the recess, he preferred that action on both be delayed until lawmakers return Aug. 1.

The major problem appears to be the size of this year's budget surplus, $2.5 billion, which is about $1 billion more than anyone suspected.

When the extra money is used to create new programs or radically enlarge old ones, it also assures massive new costs in years to come. However, there is no assurance that there will be enough revenue then to meet those costs.

Delay of the school bill was a defeat for public school lobbyists, who had been campaigning for enactment of a measure before the recess, thus giving the state's 1,042 local school districts a chance to assimilate the extra funds into their planning for the new school year.

Generally speaking, most districts must fix their budgets and tax rates for the upcoming year in August. If the Legislature fails to act early in the month, the extra money cannot easily be put to use.

Currently, lawmakers are considering two school bills, one backed by Brown and the other by the public school lobby. Although both are designed to bring the school finance system into compliance with the state Supreme Court's Serrano decision of last December, Brown's measure also would finance instructional reforms.

Please Turn to Page 23, Col. 1

THE WEATHER

National Weather Service forecast: Low clouds late night and early morning hours, otherwise fair today and Thursday. Highs both days near 80. High Tuesday 78; low 61.

Complete weather information and smog forecast in Part 2, Page 4.

FEATURE INDEX

Plan to Let Aliens Work in Crop Emergencies Studied

BY JACK NELSON
Times Washington Bureau Chief

WASHINGTON—The Carter Administration is considering legislation which would permit Mexicans to cross the border and work in special situations where U.S. labor is not available and help is essential to harvest crops, The Times has learned.

The legislation would require decisions on a case-by-case basis and apparently would not signal a reversal of the Administration's announced intention of stemming the flow of illegal aliens into the nation's labor market.

A comprehensive set of proposals for dealing with the complex issue of illegal aliens is now under consideration at the White House and President Carter is expected to reach final decisions this summer.

If adopted, the proposal to admit Mexican farm workers temporarily to deal with local emergencies would be part of this comprehensive package, a special provision designed to deal with a ticklish and long-standing problem for U.S. farmers along the Mexican border.

The problem, and the Carter Administration's inclination to provide help for the farmers, was highlighted earlier this month in a White House decision involving vegetable growers in Presidio, Tex.

When farmers in that southwestern section of Texas planted this year's crop of onions and cantaloupes, they did what they have long done: used labor from across the Mexican border about a mile away. It was a practice going back many years.

But when the Presidio growers got ready to harvest their crop this year, they found that a new Immigration and Naturalization Service crackdown on illegal aliens had sealed the border.

With the $6 million crop beginning to rot, the farmers turned to Wash-

Please Turn to Page 16, Col. 1

Post editor Kendrick explains, "People will always read about people."

Supermarket Sensationalism

The largest selling newspaper in America, the *National Enquirer* (4.4), and its imitators, *The National Tattler* and *Midnight* (4.5), can usually be found at supermarket checkout counters. For this reason they are called "supermarket journals"; their marketing method guarantees them enormous exposure. Their subject matter, too, is designed to appeal to the largest possible audience. They feature gossip about Hollywood stars and other national and international celebrities like Billie Jean King and Jackie Onassis. In addition, there are weekly stories about cancer discoveries, arthritis breakthroughs, and common but overlooked diseases "you can diagnose by taking a simple test right in the privacy of your own home." There are stories involving UFOs and astrological predictions. Faith healers who routinely perform miracles are also given space. In each issue, the *Enquirer* polls readers about their favorite TV shows. Every subject is chosen for its popular appeal. *The National Tattler* calls it "people-to-people journalism."

Publisher Generoso Pope paid $75,000 for the *National Enquirer* in 1952, when its circulation was only 17,000. Right away the *National Enquirer* began to offer up massive doses of sex and gore (headlines screamed "I Cut Out Her Heart and Stomped on It" or "Mom Boiled Her Baby and Ate Her"), and in time circulation rose to just over one million, where it stayed for a while. Then, in a stroke of marketing genius, Pope "cleaned up" the *Enquirer* in 1968, and circulation has been climbing ever since. Today, "America's liveliest newspaper" sells about four million copies a week.

Pope explains his success by saying the *Enquirer* gives the people what they want. "What you see on page one of the *New York Times* does not really interest most people, and interest is our only real rule." As for his critics, he says, "I don't care if other media respect us or not, a Pulitzer Prize ain't going to win us two readers."

The *Enquirer* relies heavily on human interest stories. Unlike new j, supermarket journalism seldom lets the reporter become part of the story. Instead, reporters try to "help" subjects tell it in their own words. One memo from Pope's office told writers to "prod, push and probe the main characters in your stories, help them frame their answers. Ask leading questions like, 'Do you ever go into the corner and cry?'" In fact, like the yellow papers, the *Enquirer* will do anything to get a good story. Pope admits a certain affection for the stunts of the old Hearst-Pulitzer days and pays writers up to $50,000 a year to dream them up. When Greek shipping tycoon Aristotle Onassis died, the *Enquirer* sent 21 reporters and photographers to cover the funeral. The tab was an estimated $50,000.

Enquirer stories have a definite point of view. The *Enquirer* world is one of modest heroes,

National Enquirer front page.

brutal killers, brilliant astrologers, and sophisticated stars. Research shows that these are the stereotypes that most intrigue the consumers of supermarket journalism. Like all successful mass media, the *National Enquirer* anticipates trends in popular tastes and provides gratification for the mass audience. The object, of course, is an enormous circulation, and the formula has paid off. It appears that most of us do have an interest in the occult, the unknown, Hollywood stars, and the like. The *Enquirer* also delivers dozens of moral lessons that reflect popular myths and beliefs.

Enquirer stories fulfill the hopes of their readers and justify their optimistic view of the world: The policewoman in New York teaches blind children to read in her spare time, the handicapped mother of six refuses to take welfare.

But there's a dark side too—government officials (the *Enquirer* calls them "burro-crats") are crooks living off the sweat of the working people, while the courts set criminals free to roam the streets and prey on their unsuspecting victims, who are often *Enquirer* readers. For better or worse, these beliefs are held by a

Midnight, published in Canada, is one of the many tabloids using the *National Enquirer* success formula.

lot of people, and the *National Enquirer* offers proof for only 35 cents a week.

Sorting Out the Soft News

How different is your local daily newspaper from the *National Enquirer*? Your local editors would maintain that the *Enquirer* is totally "soft" and that its only goal is financial profit, whereas their daily provides important hard news and operates by a strict set of journalistic ethics.

Yet the overwhelming amount of news in the local paper is soft: features, syndicated material, and columns. What's more, readership studies indicate that soft news enjoys a much larger following than hard news. If this were not so, there would not be so much of it, and the *National Enquirer* would not be America's best-selling newspaper.

Even in the dailies many front-page stories are not all hard news. Often there is a large photograph, a colorful description, or a human interest angle. After the first few pages, news section subject matter is typically a detailed story about drugs, or a plea for the paper's latest crusade to send poor children to summer camp.

The editorial section is filled with interpretative and passionate pronouncements on the issues of the day from both editor and reader. Most papers now run an *op-ed* page, literally: opposite the editorial page. Here there are first-person narratives, stories about "interesting" important people, and detailed discussions of cultural trends.

The real estate section contains large ads for new housing projects next to thinly disguised "news" stories about those same projects. There is an entertainment section filled with advertising for TV shows and films plus reviews of those same TV shows and films.

The family section is chock full of helpful household hints. Here you'll find columns by Erma Bombeck, Ann Landers, and syndicated gossip columnists (see 4.6).

In other words, short of obituaries, tide tables, weather, and a few paragraphs on the front pages, most newspapers deal primarily in soft news. It's their bread and butter, readers love it, and it is often the reason readers subscribe in the first place. So in that respect, the content of your local paper is really not that different from that of the *National Enquirer*, though there is probably a difference in style.

Professional journalists who feel that newspapers are primarily filled with hard news live in a fantasy world. A thriving interest in hard news and the real complexities of national affairs is not what sells newspapers. Most readers seek personalities, not politics; simple explanations, not exhaustive analyses. Faced with losses in circulation, newspaper editors have been forced to give readers more of what they want and less of what editors think they *should* have. After all, *news is entertainment,* and it has been since the days of the penny press.

Comics: You're Significant, Charlie Brown!

Among the most loved of all newspaper features is the comic strip. Arthur Asa Berger, who teaches at San Francisco State University, points out that comic strips and comic books have long "been part of the American imagination." It is strange that so little academic attention has been given them, because there is much to be learned from studying this medium and its audience. Some comics appeal to almost all of us (*Peanuts*) and some appeal to only a few (*Mr. Natural*), but in each case a special relationship forms between consumer and strip.

The forerunners of American comic strips were the great European caricaturists of the 18th and 19th centuries. James Gillray, Thomas Rowlandson, and George Cruikshank pioneered in telling stories with a *series* of pictures. Rowlandson was among the first to use speech balloons to give his characters a voice of their own. Most of these early "strips" dealt exclusively with politics. By the end of the

Ask Ann Landers

She is the most widely read news-paperwoman in the world. Her column runs in some 800 newspapers, and according to United Press International, she is one of the world's ten most influential women. On any given week, her mailbox is stuffed with more than 7,000 letters from readers, most pleading for advice.

She is Ann Landers, the queen of the advice columnists (the closest competition is her twin sister, Abi-gail ["Dear Abby"] Van Buren). Both were raised in Sioux City, Iowa, and were taught the old-fashioned American virtues of hard work, honesty, and sexual restraint. Though Ann turned 60 in 1978, there is no sign she is about to retire. She brags she can "run rings around" her secretaries primarily because they smoke and/or drink. Ann does neither.

Unabashedly she exclaims, "How do I feel about being a square . . . why I think that's just fine . . . I am a square and that squareness has paid off in ways that are very important to me." To teenagers contemplating premarital sex, she has her "three commandments": (1) four feet on the floor, (2) all hands on deck, and (3) no fair sitting in the dark.

For years her own nuptial bliss served as an example to those who felt marriage might be an outmoded institution. But after 36 years with Jules Lederer (founder of the Budget Rent-a-Car chain), divorce came in 1975. Though she gave the news to readers in one of her columns, she now rebuffs those who wonder why the answer lady had no answer for her own marital problems with a curt "M.Y.O.B.B" . . . that's Ann Landers lingo for "mind your own business, buster!"

19th century, American comic pioneer Richard Outcault was drawing a regular humorous strip for the *New York World*. Rudolph Dirks's *Katzenjammer Kids* were pulling tricks on the Captain as early as 1897 in the *New York Journal*. Many of that era's comics have disappeared as their artist/originators have died or gone on to other projects. Names like *Oliver's Adventures, The Yellow Kid, The Gungles,* and *Dixie Dugan* will ring no bells unless you are a real old-time comic buff. On the other hand, many strips that started as early as the 1930s and 1940s or even earlier are still with us today. These include Chic Young's *Blondie* (which first appeared in 1930—she married Dagwood later that same year), *Dick Tracy, Gasoline Alley, Gordo,* and a host of others.

Most of us tend to think of comic strips as either humorous or serious. Certainly *B.C., Broom Hilda,* and *Miss Peach* are humorous, whereas *Brenda Starr, Mary Worth,* and *Apartment 3G* are more serious. But what do we do with strips like *Feiffer* and the more recent *Doonesbury* (see 4.7)? Perhaps the "social" comics need a category of their own.

Another category might include the action-adventure strips like *Steve Canyon* and *Dick Tracy,* but these are seen less and less often on the newspaper comic pages. Action-adventure heroes seem to survive with greater dignity in other media. Superheroes Superman, Batman, and Captain Marvel still have a faithful audience who follow their adventures in comic books. Superheroes like Wonder Woman can also be found on television in their own series.

Many comic strips faithfully depict real-life characters in more or less realistic situations (*Rex Morgan, M.D.* and *Mary Worth*). Others caricature human facial or body features in a distinctive way (*Little Orphan Annie, Dick Tracy, Li'l Abner*). There are also strips that allow us to enter a world where animals talk and think in very human terms (*Donald Duck* and *Pogo*).

Why do most of us devote a part of our day to these cartoon fantasies? Because they are a source of diversion and escape, and for many they supply the heroes and heroines that are all too rare in real life. Action-adven-

Doonesbury: The New American Comic Strip

In 1968, the *Yale Daily News* began running an occasional comic strip by undergraduate Garry Trudeau. Initially, it depicted the antics of B.D., the mythical star quarterback of the Yale football team. The student audience quickly connected B.D. with Brian Dowling who was,

in fact, the captain of the Yale football team. Before long Trudeau was adding new characters: Mike Doonesbury, the make-out king who never quite made out; Bernie, the science major who revealed casually that he had been weird since age four when he ate an entire outboard motor; and Megaphone Mark, the campus radical.

The strip was picked up by King Features syndicate in 1970, and Trudeau began to add noncampus

characters like Joanie Caucus, the "liberated" ex-housewife; Phred the Terrorist, a lovable North Vietnamese soldier; and Uncle Duke, a drug-crazed reporter for *Rolling Stone*.

Almost immediately, *Doonesbury* became the most talked-about strip since *Peanuts*. It was earthy, contemporary, political, and funny. Real-life characters began making appearances in the strip: Dan Rather speaking from Zonker's

DOONESBURY   **by Garry Trudeau**

Copyright 1974, G.B. Trudeau. Distributed by Universal Press Syndicate.

The *Doonesbury* strip that was banned from many newspapers (including the *Washington Post*) during the height of the Watergate scandal. . .

ture comics have pure heroes and pure villains. In the end, the bad guys are caught and punished while the good guys win out. Even TV isn't that clear-cut anymore.

Another reason we read comic strips is because they give us a chance to become involved morally. Cartoonists receive hundreds of letters when they "kill off" a popular character. When Mary Worth dispenses folksy common sense to ease the troubled lives of her fellow

characters, thousands write to agree or disagree with her advice.

The comic pages are replete with perennial losers. Charlie Brown and Dagwood cannot seem to win no matter how they try. Often they are rejected by their friends for reasons beyond their control. We sit helplessly by and watch it happen, but perhaps we chuckle. We have been in similar situations, and it's good to see somebody else lose for a change. We television set and Richard Nixon, Gerald Ford, and Jimmy Carter from inside the White House. A series of strips on Watergate won Trudeau the first Pulitzer Prize for editorial cartooning ever given to a daily comic strip artist.

For all of this, Trudeau's satire is seldom vicious. *Doonesbury* expert Garry Willis points out that "although his satire bites—it remains kindly." No one is safe from a playful poke now and then, but no one is really hurt either. Trudeau has a unique way of making the reader sympathize with a character, whether that character is Richard Nixon or Phred the Terrorist.

Trudeau himself remains rather a mystery. He enjoys his privacy and seldom grants interviews, though he did agree to do a bicentennial minute for CBS in 1976. The only information available on him is in the biographical blurbs in his books; perhaps they offer some insight:

Garry Trudeau, twenty four, is a loner. He knows no home and his only companion is an old collie. . . .

Garry Trudeau still resides in New Haven. He is often seen cruising for girls in his blue station wagon.

Garry Trudeau, Yale '70, still disagrees with those who feel he has a professional obligation to learn how to draw.

DOONESBURY by Garry Trudeau

. . . and the 1974 strip that ran the day after Nixon resigned and Ford took office.

can identify because we've all been rejected, lonely, afraid.

It is no secret that most of us derive a certain pleasure from vicarious experience. We like to look in on other people's lives, to share in their victories and defeats. Comic strips afford us that opportunity in a safe and comfortable way. We take a daily peek into the lives of our favorite comic strip characters at our convenience.

Issues and Answers

Love, Law, and Libel— The Private Lives of Public People

Late one July night in 1975, reporter Jay Gourley stepped very carefully onto the patio of a Georgetown home. His mission: to steal the garbage of Secretary of State Henry Kissinger. His employer: *National Enquirer*. When Gourley was confronted by several burly secret service men, he explained he was engaging in "garbology," the study of notables according to what they throw away.

His was not the first garbage search. Some time before, an article had been written about Bob Dylan's trash. Dylan ignored it, but Kissinger was not so charitable. Threatening a lawsuit, he demanded his garbage back and got it. Most of it anyway.

These incidents involve a fundamental question in reporting: Where does the public's right to know or the reporter's right to find out end, and the privacy of a well-known personality begin?

Libel laws were designed to give the individual recourse against unfair attacks from the press. Since all parties may not agree on what is fair and unfair, the courts have handed down three guidelines for the reporter anxious to avoid libel suits.

1. Is it true?
2. Is it privileged?
3. Is it fair comment and criticism?

Truth was established as a defense of libel in 1735. That landmark decision acquitted New York printer John Peter Zenger of libel charges brought by the Royal Governor, who had often been a target of criticism from Zenger's press. Though existing law forbade such criticism, Zenger's lawyer argued that the statements were true and therefore not libelous.

Privileged information includes charges or statements made as part of the official record during court trials or legislative sessions. If one senator calls another a dishonest crook during a speech on the floor of the Senate, a newspaper may print it without fear of libel. If the senator does so outside in the hallway, reporters publishing it *could* be subject to a libel suit, even though they are quoting a source.

The standard for "fair comment and criticism" rests on intent. In *New York Times Co.* v. *Sullivan*, 1964, the Supreme Court held that the Constitution "prohibits a public official from recovering damages for a defamatory falsehood relating to his official conduct unless he proves the statement was made with actual malice." The Court felt newspaper reporters were bound to make some errors in reporting the facts. Even if charges as printed were eventually proved false, the plaintiff must prove that the reporter knew they were false and wrote the story with "malicious intent."

New York Times Co. v. *Sullivan* started a trend giving the press every benefit of the doubt in potentially libelous situations. This decision wiped out almost any chance for public officials to recover damages in libel suits and gave the press wide latitude in covering those officials. In later years the courts have interpreted "public officials" to include not only

First Amendment: We can't let it happen.

those in government, but all public figures in all matters of public interest. This drastically reduced the number of libel suits filed against the press each year. The more liberal Supreme Court justices would like to see libel laws, as they relate to the press, completely abolished. Justice Hugo Black once wrote: "The First Amendment [freedom of the press] was in-

tended to leave the press free from the harassment of libel judgments." (See 4.8.)

When being interviewed by David Frost, former President Richard Nixon cited *New York Times Co.* v. *Sullivan* as the reason he could not sue *Washington Post* reporters Woodward and Bernstein for what he called "factual errors" in their book, *The Final Days*. Nixon and the press have never been fond of one another, and it comes as no surprise that the Nixon Supreme Court appointees may be changing the Supreme Court position. With Justice Black dead and liberal champion William O. Douglas retired, more recent decisions have allowed the press less latitude in what they may say about public and government officials.

Queries and Concepts

1. Take a hard news article from the newspaper and imagine yourself a reporter. Now write a new journalism story about the event. Then choose a new j article from the new j sampler or another source (see the readings and references at the end of this chapter). Rewrite it to conform to hard news style.
2. Get a copy of the *National Enquirer* and examine story content. Is there a particular point of view in most stories? Is it direct or implied?
3. Now use that same copy of the *Enquirer* and compare story categories (crime, violence, occult, and others) with story categories in your local city newspaper. What are the major differences?
4. What is your favorite comic strip? Would it fall into any of the categories defined in the text? Do you identify in any direct way with any of the characters? What is it about them that you enjoy?
5. Can you find at least one article in your local paper that may contain some libel? Apply the three criteria from the text.

Readings and References

What Is New Journalism?

William L. Rivers and Everette E. Dennis
Other Voices: The New Journalism in America. San Francisco: Canfield Press, 1974.
This is the best comprehensive look at all the alternative journalism trends since the 1960s. It includes chapters on the new nonfiction, new advocacy, and counter-culture movements. The final chapter deals with the future of new j.

Thomas Wolfe and E. W. Johnson
The New Journalism. New York: Harper & Row, 1973.
This is the real bible of the movement. Tom Wolfe's 50-page essay that begins the book is a convincing defense for the new nonfiction. The book includes excerpts from Gay Talese, Truman Capote, Terry Southern, George Plimpton, and others. Hunter Thompson's "The Kentucky Derby Is Decadent and Depraved" appears in full.

New Journalism Sampler

Some enjoyable examples of the new journalism:

Laura Longley Babb, ed.
Writing in Style. New York: Houghton Mifflin, 1975.

Norman Mailer
The Armies of the Night. Cleveland: World Publishing, 1968.

Hunter S. Thompson
Fear and Loathing in Las Vegas. New York: Popular Library, 1973.
Fear and Loathing: On the Campaign Trail '72. New York: Quick Fox, 1973.

Thomas Wolfe
The Kandy-Kolored Tangerine-Flavor Streamline Baby. New York: Pocket Books, 1966.

Criticism of New Journalism

Marshall Fishwick, ed.
New Journalism. Bowling Green, Ohio: Bowling Green University, Popular Press, 1975.
A delightful anthology on the social implications of new journalism. Includes pieces on the relationship between TV and new j plus portraits of Norman Mailer, Hunter Thompson, and others. Also critical analyses in articles like "What Professionals Say" and "We've Been Had by The New Journalism, A Put Down."

Supermarket Sensationalism

"Goodbye to Gore." *Time,* February 21, 1972, pp. 64–65.

"From Worse to Bad." *Newsweek,* September 8, 1969, p. 75.

Elizabeth Peer and William Schmidt
"The Enquirer: Up From Smut." *Newsweek,* April 21, 1975, p. 62.

Sorting Out the Soft News

Linda Witt
"Ann Landers: 'Let's Hear It For Us Squares.'" *Today's Health,* January 1974, pp. 38–41.

Harry F. Waters and Martin Weston
"Don't Ask Ann." *Newsweek,* July 14, 1975, pp. 53-55.

Comics: You're Significant, Charlie Brown!

Arthur Asa Berger
The Comic-Stripped American: What Dick Tracy, Blondie, Daddy Warbucks and Charlie Brown Tell Us About Ourselves. New York: Penguin Books, 1974.
The sociological end of the comic book business. Asa Berger examines some mainstream comics and explores audience identification with each. The context is popular culture. Chapters on Blondie, Dick Tracy, Buck

Rogers, underground comics, and more. In paperback, no bibliography or index.

Reinhold C. Reitberger and Wolfgang J. Fuchs
Comics: Anatomy of a Mass Medium. Boston: Little, Brown, 1972.
First published in Germany, this stands as the most comprehensive *historical* portrait of the comic strip and comic book. Most major strips are covered. Useful index and reading list.

Garry Trudeau
The Doonesbury Chronicles. New York: Holt, Rinehart & Winston, 1975.
The ultimate collection of *Doonesbury* cartoons from the early days at Yale to the present, some in color. A short but interesting introduction and discussion of the significance of *Doonesbury* as a new force in the comic world.

Issues and Answers: Love, Law, and Libel— The Private Lives of Public People

Nelson and Teeter's *Law of Mass Communications* (Mineola, N.Y.: Foundation Press, 1973) and Gillmor and Barron's *Mass Communication Law* (St. Paul, Minn.: West Publishing, 1974) are both excellent sources for more detailed accounts of libel cases and related issues. For the historical perspective, check under "libel" in the index of Frank L. Mott's *American Journalism* (Riverside, N.J.: Macmillan, 1962). For more recent cases, see *Readers' Guide to Periodical Literature.* There are usually a few major libel cases each year and court rulings constantly reinterpret existing libel laws.

5
Magazines: The Mass Menagerie

**The whole tendency of this age is
magazineward.—Edgar Allan Poe, 1824**

The Mass Menagerie

The world of magazines is a menagerie, a wild
and unpredictable collection—colorful, competitive, and *exciting*. Magazines are the *mass
menagerie* because without a mass audience,
they wouldn't survive. Magazines are entertaining, topical, conversational, stimulating,
and attractive. They also say a lot about how
we spend our leisure time, and we have more
of that than ever before.

Relationships between magazines and
readers reveal changing trends and patterns
in social behavior. Like all commercial mass
media, magazines create and reflect popular
beliefs and tastes. The success—and profits—of
a magazine depend on how well it can antici-
pate those tastes and deliver an information
package the audience will buy.

All popular magazines in America *specialize*
in some way. In fact, they are the most specialized of all mass media. Researchers John C.
Merrill and Ralph L. Lowenstein point out that
a magazine may have either unit specialization
or internal specialization. *Unit specialization*
occurs in *Playboy*, *Ms.*, and others, which
appeal to a particular group of readers who
have common interests. The magazine as a
whole appeals to a special-interest group. *Internal specialization* publications, like *Reader's
Digest*, appeal to a larger audience, offering a
wide variety of articles and letting readers
choose those they find interesting. The specialization occurs within the magazine in individual articles.

History: The Good Old Days

The earliest American magazines were local
journals of political opinion. None circulated
far beyond its geographic origin; most were
monthlies. In 1741, Andrew Bradford's *American Magazine* was the first magazine to appear
in the Colonies, beating Benjamin Franklin's
General Magazine and Historical Chronicle by
three days. Neither was successful and both
folded within six months.

For the next 130 years, magazines came and
went. All were aimed at the local audience,
and most sold advertising and were published
monthly. In 1879, Congress changed the
postal rates to encourage broader distribution
of magazines.

In 1893, S. S. McClure founded *McClure's*
magazine and priced it at 15 cents for those
who could not afford the usual 25 or 30 cents.
His strategy was simple: deliver an entertaining, easy-to-read magazine to the masses.
Thus armed with a large circulation, the magazine could make profits from advertising revenues.

His chief competitor was Frank Munsey,
whose *Munsey's* magazine dropped its price to
ten cents in 1893. Like the newspaper yellow
journalists, Munsey stopped at nothing to increase circulation. When he died in 1925, one
critic wrote: "Frank Munsey contributed to the
journalism of his day the talent of a meat
packer, the morals of a money changer, and
the manner of an undertaker." While other
publishers made speeches about getting qual-

Time Line: The History of American Magazines

1710 Several American printers collect essays and print them in newspaper format.

1741 Benjamin Franklin's *General Magazine* and Andrew Bradford's *American Magazine* are the first regularly published magazines in America; neither is financially successful.

1821 The *Saturday Evening Post* is founded, appealing to both women and men.

1824 Magazine editor Edgar Allan Poe predicts, "This is the age of magazines, the whole tendency of this age is magazineward."

1857 *Harper's Weekly* begins publication and stresses engravings to add visual depth to stories; it immediately becomes the country's largest-selling magazine.

1865 Beginning of the first magazine boom. In the next 20 years the number of periodicals will increase from 700 to 3,300.

1865 E. L. Godkin founds *The Nation,* a journal of news and a forerunner of magazines like *Time* and *Newsweek.*

1880s Women's magazines *Ladies' Home Journal* and *Good Housekeeping* begin to have major market impact.

1893 *McClure's* is the first cheap mass circulation magazine at 15 cents per copy.

1893 *Munsey's* magazine cuts its price from 25 cents to 10 cents to compete with *McClure's.*

1897 Cyrus Curtis takes charge of the *Saturday Evening Post.*

1903–12 Magazine muckrakers expose unethical practices in business and government.

1907 *Saturday Evening Post* is one of the first magazines to top $1 million in annual advertising revenues.

1918 William Randolph Hearst hires Ray Long to edit his *Cosmopolitan.* Long becomes the highest paid editor of the era and gains a reputation for his uncanny ability to predict public reading tastes.

1920 Gross annual revenues in magazine advertising top $129 million.

1922 DeWitt Wallace founds *Reader's Digest.* His idea: Take the best articles from other magazines and reprint them in condensed book form. Articles must be "constructive, of lasting value, and applicable to readers."

1923 Henry Luce and Briton Hadden found *Time* magazine, an overnight success.

1925 *The New Yorker* begins publication and becomes the most successful metropolitan magazine.

ity reading to the masses, Munsey's main interest was making money.

In 1897, Cyrus Curtis bought the floundering *Saturday Evening Post* for $1,000. That year, its circulation was 2,200 and advertising revenues were just under $7,000. *Printer's Ink,* a trade paper, called the investment "an impossible venture." But Curtis provided just the

1925 Many magazines shift emphasis from subscription to newsstand sales to increase profits.

1930 Gross annual revenues in magazine advertising peak near $200 million, then fall to less than $100 million in 1933.

1930s Magazine circulation greatly increases from sales in grocery stores.

1933 *Esquire*'s first issue appears, and at 50 cents per copy it is the most expensive of its day.

1936 *Life* magazine founded, first issue sells for 10 cents.

1937 *Look* magazine appears as a frank imitator of *Life*.

1940s The heyday of the big general-interest magazines. *Life, Look, Saturday Evening Post, Reader's Digest,* and *Collier's* show healthy profits while expanding; black and white is replaced with new color format.

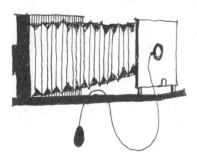

1947 *Reader's Digest* becomes the first magazine with a circulation of more than nine million.

1948 *TV Guide* founded for New York viewers, later expands to national publication.

1951 Gross annual revenues in magazine advertising exceed $500 million.

1952 William Gaines starts *Mad* magazine.

1953 Hugh Hefner founds *Playboy;* nude Marilyn Monroe is the first center feature.

1954 Time, Inc., founds *Sports Illustrated.*

1955 Rising production costs force *Reader's Digest* to accept advertising for the first time.

1956 *Collier's* is the first modern mass circulation, general-interest magazine to go bankrupt and cease publication.

1970s *Cosmopolitan* leads the way to more explicit magazines for women. Nude Burt Reynolds is the first center feature.

1972 *Life* magazine prints its final issue.

1972 *Ms.* magazine is published, devoted to women's rights and the women's movement; an overnight success.

1974 Time, Inc., founds *People* magazine, a smaller and livelier version of *Life.*

1974 *TV Guide* overtakes *Reader's Digest* as the largest-selling magazine in America.

1976 *TV Guide* circulation tops 20 million.

1978 Time, Inc., announces *Life* will begin publication again—as a monthly.

right combination of fact, fiction, and folk story. Within five years, circulation had risen to more than 300,000, ad revenues to $360,000. By 1912, circulation neared two million and ad revenues soared accordingly.

McClure's, Munsey's, Saturday Evening Post, and many more ushered in the era of the mass circulation magazine. Readers regularly supplemented news from their daily paper with the in-depth articles and fiction of their favorite magazines.

During the first half of the 20th century, many successful magazines ran quality fiction to boost sales. *Saturday Evening Post, Esquire,* and even *Look* and *Life* were showcases for the shorter fiction of writers like Ernest Hemingway and F. Scott Fitzgerald. Technical developments in photography and typography also increased magazine appeal.

From 1900 to 1950, the number of "magazine families" subscribing to one or more periodicals rose from 200,000 to more than 32 million. This magazine boom came in spite of the introduction of film, radio, television, and the paperback book.

After World War I new magazines appeared by the hundreds. *Time* presented a capsulized version of the week's news. Within a year after its first issue, it was financially in the black. *Life* appeared in 1936 at ten cents a copy. It offered bold imaginative photography and had tremendous visual impact.

At the beginning of World War II most of the earlier mass circulation magazines had died, including *Munsey's* and *McClure's.* Some, like the *Saturday Evening Post, Collier's, Cosmopolitan,* and *McCall's* remained, but many were in financial trouble. Publishers had used profits from successful magazines to finance less successful new ones. Since magazines are among the freest of the free-market enterprises, those that command adequate circulation and attract advertisers survive and those that don't perish.

These Days: Magazines Since 1950

Nostalgia buffs would have us believe that the "good old days" of magazines are gone forever. They wail that there will never be another *Look, Collier's,* or *American.* Their concern for the old has prompted special nostalgia issues of magazines like *Liberty. Saturday Evening Post* now publishes nine special issues each year, which really makes it the *Almost Monthly Evening Post.*

What happened to these magazines? The world of mass communication is one of mass change. Public tastes and information needs shift over the years; some magazines couldn't or wouldn't shift with them. Of course, the influence of television was felt by many; *Life,* for example, which had provided its audience a pictorial window on the world, was clearly upstaged by the newer medium. Other problems were increased postal rates, paper costs, salaries, and other production costs, and poor management. Most important was probably the loss of advertising revenue to other media. Why should advertisers pay almost eight dollars to reach 1,000 *Life* readers when a minute of television time cost approximately four dollars per every 1,000 viewers?

Circulation of Leading U.S. Magazines

Magazine	Circulation (in millions)	Magazine	Circulation (in millions)	Magazine	Circulation (in millions)
TV Guide	19.2	McCall's	6.8	Senior Scholastic	2.9
Reader's Digest	18.1	Playboy	5.7	American Legion	2.7
National Geographic	9.0	Good Housekeeping	5.3	American Home	2.5
Family Circle	8.4	Redbook	4.6	Sports Illustrated	2.3
Woman's Day	8.2	Time	4.3	Cosmopolitan	2.1
Better Homes and Gardens	8.1	Penthouse	4.2		
Ladies' Home Journal	7.1	Newsweek	2.9		

Of course, not all the older magazines have died. Among those still doing well are *National Geographic, Family Circle, Woman's Day, Better Homes and Gardens,* and *Ladies' Home Journal.* And if some former giants have died, hundreds of new magazines have sprung up to take their place (or part of their place) or establish new places of their own (see 5.2). Recent success stories include *Playboy, Ms.* (see 5.3), *Penthouse,* the new *Cosmopolitan, TV Guide,* and *People.* The point is that magazines are not dying, but reader needs are changing.

Figures alone don't tell the survival story in today's mass menagerie. Magazines are people: owners, editors, writers, and readers. These people represent a coalition of diverse interests that make a magazine live. Two of the biggest stories during the menagerie's last 30 years have been the rise of *Playboy* and the death of *Life.* The *Playboy* story is one of manners, morals, and ingenuity (see the guest essay by John Brady, p. 80). The *Life* story is one of visual splendor and harsh fiscal reality.

A Portrait: The Death of Life

To see life; to see the world; to eyewitness great events . . . to see strange things—machines, armies, multitudes, shadows in the jungle and on the moon; to see man's work—his paintings, towers, and discoveries; to see things thousands of miles away, things hidden behind walls and within rooms, things dangerous to come to; the women that men love and many children; to see and take pleasure in seeing; to see and be amazed; to see and be instructed. Thus to see, and to be shown, is now the will and new expectancy of half mankind.

—Henry R. Luce, 1936

Henry Luce, co-founder of Time, Inc., shared this vision for a new magazine with potential advertisers and financial backers in 1936 (see 5.4). The nation was still in an economic depression, but Luce sensed that technological development had made possible a new kind of journalism. Paper was cheap and photographs were increasingly appealing to readers. Why not a magazine that would provide a weekly "window on the world" for a mass audience starved for visual information?

Life's initial success was so overwhelming that it nearly killed the magazine. Luce had contracted with advertisers anticipating a circulation of 250,000 for the first year. To his dismay and delight, circulation was twice that almost immediately. This meant double pro-

Ms. was practically an overnight sensation. There was an audience ready and waiting for such a magazine—*Ms.* filled the need. It celebrated five years of successful publication in 1977.

duction costs without higher advertising rates. *Life* lost $6 million before appropriate adjustments could be made. Luce should have learned a lesson from *Munsey's* and *McClure's;* both magazines had experienced the same problem 40 years earlier.

In its early years *Life* was often controversial. A 1938 issue featured a *photo essay* (the term itself was a *Life* invention) of the birth of a baby. Some readers were shocked and the magazine was banned in 33 cities. Though Luce maintained that *Life*'s photo essays would "begin in delight and end in wisdom," some critics disagreed. One described the *Life* photo formula as "equal parts of the decapitated Chinaman, the flogged Negro, and the rapidly slipping chemise." As years went by, *Life* did provide a certain amount of sex appeal, and pin-up pictures of Rita Hayworth and others often created a stir.

Henry R. Luce, founder of *Life*, having dinner with Elsa Maxwell.

Life was also a news magazine. During the Spanish Civil War, World War II, and the Korean War, readers depended on *Life* to be there, to help them witness these important world events in a way no other medium could. In 1969 *Life* brought the Vietnam War home by running pictures of 217 Americans killed during a single week of combat.

But there was more to *Life* than news and photographs. Some of the world's first-rate authors published original stories there, including Ernest Hemingway, Graham Greene, Norman Mailer, and James Dickey. *Life* carried the memoirs of the famous, including Winston Churchill, Harry S Truman, Charles de Gaulle, Dwight Eisenhower, and Nikita Khrushchev.

A generation that had grown up with the institution called *Life* was dismayed when Time, Inc., announced abruptly that *Life*'s 1972 year-end issue would be its last (see 5.5). Many *Life* staffers were no less surprised, though

rumors had been circulating for some time. *Look* had stopped publishing in 1971 and many had said that *Life* would soon follow.

What really killed *Life*? *Life* writer and long-time staffer Tommy Thompson said: "We lost our focus, we didn't know who we were writing to. We continued to try to put out a mass magazine when America was not a *mass* any more, but divergent groups of specialized interests." Perhaps the needs of a "mass" audience were now better served by television. In 1952, when *Life* published color pictures of the coronation of Elizabeth II in only ten days, readers were amazed; but a few years later, television was bringing viewers similar events instantly. Of course, television is not exactly, nor can it replace, photojournalism. *Life*'s pictures captured the moment and could be enjoyed again and again.

Columnist Shana Alexander rejected the doomsday theories of those who felt *Life*'s

The Nude Journalism

John Brady is editor of Writer's Digest *and author of* The Craft of Interviewing. *This is an excerpt from an article that first appeared in* The Journal of Popular Culture.

For the past 25 years, a gaunt, pipe-smoking, Pepsi-swigging man in Chicago has edited a magazine that was never intended for female chauvinist sows or for the little old ladies of Dubuque. Along the way he has been called—among lesser delicacies—"the Crusader Rabbit of Sex," "the Norman Vincent Peale of Erotica," and "the man who started the loosening of sexual attitudes in America." If, as Emerson suggested, "an institution is the lengthened shadow of one man," *Playboy* magazine is surely one Hugh Marston Hefner.

Hefner's success is even more remarkable because it came at a time when American magazine journalism was, at best, risky. The period, in fact, is a mausoleum for once-successful publications—*Collier's, Saturday Evening Post, Look,* and *Life*—while hundreds of lesser magazines slipped quietly into unmarked graves. Yet *Playboy* prospered. The Hefnerian secret? "I invented sex," the publisher wryly observed on a recent TV talk show. And, to an extent, it's true—at least insofar as publishers are concerned. Hefner led the way. He gave popular culture a sex life. The Nude Journalism. But of course!

No other magazine in America has had an impact to match *Playboy*'s. "*Playboy* is probably the most influential publication of my lifetime," says Gay Talese, now working on a book of his own called *Sex in America*. "It has influenced middle America. It has recorded and been in the vanguard of change, sexually, in this country. . . . Hefner will probably go down in modern history as one of the most influential men of the 1960s and 70s."

Whether the magazine fostered the revolution, or the revolution nurtured the magazine, is debatable. "*Playboy* came at the right time, when the United States was experiencing a sexual revolution," says Hefner. "My naked girls became a symbol of disobedience, a triumph of sexuality, an end of puritanism." It seems safe to conclude, however, that *Playboy* at least helped bring about a cultural change in our society much more rapidly than would have occurred otherwise. Hefner's magazine became the foremost chronicler of sexual change throughout this period. Thus, following closely on the heels of Dr. Kinsey, and paralleling the development of The Pill, *Playboy* served as midwife while the age of sexual candor was born unto the popular press in America.

In 1952, only two major publications could be called general magazines for men—*Esquire* and the now-defunct *Gentry*. Other magazines that featured female nudity were a pretty seamy lot in general. The remaining men's magazines emphasized the great outdoors. Hefner found them "asexual at best, and maybe homosexual. With the outdoor and hunting and adventure things in which the place for the woman was in the kitchen while you hung out with the guys and played poker or went out on a hunting trip to chase the abominable snowman."

The first issue of *Playboy* was put together with paste pot and scissors on a bridge table in Hefner's kitchen. The publisher's personal investment was $600, which he obtained by mortgaging furniture and borrowing from friends. He also sold $10,000 in stock to random social acquaintants.

"I'm sitting in my studio one day and in comes this skinny, intense wild-eyed guy," recalls Arthur Paul, then a young Chicago free-lance artist. "He showed me this magazine he had put together. He had done all the art work by himself, and it was awful. But he looked at

demise foretold shifting trends in American taste: "Photojournalism is not dead, and the American people have not stopped reading, nor have they lost interest in the world around them. What died at *Life* was an appropriate and responsible relationship between editors and management."

During its final three years *Life* swam in a sea of red ink, losing some $30 million. A conservative management rejected numerous my work and asked me to redesign his magazine." Of course, Hefner had no money. "I took on the job," adds Paul, "accepting private shares of stock in the company he was founding, instead of salary"—and it was probably the best thing that ever happened to him.

Sales mushroomed. By the end of 1954, monthly circulation was 104,189; one year later that figure had more than tripled, and by December 1956, sales averaged 795,965 monthly.

Each month the book became thicker and slicker as profits were plowed back into the product. Not until 1956, though, did *Playboy* attract advertisers in large numbers—partly because conservative accounts were reluctant to be associated with a "skin" magazine, but mostly because Hefner rejected some 80 percent of the advertising submitted for publication, including ads for firearms, weight reducers, acne and baldness cures, correspondence courses, trusses, athlete's foot powder, sex manuals, "life-like" inflatable dolls, vibrators, and whatnot.

"Right from the start, he knew it would be fatal in the long run to carry the kind of schlock ads that usually go in pin-up magazines," says a long-time associate of the publisher. "It was the best decision he ever made." *Playboy*'s former

advertising director Howard Lederer added: "We create a euphoria and we want nothing to spoil it. We don't want a reader to come suddenly on an ad that says he has bad breath. We don't want him to be reminded of the fact, though it may be true, that he is going bald."

Now that the field suddenly belonged to *Playboy,* the magazine began to change. "I've always edited on the assumption that my tastes are pretty much like those of our readers," said Hefner in 1955. "As I develop, so will the magazine." One of the first things to develop was the centerfold. Although the feature had begun with Marilyn Monroe as "Sweetheart of the Month" ("Playmate" did not appear until the second issue), subsequent centerfolds were nameless. "In the early days, when it was hard to get a decent girl to pose in the nude," observed J. Anthony Lukas, "a few of the playmates looked as though they might feel at home on a barstool."

Critic Benjamin DeMott pointed out that the playmate, generally chosen from a middle-income background, could be *any* girl with an attractive figure. *Playboy,* he said, undertakes "to establish that the nude in Nassau and the stenotypist in Schenectady—the sexbomb and the 'ordinary girl'—are actually one creature. Essential Woman."

Today, of course, when one passes the men's magazine section of a newsstand, *Playboy* is pictorially tame compared with publications that seem to have staff gynecologists rather than art directors. "*Playboy* has become part of the Establishment," says Bob Guccione, editor of *Penthouse,* a younger, more virile *Playboy.*

Whether *Playboy* has gone Establishment is debatable, but clearly many of the causes the magazine once fought have either been won or forgotten. The magazine's circulation, which once flirted with seven million, has fallen back to some five million monthly–mostly because *Playboy* has fallen behind in the commodity its publisher invented: sex. Despite the criticism, the competition, and the awareness that the *Playboy* phenomenon has probably peaked, Hugh Marston Hefner's place as a journalist of distinction and of influence is rather secure. "All history," said Emerson, "resolves itself very easily into the biography of a few stout and earnest persons." In the annals of popular culture and The Nude Journalism, Hefner is surely the publisher who led the change. "I'm sure that I will be remembered as one significant part of our time," Hefner told an interviewer a few years ago. "We live in a period of rapid sociological change, and I am on the side of the angels."

plans from editors and other staffers to "save" the magazine. *Life* could have gone to a smaller format (its large size made postal increases disastrous) or shifted its balance between photo and story content. It could have trimmed

from its circulation list those whom demographers did not consider prime targets for potential advertisers, thereby cutting circulation costs and increasing advertiser appeal. But this would have meant a major shift in editorial

Life magazine cover, December 29, 1972.

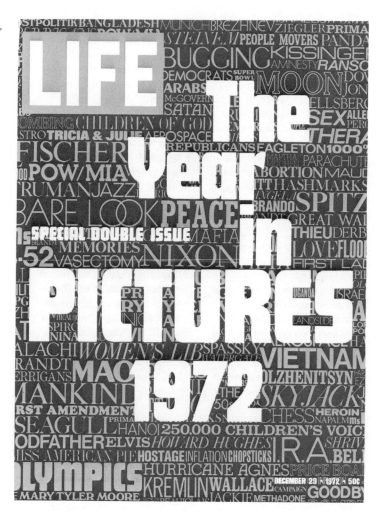

policy and the very concept of the magazine. In the end, *Life* did nothing, and died.

In death it was remembered as a social force of unparalleled magnitude. William Shawn, managing editor of *The New Yorker*, said: "*Life* invented a great new form of journalism. It contributed much to the American community that was valuable, often reaching moments of brilliance and beauty." Poet James Dickey noted, "I can't begin to calculate all of the things I have learned from *Life*. I'm not quite the same person I was because of what I read and saw in its pages." Indeed hundreds of millions of *Life* readers had their lives transformed in some way. Its legacy is the legacy of all mass media. For 36 years *Life* was an information source that shaped the lives of its readers by expanding their vision of the world

Drawing by Ziegler; © 1975, The New Yorker Magazine, Inc.

around them. It continued that mission through a number of special issues during the mid-1970s. The success of these issues prompted an announcement by Time, Inc., in 1978 that *Life* would return as a monthly. Perhaps the reports of the death of *Life* had been greatly exaggerated after all!

Specialization and Marketing Trends

Are you a regular reader of *The Peanut Farmer?* Maybe not, but Jimmy Carter probably is, or was, along with more than 28,000 others. *Writer's Market* lists over 100 magazines that deal with farming, soil management, poultry, dairy farming, and rural life. Farming magazines are one example of special-interest publications, which account for more than 90 percent of the total number of magazines published today.

Other vocations have their magazines as well (*The Iron Worker, Bank Systems & Equipment, American Shipper*). Many magazines appeal to readers' ethnic backgrounds (*Ebony, Southern Jewish Weekly*), ages (*Children's Digest*), sex (*Man to Man*), religions (*Gospel Carrier*), geographic locations (*Golden Gate North, Gulfshore Life, Nashville!*), or hobbies (*Biker/Hiker*), or points of view (*Ideals*). While mass circulation magazines give us a sense of global participation, special-interest publications allow us to share our individual concerns with people like ourselves (see 5.6).

Special-interest magazines have flourished, partly thanks to the success of their general-interest big brothers and sisters. Since mass circulation magazines print hundreds of thousands of copies, they must charge extremely high advertising rates. Only a handful of advertisers can afford to pay $20,000–$65,000 for a full page in a mass circulation magazine. As a result, many smaller companies have turned to less expensive special-interest magazines where their ads will be seen by fewer, but more receptive readers. Of course, general-interest magazines have not calmly stood by and watched their revenues disappear. Regional "breakouts" offer a local company a page in *Time* or a similar magazine for a reduced rate. That ad will appear only

Cover of *Compressed Air*, a special-interest magazine.

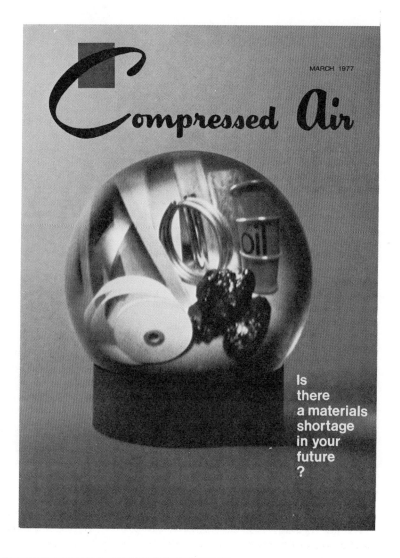

in magazines sent to a special geographic region. This gives smaller companies a chance to appear in a national magazine at a rate they can afford.

Only a handful of magazines have ever tried to survive on retail sales alone. *Reader's Digest* resisted selling advertising for more than 30 years until rising costs finally forced it to give

in. *Mad* magazine, unique in a number of ways, now stands alone as the only large circulation magazine that refuses to accept advertising (see 5.7).

In addition to ad revenues, the retail price of a magazine plays a major role in determining financial success. Like newspapers, most magazines have suffered heavily from infla-

Mad Magazine: "What, Me Worry?"

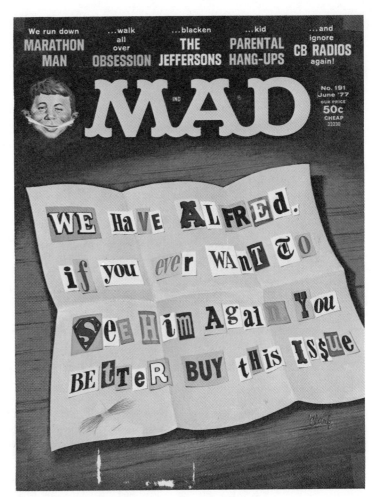

William Gaines's *Mad* magazine is mostly a journal of satire. Though it started as a comic-book-size publication in 1952, it soon grew to its present larger format. *Mad*'s growth reflects its unique ability to satirize the very products others rely on for advertising revenues. *Mad* gleefully attacks drug, automotive, and household products. Any medium is a likely target, including film, television commercials, and other magazines. *Mad* has even been known to satirize itself. These "attacks" are not malicious but, through satire, they point out the absurdity of our heavy reliance on advertising and the products it promotes. Ironically, the offices of *Mad* are on Mad-ison avenue, giving staffers a bird's-eye view of the advertising industry.

During the 1950s the "sick humor" of *Mad* was attacked by many parent and teacher groups. But what was once counter-culture has now become a part of the mainstream, and *Mad* seems harmless, if frivolous, to most parents. For them, more radical humor magazines like the *National Lampoon* pose a greater threat. *Mad*'s readers, once almost exclusively teenagers, now include people of all ages.

Alfred E. Newman, the fictitious publisher of *Mad,* has become so widely recognized that he is a cult hero. His motto, "What, me worry?" may describe the *Mad* approach to the complexities of the technological and materialistic American culture that the magazine satirizes so successfully.

tion in recent years and retail prices have skyrocketed. And no wonder—magazine production is a very costly business. The paper must be better quality than newsprint and it is considerably more expensive. Virtually all general-interest magazines and many special-interest magazines have four-color capability. This means every page must run through the press four times, an expensive and time-consuming task.

Writing for Magazines

A local newspaper will always have some loyal readers simply because it covers events in a given geographic area. For the general-interest magazine, the "local area" is the entire country. To get readers, each magazine develops a "formula" for the type of material it publishes. This formula is passed along to staff writers and to the free-lancers (independent writers who are paid by the article) who write the majority of magazine stories.

Most beginning free-lancers shoot for the big mass circulation magazines which, they assume, pay well for the stories they use. Often they do. *Reader's Digest* and *Playboy* pay $2,000–$3,000 per story; *TV Guide*, however, may pay as little as $250. More likely markets for the beginner are the special-interest magazines, which pay anywhere from nothing to $150.

Any would-be author should pick up a copy of *Writer's Digest* or *The Writer*. Both are monthly magazines devoted to the problems of free-lancing. *Writer's Market*, published yearly, is available in most libraries. Even if you have no writing aspirations, you will find it fascinating. It lists more than 5,000 markets for free-lancers. Editors describe the exact formula for their magazine, as in 5.8. These descriptions are often interesting, amusing, and even shocking to the uninitiated.

Unfortunately there is much more to free-lance writing than sending in a story and waiting for the check. Editors are highly selective about what they buy. Name magazines may receive more than 100,000 unsolicited manuscripts every year. That's an average of almost 300 a day! This year fewer than 1,000 writers will have their work published in mass circulation magazines. About 30,000 will be rejected. Only a few hundred will be able to live solely on their free-lancing incomes.

The prices that magazines pay for their articles comprise only a small fraction of their total production costs. Acceptance of an article is only the beginning. In most cases, the stories are carefully edited to conform to style. Graphic design and pictures are often added. A decision about typeface and the size and visual impact of the story is also necessary. Will the story appear early in the magazine or in the last few pages?

Writers are often unhappy with any or all of these processes, since they so vitally affect the finished product. But unless you are Truman Capote or Kurt Vonnegut, you have very little control over the story as it finally appears. In general, it is very difficult to keep the editor's blue pencil still. Yet in all fairness, the editor is often in a much better position to know what will appeal to the readers. Often, writers are too personally involved with their material and feel that each word

Writer's Market: A Peek Behind the Editor's Desk

For over half a century, *Writer's Market* has provided descriptions of magazine formulas for the free-lance writer, in the editor's own words. Some examples:

Bronze Thrills
Monthly magazine, 96 pages, circulation 80,000. All material must relate to blacks. Romance or confession/black oriented. Particularly interested in occult themes or anything concerned with UFOs. Does not want anything dealing with pregnancy or virginal girls getting pregnant after "first mistake." No old woman/young man love affairs unless story has unusual angle. Pays $30.00.

Compressed Air
Monthly magazine, established in 1896, circulation 150,000. For management and upper management men concerned with reproduction, distribution, and utilization of compressed air and other gases in all industries . . . case histories of pneumatic applications, in-depth articles about companies using pneumatics in construction and mining projects. Pays $10.00–$25.00.

Faith at Work
Eight times per year, established 1888, circulation 40,000. Personal experience articles relating to Christian conversion, growth, and ministry. Must reflect a particular Christian life-style and commitment to Christ. Pays $50.00–$100.00.

The American Blade
Every two months, established 1972, circulation 75,000. Main interest is in the history of cutlery, also collecting tips, material relating to knives, bowie knives, swords, etc. For the well-educated professional people. Pays $50.00–$200.00.

National Informer
Circulation 500,000. For the sophisticated mature adult who likes to be informed on topics he usually doesn't find in the daily papers. . . . Our readers like human-interest, self-help, and do-it-yourself type of features, particularly if these are sex-oriented. Also our readers like to be shocked by sex exposé features. We're looking for shocking features which expose and titillate. Pays two cents per word.

Though most of its space is devoted to magazine articles, *Writer's Market* also lists greeting card companies that buy lines of verse, along with poetry publications, regional newspapers, book publishers, and foreign markets.

is inviolable. Good editing is essential to the finished product.

Issues and Answers

Professional Print— The Curious Collective

Since editors, writers, and others all work on magazine stories, what we read is the result of a collective or collaborative effort. Yet reading is something we do alone. You can't simultaneously share a magazine with someone else the way you can share a film or a television program. Often the most successful stories are those in which the reader vicariously shares the writer's personal experiences. Yet, this one-to-one communication is really a myth. Even the greatest writers have editors who offer suggestions and make changes.

All of the print we consume daily is edited, rewritten, and recycled many times before it reaches us. Take this book for example. It may be different from other texts you've read because I am speaking directly to you, just as I would if you were in my office. I'm sharing personal experiences with you and hoping they will help you recall your own media experiences. Yet despite all of this, the words you are reading now are not all mine. Some belong to my editor, others to colleagues who have read earlier drafts and offered sugges-

tions; students have read many chapters and suggested that I add or delete material. In short, virtually all books, magazines, and newspapers are written "by committee," even though they are perceived as being written by individuals.

Time magazine has used this one-to-one illusion to its advantage for years. From the beginning it presented the news as if it were written *by* one person *for* one person. For years *Time* staffers never received a byline. Recently that policy has changed, and bylines are now permitted on some stories. Editors are hoping the new policy will give stories more credibility in the face of competition from the personal style of electronic media reporting. *Time*'s basic formula remains the same, however, and it is an obvious success.

True confession stories are almost always written in the first person singular to emphasize the "personal" and emotional impact of a "this-happened-to-me" experience. On the other hand, the "Talk of the Town" section of *The New Yorker* is always written with a collective "we," even when it is obviously the experience of a single person: "We went to the dinner and danced alongside Jimmy Carter," for example, or "We cracked open our oysters and talked with the old curmudgeon."

Academic texts often say, "One needs only to read this," instead of "You need only to read this." The feeling is that "one" will bring about a kind of detachment from the subject. What may result is a detachment from the reader. Curiously, this is often just the opposite of what the writer might be trying to achieve. The purpose of a text should be to get the student involved with subject matter.

This is not to say that all textbooks, magazines, newspapers, and printed material should be written the same way. Authors must make decisions based on what they think is best in a given situation. Still, decisions made on the basis of tradition alone are often blind to the real needs of the reader. The consequence is poor communication.

Queries and Concepts

1. What does your favorite magazine supply you with that you can't find anywhere else? Borrow a copy of *Writer's Market* and look up the listing for that magazine. Do you "fit" the editor's description of a typical reader?

2. In the library there are bound editions of many magazines like *Look* and *Liberty* that have quit publishing except for occasional special editions. Pick one and read a few issues. Venture some guesses as to why it failed.

3. Is *Playboy* a legitimate magazine or still a "skin" mag? Does your local library carry it? Does your school library carry it? Should they?

4. Do you have any special-interest magazines in your house? If not, pick one at random off the newsstands and do a brief analysis of what you think the audience might be like. Then check your version against the one in *Writer's Market.*

5. Pick up the latest copy of *Reader's Digest* and select an article that interests you. Now go to the library to read the original version (most *Digest* articles are severely edited). What parts were omitted and why? Does this say anything about what the *Reader's Digest* subscriber is looking for?

Readings and References

The Mass Menagerie

John C. Merrill and Ralph L. Lowenstein
Media, Messages and Men: New Perspectives in Communication. New York: David McKay, 1971.
A text on the changing relationships between media, messages, and audience. See Section One, "Media: A New Look at Changing Roles." Particularly effective regarding models and theoretical approaches to media specialization trends.

History: The Good Old Days

Theodore Peterson
Magazines in the Twentieth Century, 2d ed.

Urbana: University of Illinois Press, 1964.
A good comprehensive look at magazines from the beginning to the 1960s. Many stories about colorful early publishers; also sections on advertising and the expanding magazine marketplace. Excellent index.

John Tebbel
The American Magazine: A Compact History. New York: Hawthorn Books, 1969.
This is history in a hurry, but it probably has all the information you need. The author divides the development of American magazines into four historical periods and explores each in depth. Includes a useful suggested reading list and index.

These Days: Magazines Since 1950

Roland E. Wolseley
The Changing Magazine: Trends in Readership and Management. New York: Hastings House, 1973.
The emphasis here is on problems faced by modern magazine publishers. There are also detailed accounts of the rise and fall of some of the magazines that folded after World War II. Some predictions for the future and a good supplementary reading list. One drawback: magazines are changing so rapidly that this book is rapidly becoming out of date. For more current information, check *Readers' Guide to Periodical Literature.*

Specialization and Marketing Trends

James L. Ford
Magazines for Millions: The Story of Specialized Publications. Carbondale: Southern Illinois University Press, 1969.
Magazines for Millions is an entertaining and in-depth look at all the specialized publications in the menagerie marketplace. Separate chapters for farm publications, associations, and industry and labor publications, you name it. No bibliography, meager index.

Writing for Magazines

Jane Koester, ed.
Writer's Market. Cincinnati: Writer's Digest.

Issues and Answers: Professional Print— The Curious Collective

Robert T. Elson
Time Inc.: The Intimate History of a Publishing Enterprise 1923–1941. New York: Atheneum, 1968.
The World of Time Inc.: The Intimate History of a Publishing Enterprise 1941–1960. New York: Atheneum, 1973.
Elson draws heavily on the *Time* success formula to explain the most popular news magazine of the 20th century. Includes a lot of background material on the founders of *Time.* Comprehensive index.

PART TWO
Electronic Media: Edison Came to Stay

Imagine a world without electricity. No lights. No electric ovens. No TV. No stereo. Electric circuitry is more than a convenience; it has recreated our environment and radically altered our life-styles. When the lights went out in New York City in 1977, there were thousands of incidents of vandalism and looting. Electricity seems to have become part of that thin veneer of civilization that keeps us all from reverting back to our primal selves. From the duplicating machine to the electric coffeepot, we have come to rely on electricity in virtually every facet of our day-to-day activities.

Electric information is not print in electric form but a brand new kind of information we are only beginning to understand. In an instant we find out what is happening in the Mideast or what the weather will be like this afternoon. Electric information has "plugged" us into a giant information network that is all-encompassing and all-pervasive.

In Part Two, one chapter is devoted to radio and one to film. We do not often think of film as an "electronic medium," but films do rely on electricity to operate—projectors are not the "magic lanterns" they were once called. More important, both film and television have much in common in their use of visual imagery and their consequences in our mass-mediated environment.

The discussion of television is divided into two chapters: one for prime-time programs and the second for daytime programs and other TV-related issues like cable and UHF. I have devoted a relatively large amount of space to analyzing prime-time commercial television, with the hope that it will help you become a more critical consumer of what you find there.

Chapter 7 is devoted exclusively to the phonograph and the development of American popular music—an area ignored for far too long in other texts. Like television, popular music is a part of our lives whether we listen or not. So many people *are* listening that we cannot help but be affected.

Just as Gutenberg is not responsible for all that has happened since the invention of movable type, Edison cannot be held responsible for all the developments since the light-bulb or the phonograph. But he really started something. In that sense, Edison is here to stay.

6

Radio: The Magic Medium

**If your head says forget it
But your heart's still smokin'
Call me at the station
The lines are open.—Joni Mitchell***

KYMS and the
Edward Jay Show

The summer I left San Francisco I was determined to make a fresh start and leave all of the Haight-Ashbury craziness behind. My career as an author was embodied in a novel called *No Parking*, a reflection of the San Francisco scene, but I put it aside after receiving the first couple dozen rejection slips. Perhaps there was something else? I enrolled as a journalism major at California State University in Fullerton.

An engineer in a nighttime broadcast journalism course tipped me to a job at KYMS, the local "progressive" station. There was an opening for a copywriter. The next morning I was at their door. The station manager was playing the guitar as I entered his office: "Oh—you're the guy about the copywriting job—got any experience?"

"Sure, I've written a novel, and a lot of poems and short stories. I'm a journalism major and . . ."

He interrupted me, "Is this the easiest job you ever got?"

I gulped—I was actually in radio.

A salary of $250 a month wasn't much, but the job was supposedly only part-time. Before long I was working 10 to 12 hours a day and juggling classes in between. The only thing I could think about was getting on the air. The thought dominated my mind night and day—I practiced in the car, in bed before I went to sleep at night: "This is *Edward Jay* on

KYMS-FM . . . *This* is Edward Jay on KYMS-FM . . . This *is* Edward Jay . . ."

Finally, the big break came: We were scheduled to go off the air for maintenance between midnight and five, but the engineer was busy; since nobody else was available, did I want to give it a try? I'd practiced for six months in the production room, but this was the real thing—on the air. Thousands (well, maybe dozens) of people would be listening, and I would be sailing them away on a magic carpet of music, *my* music.

The last thing I needed to worry about was falling asleep. I was so wired all night that I couldn't stop—push a cart here—cue a record there—don't forget the ID on the half hour—not too close to the mike—answer the phone—somebody wants to hear Cream—somebody wants to hear Neil Young—Grateful Dead—Jefferson Airplane—Rolling Stones. . . .

By the time morning came I was both exhausted and jubilant. I don't think there is any way to describe that incredible evening. I've done thousands of radio shows since then, but I can recall that one for you record by record, mistake by mistake. Radio is that kind of thing—it's actually magic. And the music is a big part of it—it's the sound that makes it go.

That incredible adrenal rush is still there today when I go into a radio studio to cut a commercial or do an air shift. There is so much to do, so much to remember; and in the true McLuhan spirit everything happens all at once, all the time, because sound surrounds you—it's a total environment. You see only what's in front of you, but you hear all around you. Of course, the disc jockeys are only a small part of what makes radio work, but they *are* radio for the listener. The deejay represents that real-life link with radio, the magic medium.

Pioneers and Programmers

Several 19th-century inventors paved the way for the invention of radio, but credit is generally given to Lee de Forest (see 6.1). In 1906 he invented the vacuum tube that made transmission of the human voice possible.

Surprisingly, there was little interest in radio as a commercial vehicle at first. Most early radio broadcasters were amateurs who built their own equipment. Radio was their hobby. When Congress finally passed some early broadcast regulations in 1912, it was to keep private broadcasters from interfering with government communication channels. The American Marconi Company set up several huge sending and receiving stations and successfully transmitted wireless signals across the Atlantic. By the time World War I came along, "wireless" was well established, and it played an important part in the American victory.

In 1919, after a long series of costly court battles to protect its patents, American Marconi merged with the new Radio Corporation of America (RCA). This gave RCA strong dominance in the infant industry. Today RCA is one of the world's largest electronics companies and owns broadcast stations in most of the nation's top markets, along with a publishing house and a record company.

In 1920, Westinghouse obtained a license to broadcast, and its KDKA went on the air. KDKA offered the listener regularly scheduled programs. During that first year, it broadcast the Harding-Cox election results. Soon many people began to show interest in the new medium; yet to many, radio still seemed like a fad, and almost everyone agreed that, if there was any money to be made in radio, it was in the sale of radio sets.

American Telephone and Telegraph (AT&T) had a better idea. When AT&T opened its radio station WEAF in New York in the summer of 1922, someone decided radio was really an extension of the telephone. Since AT&T charged for telephone calls, why not charge people to come on the radio and say whatever they want? A Long Island real estate firm bought ten minutes to tell listeners about available properties and the response was overwhelming. Radio advertising was born. By the end of the decade, WEAF was grossing almost $1 million a year in "toll charges." It didn't take other stations long to get the message. Soon the airwaves were flooded with a barrage of advertisements for everything from

Lee de Forest, the "father" of radio. He lived long enough to see his cultural vision for the medium replaced by the commercial system we have today.

gasoline to hair oil. It has been that way ever since.

At about the same time AT&T began experimentally to link up stations for simultaneous broadcasting. Suddenly a *network* was possible. This had a tremendous impact on advertising practices and on the listening habits of Americans. More important, it paved the way for the coast-to-coast broadcasting that followed.

The Golden Age of Radio (1926–1948)

In 1922 David Sarnoff of RCA (see 6.3) wrote a memo to his staff arguing that the novelty of radio was wearing off; to convince people to keep buying radio sets, better programs would have to be offered. Sarnoff's idea was a revolutionary one. Why not a "specialized

Time Line: The History of American Radio

1901 Marconi is successful in sending "wireless" signals across the Atlantic Ocean.

1906 Lee de Forest invents the vacuum tube, making voice transmission possible over wireless.

1919 Radio Corporation of America (RCA) is formed.

1920 Westinghouse obtains a license for KDKA, the first radio station to offer continuous, regularly scheduled programs. KDKA covers the presidential election.

1922 WEAF begins selling air time to advertisers, opening the door for advertiser-supported electronic media.

1925 President Coolidge's inauguration is heard coast to coast through a 21-station hookup.

1926 AT&T sells out its radio interest; NBC eventually gains control.

1927 The Radio Act of 1927 is passed, and the Federal Radio Commission (FRC) is established.

1927 The United Independent Broadcasters radio network, later named CBS, airs its first broadcast; it is heard from Boston to St. Louis.

1930 *Amos 'n' Andy,* first heard in 1928, is the first successful radio situation comedy.

1931 FRC refuses to renew the license of KFKB, citing dishonest programming as the reason.

1932 Al Jarvis's *Make Believe Ballroom* on KFWB becomes the first successful deejay show.

1933 President Franklin D. Roosevelt begins his radio fireside chats, talking directly to the American people.

1934 The Communications Act of 1934 includes provisions for a new seven-member Federal Communications Commission (FCC) to regulate radio, television, and telephone communication.

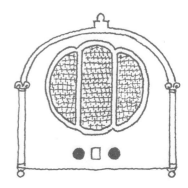

1938 Orson Welles's *War of the Worlds* creates panic among thousands of radio listeners and a government investigation follows.

1939 First experimental FM station goes on the air in New Jersey.

1940 A government court of appeals rules that records purchased by radio stations may be played on the air with no prior consent from record companies or artists.

organization with a competent staff capable of meeting the task of entertaining the nation?"

In 1926 RCA formed e National Broadcasting Company (NBC) "to provide the best programs available for broadcasting in the United States." It was so successful that NBC formed a second network a year later to accommodate increasing demand. The two networks were identified by the color of pens

1940 Edward R. Murrow brings the war in Europe to radio listeners in America.

1943 NBC sells its second network; this eventually becomes ABC, the third major network.

1945 The FCC encourages the development of television, to the detriment of FM radio.

1948 Radio's biggest money year; from here on television begins to take a larger share of advertising revenues.

1949 The FCC allows licensees to present editorials as part of regular programming and requires time for opposing views.

1951 Hundreds of radio stations switch to the deejay format and scramble to make up for lost revenues as network feeds diminish.

1955 Bill Haley and the Comets' *Rock around the Clock* becomes the first rock 'n' roll hit to make it to number one. The rock era of radio begins.

1959 With the payola scandal uncovered, deejays admit receiving money to "plug" certain records. The rise of the program director follows.

1966 KSAN-FM in San Francisco and KPPC-FM in Los Angeles become the first "underground" FM stations playing album cuts. Deejays are again given power to select music.

1970 The FCC issues a statement warning that broadcasters are liable for obscene or drug-related lyrics in songs they air.

1970s ABC radio successfully breaks into various "networks" with news, information, and entertainment designed for specialized audiences.

1972 All-news formats go on the air in New York, Washington, and Los Angeles.

1975 Don Imus, controversial and often abusive New York deejay, snares top ratings in the nation's most competitive radio market.

1976 C.W. McCall's hit single "Convoy" celebrates the new era of citizens' band (CB) radio. The FCC opens up 17 new CB channels and more than 20 million Americans are CB users.

1978 Pressure for a new Communications Act mounts in Congress, but most broadcasters are reluctant.

---

used to trace their paths in stockholders' meetings, the *red* and *blue* networks. Initially they linked only the Midwest and the Eastern Seaboard, but by the end of 1927 NBC had leased a transcontinental wire to bring its programs to the West Coast. Simultaneous coast-to-coast broadcasting was a reality.

Young Bill Paley, a 26-year-old heir to the Congress Cigar Company, had been fascinated by the way radio advertising had boost-

David Sarnoff Broadcasts the Disaster of the Decade

On April 14, 1912, young David Sarnoff in New York was casually listening to the flood of dots and dashes that made up radio messages. Suddenly a dim message, barely audible through the static, startled him. It was coming from the S.S. *Olympic* some 1,400 miles away:

S.S. *Titanic* ran into iceberg, sinking fast.

The *Titanic* was the pride of British shipbuilders who thought her unsinkable. This made the news all the more amazing and word of the disaster spread quickly. Many amateur radio transmitters were soon trying to make contact with the sinking ship. To avoid jamming the airwaves and to keep interference to a minimum, President Taft ordered them shut down except for one. David Sarnoff remained on the air.

For three days and nights he received and transmitted messages. There was little time for food or sleep. The first reports included names of survivors. Later came the long list of casualties. Sarnoff's wireless became the nation's information link with the disaster of the decade.

It was also electronic media's first "scoop." Newspapers took their information directly from radio. Many years later Sarnoff recalled, "The *Titanic* disaster brought radio to the front . . . and incidentally me." The 21-year-old boy who was there when the importance of wireless was first dramatized to the nation went on to become the driving force behind RCA and the National Broadcasting Company.

---

ed his father's cigar business. In 1928 he bought a 16-station "network" that then dared to challenge the mighty NBC. His United Independent Broadcasters eventually became CBS. Despite Paley's efforts during the 1920s and 1930s, NBC's two networks aired the most popular radio shows. During that time, a number of other small networks tried to challenge NBC's dominance, but none was entirely successful. After CBS, the Mutual Broadcasting System probably came closest to success, thanks largely to several popular radio shows, including *The Lone Ranger*.

NBC's greatest hit in the early days was *Amos 'n' Andy*. It was a situation comedy of sorts, featuring the adventures of a group of black workers, one of whom owned the "Fresh-Air Taxicab Company." The show was loaded with black stereotypes. Ironically, the voices of Amos and Andy were really those of two white men.

Probably the most popular genre of radio entertainment during the golden age was the mystery or action-adventure series. Among the most successful were *Gangbusters, Calling All Cars, Ellery Queen, The Fat Man, Sam Spade, The FBI in Peace and War*, and *The Green Hornet*. The action-adventure format first developed for radio has been carried on by TV shows like *Kojak, Starsky and Hutch*, and *McCloud*. In both media, action-adventure series have been tremendously popular.

Like daytime TV today, daytime radio had its soap operas, including *Our Gal Sunday, The Romance of Helen Trent*, and *Pepper Young's Family*. For the kids there were *Jack Armstrong, the All-American Boy, Superman, Uncle Don*, and of course, *The Lone Ranger*. There were quiz and talk shows as well. If all of these formats sound familiar, it's because television borrowed so heavily from radio. The names have changed but the genres of television and radio programs are almost identical. Some critics contend that television has supplied very few new ideas in broadcast entertainment.

But radio in the golden era was full of new ideas. It was the magic medium, and everybody loved it. Listeners from coast to coast

War of the Worlds and World War

It was a dark rainy night over most of America, October 30, 1938. In Europe Hitler was invading Czechoslovakia and was turning his eyes toward Poland. There was a definite tension in the air. Millions of Americans tuned in their radios to CBS's *Mercury Theatre of the Air.* Instead there was a late news bulletin—aliens had landed in New Jersey—America was being invaded by men from Mars! Thousands of calls poured in to newspapers and radio stations—was it true??? Were there really men from Mars? Army personnel were called back to their bases—this could be serious.

Orson Welles's Halloween production of H. G. Wells's *War of the Worlds* set off a genuine panic. There were traffic jams near the "landing site," and many people reported spotting the aliens. Public reaction was overwhelming. Some listeners had tuned in late (Edgar Bergen's show on another network had far more listeners), which added to the confusion. Welles attempted to avert disaster by broadcasting repeated warnings that this fictional radio play was not to be taken seriously; it was only *entertainment.*

That broadcast has been called the most famous of all radio programs, and perhaps it was. It is the one that had the greatest *immediate* impact on its listeners. The FCC investigated and new regulations were passed: there would be no more "fictional" news bulletins.

In a larger context, *War of the Worlds* demonstrated the awesome power of radio. No newspaper or magazine had the ability to evoke such immediate emotional response. Radio was an infant medium, but many people began to wonder—this could be more than just an "entertainment" device after all. . . .

---

could hear music (and fill in the visual picture with their imagination) from the great concert halls in Boston, or they could be transported to the Grand Ballroom at the Waldorf-Astoria Hotel in New York City. For those who lived in rural America, radio provided a link with the world outside their own small town. Radio brought everyone into the cultural and social mainstream of America.

Of course, entertainment was not the only way radio served the American people. It also remained what it had been since the *Titanic* disaster: a way to keep people informed. President Franklin Roosevelt made the most of the medium in the early 1930s, speaking directly to his constituents and urging them to support his new and controversial programs (see 6.5). His "fireside chats" gathered most Americans around the radio. The President of the United States was speaking to them!

Radio also made Americans acutely aware of current events in Europe in the late 1930s and early 1940s. Broadcasters like Eric Sevareid and Edward R. Murrow were on the scene, bringing listeners the sounds of war as they actually happened. Murrow's reports from London during the bombing were the ultimate in believability—bombs exploded in the background as he reported the latest war news. Those pre–Pearl Harbor broadcasts by Murrow prepared Americans for the war to come. Sentiment shifted rapidly from neutrality to a full commitment to England by 1941. Somehow, the war did not seem very far away, and radio was the reason.

In 1943, NBC's reign as king of network radio suffered a serious blow when the FCC decided to ban the operation of two networks by one company. NBC sold its blue network for $7 million to Edward Noble, who renamed it the American Broadcasting Company.

NBC radio stars began to defect to CBS in the 1940s, lured away by "Bill Paley's checkbook." The CBS president offered big money contracts to Jack Benny, Burns and Allen, Ozzie and Harriet Nelson, Red Skelton, Bing Crosby, and others. This stroke of genius gave CBS a nucleus of talent for its new television

President Franklin Delano Roosevelt spoke on the air often to bring his message to the people.

network in the late 1940s, and it helped establish CBS as the top network in the newer medium.

The Big Change: Radio After Television

Just as many think the "good old days" of magazines are gone forever, some contend that radio will never be what it was during the golden era. In a way, they are correct. The *Gasoline Alley* strip offers an interesting peek at how Walt and other members of the "golden era" generation feel about the current rock formats of radio stations. Radio will never be what it was, but it will continue to be what it is, and that is constantly changing. Radio has not really become better or worse since television, but it has undergone tremendous change in content.

In the mid-1950s television was using many radio programs and radio stars. In radio, an industry-wide panic set in. In their heyday, national radio networks provided programs from 9:00 A.M. to 11:00 P.M. Local stations simply pulled the switch and raked in the profits. When the networks deserted them, the locals looked for the least expensive format that would allow them to stay on the air and sell advertising time. The day of the deejay had arrived.

Of course, music had been played on radio since the beginning; and as early as 1932, Los Angeles radio personality Al Jarvis began playing a few records from a tiny studio at KFWB which he called "The World's Largest Make Believe Ballroom." In New York, Martin Block picked up the idea three years later and made believers of his skeptical bosses at WNEW by arranging sponsorship for the show himself. The program proved successful, but there were problems. Performers fought airing of their songs on radio, fearing it would dilute the product and make record purchases unnecessary. In 1940, however, a government appeals court ruled that broadcasters who had bought a record could play it on the air without prior permission from the artist.

The idea of mixing records, chatter, and commercials—creating a *complete* sound environment—was just what radio stations needed in the early 1950s. Before long the local disc jockey format had replaced the network provisions as the most common radio commodity.

During the mid-1950s the transistor reduced the size and price of the portable radio. Now it was truly a medium that "goes where you go." What's more, Americans *were* on the go. A record number of automobiles were sold during the period, and most of them were equipped with radios. The most popular deejays appeared in "drive time" from 6:00 to 9:00 A.M. and from 3:00 to 6:00 P.M., keeping commuters company to and from work. Drive time became radio's prime time and helped give the medium a much needed financial boost. Yet the deejays themselves—colorful, provocative, and eccentric—were largely responsible for keeping radio alive.

Meet the Deejay

Though I have had professional experience in many areas of mass media, it is my years as a Los Angeles deejay that seem to provoke the most student questions. What are deejays really like?

Real-life deejays are often the proud possessors of giant egos (see 6.6). Most of the male deejays I've known were five or six inches shorter than the norm and had three things

Imus in the Morning

Which New York deejay had as his regular guest the Reverend Dr. Billy Sol Hargis, who sells his "angel hair cloaks" for the "long trip to heaven"? Whose guests included Judge Hangin, who stated flatly that police brutality is the "fun part" of law enforcement, and Ronald American, who is "110 percent American" and promises to rise and walk from his wheelchair if elected President?

If you have ever spent any time in New York City, you know that this description fits only one air personality, the sometimes foulmouthed, always controversial Don Imus, former morning deejay for WNBC. John Donald Imus, Jr., started at KUTY in Palmdale, California, and was fired from his next job at KJOY in Stockton for running an Eldridge Cleaver look-alike contest. Somehow within a year Imus was in the crucial "morning drive" slot for the network-owned WNBC in the nation's top radio market, loving every minute of it. Imus's usual patter included racial slurs, which he insisted were "all in good fun." He thought nothing of spending a few moments talking with his engineer during the middle of a live commercial, or criticizing his bosses, all while on the air, of course.

Often Imus could be heard laughing through a newscast or putting down his fellow deejays. All these

Controversial New York deejay Don Imus responds to his critics.

antics violate every known code of conduct for a Top-40 deejay, but through it all "Imus's Army" of listeners remained faithful. By 1975 he had more listeners than any other deejay in New York. Yet success was fleeting. WNBC let him go in 1978 after a fall in the ratings. Radio listeners and radio executives seem to be a fickle lot, but I doubt that we've heard the last of Don Imus.

in common. They were generally insecure, usually divorced, and almost always hyperactive.

One Los Angeles disc jockey refuses to take a vacation. He works 52 weeks a year because each of his last three vacations cost him his job. Program directors slotted in a newer, younger, and less salaried deejay in his place. When listeners liked the new voice, the old one was off to the unemployment line. Being on the air is a risky business, because there is always someone willing to do your job for less, or even for nothing. Being a disc jockey is a coveted profession, and this does not encourage job security.

One reason disc jockeys are often divorced is because many stations are knee deep in something called "groupies." The deejay, whether male or female, is likely to be accosted by these warm and loving creatures at any moment. The groupie is usually young and is always caught up in the magic of the music and the people who make it or play it on the radio. In doing research on groupies, I asked my father—who did a radio show in Portland, Oregon, during the late 1930s—if there were groupies even then. He confirmed that there were, smiled quietly, and got a far-away look in his eyes. Finally he added that most of them "wanted to be vocalists with a band" but would settle for a love affair with a disc jockey.

Hyperactivity, the third professional trait, is a necessity. Deejays must be able to play a cart (a tape cartridge with a commercial or prerecorded message), cue up a record, give the time and temperature, and answer the phone—all at the same time. They must do it with a smoothness that never lets the listener know how hectic things really are. As far as the listeners know, the deejay is listening to the music right along with them.

In the early 1950s, disc jockeys programmed their own shows, selecting the records and planning whatever additional material they wanted. More recently, the program director has taken over, dictating the content of the show right down to the last supposed ad lib. The rise of the program director came in response to the "payola" scandal of the late 1950s. Once record companies discovered that air play boosted record sales, there was no stopping them. Disc jockeys would receive cases of liquor, free passes to concerts and films, and finally lump cash sums to "promote" a song by giving it air time. The net result was a government investigation in 1959, which uncovered this payola. There followed a brief rift in the public's love affair with the deejay.

But the 1960s saw little payola. Is the payola problem solved forever? Probably not—one record industry executive admitted privately to me over drinks, "It's a lot cheaper to get to one program director than to get to half a dozen jocks." "Drug-ola"—the exchange of drugs for preferential treatment of a song—is not unknown in major markets.

The authoritarian rule of the program director was challenged briefly by the appearance of the "underground" FM stations in the late 1960s. These stations played longer album cuts instead of singles, and control by a program director did not fit with their "loose and free" image. For a short time, these disc jockeys were given back the power to select the songs they aired. The program director's role was limited to riding herd on the erratic underground deejays who were often likely to forget a commercial or swear on the air. The commercial success of some underground formats led to the similar but slicker and more organized "progressive" stations, which reinstituted the program director's power to select the music.

Of course, all markets are different. In many small stations the deejay may pick all the music and there may not even be a program director. But, even this is changing as small-market owners are finding that using prerecorded syndicated shows is cheaper than hiring live deejays. Deejays, themselves a product of "the big change," are finding that new changes in radio technology are drastically altering their roles in radio programming.

The People You Never Hear

The radio world to most listeners may consist of the disc jockey, the newsperson, and the commentator; but the real world of radio is quite different. The "on the air" people may represent only about 10 to 15 percent of the total staff of most stations. In metro markets they may make up less than 10 percent. Who are the rest of the people?

Management personnel are at the top of the ladder. Each station has an owner or owners and a general manager (GM), who supervises all station activities. The GM's word is law and the decisions are final. Under the GM are the heads of the major departments.

Programming is the first department you might think of. The program director (PD) keeps track of air personnel, schedules shifts, and settles disputes involving the on-the-air staff. It is the PD's job to make sure that air personalities are slotted in at the proper times to elicit maximum audience response. If the ratings for the entire station are poor, the PD is likely to go.

Sales is often the most financially rewarding of all station jobs. Usually sales people have a guaranteed minimum "draw" of only a few hundred dollars per month, but they make up the difference by selling air time on commission. If they don't sell, they don't eat. There is usually a sales director or sales manager in charge who reports directly to the GM. In major markets there may be a few highly paid stars on the air, but at most stations it is the sales people who take home the most money.

Traffic is the department least known to the average radio listener. The traffic staff must schedule all the commercials. Only a fixed number are allowed each hour and competing products must not be placed back to back. It wouldn't be a good business practice to have a spot that urged you to "buy a Chevrolet today" played after one that told you "Ford has a better idea!" Traffic people make up the program logs, minute-by-minute projections of all commercials, IDs, promos, and other non-music materials. Air staff and engineers follow these logs exactly.

Engineering people are usually found poking around with screwdrivers and soldering irons, repairing broken station equipment. Again, there is usually a chief engineer who reports directly to the GM. Engineers keep the station running well, and they can often be heard mumbling that nobody notices them "until something goes wrong."

The *production* department is vital to the overall "sound" of the station. Copywriters and "talent" people produce the jingles, IDs, promos, and, most important, commercials. A salesperson will sell time to a local merchant and then order a spot for production. A copywriter works with information supplied by the salesperson. The "talent" goes into the studio and reads the spot. At a larger station there is an engineer who works exclusively in production (see 6.7). At a smaller station the copywriter, talent, and engineer may be one person. At a very small station, that same person may do the selling as well.

Large metro stations have separate departments for editorials, publicity, public relations, and so on. Still, most of the 8,000 AM and FM radio stations in America have fewer than 50 employees—and there never seems to be enough people to get all the work done.

As with other media outlets, the environment of most radio stations is frantic and chaotic. From morning to night everyone is on the go, typing up commercials and getting things on the air at the last minute. Coffee makes the American free-enterprise system work; I've never been in a radio station that didn't have a gigantic coffeepot that needed constant refilling. Chaos just seems to be the nature of the medium. Almost everyone who works in radio complains about it, but no one would really have it any other way.

In direct contrast to this are the new "automated" stations where all music and talk are taped ahead of time and selected by a computer. The atmosphere in the automated stations is more like that in a library or a museum.

Music Formats

As we have seen, the business of today's radio is music. Though rock is the most popular musical form of all and the one that represents the greatest share of advertising revenues, there are dozens of others. Many, like "middle of the road" and "chicken rock," are variations on rock, but others, including classical, easy listening, and ethnic music, are making inroads in major markets.

Top-40 Top-40, much more music, hit parade, boss hits—by any name this format is the most listened-to and most talked-about format in radio today. It emerged when programmers called record stores to find out what the public was buying; then they mirrored

Bob Keyker, KFWB Production Engineer, working in the master control room of the Los Angeles studio.

public taste by playing those same songs over and over. Today Top-40 radio has become Top-20 or Top-25 at many stations. The same few records receive repeated air play while thousands of others are ignored.

There are a few giants in this genre. Bill Drake's success came in the early 1960s with KHJ, a Los Angeles Top-40 station. While sitting around his pool at Malibu Beach, he picked the songs that were to be played on his station. His method was simple—play only the very top singles and play them more often than anyone else. Paul Drew, who now programs KHJ and 12 other stations, is in his forties, balding, and walks with a slouch. Yet, it is said that no group can expect a single to hit the top of the charts without his blessing.

Another giant is Kasey Kasem, who formed Watermark Productions to begin his syndicated *American Top-40* (see 6.8). Kasey gets his hits from the number one authority in the industry, *Billboard* magazine. Every week he "counts 'em down in order" to thousands of listeners in hundreds of cities from New York to Newberg, Oregon. His trademark is airing little-known facts about the group or star:

A certain singer sold his guitar and then decided he had to get it back and spent three weeks wandering around the streets of Columbus, Ohio, until one day, tired and discouraged, he stopped in Winchell's to have a doughnut and there, lo and behold, was the man to whom he had sold it! He went on to form a new singing group and this week they have the number one song on *American Top-40*—Who is it? . . . Well, we'll find out right after this message. . . .

Chicken Rock In the 1960s chicken rock appeared. Chicken rock stations play softer rock music and stay away from controversial songs or those with a heavy beat or indiscernible

Kasey Kasem of *American Top-40*.

lyrics. The Carpenters, Carole King, Chicago, and Art Garfunkel are acceptable in chicken rock, but you seldom hear Led Zeppelin, Grand Funk Railroad, or the Steve Miller Band.

Middle of the Road MOR stations sandwich a little of the softer rock between Frank Sinatra, Perry Como, and the show tunes. MOR is modern radio's attempt to be all things to all people. Often personality, not music, is what makes MOR work. The MOR deejay may use air time to talk about personal experiences or deliver one-liners from a deejay joke book. Gary Owens (the "pronouncer" with one hand cocked over his ear from *Laugh-In*) is a good example. He does an afternoon drive-time show in Los Angeles, and music simply gives him a break from chatter and commercials.

Progressive Rock Progressive rock stations are usually found on the FM dial, though a few AM progressives have popped up, particularly on the East Coast. Progressive rockers play an even balance of album cuts and Top-40 material. However, the "bubblegum" sound that is often popular with teenagers is out, as are extremely long album cuts and songs that may include obscenity or political controversy.

Country and Western Next to rock, the C&W format is probably the most commercially successful. More than 50 percent of all popular music radio stations play some country music. Every major metropolitan market has at least one C&W station. C&W is common in the rural western states. In the Deep South, it competes with Top-40 for the highest ratings.

For years, it was easy to separate country music from Top-40, but the more recent country influence on rock groups has made the distinction less clear. In addition, many country singers have found success on the Top-40 charts. The result has been an introduction to country music for many listeners. Several stations now follow a "popcorn" formula, alternating country and rock hits, hoping to attract listeners from both camps.

Easy Listening Easy listening or "beautiful music" is the next category. Often, radio is something we listen to while we are doing something else. It provides a sound backdrop in our ear or helps us study or wash the dishes. This is the secret of success for easy listening, which plays soft instrumental versions of songs that were popular five, ten, or even fifty years ago.

Easy listening fans see their stations as an oasis from the frantic "noise" of the other stations that play all that "junk." Easy listening announcers display little emotion or personality, but simply and softly announce the songs. News and commercials (when possible) are done in the same soft-spoken way. The idea is never to violate the listener's trust by starting to sound like "those other stations." Groups like the Percy Faith Orchestra play a song or two, and there's an occasional vocal by Perry Como. Easy listening formats are usually "automated" or prerecorded, with the computer selecting the songs according to some preset formula (three instrumentals, one vocal, two commercials, and so on).·

The competition among easy listening stations is fiercer than the name might suggest, because, although easy listening fans are often as devoted to their own stations as Top-40 listeners are, they tend to be less tolerant of commercials. Typically, a new easy listening station will enter a market with few sponsors. As the ratings grow, so does the number of commercials. First thing you know, the listeners are tuning elsewhere.

Easy listening is usually piped into dentists' and doctors' offices. Sometimes these offices pay to receive a closed-circuit broadcast of easy listening music, such as one called

Drawing by Ziegler; © 1976, The New Yorker Magazine, Inc.

"Muzak." The Muzak format is the easy listener's dream—no commercials, no disc jockey, no interruptions, just music. Critics contend that Muzak isn't music at all, but simply a pleasant, mindless noise.

Jazz In a few markets, the jazz format receives a comfortable chunk of the ratings. Jazz stations were once quite popular, but enthusiasm dwindled in the 1960s along with the number of jazz buffs. Those that remained were hardcore fans, however, and went to great lengths to find a station that offered what they wanted. Now there is some indication that young people are becoming interested in jazz again. Popular performers combine traditional and experimental jazz sounds with rock.

Ethnic Soul stations cater predominantly to blacks, though they are often owned and listened to by whites. "Wolfman Jack," a famous deejay, got his start on XERB, a Mexican-based station that programmed predominantly for black and Mexican-American audiences in southern California. His gravel voice and "soul talk" had most listeners convinced he was black until he began making television appearances. Other ethnic stations offer programs in foreign languages. Of these, the

Spanish-speaking stations are most plentiful, particularly in New York and the Southwest.

Classical The commercial classical station, once a respectably established format, is now virtually extinct. There are about 30 full-time commercial classical stations today, down from more than 50 in 1965. Classical music may be alive and well, but teaming it with the financial realities of commercial radio seems an impossible task. Often classical music stations are subsidized by listeners or survive because a wealthy owner writes off station losses at income-tax time.

These are the basic music formats in radio today. Many stations offer a smorgasbord of two or more formats. Often program directors claim their sound is a significant variation from established norms in order to convince advertisers that they are offering something unique. But in truth, most stations stay pretty well within the boundaries of established formats. These boundaries were set up in the 1950s and have spelled success for many stations. While station programmers always think they should be allowed to experiment, station owners are usually more concerned with the bottom line. If the station is making money, let's keep it the way it is; if it's not, *then* we can talk about change.

According to *Broadcasting* magazine, there are more commercial music stations reporting losses rather than profits each year, but those figures can be misleading. Owners often pay excessive salaries to themselves or their top executives to avoid heavy profit taxes at the end of the year. Actually, as soon as a station is a real money-loser, it will change formats, go up for sale, or both.

Non-Music Formats

Some stations do not play music of any kind. They make up the world of radio "talk." Many are *noncommercial*, and feel it is their duty to offer an alternative to music. Noncommercial stations run rebroadcasts of speeches, documentaries, and discussions. While none of these is popular with the mass audience (ratings indicate that what they offer is not what most of the public wants to hear), most noncommercial broadcasters feel they are having an impact. They are, in a sense, fulfilling de Forest's dream of radio as a device for mass education. Since 1945, the FCC has set aside 20 of the 100 FM channels exclusively for educational and noncommercial stations.

Commercial non-music stations have a far greater impact on the mass market. Of these, the *all-news* format has become the most popular. All-news programmers do not expect the audience to listen to news forever, just long enough to pick up a couple of stories and hear a few commercials. Los Angeles's KFWB has a slogan typifying this philosophy: "Give us 20 minutes and we'll give you the world."

Talk radio is not new. For some time many stations have featured discussion shows where personalities debate current issues with the listening audience. What is new is the *all-talk* format, devoted exclusively to talk. Like all-news radio, all-talk has become possible only recently as the radio audience continues to diversify.

Other non-music formats are constantly being tried in various markets. One FM station received a special permit from the FCC to carry nothing but commercials 24 hours a day. The idea was for it to become a "classified of the air." It folded after a couple of months, apparently because the public was not ready for all-ads radio.

Two-Way Radio

While the talk radio format offers a limited form of two-way radio, citizens' band (CB) offers a chance for direct feedback. Two-way communication is rapidly becoming a vital electronic communication network for America's citizens. The citizens' band is a small part of the radio spectrum set aside for personal two-way communication. CB has been around since 1945, but in 1972 there were only 850,000 CB users. In the next five years more than 15 million sets were sold. Unlike other types of radio permits, the CB license is readily obtainable by all.

For years most CB users were truck drivers who used their radios to help each other by spotting "Smokies" (police officers) or looking for "Kojaks with Kodaks" (highway patrol officers with radar units). Now CB is used by all kinds of people who spend time on the road. What's more, CB units have become popular household items. CB users with colorful "handles" (nicknames) like "Kissey Face," "Huggy Bear," "Pig Pen," and "First Momma" are everywhere.

The words of the CB enthusiast are often earthy. It is not unusual to hear a string of obscenities on the air. Enforcement of normal broadcast standards is almost impossible, at least for now. CB radios caught on so quickly that the FCC, already understaffed, was caught unprepared. The seven FCC commissioners did approve 13 new channels for CB use in 1977, bringing the total number to 40 (see 6.9). Still, overcrowding on the band remains so serious that more channels are needed.

Why the sudden CB craze? CB offers the radio enthusiast a chance for direct involvement with "the magic ear." CB is two-way communication in an era when radio stations often offer largely prepackaged and redundant one-way information. CB also represents a return to the kind of personal involvement with media that characterized radio's early years. With its own colorful language and technical terms, the CB world is akin to a "private club," albeit a club whose privacy is

"This is Woolly Caterpillar. All you good buddies can put that old hammer down,' cause 303 is Smokey-free from here to T-town—ten-four!"

increasingly threatened by its own expanding membership list.

Whither Radio?

From early experimental stations run by devoted amateurs to the computerized programming of today, radio has undergone a number of metamorphoses since the turn of the century. It is a tremendously fluid medium, able to adapt immediately to the wants and needs of its audience. In the 1950s, when television was stealing radio stars and programs, radio rediscovered music programs and business boomed. Similarly, just as the impersonal

Hy-Gain was one of many manufacturers to quickly offer 40 channels of CB after the FCC approved 13 new frequencies in 1977.

Introducing the CB system that's ready for 40 when you are.

Now you can have the Hy-Gain Personal Communications System that's ready for 40 channels when you are. It's our Hy-Gain II (Model 2682) citizens two-way transceiver and Hellcat X trunk lip antenna.

The 23-channel Hy-Gain II gives you clear, quiet performance. The incredible frequency stability of advanced Phase-Lock-Loop circuitry. And a certificate for remanufacture to 40-channel specifications. It's your guarantee your new radio will be 40-channels ready.

If, after January 1 and FCC acceptance, you decide you want all 40, send us your radio. The certificate. And $25 for remanufacturing. We'll send your radio back with all 40 channels (offer expires June 30, 1977).

With the Hy-Gain II you also get extra cost features like switchable automatic noise limiter. Mic preamp. Separate AF and RF gain controls. Automatic modulation control. And PA provision to let you convert the whole thing to a powerful Public Address System. There's exceptional sensitivity and selectivity. And superb adjacent channel rejection, too. So you don't get the whole gang when you place a person-to-person call.

And for the budget-minded CBer there's our Hy-Gain I (Model 2681). With automatic gain and modulation controls. Excellent noise cancelling. Mic preamp. The same great Hy-Gain performance. And like its big brother it can be remanufactured for 40 channels.

Complete your system with our Hellcat X. The perfect 40-channel antenna for either radio. Comes in three versions. Trunk-lip mount. Magnetic. And claw (requires 3/8-3/4" hole). All are quick and easy to install. And the Hellcat X is completely adjustable to keep the 54" stainless steel whip upright and efficient. So you get all the performance your Hy-Gain radio can deliver.

So get the Personal Communications System that's ready for 40 when you are at your Hy-Gain dealer. And ask about our 300 other fine two-way communications products. Call 800/447-4700 for your nearest Hy-Gain dealer. In Illinois 800/322-4400.

Hellcat X 40-channel antenna for citizens two-way transceivers

hy-gain
We keep people talking.

Hy-Gain Electronics Corporation   8601 Northeast Highway Six; Lincoln, NE 68505
Hy-Gain de Puerto Rico, Inc.   Box 68: Naguabo. PR 00718

The following Hy-Gain 23-channel radios can be remanufactured to FCC 40-channel specifications after January 1, 1977.
681, 682, 2680, 2681, 2682, 2683, 2679, 3084.
If you currently own one of these radios, a 40-channel certificate may be obtained from your Hy-Gain dealer.

© 1976 Hy-Gain

computerization of the 1970s began growing, CB radio ushered in a whole new era of personal radio use.

Mark Twain once quipped, "The reports of my death are greatly exaggerated." The same is true of radio. The death of radio was predicted at the end of the golden era, in the late 1940s, when rock music took over in the 1950s, and in the wake of extensive commercialization in the 1960s and 1970s. But like the famous watch, radio seems to be able to "take a licking and keep on ticking."

There are now more than 8,000 radio stations in America, which continue to offer a great diversity of information. Radio ad revenues are over $1.7 billion yearly and profits exceed $90 million. There are over 400 million radios in America—about two for every man, woman, and child in the country. Radio offers many music formats as well as all-news and all-talk stations. Radio futurists envision the day when some stations will be all-sports or even all-weather.

Issues and Answers

"Puff the Magic Dragon" and the Regulation of Radio

But if I really say it
The radio won't play it
Unless I lay it, between the lines

"I Dig Rock and Roll Music"
Paul Stookey, James Mason, and Dave Dixon

By 1927 there were more than 700 private radio stations in operation. Until that time, licensing procedures had been rather loose and stations could go on and off the air at will. This was detrimental to both listeners and other stations, so Congress passed the Radio Act of 1927. It created a five-person Federal Radio Commission (FRC) to oversee licensing of radio stations. Each station was given permission to broadcast for three years and was assigned a specific frequency.

The act established a policy that no one had a "right" to broadcast in the same way that there is a "right" to print. While the supply of paper and ink may be unlimited (though we know today this may not be the case), the airwaves contain only a certain number of channels. These channels cannot belong in perpetuity to any individual; like some lands and minerals, they are a national resource that must be operated in the "public interest, convenience, or necessity." This clearly established the FRC's power to make decisions about who could and who could not broadcast. These laws remain today, despite technological innovations like cable and the laser, which may mean that there are actually an unlimited number of channels available.

The FRC decided to include the quality of programming as one criterion in making license decisions. Though this was not always a major determinant, some licenses were awarded to those who promised the highest-quality programs.

"Aha!" you exclaim. "Then, what happened to radio—why don't we have better programs?" The problem is, what is "quality" programming for you may not be "quality" for someone else. Some people would like to banish Top-40 music from the face of the earth. Others couldn't live without it. The FRC didn't help much; it never actually defined "quality." In fact, we still don't have a real working definition for it and perhaps we never will.

An important precedent was set in 1931 when the FRC refused to renew the license of KFKB. The station had been selling patent medicine over the air and phony "doctors" had been telling would-be patients about "miracle" cures. KFKB took the FRC to court, contending it had the right to broadcast anything it liked and that the FRC could not restrict the content of radio programs. KFKB lost the case. The courts ruled that the "public interest, convenience, or necessity" clause gives the FRC the right to control certain kinds of programs.

A few years later Congress passed the Communications Act of 1934, which included provisions for telephone, telegraph, and television as well as radio. To administer this, a seven-person Federal Communications Commission (FCC) replaced the FRC. The FCC commissioners have seven-year terms. Each year one retires and a new one is appointed by the President. FCC decisions are often split since, like the Supreme Court, FCC commissioners reflect the political philosophy of their party. These appointments are among the most important a President can make, since an FCC commissioner has the potential to influence every piece of information we receive from electronic media.

However, that potential is seldom realized. Traditionally, FCC commissioners excercise little power over broadcasters. Almost 60,000 applications for broadcast licenses and license renewals have been reviewed since 1954. Only about 100 have ever been given less than a complete renewal. Of these, just a handful have been revoked entirely.

Why is the FCC so reluctant to act? One reason is that the commissioners are under tremendous pressure from the media industry. Another reason is that radio stations do their best to behave themselves. Owning a TV station has been called a "license to print money," and ownership of radio stations is also usually quite lucrative. Obviously nobody wants to lose such a valuable license. Licensees do everything they can to ensure that the FCC will not be displeased, and this often means going along with every FCC whim.

This can be both good and bad for the public. The FCC, as an agent of the government and the people, can ensure that phony patent medicines are not sold over the air. But also, the seven FCC commissioners, who are often advanced in years and sometimes out of step with the tastes of the general public, may heavily influence programming. Broadcasters often overreact to FCC "suggestions" and bend over backward to ensure dull, noncontroversial content. For example, during the early 1970s when the FCC attempted to "crack down" on stations playing songs with drug-related lyrics, Peter, Paul, and Mary's "Puff the Magic Dragon" was banned on many stations. Station owners thought "Puff" might be about marijuana and they weren't taking any chances.

At about the same time, Los Angeles deejay Bill Balance was pioneering a new kind of radio talk show. His *Feminine Forum* invited female listeners to call in and talk about their most intimate sexual problems. Quickly dubbed "topless radio," the *Feminine Forum* and its imitators soon spread to every major radio market. The FCC soon made it clear that there might be action against radio obscenity if the content was not moderated. Balance was issued a set of guidelines by his bosses and the more outrageous topics were deleted. He complained on the air that his freedom of speech was being violated, but to no avail. No matter how popular the show, the station simply did not want to risk a run-in with the FCC.

In a 1975 case, the FCC placed a sanction against WBAI-FM in New York for airing a George Carlin monologue that contained a number of four-letter words. Previous court decisions had ruled that it was not the commission's place to set obscenity standards for broadcasters, but this didn't seem to deter the FCC. In 1978, the U.S. Supreme Court upheld their action in the WBAI case.

In all of these cases it can be argued that the FCC has set standards for broadcasters that may not be in the best interests of listeners. Perhaps the FCC has outlived its usefulness. It may be that a review of the entire Communications Act of 1934 is needed. In 1934, there was no network television or cable TV. Radio stations were all network affiliated and most recordings were not permitted on the air. The FCC has tried to adjust to the tremendous changes since then by reversing a decision here and patching up a problem there. As a result, no one is happy.

Commissioners require each licensee to submit mounds of paper, including program-ming logs, replies to any license challenges, copies of listener complaints, community ascertainment studies, and much more. Some of these are necessary and proper; some are a waste of time. There are so many hundreds of rules and amended rules that broadcasters are running in circles trying to comply. Meanwhile the public is unhappy with the quality and lack of diversity in the programs it receives.

Perhaps a new communications act incorporating a realistic view of contemporary public tastes and modern station practices would not solve all of these problems, but it would be a start.

Queries and Concepts

1. Listen to the CBS *Mystery Theatre* on the air (if it is aired in your market) or dig up a recording of an old radio drama. How does it compare with its TV counterparts? Which is the more effective story-telling medium? Why?

2. Dig up what material you can on the Franklin Roosevelt fireside chats and compare them with Jimmy Carter's fireside chats and radio call-in shows. What are the similarities and differences?

3. Interview a selected audience of people over age 50 about radio's golden era.

Design a questionnaire to measure their attitudes about how early radio programs compare with today's TV and radio programs.

4. Pick an hour of the day when you are usually free. Listen to a different disc jockey each day for three days in a row. How do they differ? Are there any differences in music? What kind of audience might each be appealing to?

5. Identify the top five radio stations in your market. Write a two-paragraph description of each format.

6. Do you know anyone who has a CB radio or is tuned in to CB? That person could be the subject of an interview about CB. What has CB done for that person? What does it hold for the future?

7. Come up with your own list of *must* items for "quality" radio programs. Compare with others in the class. Are there any items that *everyone* considers essential for "quality"?

Readings and References

Pioneers and Programmers

Erik Barnouw
A History of Broadcasting in the United States, 3 vols. *A Tower in Babel: To 1933*. New York: Oxford University Press, 1966. *The Golden Web: 1933 to 1953*. New York: Oxford University Press, 1968.
Easily the most comprehensive and often-quoted historical account of the rise of radio in North America, from an amateur toy to a dynamic social institution. The books are tough going in places but full of radio folklore and legend that keep the reader interested. A definitive bibliography and index.

Sydney W. Head
Broadcasting in America, 3d ed. New York: Houghton Mifflin, 1976.
Chapters 6–9 condense the history of radio. Though this edition covers major events in radio to 1976, the text was written in 1956 and it shows. There is particularly interesting coverage of radio during the golden era. One of the most referred-to texts on the history of broadcasting. Excellent bibliography.

Christopher H. Sterling and John M. Kittross
Stay Tuned. Belmont, Ca.: Wadsworth, 1978.
Offers a chronological look at the development and evolution of radio and television in America. Covers all important aspects of broadcast history, topically and up to date. Interesting narrative bibliographies at the ends of chapters; excellent index.

Harrison B. Summers, Robert E. Summers, and John H. Pennybacker
Broadcasting and the Public, 2d ed. Belmont, Ca.: Wadsworth, 1978.
This textbook is used often for introduction to broadcasting courses. History is covered in Chapters 3–5. There is much useful informa-

tion regarding the role of government in the broadcast industry (Chapters 12–14).

The Golden Age of Radio (1926–1948)

Frank Buxton and Bill Owen
The Big Broadcast: 1920–1950. New York: Viking Press, 1972.
A catalog of programs and stars from radio's golden age, complete with a short synopsis of each program.

Irving Settel
A Pictorial History of Radio. New York: Grosset & Dunlap, 1967.
An entertaining visual exploration into the people who made radio during the early years. It is a profusely illustrated and informative text. Radio's history is neatly broken down decade by decade. A must for old-time radio buffs, the book includes particularly thorough coverage of the 1930s and 1940s. Useful index.

There's an excellent gripping account of the war years and the part radio played in *Prime Time: The Life of Edward R. Murrow* (New York: Avon Books, 1970). See especially Chapters 5 and 6, "Hello America . . . Hitler Is Here" and "London Is Burning, London Is Burning."

The Big Change: Radio After Television; Meet the Deejay

Donald Pember
Mass Media in America, 2d ed. Chicago: Science Research Associates, 1977.

Although this book is an introduction to all mass media, I am particularly fond of the treatment of radio. Chapter 6, "Radio or Come On Let Me Show You Where It's At," emphasizes radio after television, an area long neglected by traditional text writers.

The People You Never Hear

Broadcasting Yearbook. Washington, D.C.: Broadcasting Publications, Inc., published annually.
This is the number one reference book for professional broadcasters. Statistics of every conceivable kind are found here, including ownership and other information for every radio and TV station in the country. Available in most libraries.

Joseph S. Johnson and Kenneth K. Jones
Modern Radio Station Practices, 2d ed. Belmont, Ca.: Wadsworth, 1978.
Not the most exciting text you'll ever read, but one that covers every department of the radio station and what makes it work. Some interesting reading in the "Station Profiles" section. The only one of its kind, this thorough book includes chapters on radio production, equipment, programming, news, and other topics.

Music Formats

I don't know of a single source that adequately covers this area. It's another one that has been long neglected in print. The best bet is to check

Readers' Guide to Periodical Literature and the *Popular Periodical Index* under "radio." *Rolling Stone* is the best single source for up-to-the-minute news of rock and Top 40. *Billboard* supplies charts for classical, country and western, rock, easy listening, and other formats plus in-house industry news.

Non-Music Formats

John R. Bittner and Denise A Bittner
Radio Journalism. Englewood Cliffs, N.J.: Prentice-Hall, 1977.
This text is the first comprehensive effort designed for radio classes. There are chapters on "News Sources and Covering Radio News" as well as on writing, production, and programming. See especially Chapter 10, "Landing a Job," if you are interested in breaking into radio news.

Two-Way Radio

"The Bodacious New World of C.B." *Time,* May 10, 1976, pp. 78–79.

Issues and Answers: "Puff the Magic Dragon" and the Regulation of Radio

Sydney Head's *Broadcasting in America* (New York: Houghton Mifflin, 1976) covers a number of pivotal FCC rulings on the legal implications involved in censorship of broadcast media. For more detailed accounts, see Nelson and Teeter's *Law of Mass Communication* (Mineola, N.Y.: Foundation Press, 1973) or Howard Simon's and Joseph A. Califano's *The Media and the Law* (New York: Praeger, 1976).

7
The Sound of Music

**The effect that pop music has on society is incredible. . . .
If everyone that was thinking in pop music terms were to stand
end to end, they'd go around the world ten times. . . . Pop music
is basically big. It concerns far more than 20-year-olds. It's
lasted too long. It concerns everybody now.—Peter Townshend**

Popular music is a global language that leaves a personal and permanent impression. With little effort you can probably think of many songs that have a very special meaning for you. One represents a summer romance. Another reminds you of someone far away. Perhaps there's a song you still can't listen to because you have associated it with an unpleasant experience. Have you ever broken a record in frustration because the dream you associated with it never came true?

Records are a medium we can enjoy alone or with others. They seem to grow and take on new depth as we become more familiar with them. When we share that experience we seem to enjoy it even more. There is a special feeling in playing a favorite album for someone who is hearing it for the first time. You want so much for that person to enjoy it, to hear what you hear, and experience what you feel.

If live concerts are like motion pictures, records are like still photos that we can return to time and time again. We may join Joni Mitchell or Alice Cooper at a moment's notice simply by putting a needle on a piece of vinyl. Records are, literally, a "record" of our important thoughts and feelings.

For the generation that has grown up after World War II, popular music seems to have a very special meaning. Many of this generation's heroes—Bob Dylan, John Lennon, Elton John, Rod Stewart, and Joni Mitchell, to name a few—are recording artists. The lyrics of their records convey folk tales and cultural clichés. The beat matches their emotional *feelings*.

"And the beat goes on."

The Fabulous Phonograph

In 1877 Thomas Edison's carbon transmitter had greatly improved Bell's telephone and gave the young Edison ample funds to experiment with a "talking machine." The best use for such a talking machine, he reasoned, would be to improve the telephone. After all, the telephone was reserved for only those who were affluent. Those unable to have one in their own home might buy a unit that would allow them to record a message. That message could go to a central receiving station where it would be "rebroadcast."

Edison's talking machine was a metal cylinder with a spiral groove impressed on it (see 7.1). A piece of tinfoil was wrapped around the cylinder. The first words ever recorded were "Mary had a little lamb." When Edison played them back, he recognized his own voice and it startled him (see 7.2).

No time was lost exploiting this marvelous new invention. By 1878 the Edison Speaking Phonograph Company was formed to conduct exhibitions of this new talking machine all over the country. As a curiosity, the phonograph was a success. In June 1878, Edison predicted ten ways in which the phonograph

Edison's original phonograph.

would benefit humanity. These proved re-markably accurate:

1. Letter writing and all kinds of dictation with-out the aid of the stenographer.

2. Phonographic books, which will speak to blind people without effort on their part.

3. The teaching of elocution.

4. Reproduction of music.

5. The "Family Record"—a register of sayings, reminiscences, etc., by members of a family in their own voices, and of the last words of dying persons.

6. Music-boxes and toys.

7. Clocks that should announce in articulate speech the time for going home, going to meals, etc.

8. The preservation of languages by exact repro-duction of the manner of pronouncing.

9. Educational purposes, such as preserving the explanations made by a teacher, so that the pupil can refer to them at any moment, and spelling or other lessons placed upon the phonograph for convenience in committing to memory.

10. Connection with the telephone, so as to make that instrument an auxiliary in the transmis-sion of permanent and invaluable records, in-stead of being the recipient of momentary and fleeting communication.

By the turn of the century, home phono-graphs were being marketed with great enthu-siasm. They were crude by today's standards, with large hornlike protrusions to amplify the sounds. Still, the early cylinder records con-tained some great music and the well-to-do family had to have one. Prices started at 25 dollars. There were no plug-in models, of

Thomas Edison and an early phonograph.

course; all phonographs had to be wound up by hand.

Enrico Caruso, a famous opera singer at the turn of the century, lent prestige to the new invention by allowing his operas to be recorded. He was perhaps the first record star, and his recordings were enormously successful. In the two decades following his first recording session in 1902, Caruso earned more than $2 million from record sales.

The Victor Talking Machine Company developed and promoted the flat disc (forerunner of today's record), which eventually made the cylinder obsolete. At first cylinders were of far superior quality, but the disc was more transportable and easier to use. Were it not for the rise of the disc, today's radio announcers would be cylinder jockeys!

After World War I some of the early Edison patents ran out and the record field became more competitive. There were more than 200 phonograph manufacturers by 1920, up from just 18 before the war. The heyday of the phonograph record had begun, and that heyday coincided with what was known as "the jazz age." Jazz was really the first popular music to gain status with the aid of the medium. The record industry boomed; 100 million records were sold in 1927.

An important technological barrier was overcome in 1931 when Leopold Stokowski's Philadelphia Orchestra recorded Beethoven's entire Fifth Symphony on a single record without a break. Music fans could look forward to the day when their favorite operas and symphonies would no longer be cut up to fit on four-minute records.

But the Depression and the rise of radio popularity in the 1930s seemed to cripple the growing phonograph industry. By 1932 record sales had dropped to six million, and magazine writers wrote of the "rise and fall of the phonograph." Record collectors were akin to antique dealers. Few people thought there was a future in the phonograph record.

Popular Music in the 1940s

In 1939 famous big-band leader Harry James went to the Rustic Cabin in Teaneck, New Jersey, and happened to hear a new singer. James liked what he heard and hired Francis Albert Sinatra to sing for his band for 75 dollars a week. Within a year Sinatra had left and signed with Tommy Dorsey's Orchestra. He was described by critics as "a skinny kid—not much to look at—but he really had a sound."

By 1943 Sinatra was the most familiar vocalist in America. His national fame came when thousands of "bobby soxers" mobbed New York's Paramount Theatre to see him. His was dubbed "the voice that thrills millions." Fans were actually screaming and passing out during Sinatra's performances. No one had ever seen anything like it. But not everyone could be in New York or afford to see the singer in person. Record prices had dropped and mass production kept them down to about a dollar each, so now the whole country began listening to Sinatra on their phonographs.

There had been other "popular" recording vocalists, among them Bing Crosby, Al Jolson, and Rudy Vallee. But Vallee had been called the "megaphone man," while Sinatra's intimate style seemed more suited to the microphone. He was exclusively the product of a new technology, a new electric sound.

Not too much is made of it now, but Sinatra was also a social hero to young people of his day. He made a documentary film attacking racial prejudice even though his business managers warned him it could cost him the support of some influential newspaper columnists. The film alienated some critics but won the hearts of young people everywhere. Sinatra didn't need the newspapers, the magazines, or even the radio. His records were instant hits.

Young people and bobby soxers took over the record market. Record promoters discovered that most record buyers were in their teens. These new record buyers were not as interested in *songs* as they were in *artists*. "Do you have the latest Sinatra record?" became the request at the record store. It had never been like that before.

During the 1940s a number of popular vocalists enjoyed success, including Frankie Laine, Perry Como, Mel Torme, Dick Haymes, Vic Damone, Peggy Lee, Doris Day, Jo Stafford, and Dinah Shore. The songs were ballads, love songs mostly. Boy meets girl, boy falls in love with girl, boy can't live without girl, etc., etc. But you could always understand the words and most lyrics seemed to make sense.

The Birth of Rock

In some ways, the origin of rock and roll can be traced to a rivalry between two economic organizations in the music industry: ASCAP and BMI. The American Society of Composers, Authors, and Publishers (ASCAP) was formed in 1914 to guarantee that its members received a fee for the playing of their songs. ASCAP's right to collect this fee from the radio stations stood one court test after another. ASCAP charged each radio station a blanket amount to use its material. In 1941 it announced a 100 percent fee increase. Radio stations refused to go along, and as a result all songs protected by ASCAP were taken off the air. This included the work of many of the popular songwriters of the time and left radio stations with very little music. The dispute was settled, at least temporarily, toward

the end of 1941, but by that time radio stations had begun to rely on music provided by a new guild of composers.

Broadcast Music, Incorporated (BMI), was formed to scout for fresh talent who could provide radio stations with music. This became increasingly important as more stations switched to the deejay format. BMI was looking for a new sound. The sound they found was rock and roll. By the mid-1950s BMI was a powerful force and so was the new sound.

In 1956 the Anti-Trust Committee of the House Judiciary Committee investigated BMI's domination of the recording industry. Songwriter Billy Rose, an ASCAP member, outlined BMI's role in the rise of rock and roll:

Not only are most of the BMI songs junk, but in many cases they are obscene junk pretty much on a level with dirty comic magazines. . . . It is the current climate on radio and TV which makes Elvis Presley and his animal posturings possible. . . .

When ASCAP's songwriters were permitted to be heard, Al Jolson, Nora Bayes, and Eddie Cantor were all big salesmen of songs. Today it is a set of untalented twitchers and twisters whose appeal is largely to the zootsuiter and the juvenile delinquent.

But of course there was much more to it than that. Rock and roll had come at a time when young people were finding it difficult to relate to the likes of Doris Day and Patti

Page. There had been too many "adult" bands and too many tired crooners. Youth now wanted a sound of its own—something new, different, and vital.

Rock was actually a blend of country music and rhythm and blues (R&B) that was popular among black people during the early 1950s. But record producers suspected that national white audiences would never idolize a black popular singer, no matter how much they liked the R&B beat. Sam Phillips, a lawyer and former disc jockey who formed Sun Records in the early 1950s, was a tireless researcher. He drove all over the South looking for new talent and promoting his records. "What I need," he said unabashedly, "is a white boy who can sing colored." In 1954 he found him. Elvis Presley recorded "That's Alright Mama," and the song enjoyed moderate success on the country music charts. Within two years Presley became the Sinatra of the 1950s, and by the end of the decade, the older generation was explaining to the young that Sinatra had been the Elvis Presley of the 1940s.

The father of rock and roll was Cleveland deejay Alan Freed, who had started mixing R&B songs with Al Martino and Frank Sinatra records as early as 1951 on WJW. It was he who coined the term *rock and roll* to make R&B palatable to his white audience. In 1954 Freed moved to WINS in New York, where his *Moondog's Rock and Roll Party* was an instant success. WINS was soon the number one station in New York. Freed helped introduce Bill Haley's "Rock around the Clock," the first rock and roll single to reach the top of the charts.

The Blackboard Jungle, a film about juvenile delinquency, featured "Rock around the Clock" as part of the soundtrack. The pulsating, uninhibited new sound was linked with restless, rebellious youth. Young people flocked to the screen to see that film and others in a similar vein. Radio, movies, and print media all contributed to the rise of rock and roll as the king of popular music.

"Rock around the Clock" was the best-selling song of 1955. In 1956 Elvis Presley had five of the year's 16 best sellers, including the number one and number two records: "Don't Be Cruel" and "Heartbreak Hotel." I was one of millions of kids who stood in front of the mirror with a plastic guitar and tried my best to imitate his wild pelvic movements.

Dick Clark's *American Bandstand* sent the latest songs out to millions of America's teenagers. Many artists like Frankie Avalon, Fabian, Paul Anka, Bobby Darin, and Bobby Rydell used the dance show as a stepping-stone in their careers. Every one of them was a teenage idol in the mold of Sinatra and Presley; all made millions of dollars and were worshiped everywhere they went. But none surpassed Presley; he remained "The King." Though he died in 1977, his music and the impact it had on American youth will be felt for decades to come.

Another change that happened during the 1950s was the disappearance of the 78-rpm discs that had taken over from Edison's cylinders. The 78s were too large and too break-able, so they were replaced by the smaller, more durable 45-rpm records. Teenagers could pick up a couple of dozen of these and take them to a "sock hop." This helped records and the music to become an important part of the youth culture.

Despite the anguished pleas of the older generation and of songwriters like Billy Rose, rock and roll was here to stay. Danny and the Juniors, a popular rock group, sang it this way in 1958:

> Rock and roll is here to stay
> I'll dig it to the end.
> It'll go down in history
> Just you wait my friend.
> I don't care what people say
> Rock and roll is here to stay.

The British Are Coming!

By 1964 rock music had topped the charts for almost a decade, solidifying its position as the most important "new sound" in popular music. But was it still new? How long would the American public stay enchanted with the same old rock and roll?

If the fickle pop audience was looking for something new, they found it in the Liverpool sound. The Beatles led the "English invasion" of American popular music. On April 4, 1964, the top five singles in the nation were (from Rohde, 1970):

1. "Twist and Shout"	The Beatles
2. "Can't Buy Me Love"	The Beatles
3. "Please Please Me"	The Beatles
4. "She Loves You"	The Beatles
5. "I Want to Hold Your Hand"	The Beatles

No musical artists had ever so dominated the hit parade. Clearly, the Beatles had a virtual lock on top honors for the year. They brought a fresh new sound and a fresh new culture to the pop scene. Dressed in matching suits and featuring similar mop haircuts, the "fab four" stirred up tremendous excitement among America's youth (see 7.3). Ed Sullivan featured them on his Sunday night variety show just as he had featured Presley the decade before.

Why the sudden Beatlemania? Perhaps rock fans needed new love objects or idols, or maybe it was the appeal of a "foreign" culture. The older generation greeted the Beatles with the same hostility they had earlier reserved for Presley. Fundamentalist preachers urged their congregations to burn Beatle records; they considered the new music a sacrilege. But Beatle fans were too engrossed in the sound to worry.

The first Beatle tours in America brought back memories of Presley and Sinatra. Young women mobbed the stage and fainted at the sight of the Liverpool quartet. Young men wore Beatle haircuts. But the Beatles were not the only British invaders. Herman's Hermits, the Dave Clark Five, and Peter and Gordon all had Top-10 hits that year.

Masters of the Mersey Beat

It all began in a strip joint in Germany in 1962. Brian Epstein, a London music promoter, found four young men playing there. Their music was just loud enough to be heard over the din. "Their act was ragged, their clothes were a mess," he said. "And yet I sensed at once that something was there."

That something was called the "Mersey Beat," a new sound that was sweeping Britain. The American press found the Beatles curious. *Newsweek* said, "The sound of their music is one of the most persistent noises heard over England since the air raid sirens were dismantled. . . . Beatle music is high pitched, loud beyond reason, and stupefyingly repetitive. . . ."

Time predicted flatly that the Beatles stood little chance of making it with the American audience:

"Though Americans may find the Beatles achingly familiar (their songs consist mainly of Yeh! screamed to the accompaniment of three guitars and a thunderous drum) they are apparently irresistible to the English."

Irresistible indeed. "Beatlemania" was already part of the English vocabulary in 1963 . . . and that was only the beginning.

The British invasion also marked the transition from the popular *single* singer of the Presley era to the popular *group*; among the giants were Diana Ross and the Supremes, the Four Seasons, and the Four Tops. In 1956 groups and duos accounted for just 15 of the year's Top-50 songs. In 1964 they accounted for 31.

Rock Comes of Age

At the end of 1964, one fan magazine held a contest among readers to decide which of the new British groups would be around ten years hence. The readers voted for the Beatles, who barely won over the Dave Clark Five. That seems absurd now, but one of the reasons the Dave Clark Five were not able to sustain their initial fanatic following was because their music remained the same. The Beatles, on the other hand, dared to change. They saw that rock was growing up, and they grew with it. Even if the Beatles didn't last ten years as a group, John, Paul, George, and Ringo are still performing. And they haven't stopped changing.

When I moved to southern California in the summer of 1965, I tuned in Top-40 radio and heard a new kind of rock lyric. Rock artists were attempting to go beyond traditional clichés to actually communicate something meaningful with their songs. The Rolling Stones sang of social discontent and alienation in "I Can't Get No Satisfaction." The Byrds' "Mr. Tambourine Man" (written by Bob Dylan) was a strange lyrical journey with heavy spiritual overtones. Barry McGuire's "Eve of Destruction" was a genuine protest ballad and urged the young audience to:

Look at all the hate
There is in Red China,
Then take a look around, to Selma, Alabama.
You may leave here for four days in space
But when you come back it's the same old place. . . .

In September Bob Dylan's "Like a Rolling Stone" became the number one song. It was an extraordinary, long, and cryptic song, and understanding the lyrics meant trying to put together the pieces of a mysterious puzzle. Dylan, a wandering poet from Hibbing, Minnesota, by way of New York's Greenwich Village, clearly had a message that was unlike any other in pop music.

In the next year Simon and Garfunkel's songs of quiet social protest and personal bitterness also hit the top of the charts. The Beatles joined this movement with their *Revolver* album. One song urged listeners to "turn off your mind, relax, and float downstream." In 1967 the Jefferson Airplane's *Surrealistic Pillow* pointed the way toward San Francisco. Haight-Ashbury was the gathering place for a generation looking for a better way. Scott McKenzie sang, "If you're going to San Francisco, be sure to wear some flowers in your hair." Eric Burdon and the Animals advertised those "warm San Franciscan nights."

This was the rock renaissance. During the period from 1965 to 1968 rock came of age. Lyrics dealt with the grim realities of war, hatred, racism, and the infinite complexities of interpersonal relationships. To be sure, the simplistic lyric of old was still around, but all over the country people began to take rock seriously for the first time. Perhaps the new music had something to say after all.

Rock Enough for Everyone

Of course if anyone actually counted on the rock renaissance to solve the world's problems, they were in for a big disappointment. Despite antiwar protest ballads of the 1960s, the war in Vietnam continued into the 1970s. And as rock continued to develop, it didn't stay preoccupied with complex social problems. Even the great crusader, Bob Dylan, brought out a 1969 album of simple country ballads aptly entitled *Nashville Skyline*.

The early 1970s saw a trend toward a gentler rock style, with stars like James Taylor, Gordon Lightfoot, and Crosby, Stills, Nash, and Young. Their music was often soft and melodic, and the words, while simple, seemed conciliatory. The success of Joni Mitchell, Carly Simon, Carole King, and Linda Ronstadt in the 1970s gave women more voice in popular music than they had had since the 1940s. These women rode the crest of the softer rock that purists claimed was not rock at all but some sort of new folk music set to an electric beat.

"Soft rock" had hardly arrived when Alice Cooper, Kiss, and David Bowie appeared on the scene. Alice Cooper's favorite stage antics included cutting off the heads of live chickens, something that did not endear him to critics who had decided that rock had grown up. But the success of these groups points out that rock is flexible enough to offer something for everyone in the pop audience. If rock gets a little too staid, there is always a new group to turn it on its ear.

The late 1970s brought "disco music," perhaps the antithesis of the complex lyrics of the 1960s. Disco is listened to strictly for the beat. Disco music revived dancing, which had been very popular during the early 1960s, when the twist, the fly, and the loco-motion were the rage. One enthusiast reported turn-

"And now let us all rise and join Alice Cooper in singing our national anthem."

Drawing by H. Martin; © 1976, The New Yorker Magazine, Inc.

ing down a college basketball scholarship to continue his daily ritual of sleeping all day and dancing all night. "I'd rather disco," he said. "If it wasn't for the music I wouldn't want to be in the world."

If there was any unifying rock trend in the 1970s, it was that there was no trend. Those who gyrated to "Rock around the Clock" were in their thirties or forties by the end of the decade. Many of them preferred to sink nostalgically back into the "good old" rock and roll of the 1950s, and that too enjoyed a revival (see 7.4).

The appearance of punk rock or new wave music in the late 1970s can also be traced to the roots of rock. Just as the first rock singers had rebelled against the established crooners, new wave bands rejected the smooth sounds of established rock stars in favor of their own unsophisticated tunes. Critics, while dismissing most of punk rock music as "sheer noise," still admitted grudgingly that a new burst of raw energy had appeared on the rock scene, perhaps the first in the decade.

From the soul blues of Stevie Wonder to the urban blues of Paul Simon, the 1970s

Drawing by Ziegler; © 1976, The New Yorker Magazine, Inc.

brought rock enough for everyone. As the rock audience has grown in number, its needs have diversified. In the best traditions of commercial mass media, there has been a rock product to fit every need.

Rock and Rote: The Themes of Rock Music

To a generation raised in the golden era of radio, rock remains a mystery. What is it all about? How does it work? Bob Dylan's words, "You know something is happening here but you don't know what it is, do you, Mr. Jones," come to mind. I vividly recall my father's description of his first brush with rock. Though he was a professional musician most of his life, the music of the 1950s baffled him; he called it "pots and pans . . . because it sounds like pots and pans banging together." After that I could expect to hear, "Edward, turn

down the pots and pans!" whenever my radio was on top volume.

When critics complain that rock and roll "all sounds the same," they mean the *form* sounds the same. To the untrained or uninterested ear, all rock songs do sound very similar. This makes examination of content even more important since lyrics contain a rich diversity of ideas that parallel the social and emotional concerns of the youth culture. These are similar to patterns emerging in other media. The themes of rock lyrics can also be found in magazine advertisements, the great Shakespearean plays, and popular American novels.

Rock lyrics are learned by rote, that is, through repetition. Lyrics that may be barely recognizable the first time around usually become quite clear by the 10th, 20th, or 200th time. Both AM and FM stations tend to play relatively few rock songs, most of them by just a handful of superstars. That way we tend to hear the same songs over and over again,

The Way It Was: Rock 'n' Roll Gold

"Here's a new record, this morning it was a 'pick of the click,' this afternoon it's number one, and tomorrow it'll be a golden oldie!" These words from George Carlin's "Wonderful WINO" routine satirize the short life of the hit single. Since rock appeared in 1954 thousands of songs have made it to the charts—and hundreds have been number one.

A few weeks back I went to talk with my father about music during "the good old days" of the 1930s.

I wanted to check out a hunch. He told me that people would always request songs from him back then which "reminded them of the good old days," even though those *were* the good old days. The lesson is obvious: The good old days are never now, but always represent a past period in your life when you were happier, or at least think you were happier.

This explains the success of films like *American Graffiti* and a recent phenomenon—the "solid gold" radio format. Solid gold stations, called "nostalgia radio" and "total gold," have now appeared in most major markets. They play nothing but rock and roll hits from the 1950s and early 1960s.

Often the most recent hits come from 1963. This is significant because that year was the last gasp of the old rock and roll before the Beatles. If someone entered high school in 1959, they turned 33 in 1978. Listening to solid gold rock and roll reminds them of a time before they had kids and responsibilities—nothing to worry about but acne and getting a date for the senior prom.

Every year that has passed since 1954 has given us another year of rock history. Rock now has enough history so that people can talk about "the good old days of rock and roll." Though those days may be gone, their memory lives on in solid gold nostalgia radio.

and we can't help learning the words. Millions of Americans share the same words and ideas simultaneously.

Though early rock is defended by some, both the musical form and content were often pretty dismal. Rock fell into predictable categories. The music of Chuck Berry, Buddy Holly, Richie Valens, and Little Richard often told a story of some kind, usually involving a woman. "I love my baby," "I lost my baby," "I need my baby," or later, "My baby got run over by a train," were all common varieties.

Rock has grown up since the 1950s and examination of its content yields some interesting patterns. These patterns help unravel what rock is about. Like the early "I love my baby" lyrics of the 1950s, many rock songs still revolve around love and relationships with the opposite sex. Of course, none of this is new. What else have we been singing about since the beginning of civilization? The simplest songs may be about the joys of discover-

ing that someone cares about you (Paul McCartney's "Maybe I'm Amazed") and that you feel the same way. Hall and Oates' "She's Gone" talks of someone special who's gone away. Paul Simon's "April Come She Will," "Dangling Conversation," and "50 Ways to Leave Your Lover" all tell sad stories of love affairs gone wrong. (Simon is of particular interest since his lyrics use traditional literary tools like allegory and metaphor. He weaves these carefully into the music to give it a depth that is rarely matched in rock music.)

But in recent years rock has begun to offer some new views on the subject of love. David Crosby's "Triad" suggests to two women who love him, "Why don't we go on as three?" Another topic frequently discussed in rock lyrics is homosexuality. Lou Reed's "Walk on the Wild Side" paints a graphic picture of the transvestite jungle of New York City. The Kink's "Lola" tells the story of a guy who took home a gal and found out she was really another guy. In a touch of naiveté he notes that it's "a mixed-up shook-up world." More recently, Rod Stewart sings of "Georgie," his homosexual friend.

With an occasional exception, the rock of the 1950s and early 1960s was concerned with love, going steady, and other self-centered problems. Bob Dylan helped change all that. His lyrics were complex where others had been simple, mysterious where others had been transparent, socially significant where others had been self-centered. Many of the Dylan songs from the mid-1960s were scathing indictments of society. Most often they had something to say about war ("Blowin in the Wind," "Hard Rain's a Gonna Fall," "Talking World War Three Blues") or racial injustice ("Oxford Town"). Dylan's intensely personal and politically packed lyrics, coupled with his unwillingness to be packaged, promoted, or even interviewed seemed to contribute to his success. Of course, it is difficult to talk of rock as one voice or one spirit. The music and its musicians are so diversified in their own ideologies that the best anyone can do is spot trends or patterns in lyrical content that appear from time to time. Clearly the ascent of Bob Dylan on rock music's horizon was a significant turning point.

The Dylan breakthrough opened the doors for other serious themes as well. Dylan's "Father of Night" was a hymn of praise for a supreme being. The Band, a group closely allied with Dylan, recorded "Daniel and the Sacred Harp," which relied heavily on biblical images. The overriding concern for the environment is evident in the hundreds of rock, blues, and country and western songs that offer an escape from the city ("Goin up the Country," "Thank God I'm a Country Boy," "Rocky Mountain High"). Paul Simon's "America" and "An American Tune" are critical of American values and social norms.

Another frequent concern of rock music is the relationship between the artist and society. Don McLean's "Vincent" describes the tortured world of Vincent van Gogh, and Joni Mitchell's "Judgement of the Moon and Stars," subtitled "Ludwig's Tune," is a portrait of the agony Beethoven felt as he was going deaf, losing the ability to hear the very music that was making him famous.

In developing the theme of the artist's alienation, rock artists often describe their own situation. Hence, we have rock songs that describe what it's like to be a rock star or a would-be star. That star is a product of the jet age, often doing dozens of concerts all over the world in the same month. There are moments of loneliness ("Holiday Inn," "Come Monday," "Goodbye Again") and songs about the ever-present groupies ("String Man," "Guitar Man," "Blonde in the Bleachers"). In an age when artists are bought and sold in a maze of record contracts and highly promoted concert dates, they sometimes feel like prisoners of the system. Joni Mitchell's "For Free" laments the plight of a musician who couldn't attract an audience because "they knew he'd never been on their TV so they passed his music by." James Taylor tells an unbelieving patron in a neighborhood cafe: "Hey mister, that's me upon the jukebox."

The themes of rock music are as diverse and rich as those of any medium. Of course, there are hundreds of songs that could have been included in these categories, and hundreds more categories exist. The music is out there every day, churning away on the radio, spinning around on the record player. It remains one of the most important and most overlooked social forces in mass communication.

Country and Western Music

Though rock has been the most listened-to popular music of the last two decades, that period has also brought an amazing growth in country and western (C&W) music. In 1961 only 81 radio stations were playing C&W, but by 1975 there were more than 1,000 full-time country stations and 1,500 more stations that played at least three hours of C&W daily. Country fans now claim their music is more popular than jazz, soul, or classical, and sales figures back them up.

Nashville, home of the "Grand Ole Opry" and center of the country music business, now boasts the most sophisticated recording studios in the country. More songs are now recorded in Nashville than in New York City, Los Angeles, and Detroit combined. In fact, over *half* of all the music recorded in America is recorded at Nashville. Robert Altman's film *Nashville,* an overwhelming critical success in the mid-1970s, familiarized many with the city and its music.

The country sound has come a long way from the days of the hillbilly fiddle and banjo music. Country artists now often record with full orchestras, and their sound is as sophisticated as that of rock. Indeed, during the 1970s many country tunes like Charley Rich's "Behind Closed Doors" and C. W. McCall's "Convoy" hit the top of the pop charts. "Underground country," a synthesis of rock and C&W sung by stars like Waylon Jennings and Kris Kristofferson, combines acoustic sound with electric instruments and Moog synthesizers. Often these sophisticated recording techniques have sophisticated lyrics to match.

If country music has been influenced by rock, the process has gone the other way, too. Successful rock groups like The Grateful Dead and New Riders of the Purple Sage were heavily influenced by C&W. Judy Collins and Joan Baez (probably the two most successful women vocalists of the folk era) usually include at least a couple of country tunes on each new album. No one is really sure whether John Denver is C&W or rock, but his simple songs about country living obviously struck a responsive chord. Every one of his albums has "gone gold" (more than $1 million in sales).

Why the sudden rush to the country? John Colley, who teaches English literature at Yale University, puts it this way: "Country music

Guest Essay by Don Weller

Issues and Answers: "And the Hits Just Keep on Comin' "

Don Weller has been associated with rock music all his life. He has taught college courses in rock via radio and is currently a rock critic for the Honolulu Star Bulletin. *In addition, Dr. Weller teaches in the Communication Department at the University of Hawaii.*

"AND THE HITS JUST KEEP ON COMIN'." Those words. How many times have they made their way into your brain? Have you ever wondered just *how* those hits keep on comin'? Have you ever thought about having your very own hit single on the charts—making your own livingroom (basement?) tape, sending it to a record company, and ZAP! . . . instant stardom? Most of you know one basic thing about the record industry and landing a hit record—it isn't easy or simple.

The process involves *gatekeepers,* organizations and individuals whose job it is to act as a *filter,* letting a few items into the big spotlight while blocking out the others. As rock critic R. Serge Denisoff aptly puts it, "Gatekeepers in the music industry are the Berlin Wall between the manufacturer and the audience." They are hurdles, barriers, and fences, and musicians who want to see their record rise up the top charts have got to overcome them.

It is not unusual to find 100 LPs released *in any given week,* and hundreds more 45-rpm singles. Only a very tiny minority of them will ever be blessed with radio air play, press reviews, or jukebox in-

clusion. Question: Who's Mr. Big who determines which ones get to the turntables, jukeboxes, and magazines? Answer: There's no *one* Mr. Big, but rather a *number* of influential people in a *number* of organizations who make those decisions. Together with mass audience response in target geographic areas, their decisions determine which songs are hits and which are flops.

The next step involves your imagination. Picture, in your mind, a game board. On the board near the top is the *winner's circle*—the gold record—the hit single—the hit album. There are a number of paths leading to that circle and each one has a different width. The wider the path, the greater the influence of that path in getting the record to the winner's circle.

One of the widest paths is labeled "trade papers." Trade magazines and newspapers (like *Billboard* and *Cashbox*) are subscribed to by record company personnel, disc jockeys, and record reviewers to keep up with "industry happenings." In addition they provide up-to-the-minute lists of "hot" songs. In *Billboard* there is a page called *"Billboard*'s Singles Radio Action: Playlist Top Add Ons / Playlist Prime Movers / Regional and National Breakouts." It is from here that program directors learn who is playing what and where. Armed with this information they decide what to add to their own small "playlist," or list of records receiving air play.

Artists can get their product to the gatekeepers via print media by receiving favorable reviews from critics in magazines like *Rolling Stone.* In addition, most metropolitan daily papers now have at

least one staffer who turns in regular record reviews. Each record company has a publicity or public affairs department whose job it is to make sure that promotional free copies of their product are provided to the reviewers. This free service makes the reviewers a rather "elitist" group to be sure, and they tend to become a little jaded. Along with the albums comes a plethora of other "goodies"—biographies, stickers, 8x10 glossy pictures, buttons, personalized T-shirts, personalized matches, you name it. The goal is simple—to get the album public attention, preferably with a favorable review.

The music industry is overstaffed with people and overstuffed with record products. There is much more expensively recorded music than the fickle public could ever consume. What happens when that public trots off to their local record store to pick up an album? The store owner may be still another gatekeeper. Chain-store czars may agree to cut the prices of certain albums for a time. There are extra displays, provided by the record company, of course, that can increase the sale of an album. Usually, record store owners are not concerned so much with what they sell, just as long as they sell something.

So the next time you hear a strung out, caffeine-soaked boss deejay wail "AND THE HITS JUST KEEP ON COMIN' . . ."—remember only a few of the hundreds of records released today will ever sell very many copies. That leaves a lot of wasted polyvinyl chloride lying around in the bins at supermarkets and swapmeets!

The Billboard "Hot 100" are watched closely by artists, record executives, and everyone else in the recording industry.

Jim Bouton and the Ultimate C&W Song

Since its release in 1970 *Ball Four* has become one of the best-selling sports books ever written. It's a diary, an intimate glimpse into the locker-room world of the professional athlete. There, we find that country and western music is the order of the day. When Bouton objects and insists on equal time for rock, he and pitcher Larry Dierker write the ultimate country and western song. Bouton reveals: ''It took us about two innings . . .''

I want my baby back again,
She done left town with my best
  friend,
And now I lie here all alone,
I'm just awaitin' by the phone.
Her lips were sweet as summer
  wine,
And when I held her hand in mine,
I thought she'd never be untrue,
But now she's broke my heart in
  two.
The mailman let me down today,
And so I made that mother pay,
And now I'm locked in this old jail,
And my dog died and there's no
  bail.
My teardrops fall like pouring rain,
The bottle doesn't ease my pain,
And no one gives a hoot for me
Since Billy Joe took my Marie
And ran away to Tennessee.
I wish I had someone to tell
'Bout how I'm locked up in this cell,
And all my kinfolk dead and gone,
But with the Lord I'll carry on.

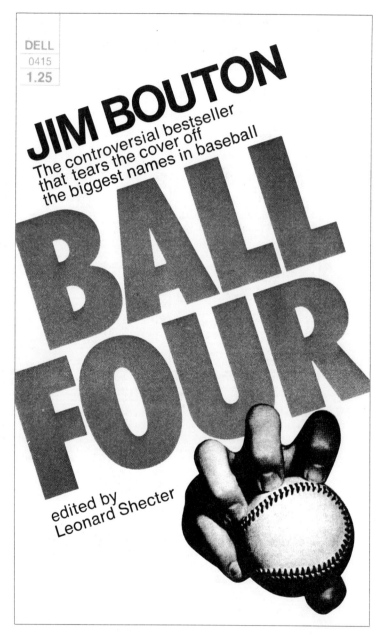

is becoming the *soul* music of white, middle, and working class people. It reminds them of quieter and more peaceful times and it describes their everyday life as they see it—as an epic adventure, full of dangers, tragedies, and triumphs." (See 7.5.)

Soul Music

Like rock and country, soul music seems to have as many definitions as there are those who sing it, although all agree that soul is associated with blacks. The term *soul* was first popularized in the 1960s, at a time when black pride and black power were first recognized as a strong social force. White "folk" music and the complex arrangements by the Beatles and Bob Dylan were then receiving wide critical acclaim and public acceptance, and there seemed to be a need for a term to describe the more fundamental beat practiced by artists like Otis Redding and James Brown.

Soul grew out of rhythm and blues, a traditional black sound that was rearranged by white musicians like Carl Perkins and Elvis Presley to contribute to the early development of rock and roll. But soul was something different from both R&B and rock and roll.

Soul was far more than a kind of music. Little Richard explained: "To me, soul is when a man sings from his heart and it reaches another heart. When you sing with feeling and you really feel what you are singing, that's soul." Black artists were fed up with trying to imitate whites or reach the white audience, and instead they sang what they felt. Nearly everyone agreed that if you had to *explain* soul to someone, they didn't have it.

Whatever soul music is, it has been tremendously popular, and not only with the black audience. Many songs "cross over" from *Bill-board* soul charts to the Top-40. Stevie Wonder, for example, is not just a soul star, he's a *superstar*, considered by many critics to be one of the most creative and important *popular* music artists. Rhythm and blues was here before rock, and soul music may still be around long after rock, as we know it, has disappeared.

Queries and Concepts

1. How many songs can you name that mark a special place or time for you? Can you remember the first time you heard them? The last time you heard them?

2. Check *Billboard* for the top ten songs of today. Can any of them be traced logically back to the roots of early rock? How do the lyrics compare with those of the 1956–1960 birth of the rock era? Other eras?

3. Do a content analysis of those same top ten songs. What kinds of issues and emotions do their lyrics deal with? Are they largely interpersonal or political? How many deal exclusively with love relationships?

4. "The most creative era of rock was the coming of the Beatles and the more complex lyrics of Bob Dylan. Since that time,

rock has made no major steps forward." Support or refute this statement using today's popular songs as evidence.

5. Country and western and rock have borrowed heavily from each other during the last decade. Which has borrowed the most from the other and why? Back your answer with specific songs and lyrics.

Readings and References

The Fabulous Phonograph

Roland Gelatt
The Fabulous Phonograph: 1877–1977, 3d ed. New York: Macmillan, 1977.
This book covers the development of the phonograph from Edison to stereo with many personal stories about the men and women who made it happen. Particularly good chapters on the development of the phonograph and phonograph record during the early years.

Popular Music in the 1940s

Ian Whitcomb
After the Ball. New York: Simon & Schuster, 1973.
You may recognize the author's name. He's a former rock star who took to writing about music after his fall from the charts. This is a panorama of popular music "from rag to rock," written in an entertaining style. There are sections on jazz, swing, ragtime, and Tin Pan Alley. Highly recommended.

The Birth of Rock

Carl Belz
The Story of Rock, 2d ed. New York: Oxford University Press, 1972.
I prefer this to Charlie Gillett's *The Sound of the City: The Rise of Rock and Roll* (New York: E.P. Dutton, 1970), though both do an admirable job chronicling the rise of rock from rhythm and blues to the age of the superstars. Belz is the more meticulous writer with his cautious assessment of the contributions of many "sacred cows," including Bill Haley, Chuck Berry, and Elvis Presley. Excellent annotated bibliography.

H. Kandy Rohde, ed.
The Gold of Rock and Roll, 1955–1967. New York: Arbor House, 1970.
A year-by-year account of *Billboard's* top songs. Included are the Top-10 for each week during the 13 years covered as well as the Top-50 songs (in terms of retail sales) from each year. There are also a brief introduction and some commentary for each year.

Rock Comes of Age

For a nostalgic look down memory lane, pour over the hits in H.K. Rohde's *The Gold of Rock and Roll, 1955–1967* (New York: Arbor House, 1970). See Alan Aldridge, ed., *The Beatles Illustrated Lyrics* (New York: Dell, 1972) and Bob Dylan's *Writings and Drawings* (Westminster, Md.: Knopf, 1973) for the complete works of the two most influential forces on rock in the 1960s.

Rock Enough for Everyone

Again, things change so rapidly in this area that you are better off going to *Readers' Guide to Periodical Literature* and *Popular Periodical Index. Rolling Stone* is, again, the number one source.

Rock and Rote: The Themes of Rock Music

Richard Goldstein, ed.
The Poetry of Rock. New York: Bantam Books, 1969.
A good anthology of significant rock lyrics. These kinds of books are rare since rock artists demand an arm and a leg for reprint rights to lyrics of their songs. It includes some interesting illustrations.

Edward Whetmore
The Role of Rock. Englewood Cliffs, N.J.: Prentice-Hall, 1979.
The history of rock is divided into three "eras," then each is examined from a social perspective. Other chapters deal with the business of rock, recurrent lyric themes, and a theoretical approach to understanding popular music by examining audience needs.

Country and Western Music

"Why Country Music Is Suddenly Big Business." *U.S. News & World Report,* July 29, 1974, pp. 58–60.

Issues and Answers: "And the Hits Just Keep On Comin' "

R. Serge Denisoff
Solid Gold: The Popular Record Industry. New Brunswick, N.J.: Transaction Books, 1975.
This book is best when describing how the record industry works, how a record becomes a hit, and other processes. Particularly informative regarding the business end, its history and current trends.

8
Television, Part One: Patterns in Prime Time

The problem with television is that people must sit and keep their eyes glued on a screen; the average American family hasn't time for it. Therefore, the showmen are convinced that for this reason, if no other, television will never be a serious competitor of broadcasting.—New York Times, March 19, 1939

And Now Back to Maverick

I have always been preoccupied with gambling, particularly cards and the track. I keep coming up with schemes and plans to break the bank. (So far the bank is still intact.) It started when I was 14—I would sneak into the race track (no one under 21 was admitted without a parent) and find kindly old men to place bets for me.

In my high school, the highest status belonged to whoever could beat up everyone else. I was at the bottom of the ladder since I couldn't beat up anyone. What's worse—everyone knew it and they beat me up!

Travel: At 16 I dropped out of high school and took my old Pontiac thousands of miles—crisscrossing the country like a madman looking for . . . anything, action, adventure, whatever. There was something glamorous about being "on the road," traveling from town to town.

Work: I had always hated it. Not a day went by when I wasn't up to some scheme, legal or slightly illegal, to beat it. I looked around at everyone doing an eight-hour shift at the sawmill and thought—my God—this isn't for me. A job may be fine temporarily, but I couldn't do it for a living!

I was thinking about all of this a few months ago and wondering how such an antisocial set of values could have evolved—everything seemed so contradictory to the American spirit. Then I turned on the television. There was a rerun of the old *Maverick* series, starring James Garner. It had been my favorite when it was first aired in the late 1950s. I can vividly remember my brother and me keeping time on Sunday afternoons by "how many hours it is till *Maverick*." Now that's devotion!

James Garner was the antihero of the old West. A hero was virtuous, but Bret Maverick was expedient. A hero was strong, stable, and hard-working; Bret abhorred work. He always took the coward's way out; whenever trouble developed he left town. A home was something he never needed; he just wandered around from place to place meeting beautiful women and playing poker. He always had fine clothes and plenty of money; his was the life of action, adventure, and above all, leisure.

Suddenly it struck me. My entire life had developed around *Maverick!* All of those inexplicable urges, those strange frustrations; it was as if I had been "playing out" the Maverick role.

Television has become a vast resource, the ultimate educational device, not because it teaches traditional curricula but because it supplies *roles*. Hundreds of characters parade through our lives each day via TV: good guys, bad guys, beautiful women, police women. Each character supplies us with bits of information about what his or her role is like. We have personal contact with a few people each day, but television gives us contact with a cast of hundreds. These roles may have a direct impact on how we perceive ourselves and our own roles in REALIFE—that is, our personal day-to-day environment.

Our lives are made up of many social experiences. Some of those are interpersonal. Our parents and friends all have an influence on the attitudes we develop and the decisions we make. But of tremendous impact are the hundreds of people we have "known" from TV. We carry around their images in our heads, and we can recall them in an instant.

Are you skeptical? OK, try this. Close your eyes and make your mind a complete blank—then think "Hoss Cartwright"—try it before reading on.

* * * * * * *

Now what did you see? Yes, it was Hoss, he was wearing a huge ten-gallon white hat, wasn't he? And remember his shirt, sort of an off-white? What about the brown vest? Hoss Cartwright has a very clear image in your mind, even though Dan Blocker, who played the character, is dead and it may have been years since you've seen the show. You still remember Hoss more clearly than, say, your third-grade teacher.

None of us really likes to concede that "the boob tube" affects us. It seems like such a shallow medium; the stories are so simple. But that's the problem. Forget about the story, forget about your anti-TV snobbery, instead consider the possibilities. Television is the most powerful and the most influential of all mass media; ignoring it won't make it go away. Ignoring leads to ignorance, and ignorance is dangerous.

Pioneers

The technical devices making TV possible happened long before the new medium was "discovered" by the people. In 1923 Vladimir Zworykin invented the iconoscope tube. The kinescope came shortly thereafter. These were the technical bases for television as we know it today. Historians usually give credit for the invention of television to Philo Farnsworth, who invented the electric camera, and Allen B. Dumont, who was responsible for the receiving or "picture" tube. Old-timers will remember the Dumont name; many of the early TV sets were "Dumonts" and once there was even a Dumont Network.

Television, like radio, was highly experimental at the beginning and was considered a fad. Everyone agreed that it could never replace radio, since radio was the "theater of the imagination." During the late 1930s experimental broadcasts of major political and sports events began to make more people aware of the tremendous potential of TV. In

Time Line: The History of American Television

1907 The word *television* is first used in *Scientific American*.

1923 Vladimir Zworykin invents the iconoscope tube.

1927 Philo Farnsworth applies for a patent on an ''electronic television system.''

1936 Regularly scheduled TV begins in Great Britain.

1939 RCA demonstrates television at the New York World's Fair.

1941 WNBT is the first commercial TV station on the air.

1944 Sponsors begin to buy TV time.

1945 FCC moves FM radio to another place on the band and gives part of the FM band to TV.

1946 First demonstrations of color television are given by CBS and NBC.

1948 FCC freezes granting new TV licenses.

1951 Movie attendance declines in many cities that have TV.

1951 NBC *Today* show begins and CBS airs *See It Now*.

1953 First noncommercial TV programming in Houston, Texas.

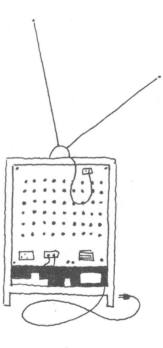

1954 The Army-McCarthy hearings are shown on TV; Edward R. Murrow challenges McCarthy on *See It Now*.

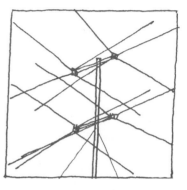

1955 *The $64,000 Question* begins, the first successful big-money TV quiz show.

1956 The Eisenhower-Stevenson presidential campaign is covered extensively by all networks.

1959 Westerns dominate the ratings, including *Gunsmoke, Have Gun Will Travel, Rifleman, Maverick,* and *Wyatt Earp.*

1959 Quiz show scandals sweep TV and networks become more responsible for programs. Sponsors have less say.

1960 Nixon and Kennedy debate is the first of TV's presidential ''Great Debates.''

1939 a Milwaukee newspaper applied for a *commercial* TV license. Since it was the first such application, the FCC pondered a bit and finally granted it in 1941, along with licenses for nine other stations.

But radio was in its heyday, films were doing better than ever, and Americans had a war to worry about. Only six of the original ten applicants for TV licenses were left in 1945. But at that time the FCC decided that

1961 FCC Chairman Newton Minow describes TV as a "vast wasteland."

1962 *Beverly Hillbillies* is the latest TV rage.

1963 The assassination of John Kennedy brings the nation together in a communal electronic experience.

1966 FCC assumes control over cable television in a precedent-setting decision.

1966 *Bonanza* is the number one prime-time show; it stresses traditional American values.

1968 *Rowan and Martin's Laugh-In* pioneers a new kind of made-for-TV comedy.

1968 The Robert Kennedy and Martin Luther King assassinations and funerals are covered by TV.

1968 Unprecedented viewer protests bring *Star Trek* back for a third season.

1969 *Smothers Brothers Comedy Hour* is canceled.

1969 There is live TV coverage of the first moon landing.

1971 *All in the Family* is the first of Norman Lear's controversial but successful sitcoms.

1971 The *Mary Tyler Moore Show* premiers on CBS.

1972 Television is blamed for death of *Life* magazine.

1973 Televised hearings of the Watergate affair give Americans a chance to see the cast of characters.

1973 *Upstairs Downstairs* is first aired on PBS.

1974 Televised impeachment hearings of the House Judiciary Committee focus the nation's attention on Watergate.

1976 The bionic man and woman help push ABC to the top of national prime-time ratings; CBS is second.

1976 Norman Lear airs the controversial *Mary Hartman, Mary Hartman* without network backing by syndicating it to local stations.

1977 *60 Minutes*, a successful news and documentary show, is aired in prime time, showing the increasing popularity of investigative electronic journalism.

1977 *Roots*, a special eight-part ABC made-for-TV movie, becomes the most watched program of all time. Its success prompts dozens of multiple-part "specials" to compete with regular weekly shows.

1978 Controversial programmer Fred Silverman takes over as President of the NBC television network.

TV was here to stay and granted band space for 12 channels. This move involved cutting back space that had been allotted for FM radio, and it made existing FM receivers obsolete. CBS, which, although experimenting with TV, had invested heavily in new equipment for FM, was badly hurt and the advantage was given to NBC in the new world of television.

By 1948, the FCC was deluged with applications and decided to "freeze" the granting of licenses until it had more time for study. By the time the Freeze was lifted in 1952, one-third of all American families had bought a TV set. Television was enjoying its honeymoon with the American people.

The Growth of Television

By the time the Freeze was over, most of the country was already involved with Ed Sullivan, Milton Berle, and *I Love Lucy.* The transition from radio to television was brief. Many radio stars went by the wayside, many switched over to the newer medium, and hundreds of new television stars were born overnight. When the Freeze ended, there were hundreds of license applications in. By the mid-1960s, there were more than 600 stations on the air, and the number grew to almost 1,000 by the late 1970s.

The numbers describing television's hold on the top spot in the media business boggle the mind. According to the 1978 *Broadcasting Yearbook,* some 97 percent of all homes in America now have at least one television set. The average home has a set turned on for just over six hours each day. More than 45 percent of all homes are equipped with two or more sets. Fifty-four million sets are color. By the time most American children enter kindergarten, they have already spent more hours learning about their environment via TV than they will spend in college classrooms getting a degree. Those hours come when the child is

considerably more open to new impressions and ideas than the average college student. Further, information presented on television is designed to keep the "learner" constantly involved and entertained, something I see rarely in a college classroom.

The FCC set the same evaluation standards for television as it did for radio. Broadcasters were supposed to be broadcasting in the "public interest, convenience, and necessity." Critics are quick to point out that TV stations more often broadcast in their own self-interest. Prime-time programs are aimed at the "lowest common denominator" with the idea that if everyone can understand a show, they'll watch it. With a large audience come better ratings and more advertising income. Some critics argue that TV programmers should be concerned with something other than ratings and, of course, they should. The fact is that they aren't (for the most part), and they won't be until it becomes financially desirable.

Those who are quick to criticize these practices forget that the average newspaper vocabulary is aimed at the 12-year-old; even the *New York Times* never prints a word that the average high school graduate can't understand. Some of the rationale here is easier to understand if you think of the term *mass medium.* Newspapers, radio, and television are all designed to be consumed by a mass audience. This audience is composed of Ph.D.'s and high school dropouts, homemakers and construction workers. Because of commercial network practices, television cannot cater to

"Who underlines the lowest common denominator, and how can they be sure they haven't slipped below it?"

Drawing by J. Mirachi; © 1975, The New Yorker Magazine, Inc.

only one segment of the audience. Newspapers have their local group, and radio stations offer programs to suit different tastes, but television is different. What other media presentation can reach 10 million homes each week and still have to worry about being a flop?

Advertisers are becoming increasingly concerned with the *demographics* of the mass audience, as well as its size. Age, social and ethnic background, and income are factors that determine how receptive a given viewer might be to the sponsor's message. But, as of right now, there is no advantage in reaching only a particular small audience via TV.

But all of this misses the point. For too long, those who study television have been concerned with what *should be* on the air and not what *is* on the air. It is hard to realize that a medium offering nonstop fun and games offers nonstop "education" as well, since that is not the kind of education we're used to. TV's real significance is hidden beneath a facade of deodorant commercials and one-liners. As we strip these obvious things away and examine the motives of the audience, we uncover the real impact of TV.

From Sitcom to Star Trek: The Genres of Prime Time

I once passed by a Chicago ice cream shop with this sign posted in the window: "31 Flavors—Instant Gratification!!!" There are few pleasures in life as sweet as taking that first bite of an exotic-flavored ice cream cone. Television is the ice cream shop of the imagination. If offers many things to "gratify" us. The list of 31 reasons for watching television in 8.2 is only a partial one. TV fills some of our needs by presenting various types of programs and, though there may be many similarities, each program is aimed at a slightly different set of needs.

Sitcom

Situation comedy has been part of television from the beginning. *I Love Lucy* was one of the first and certainly wins the longevity award. It has probably been recycled more than any other program on TV. Lucille Ball was the first of many "dingbat wives" who appeared in sitcoms on television. Desi Arnaz

31 Possible Gratifications Derived From Watching Television

Vicarious:
1. The need for vicarious, but controlled, emotional experience.
2. The desire to live vicariously in a world of significance, intensity, and larger-than-life-size people.
3. The desire to experience, in a guilt-free arena, the extreme emotions of love and hate.
4. The need to confront, in a controlled situation, the horrible and the terrible.
5. The desire to see villains in action.
6. The desire to imagine oneself a hero or heroine.

7. The need to be purged of unpleasant emotions.
8. The need to experience the beautiful and the ugly.
9. The desire to experience vicarious financial reward.
10. The desire to engage in vicarious gambling or risk taking.
11. The desire to vicariously explore dangerous territories and experience totally new situations.

Escapist:
12. The need to be distracted from the realities of life.
13. The desire to believe in the miraculous.
14. The desire to return to "the good old days."
15. The desire to be amused.
16. The desire to believe in romantic love.
17. The desire to experience "the happy ending."
18. The need to find outlets for the sex drive in a guilt-free context.

Social:
19. The need to have shared experiences with others.
20. The need to share in the suffering of others.
21. The need to feel "informed."
22. The need to see authority figures exalted.
23. The need to see authority figures deflated.
24. The need or desire to feel superior to a societal deviant.
25. The desire to see others make mistakes.

Spiritual and Moral:
26. The need to believe that spiritual or moral values are more important than material goods.
27. The need to identify with a deity or a divine plan.
28. The desire to see evil punished and virtue restored.
29. The need to explore taboo subjects with impunity.
30. The need for spiritual cleansing.
31. The need to see order imposed on the world.

---

was the husband/father. He wasn't too bright, but he patiently tried to keep the "situation" from getting out of hand. Of course, it is when the situation gets out of hand that it begins to be funny. The sitcom fulfills audience needs to be amused and entertained.

In contrast to the ever-present *I Love Lucy*, many sitcoms don't last long; the average lifespan is a season or less. Most are based on situations that seem funny at first, but writers soon run out of ideas and there is always a new show waiting in the wings. In the 1950s, a show was guaranteed a berth for 39 weeks. Now a show is lucky to make it for ten weeks—many are canceled after only six weeks on the air. NBC began something called the "second season" in the mid-1970s to pro-

mote the shows replacing the fall failures. With the TV season now less than 25 weeks long, many predict that the "season" concept will soon disappear. Shows will just come and go at will, being replaced as ratings fall.

In recent years, TV viewers have shown a marked preference for sitcoms. By the late 1970s, these programs occupied more TV time than any other genre. Many were the product of the most prolific sitcom producer of them all, Norman Lear. Lear first hit prime-time paydirt with *All in the Family* in the early 1970s. He rapidly launched a string of sitcoms based on the success of Archie Bunker and company, including *Good Times*, *Maude*, and *The Jeffersons*. Most were readily identifiable by the Lear formula: "realistic" dialogue and a tendency toward racial and ethnic controversy. There were often stories involving sex, drugs, and abortion.

Lear deserves more credit than any other single person for introducing previously taboo subjects to TV shows. In the 1970s, he forced television to grow up, contending that the audience was ready for something a little different. By 1977, there were nine different Lear productions on the air, leading more than one critic to conclude that his "fresh new approach" was no longer fresh. Even Lear had fallen victim to a TV reality: *that which is successful must be imitated incessantly.*

Nevertheless, his shows revolutionized the genre. Sitcoms had been easy-to-swallow little stories reinforcing traditional American values (e.g., the father is the head of the household). With Lear they became an active social force exploring suicide, unemployment, racism, and women's liberation. Not everyone is enthusiastic, of course; many feel such matters are better examined in a more sober context, such as a documentary. But Lear's commercial success assured him a place on TV.

Another stable of sitcoms was built by the producers of the highly rated *Mary Tyler Moore Show*. Some, like *Bob Newhart*, featured new characters; others, like *Rhoda* and *Phyllis* were spinoffs from the original show. While these did not have the constant preoccupation with controversial issues, they did raise the "state of the art" of sitcoms significantly through skillfully constructed plots and carefully written scripts. Audiences appreciated

the higher "quality" sitcom and made the programs among the most successful of the 1970s.

One trend involved scripts with multiple situations. Several subplots would be woven in while the main plot was working itself out. This lent diversity, provided new joke material, and seemed to involve the audience a little more. Sitcom producers of the 1970s were also bent on convincing the audience that their characters had depth. In doing this, they often wrote more complex scripts which allowed a character that had been stereotypically "funny," let's say, to experience a serious situation. During the seasons that the *Mary Tyler Moore Show* headed CBS's Saturday night lineup, the characters developed significantly. Mary grew from a prima donna to a capable working woman. Mr. Grant developed from a no-nonsense boss to an often troubled and sensitive person. In fact, in various episodes, the character created by Edward Asner went through a divorce (there was never a reconciliation) and became a borderline alcoholic. Hardly the kind of material for *Father Knows Best!* The character was so strong, it was spun off into the hour-long drama series *Lou Grant*, which many critics hailed as one of the best new shows on television that season.

Meanwhile, the success of shows like *Happy Days* and *Laverne and Shirley* was part of the nostalgia craze. Both were set in the 1950s and originally aimed at the audience that was in high school during that time. (People in the 25–49 age group are the most desirable audi-

"They—I repeat—they are watching the Fonz."

Drawing by Joe Mirachi; © 1976, The New Yorker Magazine, Inc.

ence since they buy most of TV's advertising products.) These shows won that audience and much more. Young people seemed to turn their record players off long enough to watch their favorite nostalgia characters, particularly Henry Winkler in his role as the "Fonz."

Happy Days and *Laverne and Shirley* were the two most successful shows of ABC's "new look" that took the network to the top of the ratings in 1976. This sudden success of ABC was attributed to their Vice President in Charge of Programming, Fred Silverman, whom *Time* called "the man with the golden gut." Silverman seemed to have an uncanny way of knowing what the public would watch.

Silverman was also at least partially responsible for the success of *Love Boat, Roots, Washington Behind Closed Doors, Charlie's Angels, The Six Million Dollar Man* and *Wonder Woman* among others. Yet his sitcoms like *Three's Company* and *Soap* created the most controversy and the highest ratings. When he signed to

move to NBC in 1978 as President of their television network, the industry was breathless. What would Silverman do next? One critic predicted cynically, "One thing's for sure, there'll be a lot more sitcoms on NBC."

Unlike other TV genres, sitcoms seem to come in only one size: 30 minutes. Hour-long sitcoms don't seem to hold the audience, though once in a while a "special episode" of an hour or longer will be aired in several parts on successive weeks.

Action-Adventure

The action-adventure program is typically about a police officer or a private eye, but you can occasionally find a science fiction or other variety. The thing all have in common is *pacing.* The audience is constantly tossed between conversation and car chase, conversation and fistfight, conversation and murder.

Drawing by Lorenz; © 1976, The New Yorker Magazine, Inc.

Since the beginning, action-adventure shows have been subject to a lot of criticism, particularly about their use of violence. There are several schools of thought here: one says that violence on television encourages violence in REALIFE, another contends that vicarious experience of violence substitutes for the real thing. If the latter is correct, it would seem the more violence on TV, the better. Generally, network executives have tried to cut down on violence over the years, but the most successful action-adventure series (like *Starsky and Hutch*) are often the most violent as well. Action-adventure series play to the audience's need to share in the suffering of others, to confront the horrible and terrible in a controlled situation, and to see villains in action.

One obvious arena where audiences find gratification is in the world of cops and robbers. Some successful action-adventure shows were *Dragnet* and *Highway Patrol* in the 1950s, *The FBI* and *Naked City* in the 1960s, and *Kojak* (see 8.3) and *Hawaii 5-O* in the 1970s. All featured plots in which stars tracked down criminals and brought them to justice with great finesse. More contemporary police dramas have emphasized the personality of the star. Scripts for *Columbo*, *McCloud*, and *Baretta* spent as much time developing the hero's character as getting the crooks.

On occasion, there is room for the private detectives, too—their work lends itself to action-adventure gratification. *77 Sunset Strip* was one of the most successful. In that program the office contained a secretary and a group of "characters" of various ages and social statuses for maximum audience identification. *77 Sunset Strip* starred good-looking, clean-shaven guys Roger Smith and Efrem Zimbalist, Jr., plus an added attraction: Edd "Kookie" Byrnes. Kookie became somewhat of a cult hero in his own right for he appealed directly to the teenage audience and helped make *77 Sunset Strip* a smash. Later, detective series *Mannix*, *Switch*, *The Rockford Files*, *Charlie's Angels*, and *Barnaby Jones* featured heroes and heroines and villains of various ages and ethnic backgrounds. There was something for everybody.

TV critic Horace Newcomb notes that new types of action-adventure characters emerged in the 1970s. They were usually part establishment and part antiestablishment. The kids of the *Mod Squad* were first, then came *Baretta*, *McCloud*, *Serpico*, and others. Though unorthodox, all worked within the system.

Telly Savalas played the hard-bitten *Kojak*, one of CBS's successful action-adventure series. His unique personal appearance and mannerisms often seemed more important than plot in determining why audiences watched the show.

Many of the action-adventure series seem to be reassuring us that even the fattest (*Cannon*), clumsiest (*Columbo*), or most severely handicapped (*Ironside* and *Longstreet*) among us can be heroes. We are *all* potential stars despite our obvious physical and mental shortcomings (see 8.4 and 8.5).

But the most talked about, most heavily watched action-adventure series was a one-of-a-kind phenomenon. *Star Trek* was on NBC for only three seasons in the late 1960s, but it still enjoys tremendous ratings as a rerun today. Its creator, Gene Roddenberry, described it as a kind of *Wagon Train* of the sky. Each week, the Star Ship Enterprise would go out into the universe and right some universal wrong. Its five-year mission was to "seek out new life and boldly go where no man has gone before."

Contrary to popular belief, *Star Trek* was not canceled because of some evil Klingon conspiracy. Rather, it was a victim of the ratings

Actor William Conrad as Frank Cannon, TV's rotund private eye, in his favorite room of the house.

system. Ratings measure the *number* of bodies watching TV, but they don't account for the emotional depth of the audience or the devotion they might have for a given show. *Star Trek*'s viewers were relatively small in number at the time, but they were intensely devoted. When the show was canceled after the second season, they set up an unprecedented howl, enough to keep it on for an extra year.

In the long run *Star Trek*'s problem was that it was a bit ahead of its time. The integrated crew included blacks, Orientals, Russians, and even Vulcans. Women were given roles as geologists and psychiatrists. Plots revolved around war, politics, racism, and the like. This would not be unusual for a sitcom of the 1970s, but for an action-adventure show of the 1960s it was unheard of. *Star Trek* got away with it for a while because it was set in the future. Wars were between planets with strange names and the names of the "races" were equally unfamiliar. In a few years, mass audi-

Character actor Karl Malden played a crook in the film *Hotel* but landed the starring role as a cop in TV's *Streets of San Francisco*. With credibility as both cop and crook he was signed by American Express to encourage travelers to carry traveler's checks instead of cash.

ence tastes caught up with *Star Trek*, but by then the show was in syndication.

Star Trek was not the only science fiction program to come to TV (others included *Land of the Giants, Lost in Space,* and *Space 1999*), but it was the only one to offer consistently believable scripts that seemed to center on *people* instead of events. None of *Star Trek*'s actors was particularly famous or talented, but the chemistry between them created dialogues that seemed genuine. There was plenty of violence and sex, but the believability of the characters was the key. It created the intense audience involvement that still brings fans out to *Star Trek* conventions and keeps them glued to their sets watching *Star Trek* reruns. As a

Although *Star Trek* ended its run in prime time over a decade ago, producer Gene Roddenberry still draws large crowds when he lectures and shows films of the series.

THE·WORLD·OF

STAR TREK

Featuring Creator and Producer

GENE RODDENBERRY

See the award winning **"Star Trek"** pilot film, never before shown in its entirety,
and the only authentic showing of the famous blooper reel, both on a full theatre-size screen.
Hear from Gene Roddenberry about the making of the new movie, **"Star Trek"**.
Ask Gene Roddenberry your own questions about **"Star Trek"**.

result, *Star Trek* flourishes (see 8.6). KTVU, an independent station in California, has been running the show for years; and according to sales manager Jim Diamond, "People just don't ever seem to get tired of the thing. . . ."

Westerns

Westerns are uniquely American and provide a large share of the programs that America exports to other countries. As a result, the myths about pioneering and gun-toting Americans get plenty of reinforcement. (Perhaps they should—Americans own more handguns per capita than residents of any other country.) At its best, the western, like all TV genres, can be entertaining, informative, amusing, and enlightening. At its worst, it can be trite, boring, and downright offensive.

Gunsmoke, the longest-running TV western ever, was a slow-moving, comfortable show with a cast of characters from every age group and varied social background. Matt (James Arness) was tall, quiet, and rugged. His sidekick Festus offered comic relief. Kindly old Doc played the grouch, while attractive Miss Kitty supplied an off-beat romantic angle. Kitty was the stereotype belle of the old West. She was a bit naughty (after all, she did run a saloon) but had a heart of gold and was very virtuous. When *Gunsmoke* finally bit the dust after 20 years, there wasn't a dry eye in the house.

Have Gun, Will Travel and my favorite, *Maverick,* merit special consideration because their scripts were often literate. Both took the genre beyond the good guys/bad guys clichés and allowed characters to develop real personalities.

The biggest western of the 1960s was *Bonanza.* Ben Cartwright and his boys dominated the ratings for years (they were finally knocked out of the number one spot by *Laugh-In*) and the show was a true believer's potpourri of traditional western values with an emphasis on home and family. Cartwright's three sons provided identification enough for everyone. There was Adam, the quiet, articulate man in black; Hoss, the comic relief—the big fella with a heart as big as all outdoors and a stomach to match; and Little Joe, the teen interest, darling of the kids who saw him as one of their own. Joe often refused to do Pa's bidding and

would strike out on his own. I doubt if there was anyone who was the "baby" of the family that didn't readily identify.

Ben himself provided a hero image for older viewers, and more than one plot revolved around his straight shooting. Ben also provided a firm, but gentle, understanding father figure. The Cartwrights were the royalty of their land. The Ponderosa was their kingdom. Owning property, of course, is a vital part of the American dream. Plots often revolved around others' attempts to infringe on the Cartwright domain.

Despite its stereotype trappings, the western format is so flexible that it can incorporate virtually all of the 31 needs listed earlier in the chapter. Perhaps this explains the enormous success of the western format during television's early years.

However, with the 1970s came increasing viewer sophistication, and westerns seemed to fade away. It was hard to have a western hero who was both a "good" guy *and* a "bad" guy. The mass audience carried around a set of expectations about the old West and there was no room for "heroes" who didn't conform to the image. The shows *Serpico* and *Baretta* worked because we knew that REALIFE people are often complex and not easily typecast. The old West was supposed to be a simpler time with simpler people. Even Paladin of *Have Gun, Will Travel* and the great Bret Maverick were too glamorous for an audience hungry for realism. As a result, the popularity of the western diminished and by the mid-1970s there were few left.

Doctors and Lawyers

Doctor and lawyer formats enjoyed great success during the first two decades of TV. *Dr. Kildare, Ben Casey,* and the more recent *Marcus Welby, M.D.* satisfied viewers who had "the desire to share in the suffering of others" and "the desire to believe in the miraculous." The success of these shows probably owes something to the high status we have given the medical profession; the genre has repaid its debt by giving the profession something extra: romantic glamour. Though these men and women were only humans, we saw them perform heroically week after week under tremendous pressure. Inevitably, their patients seemed to recover.

The hospital or doctor's office provided the proper setting for the human conflicts and intense emotions that seem so necessary in TV programs. Doctors are exalted authority figures and we want to see our trust and faith in them rewarded. Television doctors are "larger than life size." Many REALIFE patients have been disappointed because their doctors could not provide the instant cure or hours of personal attention of a Marcus Welby. This "Marcus Welby syndrome" carries over to many facets of REALIFE. We develop expecta-

tions about the roles of others from TV and are disappointed when they prove erroneous. We expect police officers to solve cases within the hour and lawyers to see justice done whether the client can afford it or not.

The best-known lawyer of television was Perry Mason. Raymond Burr played the famous counselor during the 1950s and 1960s (see 8.7). Though it was shot in black and white, *Perry Mason* enjoyed success in syndication during the 1970s and became one of television's most stable products. The plot was the same each week—someone unjustly accused would come to Mason for help. Perry, along with secretary Della Street and detective Paul Drake, would eventually unravel the mystery. Usually he would break down the real culprit on the witness stand while his client was being tried.

In the final moments, Perry would meet with the client and staff for coffee or a drink and explain how he had figured it out. That portion of the format was so successful that it had a string of imitations, including *Banacek* and *Cool Million.* None enjoyed the success of the original.

All of these shows cashed in on our desire to experience the "happy ending." Of course the illusion of the happy ending—commonly found in all media—can be a dangerous one. If we expect each episode of our lives to end happily, and if we somehow believe that everything will always turn out for the best, we may often become frustrated and discour-

Actor Raymond Burr was the leading character in two long-running TV series, *Perry Mason* and *Ironside*. Both have also been successful in syndication.

aged. Our own REALIFE may seem dull, tragic, or insignificant in comparison.

Variety

Variety shows offer something for everybody. Often they may be centered around the personality of a single star or a troop of familiar faces. Ed Sullivan was the acknowledged king of the variety format and his CBS Sunday evening show was top rated for more than 20 years. Sullivan prided himself on being a good evaluator of talent and entertainment trends.

It was he who first brought Elvis Presley to TV; later came the Beatles (see 8.8) and dozens of other rock groups. But that was only a small part of the story. No matter what your entertainment tastes, you could find something each week on the Sullivan show. There were stand-up comics, opera stars, elephant acts, talking dogs, jugglers, cartoonists, and politicians.

Sullivan himself was an enigma. Before working in TV, he had been an entertainment columnist for a New York newspaper. He had absolutely no talent as a performer and seldom got involved with his talented guests.

In 1964, Ed Sullivan introduced the most popular rock and roll group of all time to an enthusiastic TV audience.

Dozens of comics loved to do imitations of him, often while he watched. It was his very lack of talent that seemed to help him become such a success. He spent very little time in front of the camera, simply introducing the acts and getting out of the way.

Dozens of variety shows have followed. In the 1950s, there were Jackie Gleason and Milton Berle. The 1960s brought the *Smothers Brothers Comedy Hour* and *Rowan and Martin's Laugh-In*. The Smothers brothers began with the usual variety show but rapidly became recognized program innovators, and Tom and Dick Smothers, Mason Williams, and resident comic Pat Paulson became heroes to those who felt TV shouldn't shy away from controversy. They had a habit of inviting guests who were politically and socially controversial.

Often, the brothers' material was allowed because their skits were satirical and thus the audience was "not taking them seriously," but when folk singer Joan Baez made some remarks against the war in Vietnam, CBS censors snipped them out. The problem was TV, the *mass* medium. The network and some sponsors thought the brothers might alienate a part of the mass audience. The Baez incident accelerated the conflict between the Smothers brothers and the network, and after extensive discussions and lots of publicity, the show was canceled.

Rowan and Martin's Laugh-In got away with things the Smothers brothers only dreamed of. The secret of success was the special "form" of the show, composed of hundreds of pieces of video tape. There were skits, one-liners, recurring situations, and jokes. *Laugh-In* was the first program to use electronic editing devices extensively to piece together a collection of "out-takes." Dick and Dan would march out on stage at the beginning and say hello. An hour later, they'd come back to say good-bye. In between, anything could happen. There were cameos by John Wayne and Richard Nixon, cream pies and cold showers for the series "regulars." Many, including Goldie Hawn, Lily Tomlin, Ruth Buzzi, and Henry Gibson, went on to success of their own.

Laugh-In first pointed out that TV audiences could handle a lot more entertainment "information" than other shows were offering. Because it relied so heavily on editing and visual devices, *Laugh-In* was uniquely TV. The mass audience gave thundering approval and the show (originally scheduled as a 13-week summer replacement) became the most successful on TV. In addition, the critics loved it and *Laugh-In* won every top award, including a flock of Emmys.

Variety shows of the 1970s borrowed heavily from the *Laugh-In* format. Everything had to be sped up for presentation; the more elements the better. In addition, the variety shows of the 1970s depended heavily on technicians and those behind the camera to "create" the visual splendor TV had been lacking. Costuming and set decoration became key factors, as the audience expected to be visually entertained while listening to a song or laughing at a comedy sketch. *Carol Burnett, Sonny and Cher, Donny and Marie,* and others were successful because their producers realized that visual appeal, rapid pacing, and diverse guests lists were a necessity.

The 1970s also brought a flood of variety-type shows that appealed to a youthful late-night audience. *The Midnight Special, Don Kirshner's Rock Concert,* and *In Concert* all featured rock music. Many were built around major rock personalities, but occasionally a little humor would be thrown in for diversity. Though rock generally was still not popular enough for TV's prime-time audience, the late-night Friday and Saturday spots seemed ripe and ratings were good.

Meanwhile, the British import *Monty Python* had taken the *Laugh-In* formula one step further (see 8.9). This show was a nonstop barrage of satirical sketches that added extensive animation in the tradition of the Beatles' animated film *Yellow Submarine.* BBC censorship standards were considerably more relaxed than American counterparts, and nudity and four-letter words abounded. The same lack of censorship was true when the show was aired over public TV in America, as there were no irate sponsors to object. Besides, as in *Laugh-In,* everything happened so fast that

8.9

The creators and stars of *Monty Python's Flying Circus.* Front row (left to right): Eric Idle, Michael Palin, Terry Jones. Back row (left to right): Graham Chapman, John Cleese, cartoonist Terry Gilliam.

Often provocative and daring, the humor on *Monty Python's Flying Circus* is a type rarely seen on American television.

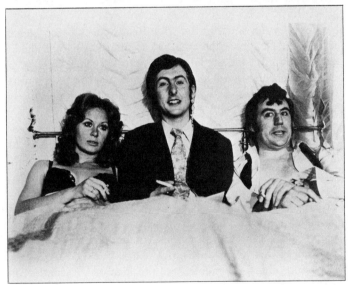

it was hard to know exactly what was being said.

Monty Python became an underground hit, particularly among young people and the public TV audience. But when one of the networks bought the rights to the shows and

aired them in competition with the late-night rock shows, regular *Python* viewers set up a howl. Whole sketches and scenes were missing. The performers themselves finally sued to stop commercial airing unless shows were aired uncut. *Monty Python* quickly disappeared from commercial TV but remained a success on the public network.

Meanwhile in America, NBC's *Saturday Night Live* was breaking ground of its own. There was no regular emcee but a weekly "guest host" whose role was often overshadowed by the antics of the "Not Ready for Prime Time Players." The comic skits offered satire with a bite, and the late-night hour kept network censorship to a minimum. Where else would TV viewers watch a sketch about a brand of soup called "Painful Rectal Itch" or see a live fish chopped to bits in a blender?

Family

The theme of family life has been with television since the beginning. Many early sitcoms were based on family situations, including *Father Knows Best, Ozzie and Harriet, Leave It to Beaver,* and others. As mentioned, the idea of family togetherness played a big part in the success of *Bonanza.* Historically, TV has always glamorized and glorified the family, never questioning its validity or the happiness found there. Even in sitcoms that emphasized family squabbles, like *I Love Lucy* and *The Honeymooners,* family harmony always won out by the time 30 minutes were up.

Television has been severely criticized for the rosy picture it paints of family life. According to many critics, the picture is grossly unrealistic, especially in modern times. According to many sociologists, the family unit, the basic component in the survival of society as we know it, is breaking down. After World War II, returning GIs married and often moved their families to another part of the country. Families that had stayed in one town for generations found their children and grandchildren thousands of miles away. When the GIs' kids grew up in the 1960s, they were not entirely convinced that marriage and a family were what they wanted. Simultaneously, the women's movement prompted many young women to ask: "Do I want to devote 20 years or more of my life to raising children?"

It was perhaps in response to these criticisms that television began to give us a different slant on family life in the early 1970s. As we have discussed; Norman Lear's sitcoms have been far bolder than the sitcoms of the 1950s and 1960s in terms of both subject matter and family discord. Other "family" shows that came into their own in the 1970s included the highly acclaimed BBC production *Upstairs Downstairs* and its short-lived U.S. imitation, *Beacon Hill.* Both were stories of wealthy, influential, fictitious families who lived near the turn of the century. Both made a conscious effort to show family dynamics realistically—sometimes happy, sometimes not. We watched their lives unfold week after week while TV critics gave their blessing. *Upstairs Downstairs* also afforded many public television stations a much-needed shot in the

8.10

A scene in the making from *An American Family:* Filmmakers Alan and Susan Raymond (right) at home with Pat Loud and her son, Grant, in their Santa Barbara, California, livingroom. For seven months, the Raymonds shared, and captured on film, the day-to-day lives of the seven-member William C. Loud family.

arm as millions of commercial TV viewers "discovered" that noncommercial TV could be entertaining.

It was also the noncommercial network that aired a controversial documentary series about a REALIFE family in the early 1970s. *An American Family* was shot by a Public Broadcasting Service camera crew in Santa Barbara, California. The crew lived with a real American family, the Louds, for seven months. The result was a 12-hour television production. The Loud family may not have been "typical." It was certainly not typical of television sitcom families. There were five children, a huge house in Santa Barbara, and plenty of problems. But they represented what most middle-class Americans were striving for—a chance to succeed and to live out "the good life" in a pleasant environment (see 8.10).

The weekly glimpse into the Loud family revealed something far more disturbing. Son Lance was a homosexual and other kids were involved with drugs. In final episodes, Mom and Dad had a series of scathing arguments which ended with separation and di-

vorce. REALIFE divorce! Meanwhile the cameras whirred away and America tuned in.

Never was the disintegration of a family unit portrayed with such accuracy and authenticity. Several years later, all were interviewed and asked whether they would do it again. Everyone except wife Pat Loud agreed they would. By that time, the family was completely scattered: the parents had obtained their final divorce decree, Pat had moved to New York, father Bill had a bachelor pad in Santa Barbara and was dating frequently, and son Lance had moved into a shabby New York apartment and was trying to start a rock group.

When pieced together, the relationship between television and family is ironic. In the 1960s, Marshall McLuhan warned that television had become the third parent, that it was a much more significant influence than mom and dad. Most parents freely admitted they used TV as an electronic babysitter. This disintegration of the family unit was then documented in *An American Family* in 1972.

Then, almost as if this kind of realism were too much for the viewing public, *The Waltons* arrived to save the day. It seemed to be time for a show that glorified the family unit. The Waltons were a Depression family with very little money, but they had a lot of beautiful land and each other. The Depression actually became "the good old days" as John-Boy recalled the hardships and obstacles that led to a weekly renewal of faith in land and family.

The Waltons took place in real time, with children growing up and getting married much as you would expect in REALIFE. Critics had a field day and lambasted its "cornball" attitudes toward social problems, but the mass audience loved it. Again, there was a broad range of ages represented. Grandparents were in their seventies, while the youngest children attended elementary school. *The Waltons* seemed to be one of those shows that transcended simplistic scripts and plots to come alive for the mass audience.

TV as Movie

TV movies did not become popular until the mid-1960s when the skyrocketing budgets of traditional formats made it cheaper to film a 90- or 120-minute "made-for-TV" movie than three or four 30-minute shows. The made-for-TV movie is generally a grade-B film and suffers when compared to those designed for theater. TV movies are filmed for 50 percent or less money than their theatrical counterparts and it shows. Still, some have been outstanding. Made-for-TV movies have con-

cerned controversial subjects like homosexuality, rape, drugs, and unwanted pregnancy. There have even been made-for-TV disaster movies. The attitude of their promoters seems to be that anything theatrical movies can do, we can do cheaper.

Despite low budgets and other restrictions, the mass audience watches made-for-TV movies. Often, a heavily promoted made-for-TV movie will outrate other shows offered at the same time, and that's what counts. Among the most popular of these are "docu-dramas" based on real-life events (Watergate, Bay of Pigs, the raid on Entebbe), which combine historical fact and scriptwriter imagination.

NBC added another twist in the early 1970s with its *Mystery Movies*. These were actually several different "series" like *Columbo, McMillan and Wife,* and *McCloud.* Each series was aired only once a month. The actors loved it because it meant a lighter work schedule, the scriptwriters loved it because it sometimes meant better-quality scripts, and the public loved it because it meant variety. The *Mystery Movie* was actually a cross between the made-for-TV movie and the series, but the mass audience perceived it as a series and was not disappointed when it didn't measure up to theatrical standards.

Movie as TV

The biggest single source of TV programming is still theatrical films. Each night there is at least one full-length feature film sliced up for commercial TV. The frank nature of many contemporary films has forced the networks to issue audience warnings before they air them. Both network censors and the public are becoming more lenient about what they will tolerate on the air, and many R-rated films arrive on TV with a minimal number of cuts.

At first, only second-rate theater films came to TV, but now the networks bid astounding sums for the right to "premiere" a major motion picture. *TV Guide* reported that NBC paid $5 million for a single airing of *Gone with the Wind* in 1976. NBC "lost" money, even though the movie had the largest TV audience ever to that date (it has since been surpassed by *Roots*). Network executives claimed that the "prestige" of being *the* network that showed the film made up the difference. In addition, that huge audience was tuned to NBC when the next program aired. The same was true when NBC bought and aired *The Godfather Saga* in 1977.

The most common viewer complaint is that these movies are cut up so badly that the filmmaker's original intent is lost between dog food and deodorant commercials. *Gone with the Wind*, for example, was 3 hours and 40 minutes long, but it was spread over two nights and interrupted by 78 minutes of station breaks and commercials. This does make a difference, but it's also important to remember that whenever there is transfer of content from one medium to another, there is change. A theatrical movie that appears on TV is no longer a movie, it is *television* with all of the things that implies. The problem is with the audience; they expect cinema and are disappointed with anything less.

There are some important reasons why TV is not cinema. While television is something we can enjoy by ourselves, a movie is a *social event*. When was the last time you went to the movies by yourself? When we enter a theater, the room is huge, darkened, and full of strangers. There is a nice curtain. The screen is large; the picture is bright, colorful, and larger than life. We *expect* a lot; after all, we paid to get in. We want to be entertained. TV is different. We may not "plan" to watch it, but flip it on when there is nothing else to do. We watch it casually and if the program is poor, well, "That's typical television for you." Besides, we can always turn it off and do something else . . . like go out to a movie!

So it is actually incorrect for the mass audience to assume they will get cinema when they watch TV. But they persist, and the networks try to accommodate, announcing films as "major events" and padding commercial introductions by saying, "You are watching the television premiere of a major motion picture: *The Thing That Devoured Toledo.*" Many local stations have gone one step further—presenting certain films without commercial interruption. They hope to sell the adjacent time immediately before and after the movie for enough money to make up the difference.

For better or worse, all types of movies are a prime source of television programming.

Drawing by C. Barsotti; © 1975, The New Yorker Magazine, Inc.

The three major networks each feed their local affiliates about 18 hours of programs per day, seven days a week, 365 days a year. That comes to about 20,000 hours every year. It takes a lot of scripts and programs and they have to come from somewhere. Movies will probably remain a significant (and relatively cheap) source of prime-time television programs. What's more, the movie studios are cranking out many made-for-TV films. Without the extra income from TV, they might have gone bankrupt years ago. This is another part of the curious symbiosis between the film and television industries.

Issues and Answers

Roots, Mass Audience, and Social Awareness

During the winter of 1977, some 130 million Americans took part in a massive sociological experiment. For eight consecutive nights, a TV version of *Roots,* the best-selling family history by Alex Haley, invaded America's living-rooms. The Nielson ratings confirmed that it was the most closely followed television program in the history of the medium. In fact, of the ten highest-rated programs of all time, seven slots are held by various *Roots* episodes.

The story of seven generations of black Americans struggling under suppression and slavery struck a responsive chord in the mass audience. It "educated" blacks and whites about black history and the struggle for freedom, and sparked a renewed interest in genealogy for everyone. While *Roots* was based on fact, parts of it were clearly fiction. But it is fiction in the tradition of *Uncle Tom's Cabin* that often brings about massive social change.

About 750,000 copies of Haley's book had been sold when *Roots* was aired, but for more than 99 percent of TV viewers it was a new story. Clearly it left a distinct impression upon them. Many observers felt it would improve race relations, and even the most skeptical admitted it left whites with a more sympathetic view of black history.

Yet, *Roots* was not merely popular, it was the *most popular prime-time show ever,* nudging aside prior champ, *Gone with the Wind.* Just as the 1939 film displayed a startling knowledge of movie "form," so *Roots* was a brilliant TV production, conceived, created, and designed for the newer medium.

Ironically, both stories used slavery and the Civil War as a backdrop for a glimpse into the lives of one family. Though both productions were based on books, the visual presentation seemed to move the mass audience in a way no book could. *Gone with the Wind* told one side of the story, *Roots* another—both had a profound effect on the mass audience.

Roots, like all prime-time television programs, was not simply a passive body of entertainment, but a complex mix of narrative, story, and visual appeal that tells us about audience needs. But at the same time television "mirrors" society, it also reconstructs it. Though *Roots* may not have set out to accomplish specific goals, it was a social experiment nonetheless. The audience was changed. Black congressman John Conyers said of the show, "It doesn't cure unemployment or take people out of the ghetto. But it's a democratic statement as eloquent as any that's ever been devised, and we've been talking about what can be done with it."

The real lesson in *Roots* may have more to do with television than with black history. For those eight nights, it was obvious that prime-time TV brought an important message to 130 million Americans. How long will it be before we realize that there are many other messages brought to us every night in exactly the same way? *Roots* was not a public television or government-structured "educational" program, it was *commercial* prime-time viewing. It made the *ongoing,* if invisible, prime-time TV education visible for a short time. It was new, and dealt with controversial material; yet the very success of every prime-time genre is based on conflict and controversy.

Perhaps nightly television program content is not always as elegant as *Roots,* yet is it so different? It is easy to poke fun at the "idiot box" but far more difficult to unravel the mysteries of prime time. Everyone agrees that *Roots* helped us realize the tremendous potential of commercial TV, but in some ways, that potential is *already* being fulfilled.

3. Check this week's TV schedule and make a list of all prime-time TV series. Then break them down in terms of genre, using the criteria found in this chapter. Does any one particular genre seem to dominate?

4. Using the 31 gratifications listed at the beginning of this chapter, pick a television show and watch it carefully, keeping the list in front of you at all times. Can you find specific plot instances that match some gratifications? Have a friend do the same and compare notes.

5. Make a list of current heroes and heroines in prime-time TV. What serious character flaws or personality quirks may have contributed to their success?

6. Reread the final paragraph of this chapter. Do you agree or disagree? Why?

Queries and Concepts

1. What is your favorite television show? Can you think of ways that it may have affected the person that you are? If you could trade places with any television character for a day, who would it be and why?

2. Name three programs currently on the air that you feel "aim for the lowest common denominator" and three that do not. Which are the most popular? Why?

Readings and References

And Now Back to Maverick

There really is no definitive work about the "roles" that TV plants in our heads. Your choice is between a set of rather stuffy academic treatises on "socialization" (see the readings and references in Chapter 14) or a lot of pop material found in the TV section of *Time* and *Newsweek.* Both regularly publish pieces about why we identify with certain TV series.

Pioneers

Erik Barnouw
A History of Broadcasting in the United States, 3 vols. *The Image Empire from 1950.* New York: Oxford University Press, 1970.
This is the third volume of the most quoted historical treatment of the rise of the electronic media. It deals with television as a societal force. There is ample material on the early TV hardware and software pioneers.

Erik Barnouw
Tube of Plenty: The Evolution of American Television. New York: Oxford University Press, 1975. This is an updated version of Barnouw's historical trilogy dealing specifically with TV. Included are sections on prime time and the rise of the major network corporations and advertising.

Note: Many of the books in the readings and references for Chapter 6 have a section dealing with television. Agee, Ault, and Emery's *Introduction to Mass Communications* (New York: Dodd, Mead, 1970) has a very useful bibliography if you want to focus on the contribution of some specific person.

The Growth of Television

Ron Lackmann
Remember Television. New York: G. P. Putnam's, 1971.
This is an interesting collection of popular television stars and shows from 1947 to 1958.

Highlights include a *New York Times* TV guide from those years, as well as a paragraph or two on all the popular shows of the era. Useful index.

From Sitcom to Star Trek: The Genres of Prime Time

Harlan Ellison
The Glass Teat. Moonachie, N.J.: Pyramid Publications, 1975.
The Other Glass Teat. Moonachie, N.J.: Pyramid Publications, 1975.
These are collections of Ellison's columns that originally appeared in the *Los Angeles Free Press.* For many of you, Ellison needs no introduction. He is a prolific writer of science fiction who has also written dozens of television scripts. He won a Hugo award for his *Star Trek* script: "The City on the Edge of Forever." Ellison has a tendency to dwell on the sexual implications of TV, but that makes it all the more fun. You'll read criticism on everything from the *Beverly Hillbillies* to *Star Trek.*

Horace Newcomb
TV the Most Popular Art. Garden City, N.Y.: Doubleday, 1974.
Includes sections on sitcom, action-adventure, western, and other genres. Newcomb is a TV pioneer, the first to write about the genres of TV with anything less than abhorrence. Instead, he offers insight into *why* these programs are popular. In doing so, he provides a catalog of American myths and values. This

may be the most important book ever written on the content of commercial television.

Horace Newcomb, ed.
Television: The Critical View. New York: Oxford University Press, 1976.
A follow-up on *TV the Most Popular Art,* this time a collection of essays on the genres of TV, plus a section on the meanings behind the myths. Four excellent pieces on the movement toward defining television in terms of mass culture.

Stephen E. Whitfield and Gene Roddenberry
The Making of Star Trek. New York: Ballantine Books, 1973.

This is the definitive book on the production of a television show, not only for those who want to produce, but also for those interested in what happens from the time the idea is born until the final product appears. Written with reverence by one of *Star Trek's* fans in collaboration with producer Gene Roddenberry.

**Issues and Answers:
Roots, Mass Audience,
and Social Awareness**

"Why 'Roots' Hit Home."
Time, February 14, 1977, pp. 68–71.

9
Television, Part Two: Other Times and Other Places

Television is one of the most powerful forces man has ever unleashed upon himself. The quality of human life may depend enormously upon our efforts to comprehend and control that force.—Nicholas Johnson

Daytime TV and the Common Cold

Last week I spent my days (and nights) at home with a temperature of 101° and the usual sinus miseries. During that week I must have seen 100 commercials suggesting remedies for my ailment.... I hadn't realized how dependent TV is on the common cold. If it is ever cured, TV is in real trouble! A lot of the cold medicine commercials are run during the day, perhaps because many of those watching are home sick from work or school.

Colds always seem to come at the wrong time, but this one came at the right time for me. It gave me a chance to make some notes on daytime TV.

1. Game shows are everything you are not when you're sick. Game show contestants are happy, elated, and competitive. It reminds me of my mother's favorite tongue-in-cheek cliché: "It's not whether you win or lose that counts . . . but the thrill of wiping out a friend." Game show hosts insist that contestants "know" each other a bit before they do battle.

2. *Hollywood Squares* features form over content. It's not the winning or losing (as with *Match Game* or *Price Is Right)*; getting there is all the fun. Some of the "stars" are people I've never heard of; that is not the case with the nighttime version.

3. This is the first time I've ever seen *Ryan's Hope* and it reminds me of prime-time shows like *Family* and *The Waltons* . . . very family oriented. Blood is thicker than (soapy) water.

4. A lot of the old reruns of shows like *Topper* are in black and white, while commercials are in *color*.

5. *The Gong Show*—how embarrassing! *The Gong Show* is like the game show in that you find yourself rooting for contestants and hoping they'll make it. You must pick your favorite contestants the way you pick your favorite sports team. "Oh, he's from my home state—I hope he wins."

6. It's surprising to see *All in the Family* being rerun during the day when it's being aired in prime time as well.

7. Programs change drastically when the kids get home from school. Lots of cartoons and western reruns are shown after 4:00 P.M.

8. *Bonanza* is alive and well . . . the episodes hold up surprisingly well. They look very "expensive" in comparison with the soaps . . . so vivid and "outdoorsy." Soap operas seldom go outdoors.

9. By the time the news comes on I am ready for something different, but the news is made up of the same elements as soaps, games, and reruns: suspense, murder, intrigue, money, violence, and uncertainty.

Richard Threlkeld and Lesley Stahl, co-anchors of the *CBS Morning News*, which straddles the line between the "straight" news broadcast and the more popular news-talk format of NBC's *Today*.

On the Fringe: Day Shows and Late Shows

All three major networks derive more advertising revenues from daytime shows than from prime time. Even though each ad costs less in the daytime, there are some 14 hours of TV that are considered non–prime time. These include the daytime hours (7:00 A.M. to 6:00 P.M.) and an increasingly longer late-night period (11:00 P.M. to 2:00 A.M.). Networks supply packaged entertainment to take care of the special audiences that watch during these hours.

In the early years TV networks supplied no daytime programs. The first major network morning effort was geared to an audience hungry for information. The *Today* show and later *Good Morning America* and the *CBS Morning News* featured extensive interviews, film footage of various public figures, and other diversions (see 9.1). The content was often more oriented to "entertainment" or soft news than were the evening newscasts, so the morn-

ing audience could be "informed and entertained" before going to work. These early morning formats have been very successful; in 1978 NBC's *Today* was still top rated.

Soap Operas

Though dozens of different daytime formats have been tried, daytime TV is still pretty much *soap operas* and *game shows*. The soaps were introduced from radio when daytime TV first began, deriving their name from the soap products that were often sponsors. The soap opera format was brought intact from radio and it's changed little over the years. Protagonists are put into conflict situations, usually involving close friends or relatives, and must make decisions to resolve those conflicts. Some soaps, like *The Guiding Light* and *The Edge of Night*, boast 20 or more years on daytime TV and a loyal audience.

The soap opera depends so much on human interaction that we may use the term to describe our own conflicts. ("Gee, my father isn't speaking to me, my sister is getting an abortion, and I'm flunking out of school. My life is really like a soap opera!") In reality, few lives are as troubled and confused as those on the soaps. As with much of TV, our real lives are dull by comparison.

Soap opera characters are carefully created for the mass audience. They are usually young (25–35), well dressed, and financially comfortable. Leading men are doctors and lawyers. Leading women are attractive and well manicured. Indoor sets are unusually large and boast wall-to-wall carpeting, plush drapes, and built-in wet bars. Soap opera characters tend to be very sophisticated and do a lot of eating, drinking, and arguing.

Regular viewers can name all the characters in a given soap and describe their history in detail. The casual observer gets lost in the plot, which has more twists and turns than a mountain highway:

Let's see . . . John's son is getting married today to the woman who used to be his father's wife, who was recently divorced from the doctor who delivered his illegitimate daughter. That illegitimate daughter is really Bill's mother, Nell, whose father was a doctor when Bill was in medical school. We know that Bill never graduated but came to town and set up practice anyway. Things were going great until he and Nell got divorced, but then she found out she was his mother and. . . .

Unlike prime-time shows, soaps are often shot only a day or two before they are aired.

This five-show-a-week schedule takes its toll on cast and crew. There is usually little budget for retakes, and sometimes missed cues and blown lines must be aired. It really keeps the cast on their toes. One advantage to the schedule is that the soap script may incorporate recent news events, while prime-time shows, shot as much as six months in advance, cannot.

Critics contend that all soaps are nauseatingly similar, but actually each is aimed at a special segment of the audience. Although 70 percent of that audience is women, there are different age groups. One hit among young viewers during the late 1970s was *The Young and the Restless*. It featured young characters and concentrated on presenting the latest fashions along with the plot.

Soap operas often set clothing and fashion trends. Most are taped in New York, and many fashion designers across the country keep an eye on the soaps to see what is happening. "What's in vogue in the soaps today will be in the shops tomorrow" is a standard saying.

Of more significance, soap operas are a fascinating study of audience-character relationships. There is no other media audience so involved with its programs and so devoted to its characters. When soap characters have an on-camera birthday, they can expect lots of cards from fans. If they are sick, thousands of viewers write and send get-well greetings. If a popular character "dies," viewers protest. And, unlike the prime-time audience, soap watchers tend to have a good handle on what they receive from their programs. The desire to believe in romantic love, the desire to see evil punished and virtue rewarded, and the desire to see others make mistakes are most often cited by the viewers themselves. Soap characters are usually good or evil, positive or negative, with well-defined personalities.

During *Mary Hartman, Mary Hartman's* airing in the mid-1970s, many viewers found themselves hooked on the genre for the first time. Norman Lear's self-described "slightly bent" soap was different. Mary's grandfather (the "Fernwood Flasher") was arrested for exhibitionism, sister Kathy went to work in a massage parlor, and Mary was about to have an affair with a local cop. For all of that, Mary retained her innocence; she was always a victim of circumstance.

While *Mary Hartman, Mary Hartman* represented a departure from traditional soap format (for one thing, it was often aired in the late evening rather than in the daytime), its real significance may be in *how* it got on the air. Despite all of his successes, Lear could not convince the three networks to give *Mary* a chance. So he brought 50 independent TV station managers from all over the country to Los Angeles for a quiet dinner on his lawn. Afterwards he screened an episode of his new soap and asked them to carry it, sweetening the pot by offering it at budget rates.

Those who accepted were probably grateful. Within weeks the show had doubled existing ratings for most stations in its time period.

It was the first time the major networks had been successfully bypassed. Now producers could take more controversial shows directly to the stations, diminishing the power of the networks to dictate what was popular. Dozens of books and hundreds of articles have been written about this problem, but it took Norman Lear's success to prove that the network stranglehold could be broken. In the midst of it all was a show from the most widely criticized genre on television.

Game Shows

Originally introduced to daytime TV to compete with the soaps, game shows now outnumber them. They are actually cheaper to produce, despite the cash they give away. Paying actors, actresses, scriptwriters, and set designers for a soap opera is expensive, but the game show requires only a couple of contestants, a limited production crew, a cheap set with a lot of sequins, and a moderator with a lot of teeth. The audience does the rest.

One game show producer, interviewed by a network TV crew, was very explicit when asked what he thought was at the bottom of his success: "Greed . . . it's American as apple pie." There is no doubt that the desire to experience financial reward, however vicariously, is at the root of the game format. Most often we can't help playing along and trying to outguess the contestants.

Each semester I bring a TV into the classroom and treat my students to a game show. In the beginning things are rather quiet, but as the show progresses more begin to participate. At the end everyone is yelling directly at the contestants and criticizing the moderator. The mood is infectious. Even in the college classroom, students who insist they "hate" TV *have* to get involved.

It is precisely this ability to involve the audience that spells game show success. By playing along, we can engage in "risk taking" in a safe and controlled way:

Do you want to keep or trade away your jogging outfit, a year's supply of frozen TV dinners, 200 pet hamsters (with cages), and four thousand eight hundred and twenty-six dollars in cash????? or ????? Do you want what's behind door number two!!!!!?????

The first game shows were a comparatively tranquil lot. *Who Do You Trust?*, *What's My Line?*, and *You Bet Your Life* were all good-natured get-togethers in which contestants were given time to get acquainted with the emcee. Playing the game was only incidental. This changed in 1955 with the introduction of *The $64,000 Question.* It was the first show to offer really big prize money, and the emphasis shifted to the game itself and the huge financial rewards that went to winners. Contestants were put in an "isolation booth" where they were unable to hear audience hints. Emcee Hal March added to the suspense

by constantly reminding the audience: "This question could mean sixty-four thooouuusand dollars!" Contestants seemed to ponder, look perplexed, sway from side to side, and then suddenly pull the answers out of nowhere. The suspense was unbelievable.

Before long, we knew it really was unbelievable! Participants had been coached ahead of time. In those days, sponsors produced programs, then "rented" space from the networks for airing. As it turned out, executives of Revlon, Inc. (which had sponsored the show and several offshoots) had decided which contestants could "win" and which were to "lose." A congressional investigation followed and most quiz shows went off the air. In 1960, networks took control of program production.

By 1960, the last big-money show was off the air and those that remained, like *The Price Is Right* and *Concentration*, gave away very little cash. Instead, prizes were furnished by sponsors in return for an on-air plug. In 1966 the *Hollywood Squares* premiered and nine well-known Hollywood personalities began trying to "bluff" contestants with right or wrong answers to questions based on material from sources like "Dear Abby" and the *National Enquirer.* Again, prizes were furnished by sponsors, but the real show was the "stars" who ad libbed and joked until there wasn't really much time left to play the game.

During the late 1970s, some big-money game shows began to reappear, including *Treasure Hunt* and *Name That Tune.* Ironically, an updated version of the old Revlon favorite, *The $128,000 Question,* was among them. But the new big-money quizzes were compulsively honest, with answers stored in a computer miles away and sealed envelopes "certified" by private detective agencies. Network officials sat in on every taping, and if anything looked even remotely fishy, they pulled the plug.

A game-show-junkie friend of mine who lives in Los Angeles attends several tapings daily. One time he got his big chance to become a contestant on the *Hollywood Squares.* After being interviewed several times, he was finally brought to the studio on taping day. The show treats all contestants to lunch at the NBC commissary. There he stood in line with Vincent Price (a *Square's* regular). He asked Price what time it was, and before the star noticed my friend's yellow warning badge, he answered the question. That was all it took; a network supervisor told my friend he could not compete on the show: he and Price may have discussed a possible answer! Disappointed, he pleaded with producers to give him another chance. They told him they'd call the next time Price was off the panel. That was in 1975 and he's still waiting.

Increasingly in the 1970s game shows seemed bent on milking every last drop of anxiety out of their frantic contestants. *The $25,000 Treasure Hunt* and the durable *Let's Make a Deal* would "play" the poor contestants' emotions until they were exhausted.

One minute they would win, the next they would lose. The emcee would tell them to sit down, then call them up on stage to "give them another chance." Audiences loved it.

The key to success is emotion—the capacity for audiences to identify with contestants and their ups and downs. Little or no skill is required to win big money, but you have to be "lucky."

Talk Shows

Talk shows usually appear late in the afternoon or late in the evening, but seldom in prime time. Many, including those that star Mike Douglas, Merv Griffin, and Dinah Shore, are syndicated or produced independently and sold to stations on an individual basis.

The granddaddy of them all is NBC's *Tonight Show.* With its hosts Steve Allen, Jack Paar, and Johnny Carson (along with countless guest hosts), the *Tonight Show* has ruled late-night TV ratings. By the 1970s Carson had hosted the show for so long that most people simply referred to it as "Carson"—"Did you see Carson last night?" Johnny Carson had become NBC's number one money-maker. The *Tonight Show's* overhead is comparatively low: the sets are inexpensive and the one production crew is not large. Guests Bob Hope, Frank Sinatra, and an obscure kazooist from Indiana are all paid the same union minimum (about $450). As the late-night audience grew over the years, so did the price sponsors paid to push their dog food or aspirin.

Carson's tremendous rise to success on the *Tonight Show* was probably due to his own affable personality. Raised in the Midwest, he seems to be "folksy" yet smooth. He seldom dominates the show but keeps things going if the guests let down. Most are Hollywood actors and actresses who need little prompting. Again, success is often a matter of chemistry: Carson's on-stage rapport with announcer Ed McMahon and overdressed bandleader Doc Severinsen is legendary.

What do audiences want from a talk show? The format offers music, stand-up comic routines, and various guests. The *Tonight Show* may offer four or five guests on a given night, some well-known, some lesser known, and some not known at all. Usually there is a vocalist, a comedian, a well-known personality, and a pop "intellectual" guest—perhaps a sociologist explaining some current social or sexual trend. Audiences like this mixed bag because there is something for everybody. The pace is not nearly as frantic as in the prime-time variety show. Viewers can nod off if they like. In most markets, the *Tonight Show* is aired from 11:30 P.M. to 1:00 A.M. and loses half its viewers by sign-off time. But that's OK; they'll be back the next night.

Over the years, both ABC and CBS have tried to imitate the *Tonight Show*'s success by offering similar fare. *Joey Bishop* and *Merv Grif-*fin each lasted less than a year. Dick Cavett gave Carson his biggest challenge. Critics loved Cavett, calling him the "thinking man's Johnny Carson." He tried to upgrade the genre by offering the audience in-depth interviews with well-known show people like Marlon Brando and Katharine Hepburn. Cavett also used something called the "theme" show. He'd bring on, say, five singers from the 1930s or six psychologists to discuss human sexuality. For all his innovations, Cavett's show didn't last. Apparently the mass audience prefers something a little more casual that late at night.

The real key to the talk format may be "talk." We all like to know something about the personal lives of those show business people who are larger than life. Are these just plain people in REALIFE, or is there some success secret that may be discovered when they come on stage to be themselves? How close are they to their media images?

A 1970s entry in the late-night sweepstakes was NBC's *Tomorrow Show.* Shown in most markets from 1:00–2:00 A.M., it began a trend toward late, late night programming. Though some affiliated stations did not carry it, those who did found there was indeed life after 1:00 A.M. *Tomorrow* really imitated Dick Cavett; each evening there were one or two guests contributing to a central theme. The success of *Tomorrow* prompted other networks to offer late, late programs (often a movie), and most affiliates stayed on the air.

Children's Shows

Of all television genres, researchers are most concerned with children's programs. They reason that children are most vulnerable to concepts they find on TV. If TV is as powerful as some say, what kinds of ideas are we putting into the heads of tomorrow's citizens?

In the beginning, there were *Captain Video, Kukla, Fran, and Ollie,* and *Howdy Doody.* These were evening shows (*Howdy Doody* was usually aired at around 5:30 P.M.). When the networks introduced daytime programs, they included *Captain Kangaroo* and other low-keyed, gentle entertainment designed to amuse the toddlers and keep them occupied (see 9.2). The commercial success of such programs in the 1950s prompted a barrage of children's shows on Saturday mornings, a logical time since children were out of school.

Most of these slots were filled with cartoon shows. Though cartoons have changed over the years (there are now fewer animals and more people), the basic formula remains the same. A central character or cast of characters is placed in conflict with another character or set of characters. Action results from the conflict. In the end all is resolved when *our* character wins.

The classic example is the "Roadrunner" series, which still runs on TV and in movie theaters. The Roadrunner does nothing but make a pleasant little "beep beep" and run up and down desert paths at 100 miles per hour. He is simple, good, and innocent. Villain Wiley Coyote plots and schemes to catch Roadrunner, but his elaborate traps always seem to backfire, leaving him the worse for wear. Yet there remains something endearing about both characters.

Occasionally the cartoon format appears in prime time, and audience researchers find that mom and dad are looking over their kids' shoulders. *The Flintstones, The Jetsons,* and *Top Cat* all made it in the 1960s. The 1970s saw a dozen *Peanuts* specials in prime time.

The only prime-time children's show that survived all three decades was Walt Disney. (Actually the Disney program has had three different names, but they have all been essentially the same show.) The Disney show offered cartoons, action-adventure, and other programs appropriate for children. Parents trusted Disney to deliver what was good for their kids, and in a sea of sex and violence, it was a relief for them to find the Disney show.

Critics have also been wary of commercials aired during children's shows. Children may be more susceptible to the advertiser's message and should be protected from the gimmicks used to sell products to adults. The products themselves were often criticized. Some claimed that war weapons encouraged kids to poke one another's eyes out, and "sugar-coated" cereals turned out to be more sugar than cereal. Parent groups were successful in convincing the networks to cut down on some violence during the hours in which children normally watch TV.

Bob ("Captain Kangaroo") Kee-shan stars in one of television's longest-running series. The CBS children's show has been on the air since 1954.

Yet parents remain uneasy about commercials and children's programs in general. That uneasiness stems from their instinctive knowledge of the power of television. They watch their children gaze hypnotically at the colorful images dashing across the screen and wonder what will become of it all. This was particularly true with parents who experienced the medium for the first time while adults. Today's younger parents grew up with TV and may not fear it as much. "After all," they say, "we watched TV all the time, and we turned out all right." What they may not realize is how much of what they are now is a product of that small screen.

Sports

In constant competition with kids for rights to the family set on weekend mornings is the sports fan. Much has been written about the impact of sports on TV and vice versa. When sports coverage began, it seemed like a natural. After all, TV could "put you there" in a way radio never could. Live sports coverage was a big part of the 1950s. Dominating all was the broadcast of major heavyweight boxing matches and baseball's World Series. The technical capabilities of TV improved to make diversified sports coverage a reality in the 1960s. An experimental broadcast of the 1940 World Series broadcast had involved one camera located on the sidelines. By the 1960s there were a dozen cameras, and by the 1970s a roving "mini-cam" had been added along with cameras in helicopters and in the locker rooms.

But the real story of TV sports is football. The game was a second-class professional sport in the 1950s; more attention was focused on college games. The average National Football League (NFL) player was earning about $6,000 a year. TV changed all that. It was impractical to televise baseball every day, no *one* game ever meant anything and besides, baseball was so long and drawn out. It was impractical for TV because a game might go on forever. Football was different; there was plenty of action with balls thrown in the air and guys running into each other all over the place. Football was so, well . . . so *visual!* What's more, when the clock ran out, that was it. No overtime meant no unscheduled preemptions of other network programs. When TV networks approached the NFL, they found them eager to talk. This was in sharp

contrast to baseball teams, which enjoyed record attendance and didn't want to "rock the boat." The television-football marriage was born.

The people of North America watch a lot of football on TV. The Super Bowl seems to break its own rating records year after year. By the middle of the 1970s, more than half the men and women in America were tuning in for the annual spectacle. Football provided just the right amount of "action" (violence, if you like) to make it the perfect TV vehicle. The status of professional football rose accordingly, and by the time the first few Super Bowls were aired, baseball was no longer "America's favorite pastime."

Football provides many of the same gratifications as other TV genres. There is certainly the desire to believe in the "miraculous" ("That catch was a miracle, Howard"). There is the desire to imagine oneself a hero ("Mildred, did you see that—that was just like the touchdown I scored at Tech High back in '57—remember?"). There is the need to experience the ugly and the desire to share in the suffering of others ("Look at that field, it must be frozen solid, why it's below zero out there").

According to communications researcher Michael Real, football represents a microcosm of American social values. For example, it is a game of territory and the winner is the one who gains the most. Football is competitive, played by the clock, and full of "deadlines" and penalties, much like REALIFE. Of course,

"Why are they doing that?"

Drawing by Opie; © 1976, The New Yorker Magazine, Inc.

football also supplies the heroes with whom we can identify. The Super Bowl in particular is a communal festival. Many Super Bowl watchers interviewed admitted that they seldom watched other football games on TV or in REALIFE but felt that they *had* to watch this one because "everyone was doing it, and everybody will be talking about it tomorrow."

This tremendous sense of participation, of being involved with everyone else in experiencing a spectacle, explains a lot about the popularity of football and all sports on TV. ABC figured this out in the late 1960s and began quietly buying up rights to air the Olympics. By the 1970s ABC had pulled off a ratings coup, putting night after night of the games in prime time and outrating the competition.

Though the Olympics had been aired before, ABC showed them with a clearer understanding of TV "form." The TV audience never had to wait for any event. Olympic schedules were altered so that one event would take place here, another five minutes later somewhere else. Cameras were set up at every location and viewers were treated to colorful nonstop action supplemented with "personality profiles." Interviews with Olympic stars were taped in advance but aired just before the crucial moment of "the thrill of victory" or "the agony of defeat."

Sports purists decry such manipulative actions, saying TV has forever altered the true spirit of sport. They point to football games televised in prime time where referees work directly with TV crews, calling "time out" whenever there is need for a commercial. But these critics miss the point: football is not a game played on the gridiron for a few thousand fans, it is a game played on television for millions of fans. Football *is* television, in the truest sense of the word, for many, many viewers. And so are tennis, golf, bowling, basketball, and even baseball.

The Media Experience

I was struck by this at a recent baseball game. It was San Francisco at Cincinnati, and we had choice seats just over home plate. I noticed that the guy next to me had a portable television set and a radio. Both were tuned to the game we were watching. After a few beers I got up the courage to ask him, "Why all the paraphernalia?" He looked up from the TV, turned up the radio, and gazed at the field through his binoculars, "Whadya mean?" he said impatiently. "Why, without this stuff I wouldn't have any idea what was going on."

We need to have REALIFE put through mass media channels before we really feel that we have experienced "the total event." Particularly in sports, the media actually determine the nature of the experience. Media coverage has become more important than the event itself.

The genres of TV combine to give us everything we always wanted in REALIFE and could never have, everything we always wanted in REALIFE but were afraid to have, everything we used to have in REALIFE but lost. In doing this, they have actually become REALIFE, influencing every action we take and every word we say.

The Stepchildren

We have spent a lot of time with the most prominent aspects of commercial television,

but there is a lot more to TV than ABC, NBC, and CBS. These networks and their programs are only a phase that television has been going through since it first invaded our livingrooms. The real destiny of TV may well be locked up in public TV and UHF. These are the "neglected stepchildren" of the medium. They have gone through a long childhood and are just now beginning adolescence. As adults, they, along with exciting new technologies like cable TV and satellites, may revolutionize the very meaning of the medium.

Public TV

During the 1950s there was much excitement about a possible "educational" TV network; one that would provide traditional education materials and create a "university of the air." But educators found they could not tape lectures, put them over the air, and interest the audience, even when they offered college credit. The programs were not visually appealing. Content criteria were borrowed from print, and often too much information was crammed into too short a time.

Although the educational TV idea of the 1950s did not work, there is still public television in the form of noncommercial stations funded by government, corporate, and viewer contributions. In 1970 an alliance was formed, known as the Public Broadcasting Service (PBS). This is not a "network" in the strictest sense, since most programs are distributed through the mail rather than transmitted electronically.

At first glance it would seem that noncommercial stations have a big advantage over their competitors. After all, they offer uninterrupted programs with no hypes for the "living bra" or "iron-poor blood." Yet in every major market, noncommercial viewers total less than 5 percent of the audience. Why?

Public TV stations have not succeeded with the mass audience because their programming "form" does not live up to audience expectations created by the slicker commercial programs. In fact, to a great extent public TV programmers have deliberately avoided appearing "slick." Smooth acting, professional editing, exact lighting, and perfect timing have become the hallmark of commercial prime-time programming. Noncommercial outlets have lagged behind and presented "talking heads" (an industry term to indicate a show with two or three people sitting on stage just talking to one another). For example, picture any public TV station:

Fade in: There are two people seated in a bare room, discussing the economic implications of the currency exchange rate between the United States and Uganda. The lighting is poor, and shadows cross the faces of both participants. They talk back and forth for what seems like hours. Neither has much professional TV experience so both sweat nervously. The cameraperson can't hold the lens still and the picture is occasionally out of focus. There are only two cameras, so we change from close-up to long shot to close-up to long shot.

Since this is all live, we get every mistake and embarrassing redundancy.

Pretty soon we say, "Hey, let's turn this off and go out to a movie."

On the other hand, envision the same program as it might be handled by a top commercial television producer:

Fade in: We see some film of violence in Uganda. Quick cut to violence on the streets of New York City. Suddenly two small green spots appear in the middle of the screen, and as the music builds they get larger and larger—there they are—dollar signs! A relaxed emcee looks straight into the camera; behind him is a revolving set of books, lights, colors, charts, and world map. It whirls by as he says in perfect pear-shaped tones: "Uganda, the United States, and money. What's going on here? We'll find out, right after this message."

We say, "No thanks, Betsy, I know you have free front-row tickets to the Rolling Stones concert, but I can't go just now. I have to stay and see what's happening between the United States and Uganda."

I exaggerate, of course, but I hope you get the point. Our experiences with commercial TV have shown us that visual form is much more important than story content. *All in the Family* scripts were good, but audience reaction was strongest when those incredible exasperated looks crept across Archie's face. Without his uttering a word, we knew he'd had enough of "the dingbat." The popularity of shows like *Streets of San Francisco* and *Hawaii*

Big Bird, one of the "stars" of *Sesame Street,* PBS's highly acclaimed learning experience for children.

5-O had more to do with scene than with script. *Charlie's Angels* did not rise to popularity on the strength of its story line.

Almost any content can interest the mass audience if visual form is attractive. CBS's success with *60 Minutes* in the 1970s proved that the mass audience could be drawn to documentary material if it was packaged in a form that met their expectations. And when public TV does air material of professional (commercial?) quality, it is often a success. English imports like *Upstairs Downstairs* and *Civilisation* had surprisingly strong ratings. *Sesame Street* was a collage of bright colors,

Judy Graubart's gesture tells young viewers that the ''e'' is silent in this scene from *The Electric Company.* Like *Sesame Street, The Electric Company* uses exciting visual form to teach traditional language content to children.

clever editing, and professional production techniques (see 9.3). Its form became a model for commercial children's programs.

If public TV programmers ever want to live up to their name and serve "the public," they are going to have to borrow a lot of techniques from commercial broadcasters. And, of course, such productions can be more expensive than simple "talking heads." This expense means that public TV stations must be funded adequately if they are going to compete for the mass audience. But Congress is getting tired of funding a television network that serves so few citizens; and without adequate funding, no public TV station can be expected to compete for the mass audience. If this vicious cycle continues, there will be no public television in America, and a great opportunity will have been lost.

Not everyone would agree that public TV has failed. Some contend noncommercial stations exist to offer an alternative to commer-cial fare. If only one person is watching, they have succeeded. But again, television is a *mass* medium, and the *mass* audience is what it's there for.

All TV is educational. It teaches us cultural norms, speech patterns, buying habits, and interpersonal strategies. It is possible to teach any social, moral, or political content via TV if programs are packaged properly. So far, only a few attempts have been made to *really* teach using all the facilities television has to offer. *Sesame Street* and *The Electric Company* are the only large-scale examples, and their success may finally shake the educational TV establishment awake (see 9.4).

UHF TV

Of the more than 700 commercial TV stations on the air, about 25 percent are UHF or ultra-high frequency, channels 14–83. UHF also accounts for more than half of the 250 noncommercial stations. When the FCC ended the Freeze on new licenses in 1952, it added 70 new UHF channels to the 12 existing very high frequencies (VHF), channels 2–13. But there were already millions of TV sets in America not equipped to receive the new channels. It wasn't until 1964 that it became mandatory for manufacturers to add UHF. By the late 1970s some commercial UHF stations were earning a profit, particularly those in smaller cities where they were the only outlet for local TV advertising.

Most UHF stations in major markets have had an uphill battle. Many commercial UHF stations are independent, since they entered the market too late to be affiliated with one of the networks. This means they must pay for the programs they air, limiting them to syndicated network shows that ran in prime time years ago, old movies, or locally produced stuff hardly up to network standards. Ten percent of the TV sets in service are still without UHF, and all sets need a special antenna to receive the higher channels. It's just a lot of extra hassle to tune in UHF, so most viewers stay with VHF channels.

UHF has only one distinct advantage: there is a lot more room for growth. Many predict rapid growth for UHF when cable TV comes of age. Viewing patterns could diversify as more channels become available. The pattern would be like radio in the 1950s. Rather than relying on a few mass-audience stations, viewers would seek out those more closely in tune with their own diverse tastes and interests. The FCC requires all cable companies to carry all VHF and UHF stations in a market. Hence cable subscribers can tune in any station with equal ease and every station's reception is equally clear.

CATV: The Gray-Haired Child

Much has been written about the "revolution" cable TV will bring to television. That revolution has been a long time coming, and many broadcast professionals have now decided it will never come.

Currently, there are about 3,000 community antenna TV (CATV) systems in America, and Arbitron TV estimates that more than 10 million homes are hooked up—that's one in seven. As always, we tend to make the new medium do the work of the old, so CATV is used to rebroadcast existing "over the air" stations. Actually, CATV is an entirely new medium with new possibilities.

CATV means the end of bad reception and the end of the three major networks as we know them. It means the beginning of video access for every political, social, and commercial group that desires it. It means a reduction of the huge costs involved in getting your video message over the air. It means a reconstitution of audiovisual entertainment and communications channels along community lines instead of national lines. It means increasing fragmentation of viewer preferences. Coupled with new video retrieval systems, it means an increasing tendency to store vital cultural information in video form, hence a decrease in our reliance on print.

Great, you say. How long till the revolution is upon us? Well, don't rush out to buy a cable company yet. While the FCC has discouraged ownership of CATV franchises by broadcasters, many are owned by corporations that also maintain broadcast interests. Just as we did not move into TV until the networks were sure they would profit by leaving radio behind, so CATV will not "arrive" until broadcasters are ready and can be sure of steady profits.

Most of you think of CATV as a way to get better reception of broadcast stations, so even if you had CATV, your viewing habits would probably not change. When I lived in Honolulu and was hooked up to Oceanic Cablevision, it supplied 32 channels of programming. These included financial news, surf reports, a channel with nothing but old movies from the 1930s, and a "public access" channel that aired poorly produced discussions about homosexuality and Krishna consciousness. What did I watch? The three major networks, of course! My viewing patterns were established long before I moved to Hawaii. If I was going to the beach, I might glance at the surf report, but only for a moment—who wants to watch a surf report for an hour?

So our viewing habits are set. We are *used* to receiving gratification from the form and content we find on network TV. Until that changes, or until CATV programmers realize it and do something, we will continue to be held captive by the three networks.

Satellites

In Hawaii, most network programs are aired at least a week behind schedule. It's rather unnerving; after all, who can enjoy a Christmas special on New Year's Eve, or a baseball game decided last Saturday? The only "live" programs from the rest of the country come via satellite.

At first, local station owners found that only football and a few other sports events provided an audience large enough to pay satellite costs. Yet that is changing. At this writing, two networks are airing their nightly newscast via satellite. Satellite transmissions, once a subject of great promotion, are becoming routine.

Around the world, more than 100 satellites are launched every year, and they do much more for us than help predict the weather. We can already beam our voice messages to anywhere on the globe, thanks to satellites and the telephone. Video messages may be handled the same way in the very near future. The orbiting relay systems already in operation have the potential to reach every country on the globe. When decreasing satellite costs make possible two-way televised communi-

"Naturally, neither Edwina nor myself is your ordinary, run-of-the-mill, average televiewer."

Drawing by Mulligan; © 1976, The New Yorker Magazine, Inc.

cation, we will be able to bypass traditional "lines" of communication, i.e., the networks.

Naturally, the networks don't plan to sit by and watch this happen. Former CBS president Frank Stanton has suggested that networks pool their resources and come up with their own satellites if they are to continue to be a force in televised communication. In any event, it is clear that satellites will help shape our communication future in ways we can only imagine today.

Issues and Answers

Who's in Charge Here?

Eric Sevareid has pointed out: "Until a few years ago every American assumed he possessed an equal and God-given expertise on three things: politics, religion, and the weather. Now a fourth has been added—television." Television, like the weather, is some-

thing that everybody talks about and few people do anything about.

It's hard for the average TV consumer to understand how so many poor-quality programs get on the air. It's equally hard to understand how a station pledged to operate in the *public* "interest, convenience, and necessity" can devote so much air time to commercials touting the *private* enterprises of thousands of sponsors. For that matter, a sizable minority of TV's potential audience finds nothing in the medium that interests them, so they watch little or none at all.

But what can the public do about such matters? And isn't the FCC supposed to act as a watchdog over TV stations and make sure they are programming in the public "interest, convenience, and necessity"? Why isn't the FCC doing its job?

Some of the most salient criticism of network television practices has come from Nicholas Johnson, a former FCC commissioner during the Johnson administration. His book *How to Talk Back to Your Television Set,*

A book for all television viewers.

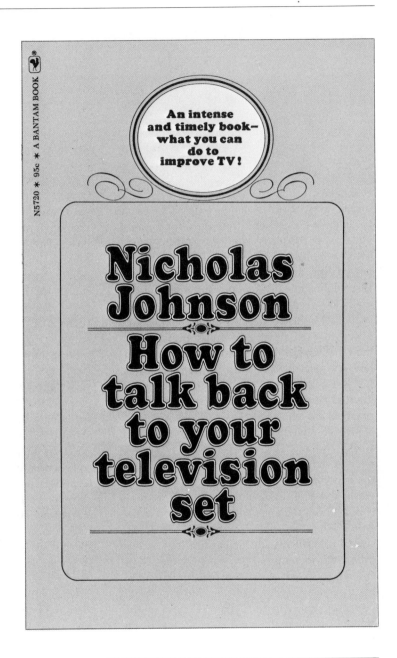

which deals with the whole issue of who really controls television, will never *really* be dated as long as broadcast license procedures stay the same (see 9.5). And they have changed very little since 1934, when the present system was set up.

As with radio, TV channels have practically become the property of the licensees. Only on the rarest of occasions does the FCC refuse to renew a license, and then only for flagrant violation of broadcast law. More often "warnings" will be issued or licenses will be renewed for one year instead of the usual three. Johnson's book points out that there is really no deep dark conspiracy between the broadcast industry and the agency that is supposed to regulate it. It's much more subtle than that. Over the years, friendships develop; lawyers meet lawyers and go out to dinner. It's just a lot more "pleasant" if licenses are granted as a matter of course and a lot more practical as well.

License renewals involve mounds of paper work, and the FCC does not have a large enough staff to review every word or to monitor every program. In addition to the paper work, the FCC budget must sustain a small core of field engineers whose job it is to make sure stations are not straying from their assigned frequencies and power limits. There is little time to monitor program content; it is enough to worry about outright violations of broadcast law, without getting into gray areas like program "quality." The FCC takes the stations' word that "good works" are being done for the community.

Johnson concludes that if the public wants change, it is going to have to invest its own time and energy, do the necessary research, and submit findings to the FCC, the press, and anyone else who will listen. He suggests that though the FCC responds to pressure from the broadcast industry, it also responds to pressure "from anybody." Ralph Nader has shown just how much impact citizens' groups can have. The 1970s were an era when citizen lobbies made significant inroads into corporate America. Many groups have used the courts in their quest, and class action suits have appeared with greater frequency. Perhaps it is a fantasy to envision citizens banding together to sue local stations for presenting inferior programs, but after all, the local station is legally pledged to operate in your "interest, convenience, and necessity." If you feel that it's breaking that pledge or could be doing a lot better, there are ways to bring about change.

Letters to the local station are not thrown away but are carefully filed. You will get a response, particularly if you mail a carbon copy to the FCC, which also keeps all letters it receives. This material is reviewed when the station comes up for license renewal. Be as specific as you can about your complaint; write one letter for each practice or program you find objectionable. Sponsors are particularly sensitive to letters of this type.

Your letters take on increased significance when you have collected data to back your value judgments. Is your local station airing too much advertising? Get out a stopwatch: just exactly how many minutes of commercials are aired per hour? Is enough time devoted to public service announcements? What about the balance between news, entertainment, and other types of programs? A quick check of the TV schedule will tell you how many hours per week are devoted to various program types.

Many women's groups brought about change by taking apart the content of the shows themselves. Are minorities fairly represented? Remember that even if a show is piped in by the network, *your local station* is responsible. The FCC does not license networks; it licenses local stations.

Most stations are members of the National Association of Broadcasters (NAB) and as such subscribe to the NAB code, which has rules of conduct governing news/editorial practices and limitations on commercials. Unfortunately, the NAB has no staff to monitor stations, but again you can be of service. It's no secret that many stations operate in direct violation of the code by running excessive amounts of commercials and making few attempts to bring diverse programming to their viewers. If a station is violating the code, the NAB should be notified and the seal of approval withdrawn.

There are many organizations that have been formed by citizens determined to improve television offerings. All provide literature and suggestions about what you can do to improve TV.

All of this may sound like a lot of work and bother, and perhaps it is. Still, one letter can sometimes make all the difference. Take heart from the story of John Banzahaf, a lawyer who tired of seeing all those cigarette commercials on TV in the 1960s. He reasoned, if stations are forced to give various political partisans "equal time," why weren't antismoking forces given air time, too?

He challenged all stations indirectly but narrowed his focus on one. He authenticated his claim by monitoring New York's WCBS-TV and citing specific commercials. That one letter, carefully documented, opened the door for a new FCC ruling; stations had a responsibility to air the "other side" of the smoking question. Millions and millions of dollars worth of broadcast time was offered to antismoking groups who produced a series of rather clever antismoking ads. (Remember "Johnny Smoke"?) Eventually, of course, *all* cigarette commercials were banned from radio and television. And it all started with one letter.

Talking back to your TV set may seem like a revolutionary task, but it is something that every media consumer has the *right* and the *responsibility* to do. The concept that the airwaves belong to everyone is beautiful, but often our airwaves, like our beaches, forests, and other natural resources, are misused. Only the "rightful owners" can put a stop to it before the damage is irreparable.

Queries and Concepts

1. Skip school and stay home pretending that you are coming down with a cold.

Turn on the TV set at 9:00 A.M. and leave it on all day no matter what. Make notes about what you find. Discuss.

2. Check the TV schedule for the total hours of programming available in your market. How many of those hours are network feed? How many are devoted to news and public affairs programs?

3. Enter the world of children's programming; pick a Saturday morning, turn on the set, and tough it out. Can you spot the shows that appeal to specific age groups? Ask your little brothers, sisters, or neighborhood kids about their favorite programs. Their answers may startle you.

4. What is the total amount of weekend TV time devoted to sports programs? Would you rather watch a favorite sport on TV, view it in person, or directly participate in it?

5. Do you have cable TV in your area? How much does it cost per month? What does the cable provide that broadcast TV cannot? What percentage of homes in your area are on cable? Many cable outlets offer you the chance to produce, direct, and star in your own TV show. Investigate.

6. Compare and contrast a random hour of public TV and an hour of commercial TV. What could commercial programmers learn from public programmers and vice versa?

7. You have just been appointed chairperson of the FCC. What immediate changes would you make to improve the "quality" of TV programming? Remember the public "interest, convenience, and necessity" guidelines.

Readings and References

Daytime TV and the Common Cold; On the Fringe: Day Shows and Late Shows

Charles Sopkin
Seven Glorious Days, Seven Fun-Filled Nights. New York: Simon & Schuster, 1968.
This bible of commercial TV complaints was created in seven days and nights, but the author never rested. Entertaining and informative.

Soap Operas

There are several magazines like *Soap Opera Digest* that print the plots along with real-life facts about their stars.

Game Shows; Talk Shows

TV Guide is a good source for current trends in these areas. You'll find it included in the *Popular Periodical Index.* Some back copies are available from the Triangle Publications, Radnor, Pennsylvania, 19088.

Children's Shows

Ray Brown
Children and Television. Beverly Hills: Sage Publications, 1976.
A thoughtful empirical analysis of the impact of children's TV programs. Up to date and full of insight, this anthology covers all the bases—violence, advertising, and social trends.

Sports

Michael Real
"Super Bowl: Mythic Spectacle." *Journal of Communication,* Winter 1975, pp. 31–43.

The Media Experience

Michael R. Real
Mass Mediated Culture. Englewood Cliffs, N.J.: Prentice-Hall, 1977.
The author discusses a number of mediated experiences including Disneyland, Marcus Welby, Billy Graham, and others. Fine introductory chapter on the significance of mass mediated culture. Highly recommended.

The Stepchildren

There are dozens of books available on cable and public television, but not much on UHF. I chose those listed below because, when taken together, they represent some rather exciting ideas about the possibilities of the "new media."

Brenda Maddox
Beyond Babel. Boston: Beacon Press, 1972.
There are sections on satellites, cable, telephones, and much more in this down-to-earth, descriptive work. It is balanced between hard-headed reality and a kind of unorthodox optimism. Enjoyable reading, packed with information.

Barry N. Schwartz, ed.
Human Connection and the New Media. Englewood Cliffs, N.J.: Prentice-Hall, 1973.
A most daring and provocative collection of essays on the possibilities of video tape, cable, and media language. Section three, "Impact of Media," is a must, especially Schwartz's three-page "The Electronic Person." This is the most confusing and startling collection of probes since McLuhan.

Sloan Commission on Cable Communications
On the Cable: The Television of Abundance. New York: McGraw-Hill, 1971.
The most complete work yet on cable TV. Lots of facts and figures, plus sections on history, impact, ownership, regulation, and community. Slow reading.

Public TV

Carnegie Commission on Educational Television

Public Television. New York: Harper & Row, 1967.

The Carnegie Commission spent 18 months reviewing the status of public television before issuing this impressive report. Their conclusion ("a well-financed, well-directed educational television system . . . must be brought into being if the American public is to be served") is as convincing now as it was more than a decade ago.

Issues and Answers: Who's in Charge Here?

Nicholas Johnson
How to Talk Back to Your Television Set. New York: Bantam Books, 1970.

This will be the book people look back on in 30 or 40 years and say: "This is where it all began. People actually started taking charge of their own media." A must.

Nicholas Johnson
Test Pattern for Living. New York: Bantam Books, 1972.

A follow-up to *How to Talk Back to Your Television Set,* with updates on some cases that were still being decided when the original was written. Johnson has become more philosophical and introspective in this second volume, and ties most of what goes on in America to "Big Business, Big Broadcasting, and Big Government." Stimulating.

Harry J. Skornia
Television and Society: An Inquest and Agenda for Improvement. New York: McGraw-Hill, 1965.

Though dated in parts, this is living proof that things change very little in the world of TV programming. Many a student has become an outraged critic of modern TV practices after reading it. There are sections on leadership, regulations, ratings, economics, and effects. The most cohesive indictment of television ever.

10

Film: The Celluloid Hero

**People tell me that the movies should be more like
real life. I disagree. It is real life that
should be more like the movies.—Walter Winchell**

America's Sweetheart

Among my most prized possessions is the black and white photo of Mary Pickford in 10.1. Mary was "America's cinema sweetheart" during the 1920s. She was the picture of innocence. Her blonde hair flowed down her back and fell to her shoulders in long curls. She *created* innocence; she planted an image in my mind of what innocence was. I'm still looking for Mary Pickford, but she doesn't exist. She's now a wrinkled old lady of 85. Still, the young star lives on because I rush to the theater to see her pictures, which were made decades before I was born. On the silver screen her innocence was captured forever.

The Audiovisual Record

Perhaps the most important thing to remember about film is that it started a complete audiovisual history of the world. We see evidence of that today. There are TV shows set in the 1930s, the 1940s, the 1950s, and so on, but none in the 1920s . . . why? Because we have formed very few ideas about what the 1920s were like. We can go back to film records of 1930 to look at the suits and listen to the voices. Film first provided a *multisensory* record of western civilization. That record began in 1927 with the release of *The Jazz Singer*, the first "talkie"—or film containing a vocal track. (Actually only a portion of it was in sound.) It combined sight with sound to give an *audiovisual replica* of its content.

To be sure, *The Jazz Singer* was not a film of the President or a documentary about life in the United States. Like most mass media content *The Jazz Singer* was part of popular culture. The movie was designed to give the audience an entertainment package it would find appealing. As such it provides a record of popular taste and, coincidentally, gives us our first multisensory historical record.

Two years later the stock market crashed and the Great Depression began. *The Jazz Singer* provides a valuable document of the carefree life and entertainment that existed before the Depression.

Life Is Like a Movie

Film is larger than life. It illustrates the values we hold most dearly. There is love and romance, the hero and the heroine. Film provides us with a giant mirror—a reflection of the values, the half-truths, and the ideals of society.

It does this because writers, directors, and producers are successful at tapping into our personal emotional treasure chests and translating them to a film. We then "buy them back" at the box office. The more closely a film approximates our own mixed bag of myths and values, the more likely we are to see it and recommend it to others.

Mary Pickford, America's sweet-heart.

Fear is a universal emotion. We have all been afraid at one time or another, afraid we were going to die some horrible, lingering, and unjust death. The "master of suspense" Alfred Hitchcock successfully plays to these fears through the story on the screen. There is universal audience identification with fear and that translates to box-office success. That success has turned Hitchcock into one of the largest legends in filmdom.

Likewise *Gone with the Wind* played on our romantic emotions. Clark Gable's Rhett Butler

Copyright 1973, G.B. Trudeau. Distributed by Universal Press Syndicate.

was the rogue who had a way with women. Vivian Leigh was Scarlett O'Hara, the beautiful, spoiled belle of the old South whose star-crossed love affair with Ashley Wilkes was never to be. We wanted to jump into the screen and plead: "Oh Scarlett, can't you see it is Rhett who really loves you?" But it was too late—Rhett was gone and Scarlett's life was ruined.

These are universal emotions—fear, love, disappointment—but few of us have experienced such total ruin, complete love, realistic fear, and utter violence. The film represents universal emotions but "blows them up" until they are larger than life. When we come upon an experience in REALIFE that is profound, we think of movies. "This is just like a movie," we say. Our ideals—our very way of perceiving intense experience—are shaped by what we have seen on film (see 10.2).

In F. Scott Fitzgerald's final novel, *The Last Tycoon*, an admirer marvels at the power a movie producer, Stahr, has had over her life: "Some of my more romantic ideas actually stemmed from pictures. . . . It's more than possible that some of the pictures which Stahr himself conceived had shaped me into what I was."

Indeed the power of the filmmaker to shape our notions about intense experience, to provide a series of fictional experiences through which we funnel REALIFE is unrivaled in all

Scarlett visits Rhett in his prison cell shortly after the end of the war. These love scenes represent our very definition of romance in America.

From the MGM release GONE WITH THE WIND © 1939 Selznick International Pictures, Inc. Copyright renewed 1967 by Metro-Goldwyn-Mayer Inc.

of mass communication. Somehow, what we see "up there" takes on an inexplicable significance.

At first glance it's easy to make a distinction between REALIFE, the events that happen to us directly, and those we experience in "reel life" via film. If I asked you what the difference was, you would probably respond rather huffily that you could "certainly tell the difference between fact and fiction." However, it's really not that simple.

Since all mass media play a large part in formulating our attitudes, beliefs, and ideals, they act as conduits through which our REALIFE experiences must pass. For example, most of us have never experienced major crime firsthand, so we formulate our ideas about these types of experiences from what we see in films or on television. If we actually do witness a crime in REALIFE, we can't help comparing it to what we have seen on mass media. We might even *react* to a given situa-

Time Line: The History of Film in America

1820s Peter Mark Roget and John Paris in England conduct experiments and publish findings involving persistence of vision.

1839 Louis Daguerre in France develops a workable system of still photography.

1882 Dr. E. J. Marey, a French physiologist, develops a photographic "gun" that takes 12 pictures per second.

1888 Thomas Edison and assistant William Dickson develop the first workable motion picture camera.

1895 Auguste and Louis Lumière perfect a projection system and exhibit films to a paying public. The theater is born.

1900 Edison, Biograph, and Vitagraph are competing companies in the new film industry.

1903 Porter releases *The Great Train Robbery.*

1905–10 Era of the nickelodeons.

1906 British inventors Edward R. Turner and G. Albert Smith devise Kinemacolor, the first practical natural color film process.

1909 The Motion Picture Patents Company is formed.

1915 D. W. Griffith's *Birth of a Nation* becomes the most successful film in the medium's history.

1922 Technicolor is introduced.

1927 *The Jazz Singer* is the first "talkie."

1929 *On with the Show* is the first all-talking color film.

1930 After just three years, almost all new films are talkies.

1933 Fred Astaire and Ginger Rogers team up for *Flying Down to Rio* and become film's most successful couple.

1939 *Gone with the Wind* is the film of the year, sweeping the Oscar awards.

1941 *Citizen Kane*, perhaps the greatest American film of the sound era, is released.

1946 Film's biggest box office year; 90 million Americans are going to the movies every week.

1950s The film audience is younger than ever. Many adults give up films to watch television.

1960 Alfred Hitchcock's *Psycho* is released.

1969 *Easy Rider* typifies youth-oriented films with a message.

1970s Disaster films *Towering Inferno, Earthquake,* and others are successful.

1972 X-rated *Deep Throat* pioneers pornography for the mass audience.

1975 *Jaws* becomes the most successful film of all time.

1975 Robert Altman's *Nashville* breaks new ground in entertainment films with the vignette approach.

1977 *Star Wars* breaks theater attendance records.

1978 A rash of movies involving popular music appear: *American Hot Wax, FM, Sgt. Pepper's Lonely Hearts Club Band,* and *The Buddy Holly Story* follow on the heels of *Saturday Night Fever.*

tion by imitating behaviors of those we have seen in a film or on TV.

Our notions about romantic love are almost completely derived from mass media, formed by what we have read and seen. All of us are waiting for that great scene when we will take that special person in our arms for the first kiss. It will be a long, smooth, beautiful kiss. Everything will be perfect. The skyrockets will explode and we will go off and live "happily ever after" just like in the movies.

The problem with this is that REALIFE can't always measure up to the expectations we have developed by consuming mass media. More often when you take a special someone in your arms, you find that person is in the middle of a peanut butter candy, your mouths are a different size, or your braces get stuck together.

The Magic Lantern

Like all mass media, film has two component parts, *form* and *content*. The form of film involves hardware components, the mechanical phenomena that make it go. The content is the story, plot line, and cast of characters that deliver the "message" to us. When we experience moving pictures, we seldom think of the form but (as with all mass media) concentrate on content to derive the message.

Moving pictures do not actually move, but they seem to because of a physiological process called "persistence of vision." When a series of still pictures is flashed before your eyes faster than you can perceive each one individually, your mind runs them together, creating the illusion of motion. Perhaps you can recall seeing cartoon books that instructed you to thumb through rapidly and "watch the characters come to life." The characters appeared to move through persistence of vision.

This was discovered almost 2,000 years ago by the astronomer Ptolemy, but it was Thomas Edison who put it to work. He invented the incandescent bulb, a light so strong it could project pictures on a wall, making them visible to a large audience (see 10.4). This is how "moving" pictures differed from the other media forms using persistence of vision which were already popular in the late 19th century. Kinetoscopes and vitascopes were one-person peep shows usually found in a penny arcade. You put in a penny and turned a crank. When turned at the proper speed, the pictures appeared to move.

In the late 1880s, one of Edison's assistants, William Dickson, developed a camera and a projecting device using the new bulb. His first effort at filmmaking was not exactly an aesthetic masterpiece; it lasted 15 seconds and recorded a man sneezing. Yet there were many films with equally dull content that played to large audiences around the turn of the century. Such is often the case with a new medium. The new form carries it for a while; refinement of content comes later. (Ask your parents about the early years of television. They'll tell you that there was only one sta-

Thomas Edison with an early version of the motion picture projector.

tion, and when they saw their first television they just stared and stared. It didn't matter what was on the screen, Howdy Doody, a test pattern, anything.)

Those early moving pictures lasted only five to seven minutes and were pretty dull. Perhaps it was seven minutes of random scenes at a downtown location or the sun rising in a cornfield. People flocked to see these new moving pictures. The admission price was usually a nickel and the theaters were called "nickelodeons."

Many who have written of this era have romanticized it or found it "cute," overlooking the seamier side of things. Albert E. Smith, who helped found Vitagraph (one of the early motion picture companies), recalls things a little more realistically. There was tremendous competition among early filmmakers to cash in on this new revenue source. Smith admits to "pirating" pictures of major boxing matches by sneaking in a huge camera under his overcoat. He "faked" pictures of major battles of the Spanish-American War and passed them off to an unsuspecting public as the real thing. At the same time Smith tells fascinating stories of legitimate photographic missions. He claims to have filmed the charge up San

Juan Hill with Teddy Roosevelt, who became the first American President introduced to the people via a nonprint mass medium, the film newsreel. Smith was filming a speech by President McKinley when suddenly a shot rang out. The President had been mortally wounded and it was all on film.

Often the most vicious film battles were fought in the courtroom by competing companies vying for patent rights to cameras and projector components. They "borrowed" on one another's inventions shamelessly. For years Edison felt he should receive *all* of the revenues from motion pictures, claiming his inventions and patents had made them possible. By the time he organized a court fight, the situation was out of hand. Too many new improvements had come along. In the end a collective was formed and agreements were reached among the major patent holders. They formed the Motion Picture Patents Company (MPPC) and "pooled" the use of all patents, giving any additional benefits to the inventors. All movie companies were required to pay a flat fee each time they shot a film. Edison held the largest number of patents and eventually his share of pool funds reflected it.

Some filmmakers were unhappy with this agreement, particularly smaller companies that operated on very small budgets and preferred to pay no fees at all. Their solution was to leave the East and go so far away that the MPPC would have a hard time tracking them down. Since all films had to be shot outdoors (indoor lighting for film had not been per-

fected), they decided to locate where there was sun all year round. Most ended up in a remote farm area just north of Los Angeles, called Hollywood. Here was the ideal location for filmmaking, a quiet sunny area close to a major West Coast town. But it wasn't quiet for long. From this farming community would spring the hopes and dreams of America.

Hollywood became a fairy tale land. Even today, for all of its tackiness and vulgarity, Hollywood remains synonymous with adjectives like beautiful, thrilling, amazing, and spectacular. You can still walk down Hollywood Boulevard reading the names of the stars on the sidewalks, or buy a "map to the homes of the stars." Films, movie companies, and stars may come and go, but the myth of Hollywood remains, kept alive by Americans everywhere who insist on having a real geographic place to accompany the fantasies they have experienced on film.

The Quiet Years

The birthdate of significant "content" in film is generally regarded as 1903. An American filmmaker, Edwin S. Porter, had experimented with moving pictures that told a story in his *The Life of an American Fireman* the year before, but it was quite by accident. Now he set out specifically to construct a "story" film—one that would convey a complete plot, not simply capture an existing event. Porter felt that by using stage actors, a script, and *joining disparate*

Director D. W. Griffith at work.

pieces of film together he could convey a story to the audience.

It hardly seems revolutionary now, but it was the first time it had been done. Many were skeptical about such a venture, but Porter went ahead anyway and his *The Great Train Robbery* was filmed and released. It was a western and the plot was pretty flimsy. In the final scene a robber shoots a gun directly into the audience for no apparent reason. Yet the film was a tremendous commercial success, paving the way for more complex subject matter.

Twelve years later, film took its greatest leap forward. Former Porter film actor, D. W. Griffith, had shot a number of short films with tremendous box-office success. Many were based on American history—pioneering, the West, Indians, and the like. When Griffith decided to make a grandiose film, one subject came to mind. The Civil War was the perfect historical backdrop because it was the most turbulent time in American history, a time when conflicting ideologies were at a peak and

unprecedented violence swept the land. But Griffith could not capture such a magnificent event while confined to the existing "form" of film. He expanded it to fit, using a large screen to reproduce marvelously photographed outdoor battle scenes. There were moving shots, extreme close-ups, and a host of other film innovations (see 10.5). *Birth of a Nation* was issued complete with a score to be performed by a full orchestra. No one had ever experienced anything like it. It became a huge box-office success and was the most popular film ever until 1939 when another Civil War epic *(Gone with the Wind)* took its place.

So advanced was *Birth of a Nation* that almost all film critics agree it was the most influential silent film ever made. It is difficult for students viewing the film today to assess its impact properly for a number of reasons. The film's heroes are members of the Ku Klux Klan. (This reflects Griffith's own racial prejudices and his rural southern background.) Though the content is socially archaic, the achievement of form remains as brilliant today as it was more than a half century ago.

Griffith continued making epic films. His next effort, *Intolerance*, one of the most expensive silent films ever made, was on an even grander scale. It contained four interwoven stories and the film skipped from one to the next. That is a common technique in today's cinema, but one that confused the 1916 audience. Griffith was ahead of his time and he couldn't take the audience with him. In 1948, he died alone and almost forgotten. It was only after his death that his film genius was truly recognized.

While moviegoers of the quiet years flocked to see short comedy films with stars like Charlie Chaplin and the Keystone Kops, epic films flourished, too. Audiences now were used to full-length feature films like *Cleopatra*, *Ben Hur*, and *The Ten Commandments*. These names may be familiar to you, since remakes were done for the sound era.

This tendency to redo existing material did not start when sound came to film. The content of film in the quiet years was largely borrowed from books and stories that were popular at the time. Griffith's *Birth of a Nation* was taken from the novel *The Clansman*. As the practice became commonplace, many discovered that stories lifted directly from print were simply not the same on the screen. We know now that they couldn't be. Whenever we transfer content from one medium to another, it must change to accommodate the new form. But in the quiet years there was little radio and no television, and audiences were not used to the process of adaptation. According to film critic Elinor Glyn, the transferral process was often painful:

All authors, living or dead, famous or obscure, shared the same fate. Their stories were re-written and completely altered either by the stenographers and continuity girls of the scenario department, or by the Assistant Director and his lady-love, or by the leading lady, or by anyone else who happened to pass through the studio; and even when at last after infinite struggle a scene was shot which bore some resemblance to the original story it was certain to be left out in the cutting-room or pared away to such an extent that all meaning which it might once have had was lost.

The Star Is Born

But critics and authors had yet to learn what the public knew instinctively: story content was only part of the film phenomenon. The film audience was becoming less concerned with *what* and more concerned with *who*. The star system was born.

Early silent film stars came from all walks of life, some like Charlie Chaplin had enormous talent, others had only tremendous *visual* appeal. Most popular of all were those who projected a romantic, sexual image. Actors Douglas Fairbanks and Rudolph Valentino were cast as romantic rogues, while actresses Lillian Gish (see 10.6) and Mary Pickford projected virginal innocence and

Actress Lillian Gish was one of the first to become a ''star'' through the film medium.

Miss Lillian Gish
Triangle.

breathtaking beauty. Soon, titles of films appeared at the bottom of the marquee—at the top was the name of the film's best-known actor or actress. People began to ask each other: ''Have you seen the new Rudolph Valentino film? *Story* had been replaced by *star.*

Cults grew around the great stars and the public became hungry for details of their lives. Fan clubs abounded. The studios were more than happy to cooperate, sensing that a bevy of stars under contract meant box-office success and financial reward. What they did not foresee were the days when stars would make exorbitant salary demands and become ''free agents'' moving from one studio to the next. Every major film studio in America was built on the star system, yet it was that same system that eventually led to a decline in big-studio control of the industry.

The Movies Learn to Talk

In the late 1920s my father played the organ for the silent pictures in one of Los Angeles's major movie houses. He made $60 a week, which was more money than he had ever seen in his life. He drove a brand new Jewett and, needless to say, this put him at the top of the social heap at Manual Arts High School.

But suddenly there was tragedy. A theater down the street began showing *The Jazz Singer*, and overnight, as he recalls it, the lines in front of his theater dwindled while people waited for hours to see (and hear) the talkies. The theater owner assured him it was "just a fad." The quality of silent pictures produced during the late 1920s was fantastic, whereas the talkies were crude and simplistic by comparison. Surely the audience would soon come to its senses! When it didn't, my father found himself out of a job and playing in bars for two dollars a night. He was understandably bitter; he had to sell the Jewett and for years refused to go into a theater to see a talkie.

Technological alterations in mass communication can often move so fast that even those closest to media are unable to fathom them. The same producers who had been successful with silent pictures were bewildered with talkies. Studios that got into sound early flourished; others perished. Stars who had commanded five-figure salaries were suddenly unwanted because their voices did not match the voices audiences had created from their visual image. As we have seen, 20 years later radio and television reversed the process. Stars who had been only a "voice" in radio could not make it in a medium where their visual image did not match audience expectations.

Such is the nature of the mass audience. Adulation for the star is often a mile wide and an inch deep. Perhaps this is because stars are part of the dream world and the stuff that dreams are made of is very easily destroyed.

Critics of the 1920s were quick to condemn the talkies. Paul Rotha, in *The Film till Now* (1930), wrote:

It may be concluded that a film in which the speech and sound effects are perfectly synchronised and coincide with their visual images on the screen is absolutely contrary to the aim of the cinema. It is a degenerate and misguided attempt to destroy the real use of the film and cannot be accepted as coming within the true boundaries of the cinema. Not only are dialogue films wasting the time of intelligent directors, but they are harmful and detrimental to the culture of the public. The sole aim of their producers is financial gain, and for this reason they are to be resented.

But the public wasn't listening to the critics; it was listening to the sound tracks of the new movies. By 1930 virtually all films appearing for general public release were talkies. The change was sudden, complete, and final.

Talkie producers found that material suitable for silent films did not always work with sound. So they looked to the stage for new stories and fresh faces whose voices were a proven success. This led to a fresh crop of stars with Broadway and other theatrical experience, including Fredric March, James Cagney, Spencer Tracy, and Fred Astaire. A precious few, like Greta Garbo and Marie

Dressler, survived the transition from silent to talkie because they had stage experience and their voices were much as silent film fans had imagined.

1930s: The Sound and the Cinema

The emphasis on sound led to the tremendous success of the musical. After all, now that pictures could talk, why couldn't they sing? Sing they did; most major studios produced a series of musical extravaganzas, each more lush and spectacular than the last. MGM's *That's Entertainment* (Parts 1 and 2) released in the early 1970s is the most complete film record of that wonderful genre which began during the period. Again it was not the story that was important, but the grandeur of it all.

No single couple dominated entertainment films of the 1930s more than Fred Astaire and Ginger Rogers. They first appeared together in 1933 in *Flying Down to Rio*. Then came a string of box-office smashes including *The Gay Divorcee, Follow the Fleet,* and the most famous *Top Hat.* Plots were secondary in the Astaire-Rogers films; emphasis was on the dance numbers sprinkled throughout. New dance steps were usually introduced at the end of each film, and though the formula was redundant, audiences of the 1930s never seemed to tire of it. Most critics argue that the last "great" Astaire-Rogers film was *Carefree* in 1938. There, for the first time, Fred kissed

Ginger on screen and that seemed to break the spell. Their later films seemed to have lost the magic.

The 1930s films of the Marx Brothers draw large audiences even today. The zany brothers were never concerned with plot. In fact, Groucho would often leave the story altogether while he communicated directly with the audience: "I told you this story would never get beyond the second reel," he'd say impishly and delve back into the action. There were a number of obligatory production numbers in Marx films, but the brothers seemed to enjoy doing them. Sound suited the Marxes perfectly, for they delivered an avalanche of dialogue filled with double and triple entendres.

Visually, of course, the Marx films were unrivaled. There were sinks hidden beneath coats, horns and harps under the table, smashed hats and cream pies. The secret of the Marx success involved their ability to poke fun at established authority figures. Kings and queens, dimestore employers, underworld bosses, rich society matrons, and military commanders were all treated with the same irreverent humor (see 10.7). Yet for all the symbolic and social implications of their films, their success is summarized in one word by film critic William Bayer: "outrageous."

The 1930s also saw a curious public preoccupation with crime. Actors like James Cagney and Edward G. Robinson were filmed fighting and killing one another in an endless parade of St. Valentine's Day Massacres. Perhaps this

Two scenes from *A Night at the Opera*, one of the Marx Brothers zaniest films. Their form-over-content approach to films has been one reason that their popularity has not diminished in 50 years.

From the MGM release A NIGHT AT THE OPERA © 1935 Metro-Goldwyn-Mayer Corporation. Copyright renewed 1962 by Metro-Goldwyn-Mayer Inc.

From the MGM release A NIGHT AT THE OPERA © 1935 Metro-Goldwyn-Mayer Corporation. Copyright renewed 1962 by Metro-Goldwyn-Mayer Inc.

is one time when mass communication simply reflected a public longing for justice. While hundreds of successful pictures like *Little Caesar* and *Public Enemy* ended with gangsters getting their just deserts, real public enemies Al Capone and Machine Gun Kelly seemed to be, literally, getting away with murder. Nevertheless these films were often criticized

A disillusioned Scarlett surveys battle casualties in this scene from *Gone with the Wind.* The Civil War has been the backdrop for several popular American films including Griffith's *Birth of a Nation.*

From the MGM release GONE WITH THE WIND © 1939 Selznick International Pictures, Inc. Copyright renewed 1967 by Metro-Goldwyn-Mayer.

for showing criminals in a sympathetic light and encouraging gangster hero worship among young people.

Gone with the Wind

The one element that seemed to thread through all the successful films of the era was escape from reality. There were few films about REALIFE because life during the Depression wasn't very entertaining. Films offered an escape from poverty and worry to a world where there was singing, dancing, laughter, justice, and fair play. The most successful film of the 1930s came during the final year of that decade and incorporated all of

these themes and more. So powerful was the fictional world of *Gone with the Wind* that it has entertained generation after generation.

Clark Gable, who played Rhett Butler, and Leslie Howard, who played the long-suffering Ashley Wilkes, were both well-known actors in 1939. Both had come into movies at the beginning of the talkies, and Howard had distinguished himself on the stage before that. On the other hand, Vivian Leigh was a relative newcomer to the screen, and her chemistry with Gable was responsible, in part, for the huge success of the film (see 10.8).

In the last analysis it really is her film; she dominates throughout and is seen sobbing the obligatory moral message in the final scene: "Tomorrow is another day!" It's easy to forgive this kind of simplistic moralizing given the prevailing standards of the time. When Rhett finally walks out on her and says: "Frankly, dear, I don't give a damn," it sends shivers up your spine. It's hard to imagine now, but the line was tremendously controversial at the time. "Damn" just wasn't said in motion pictures tailored for the mass audience.

Gone with the Wind is durable because it had everything. The mustachioed Clark Gable, the innocent but ruthless Scarlett, the "goody-goody" Melanie Wilkes, and the lovable stereotyped black mammy. Then there were the Civil War, the carpetbaggers, the Yankees, and the burning of Atlanta. The film was taken from the best-selling book of the time and produced by David O. Selznick, who spared no expense on lavish sets and period costumes. It was directed by Victor Fleming, whose *Wizard of Oz*, produced the same year, was also a classic. In short, *Gone with the Wind*, milked every cinematic cliché and success formula that had emerged in the first 40 years of the medium. It stands as a classic for in it we can see pieces of every one of its successful predecessors.

1940s: Citizen Kane and the American Dream

The 1940s was a period of abrupt change for many Americans. Along with increasing prosperity came a devastating war. The country was changing faster than ever before. Likewise, the era was a period of abrupt change in American film and in film all over the world.

In the beginning, there was *Citizen Kane*. Released in 1941, it is considered by many to be the most important American film ever made in the sound era. Like *Birth of a Nation*, it *advanced* the state of the art by developing entirely new ways of delivering a significant message on film.

In many ways the story of *Citizen Kane* is the story of one man, Orson Welles. He produced, directed, supervised casting, co-authored the script, and starred. All this is particularly impressive when you consider that the film was completed just in time to celebrate his twenty-sixth birthday.

Welles had become a national celebrity in 1938 with his *War of the Worlds* broadcast (see Chapter 6). He received several offers to do films, but according to film critic Pauline Kael, he held out until he could get *complete* artistic freedom and an ample budget. RKO finally gave him that opportunity in 1940 and he moved to Hollywood, bringing his *Mercury Theatre of the Air* cast with him. The young sensation looked over the facilities at RKO and exclaimed: "This is the biggest choo-choo train a kid ever had."

It took Welles less than six months to film *Citizen Kane*, and he did it for less than $1 million. The plot was a fictionalized version of the life of William Randolph Hearst, the newspaper tycoon whose reputation for sensationalism and subterfuge was well known to the public at the time. It's not a particularly flattering portrait, and Hearst threatened to sue RKO if it was released. The studio held out, hoping the film would catch on and become a money-maker. It didn't, at least not right away. Reviews of the innovative film were mixed and public response was lukewarm. It took many years for RKO to recoup its initial investment.

For all of its artistic virtue, *Citizen Kane* was not really a "personal statement" in the later tradition of Fellini or Bergman. Rather it was a film designed to entertain the mass audience. It tells the relatively simple story of a newspaper tycoon. In the best tradition of the entertainment film, the tycoon rises to the top and is transformed from a brash, idealistic playboy to a bitter, defeated old man. Sounds like grist for any one of hundreds of film. What made *Citizen Kane* so different?

Plot The film does not tell the complete story but gives us glimpses into the life of Charles Foster Kane. It actually *begins* with Kane's death and works backwards. A reporter from a news weekly interviews those closest to Kane and pieces the story together. Incidentally, the opening few minutes of *Citizen Kane* are done as a newsreel: "News on the March" (an imitation of the "March of Time" movie newsreels of the 1940s). This gave the audi-

ence the necessary background and it was so like an actual newsreel that many thought it was real (shades of *War of the Worlds!*).

Sound Since Welles's background was in radio, he *knew* the power of sound and its potential to influence the mass audience. Remember talkies were only beginning their second decade and the use of sound was still considered an artistic handicap to true film art. Welles turned this around by making sound work for him. He used all of the "tricks" of radio production, including echo, recorded sound effects, and music to help tell the story.

Approach Because Welles had never directed a film or even appeared in one, every decision about the storytelling function of film was rethought. Cameramen would scream, "It's never been done," but that didn't stop Welles. Since he didn't know it couldn't be done, he did it. For example, in one scene Kane's ex-wife is sitting alone in a large, dark restaurant. Outside the rain is falling; the exterior of the building is bleak and foreboding. The scene begins with a full shot of the neon sign on the roof, which says, "Susan Alexander Kane appearing twice nightly." Then the camera goes *through the skylight* on the roof and zooms in to where Mrs. Kane is talking with the reporter. Welles combined animation and live footage to give the audience the zoom impression, and the scene became the model

Citizen Kane star and director Orson Welles in a festive staff meeting scene. *Citizen Kane* may be the most important American film ever made.

for many films in the years that followed. This is but one example of the dozens of completely new techniques that *Citizen Kane* contributed to the art of film. There were new lighting effects and innovative use of mirrors, shadows, and extreme close-ups (see 10.9).

In one scene Kane and his wife are at Xanadu, their mansion in Florida. (Hearst's mansion was at California's San Simeon.)

They are having a dispute and are far apart. The distance between them is symbolically represented by the physical dimensions of the huge room; they are so far apart they practically have to shout to be understood. The camera lens distorts the distance, emphasizing it even more. An echo effect makes their voices seem to rebound against the castle walls.

No discussion of *Citizen Kane*, no matter how brief, would be complete without mentioning "Rosebud." "Rosebud" was the "hook," the one thread that wove the pieces of the Kane puzzle together. The reporter sets out to find why Kane murmured "Rosebud" just before his death. At the end of the film, the reporter concludes that he'll never find out what Rosebud was. The audience does find out, how- ever, in the last shot of the film. The use of such a "hook" was not entirely new, but never had it been so skillfully employed, and never had the screen told such a powerful story with such believable irony.

Citizen Kane was successful in bridging the gap between "popular" entertainment de- signed for the mass audience, and a personal "artistic" statement. It remains the most discussed and important American film of the sound era.

Humphrey Bogart

Meanwhile, like the 1930s, the 1940s was developing an identity of its own on the big screen. The most popular single genre of the era was not the musical but the detective story. The private detective was usually at odds with the police for refusing to divulge the name of his client, while being shot at by unknown underworld characters.

Private detective films, like television shows of the same genre, are designed to entertain and intrigue the mass audience, to offer an escape from everyday life into a world of intrigue and suspense. One of the first great detective films appeared the same year as *Citizen Kane*. John Huston directed *The Maltese Falcon* and cast in the lead an experienced but little-celebrated actor who had mainly played supporting roles in second-rate pictures. His name was Humphrey Bogart.

Bogart became the screen's leading man of the 1940s (see 10.10). His successes, *The Maltese Falcon, Casablanca, Key Largo, The Big Sleep,* and *The Treasure of Sierra Madre*, to name just a few, are as well known today as they were when they first thrilled the audiences of their day. Bogart performed equally well as a detective in *The Big Sleep* and as a mercenary in *The African Queen*. The key to his success seemed to be his role as the "loner."

An unlikely hero and an unlikely leading man, Bogart was always tough, street-wise, and looking out for number one. Yet inevitably, plots would lead him to a confrontation that pitted those self-serving values against the public good, law and order, or wartime justice. His decision was usually to opt for good in spite of it all.

No one has ever accused Bogart of being handsome in the Clark Gable or Rudolph Valentino mold. He became the screen's leading man because he projected a visual image that was unique; there was only one Humphrey Bogart. He was tough and tender, selfish and giving, irreverent and sympathetic. As with all successful stars, any picture became *his* picture. Plot was secondary.

Perhaps the ultimate detective film was Howard Hawk's *The Big Sleep*. Bogart starred opposite Lauren Bacall. The great novelist William Faulkner wrote the screenplay from the Raymond Chandler novel. The result was a film that defied understanding. There were so many bodies scattered about and so many evil characters that the audience never did understand "whodunit," but it didn't matter! The real story was Bogart, rescuing damsels in distress and trading sizzling one-liners with Bacall. The film was very tongue in cheek, but the acting was first rate, the script was exhilarating, and the audience was completely engrossed.

Dozens of newer films and television programs in the detective genre can be traced directly back to Bogart and his rendering of

Humphrey Bogart was the unlikely leading man in several important films during the 1940s.

detectives Sam Spade and Phillip Marlowe. The detective film, with its accent on action, violence, and ultimately, virtue and justice, was the most successful genre of the era.

This time saw the full flowering of films in America as far as financial success was concerned. The biggest box-office year ever was 1946; 90 million Americans went to the movies every week. The industry would never have that large an audience again.

The decline of the movie business in the late 1940s had much to do with new tax regulations, which made films less desirable as investments. Also, the house Un-American Activities Committee was looking into films, and the blacklisting of some top film stars and writers did not help the industry's image. But what really hurt was, of course, television. Within a few years, television would replace movies as America's favorite entertainment pastime. Like radio, film would undergo tremendous change to adjust to its new role as a secondary source of entertainment.

1950s: A New Film Audience

The 1950s film audience demanded that a movie deliver an evening's entertainment different from TV. Perhaps the most significant trend was not in the films but in the audience. Increasingly the movie theater became the habitat of young people. Adults stayed home and watched TV while kids went to the movies to get away from mom and dad, engage in a little heavy petting, and nibble a box of popcorn. The youth audience put pressure on filmmakers to produce movies young people could identify with. It remains so today.

The Wild One featured Marlon Brando as a mumbling motorcycle leader whose gang terrorizes a small town, pillages the local shops, and leaves folks devastated in a senseless rampage of violence and disorder. Yet Brando emerges as an antiestablishment hero of sorts, a carefree idol on a motorcycle, sought after by the local "good girl." The plot was borrowed from grade-B westerns, but horses were replaced by motorcycles. The picture was a huge commercial success.

Another hero in the antiauthority mold was James Dean. His most noted film, *Rebel without a Cause,* told the story of a "new kid in school" who is roughed up by some juvenile delin-

quent types. Dean must take his stand of course, and this involves a "chickie-run," a contest where he and a rival head their cars for the edge of a cliff and jump out at the last moment. The first one to jump is a "chicken," perhaps the most despised social role among youth of that day. More telling than any other scene in the film is the confrontation between Dean and his father (played by Jim Backus). When his son asks if he should go ahead with the chickie-run, Dad says simply: "In 10 or 15 years, none of this will be important to you." The frustration of young people is clearly mirrored here.

Like rock music, *Rebel without a Cause* seemed to strike a responsive chord with a bored teen audience. James Dean was someone they could look up to, a younger Humphrey Bogart whose main concern was his most important possession, his automobile. So strong was audience identification with Dean that he became something of a cultural hero after his tragic death in a car accident. Though he starred in only three pictures (*East of Eden* and *Giant* were the other two), he was probably the era's greatest youth hero besides Elvis.

There was also a market for a new kind of horror in the 1950s—the science fiction film. True sci-fi buffs will recoil when I use the term to describe movies like *The Incredible Shrinking Man, The Fly, The Thing, The Blob,* and *It Came from Outer Space.* Yet these films were a product of the time, representing millions of dollars in box-office revenues. Usually there was some technological disaster that transformed men and women into robots, automatons, insects, or the like. Often the culprit was a visitor from outer space, bent on conquering and destroying the earth. Usually there was a scientist in charge for us good guys, and his teenaged son/daughter/student would play a role in the victory, allowing the audience to identify. These films were often made by small, independent studios like American International Pictures. But their success caused the major studios to rethink some policies. Many ventured into the B-film business while retaining their "major" releases.

Many of the greatest western films were made during the 1950s. *High Noon* and *Shane* both drew more attention to the genre from film critics. The western remains one of the most popular movie types, though its TV heyday has come and gone. More than any other entertainment form, the western is *totally* American. The story of the American cowboy is a vital component of the American dream. Like the detective story, the western offers a platform for the vicarious violence of which Americans seem so fond.

The need for vicarious physical experience of a different kind may also explain the success of those forgettable films starring sex queens of the 1950s, most notably Jane Mansfield. Plot served as vehicle for the sex goddess to parade her wares before the camera. Like violence, sex in the cinema became a vital ingredient to the success of many movies. There

had been sex on film long before the 1950s, but it was usually an appetizer, not the main course.

1960s: The Young and the Restless

Movies in the 1960s continued the accent on youth and reflected the anxieties of a generation born into the atomic age. The period was one of tremendous social upheaval and some of it ended up on film.

Psycho was perhaps Alfred Hitchcock's greatest film. There have been hundreds of horror films, some good and most bad, but film critics and the moviegoing public agreed *Psycho* was a masterpiece.

Janet Leigh steals money from her greedy insensitive boss and absconds to a motel. But by the time a half hour has passed, she decides to turn the money back in and face the music. She steps into the shower and lets the water run down her body as if to cleanse it of this terrible sin she has committed. Then an unknown person pulls the shower curtain back and stabs her repeatedly. The audience has no idea why; it all seems so senseless. Suddenly we are transformed from one story to another far more brutal and terrifying.

The stabbing itself is a miracle of cinema. We never actually *see* the knife enter her body, but through hundreds of short quick scenes we watch the knife gleam, see the flesh gyrate, and gasp as blood mixes with the swirling water. It is probably the most violent and chilling piece of film ever shot, yet the murder happens entirely in the viewer's imagination. (I remember seeing the film shortly after it came out—I couldn't take a shower for a month afterwards.)

Hitchcock is called the "master of suspense" because he is most successful in creating that suspense in the minds of his audience. The famous director is an "artist" but says he is "merely an entertainer." Perhaps exact definitions of the two will always be blurred, but Hitchcock pays special attention to his audience, and the result is a string of commercial successes.

Stanley Kubrick's *Dr. Strangelove*, which was made not long after the frightening Cuban missile crisis of 1962, brought the possibility of nuclear holocaust home to the nervous public. Fear of the bomb had been an American preoccupation ever since 1945, and during the late 1950s and early 1960s many Americans had spent a lot of time and money building bomb shelters in their basements. *Dr. Strangelove* played on this phobia for laughs, and the humor was very black indeed. The military elite were portrayed as mindless puppets enjoying the ultimate destruction. We peek in on the action as decisions are made to destroy one city after the next. Kubrick uses the film as a forum to mock the military-industrial complex, and we laugh until we cry. *Dr. Strangelove* still attracts large audiences whenever it plays, despite frequent

appearances on television. Perhaps its popularity during the latter part of the 1960s was bolstered by the Vietnam War. Young moviegoers, suspicious of the military and its motives, approved of Kubrick's message.

In a less serious vein, three films starring the Beatles rang up box-office profits during the 1960s. *A Hard Day's Night, Help,* and *Yellow Submarine* were all tremendous commercial successes. Though the popularity of the group as rock musicians was a vital component of the films' success, film critics are beginning to realize that the "genius" of the Beatles leaked over to their other media efforts. On film the group performed very much like the Marx Brothers. There was little plot; rather, the screen was a vehicle for music and madness.

Yellow Submarine, a full-length animated film, found the "fab four" wandering around Pepperland and taking on the "Blue Meanies." Eventually they convinced them: "All you need is love." The simplicity and naiveté of their message were no handicap.

As with the Marxes, so *much* happens in a Beatles movie that you watch it over and over and find something new each time. There are puns galore along with message and music. All three films went much further than simply setting film to music. They explored how each medium could reinforce and expand the other. As such, they were unique. Rather than taking the "easy way out" (as was the case with the later documentary, *Let It Be*), the Beatles and their crew displayed remarkable talent, breaking new ground by combining rock and cinema. The significance of that contribution becomes more apparent as filmmakers discover that devotion to rock can spell box-office success.

In 1969, the commercial success of *Easy Rider* set off a wave of youth-oriented "protest" pictures. Dennis Hopper, who directed and starred in the film, may have been the first American director since Orson Welles to have so much freedom with his product. *Easy Rider* was privately financed (costing a comparatively low $370,000) and not under the direction of any major studio. Those who had the chance turned it down, feeling the experimental plot was an open endorsement of drugs and would scare away the mass audience.

What it actually did was bring them in. *Easy Rider* struck a responsive chord with the youth audience because it articulated, in the most graphic and basic way, the concerns of the 1960s. Two long-haired trippers, Captain America and Billy, set off on their motorcycles to chase down the American Dream. Along the way they visit a commune, a couple of prostitutes, and a southern lawyer (Jack Nicholson), who gets them out of the local jail. Nicholson is the first to die a violent death at the hands of the rednecks. Both Captain America and Billy die at the end of the film. In between there is talk of politics and the use of drugs. *Easy Rider* vindicated a large subculture of people who had been using marijuana for years.

Audiences leaving the theater after *Easy Rider* were often stunned by the violent ending. The film provided a warning to society and a plea for understanding. It also provided music, lots of it. The successful use of songs like "Born to Be Wild" solidified youth identification and made *Easy Rider* one of the most significant social films of the decade.

1970s: Snatching Victory from the Jaws of Disaster

The key to big box office in the 1970s was disaster. A string of hits beginning with *The Poseidon Adventure* proved the mass audience was hungry for giant films, giant stars, and giant catastrophes. *The Towering Inferno* was the story of a huge office building fire. *Earthquake* told of the inevitable destruction that finally came to Los Angeles. It also featured sound so loud it practically shakes the audience out of the seats.

But a bigger box-office success than all these disaster films was a disaster of a different color. *Jaws*, about a shark that devours random tourists at an East Coast beach resort, played to millions of people and became one of the most talked-about movies ever. It broke all box-office records and became the biggest money maker of all time. (It was surpassed in 1977 by *Star Wars.*)

Jaws was the *Moby Dick* of the 1970s. It pitted humanity against beast in the *King Kong* tradition and involved the audience in the struggle. Millions screamed in anguish as the skilled camera crew convinced them the giant shark was about to come out of the screen and eat them alive.

It was the *form* of *Jaws* that made it such a spectacular hit. The content was believable and dull. *Jaws, The Exorcist, King Kong,* and the disaster films shared one common trait: they were able to take the audience along for the nightmare. Critics argue that theatergoers are becoming jaded, that they demand increasing doses of titillation. Perhaps this is so; as soon as we thought we had reached the ultimate in vicarious thrills, along comes *Jaws* to show us we had just begun.

All of this raises a more significant issue. Are there moral implications to this symbiotic relationship between audience and filmmaker? Can audience gasps that come when the shark gobbles up a victim's leg be somehow damaging in REALIFE? Those questions have yet to be answered, and they become enormously important as audience manipulation becomes easier for filmmakers.

Nashville and Network

Many have argued that the movies of the 1970s were devoid of aesthetic merit, that films were notable only for their commercial success. Two defy this analysis: Robert Altman's *Nashville* and Paddy Chayefsky's *Network* (directed by Sidney Lumet). Altman produced a number of first-rate films including *M*A*S*H, McCabe and Mrs. Miller,* and *California Split,* but *Nashville* is his masterpiece, as innovative and entertaining as any film.

Nashville defied film convention. It was almost a documentary, tracing the paths of dozens of characters as they attempt to crawl to the top of the country and western music scene in Nashville. There is the established C&W star, the teenybopper just in from California, the bevy of C&W starlets eager to make their way in the music business, the politician who sends advance men to convince a country group that "this is a good time to support . . . ," the wife of the promotion man who sleeps with the young lead singer, and the singer himself who lives and loves one day at a time and sings his one "special" song to every woman in the room.

There's also the music—more than a dozen country and western tunes sung by superstars and would-be superstars. All the songs in the film were written by the performers, few of whom had any real professional musical experience. This didn't keep Keith Carradine from winning the Academy Award for best song with his haunting "I'm Easy."

Oddly enough, that's the only Oscar the film won, though it was lauded by reviewers. Although it was not a complete commercial failure, it failed to live up to the predictions of the critics. Like *Citizen Kane, Nashville* will make a handsome financial return over the years, but a large portion of the mass audience came away confused, bored, or both.

The form of *Nashville* is both its strongest virtue and its greatest handicap. The dozens of subplots are interwoven in a series of vignettes so the audience never has a chance to get to know the characters as well as it does in other films. Yet Altman turns this into a strength, because *Nashville* is not the story of one star but the story of the star system. It doesn't matter what kind of stardom you're after (film, C&W, rock and roll), *Nashville* tells a universal story of media power and prestige and its glorious, but arbitrary, rewards.

The film points out that arbitrary success works for singers and politicians alike. The political hero of the film, Hal Phillip Walker, is out to "use" the glitter of the stars to his own advantage. His advance men hint that C&W superstar Henry Gibson might eventually become governor if he'll "only go along."

We are still years away from understanding *Nashville* completely; perhaps we never will, but its significance will become increasingly apparent. Already critics keep mentioning it in conjunction with a new technique here, a new approach there, a whole new *kind* of film somewhere else. In the decade when the film industry seemed interested only in box-office numbers, *Nashville* stood out like a beacon.

More commercially successful was Paddy Chayefsky's *Network*. The 1976 film captured several Oscars, including those for best actor and best actress. The story involves the behind-the-scenes activities at UBC, a mythical fourth TV network. When a wild-eyed anchorman goes off the deep end on camera,

ratings skyrocket. He's left on the air despite his strange ravings because it is UBC's first hit show.

Network was often silly and sentimental. The story was told in a very traditional manner, but it was an important story. Chayefsky's animosity toward the influence of television struck a very responsive chord in the filmgoing audience. Both the real audience and the depicted TV audience seem to respond unanimously when the anchorman urges them to begin shouting (for no special reason), "I'm as mad as hell and I'm not going to take this any more!" *Network* proved that though the protests of the 1960s had disappeared, there remained a bubbling undercurrent of frustration. Ironically, the film was sold for airing on television in 1978.

The Critics, Promotion, and Success

Throughout this chapter I have continually referred to "the critics" as if they were a consolidated body of snobs who perceive film on an altogether different plane from the mass audience. Although this point of view is somewhat simplistic, there may be some truth in it. Film critics do not generally reflect the mass audience's taste, and therefore they don't have the power to "make or break" a film the way a record reviewer for *Rolling Stone* can make or break an album.

For example, there are hundreds of successful films that have received nothing but poor reviews from all major film critics. Among the top ten money-makers of all time in the following list, not one has really had the critical acclaim of *Nashville* or *Citizen Kane*. Yet they are the ten most popular films ever made. Why?

Ten Top Money-Makers (1900–1978)

1. *Star Wars*
2. *Jaws*
3. *The Godfather*
4. *The Exorcist*
5. *The Sound of Music*
6. *The Sting*
7. *Gone with the Wind*
8. *One Flew over the Cuckoo's Nest*
9. *Rocky*
10. *Love Story*

The films listed are those that have grossed the most money. Is it possible that the more recent films made more money due to higher ticket prices rather than higher popularity? Perhaps we should include inflation as a factor in this list.

Film has been around a lot longer than radio or television, and it has developed a certain artistic integrity in the minds of the cultural elite. Like the novel, film has a swarm of reviewers who make a living judging each new effort and pronouncing its "place" among all other works. Radio and television have few such critics. Broadcast media programs are noted only for their ability to get and hold a large audience. The TV and radio shows that get the most attention from critics are those known to the mass audience: *I Love Lucy, Mary Tyler Moore Show,* and *Happy Days* for example. But the films that most critics like to talk about, "artistic" films like *Rules of the Game, Jules and Jim,* and *8½,* may be virtually unknown to the mass audience. There is a clear difference between the elite interpretation of film as "art" and the mass audience perception of film as "entertainment." Film critics may abhor the public's "poor taste," but the public goes on tasting as it pleases.

For this reason, movie studios do not go overboard trying to woo the critics. Instead, they try to appeal directly to the buying public through publicity and promotion. But even these tools do not always do the job. For example, *The Great Gatsby* was released in 1974 amid one of the greatest ballyhoos of the 1970s. Everyone was rereading the Fitzgerald novel. The studio spared no expense hiring Robert Redford to play Gatsby and Mia Farrow for the fragile Daisy. *Time* magazine put it on the cover and everyone was set for a box-office bonanza. Within a few weeks most theaters showing the film were empty. Six months later it was on television. The word was out: *Gatsby* was a bomb and no amount of publicity could save it.

Drawing by Modell; © 1976, The New Yorker Magazine, Inc.

Most movie producers agree that film, more than any other medium, has one elusive requirement for commercial success: word of mouth. The audience sees a film and passes the word along to friends. They in turn see the film and pass the word along. Pretty soon there are long lines waiting to see film A, while film B, which cost the same to produce, opened at the theater next door, and enjoyed an equal amount of advance promotion and critical acclaim, goes begging.

At the heart of the problem is the intricate relationship between studio, critic, and audience. The studio would like to produce winners that are loved by mass audience and critic alike, but its primary concern is the mass audience. No amount of critical acclaim or advance promotion can guarantee money in the bank.

Issues and Answers

The Regulation of Self

The trend toward explicit sexuality in films in the 1950s culminated with a series of movies that seemed to capitalize on an increasingly permissive society in the 1960s.

Swedish import *I Am Curious Yellow* showed sexual intercourse on the screen. Parents seemed reluctant to send their children to see anything but Walt Disney films for fear the kids would be exposed to language and behavior they considered unsuitable.

Seeing a threat to their pocketbooks, the Motion Picture Association of America (MPAA), a trade organization, instituted a rating system designed to give audiences an idea of what "kind" of picture they were going to see. After some modifications, the four now-familiar "categories" of films emerged.

G: For all ages, this film contains no nudity or sex and only a minimal amount of violence.

PG: Parental guidance suggested. Some portions may not be suitable for young children. Some mild profanity may be present, and violence is permitted as long as it is not "excessive." A glimpse of a nude body is permitted, but anything more makes it R.

R: Restricted; those under 17 must be accompanied by a parent. This is an adult film in every sense of the word and may contain very rough violence, and explicit nudity, and/or love making.

X: No one under 17 is admitted with or without a parent. This rating is generally reserved for films that are openly pornographic, though some serious films by noted filmmakers have been rated X.

The ratings do not represent censorship per se, since filmmakers usually have the final say. But studios know, in most cases, that the more acceptable the rating, the larger the potential audience. With film emphasis on youth (almost half of all moviegoers are between ages 12 and 20), major studios hesitate to make films that will exclude everyone under 17. Though the absurdity of rating or evaluating a film according to the number of seconds a bare buttock appears on the screen is self-evident, the ratings seem to have accomplished what they set out to do.

Perhaps the most difficult thing about the ratings is that they have the same problem as all attempts to identify what makes a media presentation "objectionable." Guidelines must be flexible enough to incorporate shifting community standards, but which community? Frontal nudity on the screen may be commonplace in Manhattan but unheard of in Milpitas.

Millions and millions of words have been written attempting to define *obscenity*. But it's an elusive term; today's obscenity is tomorrow's art. No attempt will be made to define obscenity here, but it's worth taking a moment to think about the code itself and what it may hold in store for other mass media.

The most obvious flaw in the code is its approach to violence. Though hundreds of sexually explicit films received the X rating, it wasn't until 1974 that a martial arts film, *The Street Fighter*, received it for showing objectionable violence. The implication seems to be our society will tolerate arbitrary violence and death but objects to arbitrary sex.

FEIFFER
by JULES FEIFFER

IN THE OLD DAYS YOU WENT TO THE MOVIES TO SEE THE BAD GUYS BRUTALIZE, TERRORIZE AND MURDER.

AND THE GOOD GUYS CATCH THEM AND KILL THEM.

THAT WAS ENTERTAINMENT.

TODAY YOU GO TO THE MOVIES TO SEE THE GOOD GUYS BRUTALIZE, TERRORIZE, AND MURDER.

AND THE BAD POWER STRUCTURE BRUTALIZE, TERRORIZE AND MURDER THE GOOD GUYS.

THAT'S ART.

SO THE CHOICE IS NO LONGER BETWEEN GOOD GUYS AND BAD GUYS.

IT'S BETWEEN BRUTALIZING ENTERTAINMENT AND BRUTALIZING ART.

During the 1970's television networks began to show more explicit material (usually films) but coupled it with a "warning" to the audience that parental discretion was advised. Some TV cable companies showed uncut X-rated movies during late hours. The time slot of a network show sent a message to the audience. The family hour experiment that began in the mid-1970s was designed to reassure parents that their children would be safe watching shows during the early evening.

The "success" of the MPAA rating scheme may eventually lead to a similar code for radio and television programs. The large audiences watching controversial TV shows like *All in the Family* and listening to deejays like New York's Don Imus (see Chapter 6) mean there is a segment of the public that is ready for "adult" broadcast programs. But their desires often conflict with those determined to protect kids by keeping sex and violence off the air. A self-imposed ratings system could go a long way toward resolving this conflict.

Queries and Concepts

1. Choose three top films now showing in your local theaters. Can you make a list of myths and values that may be associated with each?

2. Make arrangements to see a silent film. (There is probably one available through your library, and public television stations show a number of silent films.) Keep a journal of observations regarding the differences between silents and talkies. Which seems to move faster? Which uses the visual aspect of film more effectively?

3. Are there any young film stars of today that enjoy the idol worship of James Dean? If so, who are they and *why* are they? If not, why not?

4. Prediction time: When the 1980s are over, we will look back and write about the film

trends of that decade just as the 1940s through the 1970s are assessed here. What will those trends be?

5. Devise a set of guidelines for self-regulation of TV programming. What type of material should not be shown under any circumstance?

Readings and References

America's Sweetheart

Raymond Lee
The Films of Mary Pickford. Cranbury, N.J.: A.S. Barnes (1970).
I bought this book on sale for one dollar . . . here's hoping you have that kind of luck. There is a very short introduction and then hundreds of incredible stills from Pickford's most famous films.

The Audiovisual Record;
Life Is Like a Movie

These areas often go unexplored in many books on film. The best single source on the emotionally lingering impact of film is F. Scott Fitzgerald's *The Last Tycoon* (New York: Scribner's, 1941). Some social approaches to film may be found in *The Movies As Medium* (New York: Farrar, Straus, 1970), an anthology edited by Lewis Jacobs, and in Arthur Knight's *The Liveliest Art* (New York: New American Library, 1971).

The Magic Lantern

Albert Smith
Two Reels and a Crank. Garden City, N.Y.: Doubleday, 1952.
This is a particularly rewarding first-person account of the early years of film from nickelodeon to the silent screen. Told with relish and conviction.

The Quiet Years

Edward Wagenknecht
The Movies in the Age of Innocence. Norman: University of Oklahoma Press, 1962.
Silent screen star Lillian Gish calls this "the best book on films I've ever read." It turns out she is a personal friend of the author, but her enthusiasm is warranted. The book concentrates on the silent film, particularly its heroines.

The Star Is Born

Richard Schickel and Allen Hurlburt
The Stars. New York: Dial Press, 1962.

Schickel has been a film critic for *Life* and *Time* so this is more than a fan's-eye view of the stars. Their lives and influences are examined in the context of their audiences. Good tight reading, plenty of lavish pictures.

The Movies Learn to Talk

Thomas W. Bohn and Richard Stromgren
Light and Shadows: A History of Motion Pictures. Sherman Oaks, Ca.: Alfred, 1975.
One of the newer historical accounts of the rise of cinema. See particularly Chapters 3–6 on the rise and influence of the silent film. Chapter 7 deals exclusively with the impact of sound.

Richard Griffith and Arthur Mayer
The Movies. New York: Simon & Schuster, 1970.
A decade-by-decade fan's-eye view that covers film into the 1960s. The largest (9"x12") and most enthusiastic history around.

Paul Rotha and Richard Griffith
The Film till Now. New York: Springs Books, 1967.
This book was originally written in 1930 and is obviously dated. Yet it was the first monumental history of film ever written, compiled before the intellectual establishment was taking film seriously. Rotha notes in an updated introduction that he would like to take back some of his earlier opinions, particularly those on sound films. (He thought it was a passing fad.)

1930s through 1970s

William Bayer
The Great Movies. New York: Grosset & Dunlap, 1973.
This is the best *single* source for great films of the sound era. Easy and fun to read. Bayer is a sharp film critic with a gift for getting to the point. It is filled with more than 300 photographs and a text that provides convincing rationale for his choice of the 60 greatest films ever made.

1940s: Citizen Kane and the American Dream

Pauline Kael
The Citizen Kane Book. New York: Bantam Books, 1973.
This includes the original review by Kael as well as the full shooting script and over 100 hard-to-find stills from the film. Once you have seen *Citizen Kane* you will probably want to pick it up. Now available in paperback.

The Critics, Promotion, and Success

Pauline Kael
Kiss Kiss Bang Bang. Boston: Little, Brown, 1968.

The *New Yorker's* incredibly witty film reviewer issues a book every few years containing her best reviews and longer pieces about film. This is one of her most entertaining.

Note: See David Shaw, "The Film Critics— Power of Pen Has Sharp Limits" from the *Los Angeles Times*, July 6, 1976 (p. 1) for a discussion of popular versus critically acclaimed films.

Issues and Answers:
The Regulation of Self

Bohn and Stromgren's *Light and Shadows: A History of Motion Pictures* (Sherman Oaks, Ca.: Alfred, 1975) gives equal time to sex, violence, and race and their roles in the MPAA ratings. There's a brief discussion of movie ratings in Agee, Ault, and Emery's *Introduction to Mass Communications* (New York: Dodd, Mead, 1970); check the index under "film."

PART THREE
The Phenomena of Mass Communication

Until now, we have concentrated on the media themselves—what they are, what they have been, and what they have done. This final section selects a few media-related areas to explore. They were picked from several possible areas after some thought about what might be of most interest and importance to you as well as to the study of mass communication.

News has always been with us, and many people still think of mass media primarily as conveyors of news. As you will see, that concept is becoming outmoded.

Advertising and public relations play unique and very controversial roles in our mass communication system. Yet without them, the system, as we know it, would not exist.

Popular culture is a new area of academic exploration that is interesting a lot of students and teachers alike. I hope the chapter devoted to it will lead you to further thought and interaction with the meaning of it in your everyday lives.

Media research of the empirical kind is being conducted daily to answer many of the important questions that have been posed in this book. But there are a lot of ways to conduct research, and lay people can be easily influenced by articles that attempt to simplify findings. Let Chapter 14 be an introduction for you and a kind of "consumer's guide" to reading about empirical research and the effects of mass media.

The final chapter is a brief glimpse into the future of Mediamerica and what may be in store for us there. I promise you'll find plenty to agree *and* disagree with. What I find exciting is that among the thousands of you who read this book some of you will write your own books about mass media sometime in the future. I hope Chapter 15 provides you with some possibilities for that book. And when you write it, please send me a copy!

11

And Now the News . . .

"It is our assumption there may be those in this country who would be disrespectful to the President but that no one would be disrespectful to Walter Cronkite," White House Press Secretary Jody Powell said.—Associated Press, March 5, 1977

Wally and Me

Every afternoon, I rush home from work in time to tune in "Wally." Walter Cronkite and I have been friends for a long time. We've weathered floods, storms, airline crashes, and Watergate. Through it all, Wally has remained as faithful, sober, and credible as any human being could. I can *count* on Cronkite to give me all the news—fairly, concisely, objectively. He never lets his emotions get in the way.

Yet, he is not without emotion. The day that Nixon resigned, I thought I saw a faint look of relief in Wally's face for just a moment. During the Bicentennial, he beamed as the gaily decorated schooners glided across the color screen.

Walter Cronkite is the final word. If there are doubts or anxieties about the world situation, he can put them to rest with the shuffle of a paper. When the day's events are done, I know that I am truly informed, for Wally assures me solemnly: "That's the way it is . . ."

Newspapers

Most of us get all our late-breaking news from three media: newspapers, radio, and television. From newspapers—at least traditional newspapers—come detailed, factual, dispassionate accounts of the day's events. Television supplies a visual depth, while radio keeps us up to the minute with the latest headlines while we drive, work, or play.

The average daily newspaper runs almost 60 pages per issue. More than half that space is for advertising, but some 25 pages are devoted to editorial content—the stuff we call "the news."

The circulation of weekly newspapers is close to 35 million. Weeklies are most often found in rural areas that cannot support a daily. Weekly readers are loyal to their product since it may be their only source of community information. Weekly readers may share geographic, ethnic, or social interests. Many religious groups publish their own newspapers, giving members a particular perspective on world events.

Staff sizes vary tremendously from one newspaper to the next. The typical large daily newspaper employs a full-time editorial staff of 75–100 people. Major dailies like the *Washington Post* may have several hundred editorial staffers. Small rural weeklies are often "Mom and Pop" operations run entirely by one family or (in some cases) one person.

The Newspaper You Never See

We all have a picture of the investigating reporter in our minds. We know about the crusading editor/publisher. But, as with all media, these people represent only the tip of the iceberg. There are dozens of lesser-known jobs; many are those where a new employee can break into the business. All are vital if

"Remember, my boy, never trust anyone."

"Not even Walter Cronkite?"

Drawing by Dana Fradon; © 1976, The New Yorker Magazine, Inc.

the paper is to get out on time. In an average metropolitan daily the major departments break down this way.

Owner/Publisher   This can be one person or many. The *Kansas City Star* was even owned by its own employees. For a number of years it was the only totally employee-owned metro in the country, though this ended when the employees sold the paper in 1977. The owner/publisher hires the editors and fills key editorial positions.

Editors   The editor-in-chief is in charge of all editorial functions but delegates the power of review to individual specialized editors in all but the most extraordinary cases. These specialized editors include the powerful city editor, managing editor, and various section editors, including sports, editorial, financial, education, science, religion, and society. These specialists make decisions about which reporters will cover a story and where it will be placed.

Business Manager   This person ranks equally with the editor-in-chief. The business manager is in charge of advertising, classified, promotion, circulation, and accounting. A good business manager makes sure the paper is earning a profit. He or she reports directly to the owner/publisher.

Production Manager   This person is in charge of the "hardware" of the paper. Under the production manager are separate departments for composition, engraving, and stereotyping. Workers in the press room are included. The production manager reports directly to the owner/publisher.

Reporters and Photographers These people work under the city editor or are assigned to an editor in a special department. There are about 15 reporters on a crew of 75, so they actually represent about 20 percent of the total editorial staff. However, like the radio disc jockeys, they are the portion of the staff best known to the average reader. There are general reporters (taking a number of diverse assignments) and those assigned as columnists or who have special "beats" like city hall or the courts. Photographers usually work with reporters and are often assigned to a story with a good "picture possibility."

Proofreaders and Copy Readers These are the unsung champions of the newsroom. Without them all copy would read strangely. I've never known a reporter who could hand in a story with every word spelled correctly and every punctuation mark in place. Copy and proofreaders "clean up" copy to get it ready for typesetting. This job is absolutely vital since readership studies indicate that spelling mistakes and grammatical errors detract from a story's credibility. The content may be correct, but if form is poor the reader is skeptical.

Stringers Most newspapers employ a shadow staff of occasional contributors. Often these are young journalists still in school or those working full time in other jobs, many of whom hope to break in as full-time reporters. Stringers are usually paid by the column inch. A newspaper with a full-time editorial staff of 75 people may use 15–20 stringers.

Naturally no two newspaper staffs are exactly alike; all functions vary according to individual editorial needs and staff abilities. Most major dailies have a separate art department with editorial cartoonists and illustrators. Often there are special correspondents at the state and federal levels to give the "local slant" to regional and national news. In large labor towns like Detroit and San Francisco, there are often a labor editor and a staff of reporters to cover the union beat. Each city has its own unique problems and readers.

What's News?

Experienced editors know that a story must have certain attributes to qualify as "news." They make decisions based on time-worked criteria. These criteria for news selection are not always what you might imagine. There is more to be asked than, "Is it important to the reader?" Actually that might be one of the last considerations. We have already discussed hard news versus soft news and the role that each plays in the content of newspapers. Comparatively little hard news may appear

"I deem thee newsworthy."
Drawing by Dana Fradon; © 1976, The New Yorker Magazine, Inc.

because editors have learned that hard news doesn't always sell newspapers.

Time Time is a key factor. Has the story already been covered by the broadcast media? What can the newspaper add? Is the story going to be of interest to the reader *right now!?*

Newsmakers Some people make news no matter what they do. The President of the United States, a wealthy Arab leader, Jackie Onassis, and other newsworthy people are always worthy of a story.

Regional or Local Interest Geographical news events are those with regional or local importance. The editor must decide if the reader will want to know about an event because *it*

happened here. If a bridge falls and two are killed in Paris, it doesn't "play in Peoria." If the Peoria bridge goes out, it's front-page news in the Peoria newspaper.

Rewards Wilbur Schramm says that news stories have either *immediate* or *delayed* rewards to a felt need. We all need to feel informed, and immediate-reward news stories provide instant satisfaction. We can laugh, cry, sympathize, or become angry about them right away. Stories concerning disaster, crime, sports, and social events all give us immediate rewards. Delayed-reward news stories may be about public affairs, business, finance, or other complex matters. These stories don't carry any immediate relevance to our lives, and increasingly, editors are finding less room for them.

*". . . and now stay tuned for Varnum Hadley and the
Six o'Clock Bad News Roundup."*

Human Interest These stories are becoming more common on the nation's news pages. They're heart tuggers; the widow with five children who refuses to accept welfare, the handicapped man who rises to an important government position. Editors are finding that an increasing number of readers desire the "human side" of the day's events. Perhaps this is a response to a general feeling of disaffiliation with government and world affairs.

These criteria are not universal or all-inclusive, but they are some of the most common. The unusual, the unique, the sensational—this is the "stuff" of the day's news.

It is also important to remember that reporters find news *where the editors tell them to look.* In this sense, the news is institutional, predictable, and likely to come from the same sources day in and day out. This is one reason editors were so shocked when readership studies indicated a large gap between what editors thought the reader *should* be reading and what the reader actually *was* reading.

No News Is Good News

One of the most frequent complaints an editor hears is, "How come you guys never print any *good* news?" It's true that reporters seek out stories about murders that did happen, not about murders that didn't.

Perhaps this is human nature. We don't usually go out of our way to tell people how *good* we feel, but if something is bothering us we let them know. Good news is its own reward; bad news has immediacy.

Chet Huntley, the former Brinkley team-mate on the NBC news, once said flatly: "Journalists were never intended to be the cheerleaders of society." For print journalists this is particularly true. Reporters often see them-

The New Muckrakers

The most widely read and famous reporters of the 1970s were those who specialized in investigative reporting, a group journalism writer Leonard Downie, Jr., calls "the modern muckrakers."

Bob Woodward and Carl Bernstein are probably the best-known newspaper reporters in America. They were instrumental in breaking the Watergate story, and their pursuit of the Nixon connection was made into the popular film *All the President's Men.* Woodward admits, "It's almost a perverse pleasure. I like going out and finding something that is going wrong

. . . and then putting it into the newspaper."

Seymour Hersh was a Washington correspondent for the *New York Times* during the Watergate era and is often disturbed by the "ground rules" of investigative journalism. "One of the bad things about the newspaper business is that the stories have to be so dry and stick to proven facts." Hersh has been given credit for breaking the My Lai massacre story, and he played a key role in the investigation of the CIA's illegal activities in Chile.

Donald Barlett and James Steele are specialists at digging into public records and focusing attention on corruption in government. One particular triumph was a 1973

series of articles for the *Philadelphia Inquirer* revealing corruption in the judiciary, routine court payoffs, and unequal dispensation of justice. The following year, they won a Pulitzer Prize for stories uncovering preferential IRS treatment of wealthy taxpayers.

Jack Anderson worked for two decades as an understudy to the famous muckraker, Drew Pearson. When Pearson died, Anderson took over his "Washington Merry-Go-Round" and has kept the famous column in motion . He has been threatened, beaten, and drugged by his enemies, but it doesn't seem to deter him. When asked why he continues, Anderson replies casually, "It's a really sexy way to make a living!"

---

selves as the thin buffer between society and government, order and anarchy. Most feel their duty is to report what goes wrong. Implicit is the feeling that if these wrongs are reported, others may learn a lesson.

Clearly this is the motivation for the investigative reporting so much in vogue during the 1970s (see 11.1). When Don Bolles, an Arizona journalist, was killed while investigating white-collar crime, a blue-ribbon panel of three dozen journalists descended on the area. After six months of exhaustive research, they published a series of articles implicating Senator Barry Goldwater and other high-ranking Arizona officials in a web of crime.

In 1977, several Hanafi Muslim leaders held 134 Washington residents captive for several days. Afterward, the news media were resoundingly criticized for "overcovering" the event. Many said such coverage encourages

others to commit crimes. News men and women responded by defending their actions on the basis of truth. "If we neglect to report some news because we think suppression is in the public interest," they said, "we'll lose our credibility as impartial news reporters." That impartiality may already be suspect, given the criteria for news selection, but the point is well taken. There is a difference between *selection* of news and *suppression* of news.

There's a new trend among journalists of all media to present a certain amount of "happy news." Perhaps this helps to balance some of the sensational "unhappy news" we see and hear so much. But journalists are not likely to quit printing the "unhappy news" or to suppress news of major events, no matter how bizarre or violent they become. Changes in these areas would require adoption of an entirely different concept of freedom of the press.

Newspaper Layout: The Eyes Have It

In 1919 Joseph Patterson decided New York City was ripe for a new kind of newspaper. For a number of years, staid papers like the *New York Times* had been tops in circulation, and Patterson thought the city was ready for a no-holds-barred journal more in the tradition of the yellow papers of the 1890s. His *Illustrated Daily News* (later simply the *New York Daily News*) sported a tabloid format and coupled it with a tremendous emphasis on photography. On some occasions the entire front page consisted of masthead, photograph, and caption.

This caught the eye of New Yorkers who had not been daily newspaper readers. While the circulation of most city papers remained the same, the *Daily News* became the largest-selling daily in the country, a position it still holds. Sensational weeklies like the *National Enquirer* later copied the layout formula and prospered. Patterson's was a new kind of journalism that seemed to typify the "jazz age" of the 1920s. It became known as "jazz journalism."

Of course jazz journalism was much more than visual appeal, but layout was an important component in the phenomenal success of the *Daily News*. Since that time all newspapers have become more aware of how important visual appeal and graphics are in holding the attention of the reader. Newspapers now have to compete with TV, a far more visually appealing medium. Graphics research is done to determine reader preference for various typefaces. Editors have found that most readers prefer bigger pictures, larger headlines, and more eye-catching lead material.

There is an increased awareness that newspaper *form* as well as *content* is important in getting and holding a large readership. The average 60-page newspaper is read in just less than half an hour. That's less than one minute per page. Readers make critical decisions about what they will read by glancing at a headline or photograph.

An awareness of this process has led to increasing specialization in most daily newspapers. In the future, your newspaper may be quite different from the one delivered next door, though both come off the same press. If your neighbors are executives, they may get a larger business section. The technology is not quite here yet, but newspaper people know they must help readers find the news they want.

There are now special magazines, inserts, and advertising supplements for individual areas of interest. In addition, there are more soft news, advice columns, and how-to and where-to news in the daily paper than ever before. All of this involves a basic shift away from what some editors think of as news and toward the news that readers demand. Editors, some grudgingly, are realizing their newspaper is a "product" that must be marketed and sold according to the needs of the consumer.

Radio: The New Kid in Town

During the early 1920s, radio broadcasters were not very interested in news. There were no radio reporters, and most news came directly from newspapers and sounded rather dull on the air. Advertisers expressed little interest in sponsoring news broadcasts, preferring to back more popular entertainment and music shows. Yet there were some news events that seemed designed for radio coverage.

The Hoover-Smith presidential election of 1928 was fully covered by the new medium. The three wire services (Associated Press, United Press, and International News Service) supplied radio with details of the campaign and official election results. Listeners found they could hear returns via radio without having to wait until the next morning for printed results. The candidates themselves spent almost $1 million in radio advertising. The age of radio news and public affairs had arrived. By the time the Depression began in 1929, some stations had as many as 10 radio reporters whose sole job was to cover the news.

Newspapers were among the first to feel the economic pinch of the Depression, and they were not about to sit by and lose advertisers to radio. They reasoned that radio was supposed to provide entertainment, but real news coverage should remain exclusively the job of print. In 1933, a majority of Associated Press members fired the first volley of the press-radio war by refusing to provide wire service information to radio networks. This forced newscasters to go to the early editions of newspapers for their news, but the AP soon went to court to stop even that practice. NBC and CBS then set up their own news-gathering bureaus.

A compromise was tried: in exchange for the networks dropping their plans to expand radio news coverage, a newly created "Press-Radio Bureau" would supply two five-minute newscasts daily, culled from wire service stories. But that wasn't enough. Radio stations and listeners demanded more. Soon there were a half dozen competing radio news services.

Radio bypassed traditional news channels to bring listeners the events leading to World War II. Edward R. Murrow organized a series of broadcasts for CBS from the capitals of Europe. As Hitler's demands became more preposterous, listeners heard reporters describe the tense situation. All this culminated in Murrow's 1940 broadcasts from London. While bombs burst all around him, Murrow told the sad tale of England's struggle to survive the war. This tremendous sense of immediacy and involvement would not soon be forgotten by the millions of Americans glued to

Radio news anchorperson Chet Douglas on the air at Los Angeles's all-news KFWB.

their radios. Radio had won the press-radio struggle and achieved its rightful place in news reporting.

Rip and Read

Despite this exciting beginning, radio news has made few major advances since World War II. No sooner had radio established personalities like Edward R. Murrow and Eric Sevareid than television came along and offered them a more exciting challenge.

Most radio networks were forced to cut back on expensive news operations when radio began losing lucrative entertainment advertising dollars to TV. Many continued to provide affiliates with five minutes of national news per hour, most of it ripped and read from the "radio wire," which provides news copy, and a limited number of actualities or taped broadcasts from reporters in the field.

In 1975, NBC merged existing news facilities with a new radio news service dubbed the "News and Information Service" (NIS). NIS provided affiliates (both NBC and non-NBC stations) with 50 minutes of radio news per hour, allowing them to become "all-news" stations overnight simply by plugging in. NIS featured imaginative interpretive reporting and a barrage of "feature" material. Despite the popularity of the all-news format in many markets, NIS folded in 1977.

The 1970s also showed one other interesting trend in radio news. Local stations more and more tailored newscasts to "fit" their program content. Top-40 stations had long used aggressive newscasters to shout out the headlines in the manner of the Top-40 deejay. And easy listening formats had found "easy listening" newscasters with a decidedly calmer approach to the day's events. Now "progressive" station newscasters began to play instrumental music under their news, matching stories with popular songs that seemed related. Sometimes they didn't have to look too far. In 1976 Bob Dylan's "Battle of Hurricane Carter" was popular just as the prizefighter was being retried for the crime described in the song.

The Commentators

Radio commentators are newscasters with a unique voice or delivery listeners can easily recognize. The voice is the most recognizable "byline" ever. This brief listing includes a few newscasters who pioneered a new brand of "audio journalism."

Paul Harvey was still going strong in the 1970s. His delivery includes long pauses that drive the point home. Seldom does Harvey have to let his audience know how he feels about a subject. His tone tells all. Harvey has said: "The cold hard facts have to be salted and peppered to make them palatable. Since objectivity is impossible, I make no pretense of it, I just let it all hang out."

His daily newscasts seem to strike a particularly responsive chord in small-town and rural America. Stories include the big news of the day as well as the story of the couple who has been married "68 years today . . . and still holding." His trademark sign-off is punctuated by five seconds of silence. "This is Paul Harvey . . . . . Good day."

Gabriel Heatter had a flair for the emotion-packed human interest story while with the Mutual network during the 1920s and 1930s. Heatter's name became a household word. He was one of the first to be strongly identified by voice and broadcast style. Along with Fulton Lewis, Jr., and Elmer Davis, he pioneered the 15-minute "news commentary" format.

H. V. Kaltenborn started broadcasting in 1922 and joined CBS eight years later. He was probably the best-known radio commentator of his day. The height of his fame came during a 20-day crisis in 1938 when Hitler made a number of demands on Czechoslovakia. Europe appeared on the brink of war and Kaltenborn set up a cot in his famous "Studio Nine" to give listeners all the latest. During those three weeks, he did more than 80 broadcasts, including a number of long commentaries. Never had Americans heard so much news and comment.

Edward R. Murrow secured his place in history during the 1940 London bombings and went on to become famous with his *Hear It Now* and *See It Now* broadcasts. Most consider him the greatest electronic journalist of all time. He died a tragic death from lung cancer in 1965. His lit cigarette and curling smoke had long been a trademark.

Lowell Thomas began at Pittsburgh's KDKA in 1925 and was still going strong in the 1970s despite his advanced age. Thomas had a unique, brash, but sincere delivery that caught on with the public. His era of reporting stretched to include the Spanish Civil War as well as the war in Vietnam. Thomas's trade-

Walter Winchell in 1944.

mark was his introduction: "From Moscow to the Suez Canal comes today's news. Good evening everybody, this is Lowell Thomas for CBS news . . ."

Walter Winchell may be remembered by some of you as the machine-gun staccato voice that introduced the old *Untouchables* series. Winchell was a New York newspaper columnist who got into the radio business as a sideline. Unlike his other radio colleagues, Winchell was strictly in the entertainment business, supplying humorous tidbits and personal "secrets" (see 11.3). His popularity among peers faded somewhat in the 1950s.

He once accused Lucille Ball of being a "communist" and sided with Senator Joe McCarthy against Edward R. Murrow in the famous 1954 TV battle.

Television News: The Tossed Salad

Television news began as a simple rip and read operation. TV newscasters delivered the script taken directly from the AP and UPI radio wires. A tremendous amount of TV news still reaches us this way. Local newscasts are often a "tossed salad" culled from radio wire copy, newspapers, and other sources. Still slides are used along with 16 mm film. None of these media is television in the strictest sense of the word.

Walter Cronkite has observed that the concept of an anchorperson unifying these separate parts may become a thing of the past:

If we can illustrate all stories there is no further need of a news broadcaster to read half the items to the public. Disembodied voices can narrate the film, reporters on the scene will be seen when the situation demands, and there will be no need for a news master of ceremonies in the studio.

Indeed, the whole idea of an anchorperson may be left over from commentators of the radio era. Yet today's news anchor people seem far less opinionated and pioneering than their radio counterparts. Of more importance is their visual appeal to the audience. According to author Irving Fang, the five most important qualities for the TV anchorperson include:

1. Speaking clearly.
2. Imparting the sense of the news.
3. Convincing viewers you know what you are talking about.
4. Keeping the newscast running smoothly.
5. Maintaining contact with the audience.

Nowhere on the list do we find skills involving more traditional journalistic practices or ethics.

Perhaps the ultimate extension of this trend came when ERA, a San Francisco research firm, was hired by Los Angeles's KNXT-TV to find out why news ratings were slipping. Viewers were chosen at random and their galvanic skin response (GSR) was measured while they were shown film clips of the station's anchor people. GSR works like a lie detector test; when viewers get excited, they begin to sweat slightly and GSR picks up the subtle difference. Newscasters that produced sufficient GSR responses were kept; those who didn't were fired.

George Putnam, a rival newscaster and long-time Los Angeles TV personality noted for his own ability to elicit emotional audience response, objected to the practice. "This ERA thing is frightening. I'm sure if they showed Adolf Hitler up there on the screen the needle would jump right out of the glass. But that's no reason to let Adolf anchor the five o'clock news!"

Nevertheless, those who anchor newscasts realize their jobs are as much cosmetic as substantive. When ABC paid Barbara Walters $5 million to co-anchor their evening newscast, it was not because they seriously felt she could add substance. What she would add (they hoped) were style and flair—that indescribable something that seemed to be working for many local male-female co-anchors.

"This is Barbara Walters. Fighting continues in the streets of Beirut..."

Drawing by Lou Myers; © 1976, The New Yorker Magazine, Inc.

Friendly Teamness . . .
Teeming Friendliness

ABC-owned stations in San Francisco and New York pioneered *The Eyewitness News* format in the early 1970s. These shows have also been called "Friendly Teamness" and "Happy News." They differ from other local newscasts in a number of ways, but most notably in the way members of the news team relate to each other. Gone is the old stiff-collared serious approach. Friendly team members are relaxed and at ease with their news.

In between stories there is light chitchat about the day's events and whatever else comes to mind. News stories emphasize "human interest." There's a group of boy scouts going on a hike in Tarzana, a new flower seller on Fourth Street.

Journalists debate the ethics of "friendly news," but no one debates its success. ABC hit the ratings jackpot in both San Francisco and New York. The network promptly sup-

plied the format outline to local affiliates, and soon eyewitness news teams began to spring up in most of the country's major markets. Other newscasts were forced to copy in hopes of winning back viewers.

In part, this is a product of the new competitiveness among local newscasts. Though the local news seldom makes money (news is very costly to produce), every station has to do it anyway. Why not offset costs as much as possible?

In addition, for many stations the local news is directly followed by prime-time offerings. If a large audience is tuned in for the news, more will stay tuned when the news is over. From a practical standpoint, "teeming friendliness" is desirable because it means a larger audience than the more traditional approach. Why?

ABC called in Marshall McLuhan to explain the phenomenon. McLuhan contends that friendly newscasters *share* the news with the audience rather than reporting it in a more objective way. The friendly talk between newscasters lets the audience in on what's happening. "The press," he says, "is concerned with what *has* happened. TV news is more successful when it concerns itself with what *is* happening."

Eyewitness news is really "I" witness news. It's a warmer, friendlier, more relaxed coverage of events that allows the viewer to participate. The news team has direct dialogue with the audience. The old newscaster says, "That's the way it is"; the friendly news team says, "This is the way *we are*." In this way, the reporting of the event *becomes* the event, overshadowing the original story. Hence the *coverage* of a sports event is really more of a story than the event itself.

The same can be true of news at the national level. Famous anchor people are stars or celebrities in their own right. When Barbara Walters goes to interview the Ambassador of Kuwait, she is actually the story since she's far better known than her interviewee.

Broadcast Editorials

The concept of the editorial was borrowed from print. Editorial expression has of course been around since the beginning of mass media, but the earliest separate editorial pages appeared in Horace Greeley's *New York Tribune* in the 1840s. Though Greeley was a great "moralist," he felt the place for opinion was on a separate page, not mixed up with the

news. The editorial page was a permanent fixture by the end of the century.

When radio appeared in the 1920s, there was no thought to giving a point of view. But as radio news went into high gear, some stations offered programs of news and comment, calling them "newspapers of the air." By 1940, WAAB in Boston was offering regular opinions on the qualifications of political candidates and other controversial public issues.

Some complaints to the FCC surfaced in 1941 when WAAB applied for a license renewal. Hearings were held. In what became known as the "Mayflower Decision," the FCC concluded that:

A radio station cannot be used to advocate the causes of the licensee. It cannot be used to support the candidacy of his friends. It cannot be devoted to the support of principles he happens to regard most favorably. In brief, the broadcaster cannot be an advocate.

WAAB saw the writing on the wall and stopped editorializing. Without ever being tested by the courts, the right to editorialize was relinquished by broadcasters. For the next eight years, there was much debate about what the rights and responsibilities of a "truly free radio station" should be. Many broadcasters were alarmed, contending that the FCC had overstepped its authority. In 1949, the commission reversed the Mayflower Decision and said that in the interest of the public's right to hear all points of view (and of broadcasters' right of free speech), editorials would be allowed. It established guidelines for those who would editorialize, reminding them that the right to editorialize carried with it an obligation to make sure those with opposing points of view were heard.

The commission said, "In such presentation of news and comment the public interest requires that the licensee must operate on a basis of overall fairness." This came to be known as the "fairness doctrine." The policy became more important in 1959 as Congress (through an amendment of section 315 of the Communication Act) began to *encourage* broadcasters to editorialize and in the 1960s, with encouragement from FCC Chairman Newton Minow. In essence, they said that it was not only broadcasters' *right* to editorialize (and offer equal time), it was also their *responsibility*. In this way, the public could hear all sides of controversial issues.

In the 1969 Red Lion Decision, the U.S. Supreme Court went even further, saying the rights of viewers and listeners came before those of broadcasters. Broadcasters may not systematically exclude a program because they fear it will be controversial or some listeners may find it objectionable. They have a duty to present provocative programs and diverse points of view.

By the mid-1970s, two of every three commercial TV stations in the country carried some sort of editorial. But only one station in seven carried a *daily* editorial or reply. What's more, the subject matter for those editorials was often innocuous or relatively trivial. Some stations still stayed away from more substantive issues for fear of offending viewers or sponsors. Two out of three commercial AM radio stations and half of the FM stations editorialized. Congress has forbidden public radio and TV stations from editorializing, fearing public broadcasting funds might be used to support a particular candidate. The constitutionality of forbidding public stations to editorialize while demanding it from commercial stations remains to be tested.

Issues and Answers

Who Owns the Media?

We are surrounded by thousands of media outlets supplying countless billions of words, sounds, and pictures in a never-ending stream of cultural information. Our right to get news and opinion from these diversified media has been affirmed by the Supreme Court. We have a tradition of a free press and a free marketplace of ideas where all can speak their mind as they see fit.

But the marketplace of ideas is also a marketplace of free enterprise. Media ownership trends in recent years have some critics worried. We know the power of media is the greatest single power in our society. Control of media means control of the information

". . . and now the news."

Drawing by Richter; © 1975, The New Yorker Magazine, Inc.

channels we use to decide political and social issues. We may try to counteract this control by subscribing to a newspaper and listening to newscasts on radio and TV stations. But if the newspaper we read, the radio station we hear, and the television programs we see are all owned by one person or corporation, where does that leave us? Are we being robbed of our chance to get more diversified information?

The proliferation of vast corporations—some owning 50 or more newspapers, some even owning two in a single market—is cause for concern. In 1977, the 12 largest owned a total of 245 newspapers with a combined circulation of 23.4 million or 38 percent of the 61 million individual newspapers distributed in America each day. To make matters worse,

many of these same chains maintain broadcast interests.

During the 1970s, a series of FCC decisions made it clear that owning broadcast and newspaper outlets in the same market was not desirable. But to break up existing combinations would mean the sale or trade of stations in 43 states and most major markets. So, while the FCC would approve no more *cross-ownership* deals, it would let those that existed remain. A 1977 U.S. circuit court decision took the FCC ruling one step further, saying that broadcasters must either prove that such arrangements are "in the public interest" or divest themselves of multiple outlets.

Former FCC Commissioner Nicholas Johnson hailed the decision as a landmark victory for freedom of speech and first amendment rights. Long a critic of those he calls "the media barons," Johnson says the FCC is our only hope of continuing diversified information. Once, he says, the FCC took this responsibility seriously.

In 1941, they ordered NBC to divest itself of one of its radio networks and in that same year, they set limits on the total number of broadcast licenses any individual can hold . . . but since the New Deal generation left the command posts of the FCC, this agency has lost much of its zeal for combatting concentration . . . atrophy has reached an advanced state.

Johnson notes that the question is very basic. Can the government or its agency really *control* an industry that in turn controls the access of government officials to the electorate? Perhaps this is why the FCC has been timid in recent years and why it took the court of appeals to prod it into doing its job.

Media owners were outraged at these events, pointing out that profitable broadcast stations often support money-losing newspapers. Without the broadcast income, they claim, many newspapers would cease publication. Yet the power of owning several media outlets in one community is awesome. It may be better to have no newspaper than to have one controlled by owners who already run AM, FM, and TV stations. If the FCC can't or won't force the issue, the problem will have to be left to the judiciary.

The Department of Justice has authority under the antitrust laws to break up combinations that "restrain trade" or "tend to lessen competition." These laws apply to media as they do to any other industry. Johnson argues convincingly that, if it is in the public interest to have different brands of steel and different kinds of automobiles, it is certainly in our interest to have diverse sources of information.

Queries and Concepts

1. Compare a local daily paper and a weekly paper. What are the differences in size? Amount of advertising? Editorial content?

2. Make up your own list of criteria defining "what's news." How does it differ from the editor's list included here? How would newspapers be better if they followed your list?

3. Dig through your library or newspaper's files to find a newspaper printed 30 years ago. Does the visual style differ from that of today? How about the use of pictures? Headlines?

4. Do a comparative analysis of newspaper, radio, and TV news. Simply list all stories in the front section of the newspaper, all stories covered by a five-minute radio

newscast, and all stories covered by a half-hour TV newscast on the same day. Which does the best job of covering the day's news? Why?

5. Check your local TV newscast for any possible influence of the "friendly team" approach. You might want to look at all TV newscasts in your market and decide which has the friendliest team!

6. Do some research on the ownership of media outlets in your market. Does any one single person or corporation own more than one? How might this affect the news you receive?

Readings and References

The Newspaper You Never See

One excellent staff chart of a typical newspaper appears in Chapter 14 of *Mass Media* by Hiebert, Ungurait, and Bohn (New York: David McKay, 1974).

What's News?

For a number of articles groping with definitions for news, see the special section, "What Is News," *Journal of Communication*, Autumn 1976, p. 4.

Newspaper Layout: The Eyes Have It

Arthur T. Turnbull and Russell N. Baird
The Graphics of Communication: Practical Exercises in Typography, Layout and Design. New York: Holt, Rinehart & Winston, 1968.
This is the complete book of newspaper design covering graphics, typography, and layout. Though it is dated, its historical perspective and basic premises remain applicable to today's visual trends.

Radio: The New Kid in Town; Rip and Read

Sydney W. Head
Broadcasting in America, 3d ed. New York: Houghton Mifflin, 1976.
First published in 1956, this is the standard text for introduction to broadcasting. There are sections on the history of radio and television, as well as brief descriptions of key legal battles involving news development in the new media. Use the index to go directly to the sections that interest you. The 1976 edition is a must; other editions are too far out of date.

The Commentators

You'll find an interesting discussion of Paul Harvey and his influence in William L. Rivers's *The Mass Media*, 2d ed. (New York: Harper & Row, 1975). Edward R. Murrow's biography, *Prime Time: The Life of Edward R.*

Murrow, by Alexander Kendrick (New York: Avon Books, 1970) is the most complete account of the highly revered newsman. See also *CBS Reflections in a Bloodshot Eye* by Robert Metz (New York: New American Library, 1976) for the "inside story" of early CBS radio and TV commentators and stars.

Television News: The Tossed Salad

Irving E. Fang
Television News: Writing, Filming, Editing, Broadcasting. New York: Hastings House, 1972.
This is the most popular text for TV news courses. Fang covers the mechanics, history, and development of TV news, current topics, and issues in the field. The heavy emphasis on social issues like the Vietnam War dates it, but perhaps there will be a new edition by the time you read this.

Alfred W. Friendly
Due to Circumstances Beyond Our Control. Westminster, Md.: Random House, 1967.
The man who co-produced *See It Now* with Ed Murrow reminisces about his broadcasting career and his final years as president of CBS News. He quit in 1966 when the network chose to air a rerun of *I Love Lucy* instead of critical public hearings on Vietnam.

Maury Green
Television News: Anatomy and Process. Belmont, Ca.: Wadsworth, 1969.
Green covers the same territory as Fang, but

I prefer Green because his book is easier to read and filled with the "newsman's-eye view." Green is a former Los Angeles newscaster with many years of professional experience.

Friendly Teamness . . . Teeming Friendliness

McLuhan's article for ABC has not been reprinted as far as I know, though I managed to get a copy. You might write to ABC.

The May/June 1977 issue of *Columbia Journalism Review* features analyses of the eyewitness news phenomenon.

Broadcast Editorials

There's a concise discussion of this in Sydney W. Head's *Broadcasting in America* (New York: Houghton Mifflin, 1976); also see Frank J. Kahn's *Documents of American Broadcasting* (New York: Appleton, 1973) for the complete annotated FCC decisions in crucial legal matters. Fred W. Friendly's *The Good Guys, the Bad Guys and the First Amendment: Free Speech Vs. Fairness in Broadcasting* (Westminster, Md.: Random House, 1977) examines the Red Lion Decision and related issues.

Issues and Answers: Who Owns the Media?

See Chapter 2 of Nicholas Johnson's *How to Talk Back to Your Television Set* (New York:

Bantam Books, 1970) for a scathing indictment of "the media barons." *Los Angeles Times's* "Outlook" section of March 20, 1977, carried the story of the U.S. circuit court decision. *U.S. News & World Report,* January 24, 1977, carried a piece on the disappearance of the independent newspaper, entitled "After a Rash of Take-Overs, New Worries About 'Press Lords,'" pp. 54–56.

Bryce W. Rucker
The First Freedom. Carbondale: Southern Illinois University Press, 1971.
This includes a thorough compilation of statistics on media cross-ownership. See especially Chapter 13, "Broadcast Control by Chains and Newspapers." Though the examples need updating, the principles and issues remain the same.

12

Advertising and Public Relations: The Pretty Package

News, by its very definition is bad; if one hears good news— it must be advertising or PR. . . .—Marshall McLuhan

Selling Out

After getting my master's degree and finding teaching jobs as scarce as smog-free air in Los Angeles, I pondered what to do with my life. Dozens of want ads later, it came down to two possibilities. An $85-a-week "page" job at NBC (which would allow me to keep my ideals intact) or a commercial position with the public relations and advertising department of a large insurance company that paid much more. I thought it over for 15 seconds and "sold out" gleefully.

The idea of someone, anyone, paying me that much money was gratifying. Shortly, I learned why advertising and public relations positions pay so well. In six months I had two ulcers, three cars, and a four-a-day scotch-and-soda habit. Hours were long and tedious, including late nights and weekends. I was about to quit when my boss took a month off, leaving me in charge to "see if I could handle it." I couldn't. By the time he got back my desk was a maze of files and buying schedules, and I was up to six scotches a day.

Gently, he hinted that I didn't really have what it takes to be a success in advertising. Later, I came down with "insurance leg," a physical illness that seemed to flare up whenever I went in to work. I resigned and went on unemployment.

In reviewing my failure to make it in the ad business, I have decided I had too much, too soon. Advertising and public relations, like sales, require one to "lay it on the line"

every day. The proof is "the bottom line," snaring and keeping the clients, who provide your daily bread. Advertising and PR require a quick wit, endless creativity, the physical stamina of a teenager, and the heart of a realist. It is a world of deadlines, challenges, and bottom lines. Advertising and PR are among the most influential and competitive media-related industries.

The Business of the Message

In some ways, advertising and PR differ little from mass media themselves. As in print, radio, and television, a message is created and designed to reach a mass audience. But the advertising message must do more than keep the audience's attention. It must influence attitudes, beliefs, and behaviors. No matter how clever a message campaign may be, if it fails to influence, it fails. What's more, you may have only 30 seconds of air time or a few column inches of space to make it happen. This makes advertising and PR particularly challenging.

Advertising is selling a product; it is designed to influence the buying habits of a target audience. PR is more subtle; campaigns are designed to influence attitudes and beliefs. This may mean reinforcing existing attitudes or creating new ones.

Let's take the case of the large oil company whose drilling operations have accidentally spilled two million gallons of oil on Miami

Beach. That is "a hell of a PR problem." The PR staff advises how to rectify any damage to the company's image. Perhaps there will be a press release explaining company efforts to clean up the beach, or advertising to counteract public outrage, or publicity concerning a new company-instituted safety regulation.

At the same time, the advertising department of the same oil company will continue as if the oil spill had never happened. Its job is simply (as we'll see, it's not really all that simple) to urge people to buy their brand of gas and oil.

Advertising and PR are *message businesses*. But these messages are often aimed at only small segments of the mass audience. For example, a PR campaign may be aimed at only those who have negative feelings about a particular company. An advertising campaign may be aimed at only those affluent enough to buy a Mercedes Benz. PR and advertising practitioners are *information specialists*.

The Advertising Business Develops

Mass advertising developed along with mass media. Advertising was rare until Gutenberg and the rise of mass literacy. Early ad forms were handbills and printed signs. As newspapers developed and circulation increased, publishers found they could supplement their income by offering space for sale. By the early 1800s there were thousands of such publica-

tions. Most transactions were made at the local level, but as marketing techniques became more sophisticated and long-distance travel more common, many businesses wanted to expand to new markets.

Into this dilemma came the advertising *agency*. Volney Palmer organized the first one in the United States in 1841. Early agencies represented publishers, not products, going to potential advertisers to offer space for sale. They were given a small fee from publishers, usually based on the total amount of revenues they brought in.

Soon the advertising business was becoming unwieldy. Companies that advertised their products were constantly in doubt as to which publication to buy and what their ads should say. Circulation figures were suspect, and advertisers had no way of knowing the real "cost per thousand" of readers reached. Into this vacuum stepped the N. W. Ayer & Son Agency. In 1875, it began offering ad counseling directly to the people with the products, advising them how to get *more* for their advertising dollar. The idea was a great success, and the basic structure of advertising remains the same today.

Advertising agencies represent clients, dream up copy for their ads, recommend media outlets, and are paid a percentage of the total advertising dollar (usually 15 percent). One additional twist makes the relationship between agency and client interesting. Though agents are paid a percentage of their client's advertising dollar, the client doesn't

"It's Ron Lassiter. He says the Mocha Munchies people don't like our presentation, and he's going through a lot of pain."

always actually pay. Most media outlets offer a 15 percent *agency discount* on all ad rates. In theory at least, clients are obtaining the services of their agencies for free.

Of course, to the advertising agency it doesn't matter *who* pays the fee. What matters is getting new clients and holding onto the existing ones. Agencies spend a lot of money making presentations to potential clients in an effort to obtain new accounts. Often this involves winning clients away from other agencies. Even the largest, most stable companies like General Foods, General Motors, and American Telephone and Telegraph may change agencies often.

Radio Advertising

There has always been a difference between public perceptions of print and of broadcast advertising. From the beginning, people seemed to take print advertising for granted. No one seemed to object in the 1800s when most newspapers developed a heavy dependence on advertising. It's easy to see the benefits to all of newspaper classified advertising, for example. But broadcasting was different. The public seemed to feel that broadcast ads were an intrusion into their own private space. Many still do.

From the time the first radio ad ran in 1922, it took only five years before radio advertising was commonplace. Advertiser claims and counter-claims were chaotic. Into all this stepped the federal government, and in 1927 the first radio act was passed. The provisions of the act made it obvious that the American system of broadcasting was to be "commercial." What might have happened had the government taken a different attitude? In Britain, all broadcasting was put under control of the national government. No advertising was allowed and listeners "paid" for their entertainment via a special tax on home receivers.

The commercial nature of American radio continued to be challenged. As late as 1929, the National Association of Broadcasters, an industry organization, was trying to discourage advertising during what we now call "prime time." Its code of ethics stated that there was a "decided difference between what may be broadcast before 6:00 P.M. and what may be broadcast after 6:00 P.M." They reasoned that before 6:00 P.M., radio was part of the listener's business day. But after that time, radio should be used for "recreation and relaxation." The 1929 code limited advertising to a dignified identification of sponsors between 6:00 and 11:00 P.M.

Such idealism soon gave way to a more pragmatic approach. It was precisely during prime time that most people were listening, and broadcasters quickly learned they could charge more for advertising time when the audience was large.

By 1930, the CBS and dual NBC radio networks were going strong. Between them, they boasted more than 100 affiliates. Programs supplied through the networks were not their own creations, but those of sponsors and their advertising agencies. Thus during the 1920s and 1930s many successful programs bore the names of products: *Lux Radio Theatre*, *The Eveready Hour*, and *The Purina Chow Checkerboard Boys*. Often the name of the product was woven into the theme song of the show.

Radio stars unabashedly endorsed everything from soap to cigarettes.

Early Excesses

Advertising practices during the first half of the 20th century were often more practical than ethical. Print media and radio stations received consumer complaints by the thousands, accusing advertisers of making exaggerated claims for their products.

In 1911, a crusade was started by advertisers to clean up the industry. This was in large part a reaction against the shady campaigns of purveyors of patent medicines. A number of organizations tried to adopt codes of ethics to encourage truth in advertising and discourage questionable practices. They reasoned that the public might come to distrust all advertising.

The 1929 code of ethics of the National Association of Broadcasters laid down guidelines for the regulation of commercials, placing the responsibility for commercial content on the broadcast licensee. Broadcasters were urged to prohibit advertising making "false, deceptive, or grossly exaggerated claims." Obscene material was to be banned. The client's business product should be mentioned "succinctly to ensure an adequate return on his investment, but never to the extent that it loses listeners to the station." That's a magic formula most stations would still like to have today!

The problem comes in defining the terms used in the 1929 code or in any of the dozens of advertising codes that followed. At what point do we reach "excessive" advertising claims? When does zealous representation of the product end and exaggeration begin? Advertising remains "advocacy" for a product. Most consumers know by now that advertising agencies exist to portray the sponsor's product in the most favorable light. A product's weaknesses are going to be ignored, but if the opposition has a weakness it is going to be exploited.

Of course it would be absurd to say that all advertising is untrue, or that the industry is not generally more "ethical" today than it was 60 or 70 years ago, but the main agency concern is selling the sponsor's product. All other considerations (like absolute truth and uncompromising ethics) remain secondary.

Television: The Ultimate Advertising Medium

After World War II television rose to become the dominant entertainment medium in America. Network radio no longer attracted the mass audience. Advertisers were among the first to perceive this change, and TV was quickly flooded with commercials. Since the new medium delivered to a heterogeneous audience, products most likely to benefit from TV exposure were those almost everyone could use: toothpaste, aspirin, soap, and cigarettes.

Television was a new challenge for advertisers since they could now *picture* the product as well as describe it. An important lesson, first learned in radio, was doubly applicable to television. In a marketplace flooded with similar products, the *form* of the ad was at least as important as the *content*. Cigarette commercials in the mid-1950s, for example, showed scene after scene of lush springtime countryside. A playful couple cavorted with each other flirtatiously while smoking. Clearly the message was that smoking (for whatever unknown reason) is like a springtime experience, embodying all the joys of youth, love, and an ant-free picnic.

In 1952 the sale of radio time still accounted for more than 60 percent of every broadcast advertising dollar, but two years later television surpassed radio with sales that exceeded $500 million. By 1956, the total spent buying network radio time had dropped to $44 million, about a third of what it had been at the beginning of the decade.

As in radio, most network television programs were *sponsored*, conceived, created, and paid for by sponsors and their agencies. In 1959, the public was outraged at having been deceived by those rigged quiz shows and blamed the networks. With some justification all three maintained they were only conduits, selling time to others who created the shows, but it didn't seem to matter.

Networks rapidly realized they would have to control more carefully the content of programs they aired. Increasingly, new shows were conceived and produced by the networks themselves. This led to a decline of the sponsorship and the rise of *spot* advertising. The spot advertiser does not buy any one show but hundreds of 30- or 60-second *spots* to be run at specified times.

Save Me a Spot

Spot advertising is the backbone of broadcast advertising. Here's how it works:

1. The ad agency meets with the client and determines media strategies most appropriate for the product.

2. A time buyer employed by the agency meets with a station representative, who may handle dozens of radio and TV stations. Together, they try to determine which "buys" will be most effective for the client.

3. The station rep designs a package of buys, specifying stations and air times.

Sometimes a client will intervene by putting other constraints on the time buyer. Often the station rep will try to stick time buyers with the less than desirable times they are under pressure to sell. Eventually the client's spot, conceived and produced by the agency, appears on the station at the time and date specified.

What I've just described is a simplified version of what happens at the national or regional level. At the local level, sponsors may deal directly with the station sales people. In very small markets, those sales people may also be on-the-air personalities, or perform some other function for the station.

Advertising: Making a Living

There are more than half a million people employed in advertising in America today. Some of these are station reps and time buyers. Some deal exclusively in print: layout, design, illustrations, and graphics. Others work for newspapers, magazines, or other media outlets. Some are involved with broadcast copywriting and production.

A typical advertising agency is run by a board of directors who choose a president. The president then deals with department heads, each of whom has a specialized staff of people designed to get their job done.

Marketing Research This is the statistical arm of the agency that informs clients of the most lucrative geographic and demographic markets for their products. Often marketing research means field interviews with potential buyers.

Media Selection Media selection is obviously crucial. It is done by the print space buyers and the broadcast time buyers who do their best to place the sponsor's message where it is likely to get maximum response.

Creative Activity   Creativity is what most of us think of when we imagine an advertising agency. It involves the people who write the copy and create the visual content of the ads we see and hear each day. There are often photographers, graphics experts, copywriters, and others employed by the agency on a full-time basis.

Account Management   These are the account executives who deal directly with the client and who are constantly on the lookout for new clients to bring into the agency fold. Account executives, like radio and TV sales people, are generally among the highest paid staffers. Without them, there would be no need for other staff members since there would be no clients.

Advertising has become so complex that many large companies hire people whose sole job is to watch over the agencies. One of my functions at the insurance company was to act as a watchdog for agency decisions, to make sure they were getting the most for the company's advertising dollar. Agency representatives would always have elaborate rationale, including charts, graphs, and demographics, that explained why they were buying this market or that one. This was usually accompanied by tickets to football, basketball, or

baseball games, free dinners and drinks. This may seem like "cheating" to the uninitiated, but I was assured that it was quite normal.

Most graduates lucky enough to land an entry-level advertising position start as sales people at local media outlets. If you go to an agency, you could start as a copywriter, particularly if you are a man. Most of the ad agency people I know still use women college graduates as clerk typists, though they adamantly insist they practice equal opportunity employment.

However, women will find that initiative is rewarded more rapidly in advertising than anywhere else in media—not because ad agencies are feminist, but because they are pro-achievement. Advertising is a very upwardly mobile business. Once you get over the demeaning lower hurdles, you'll be able to rise as far as your brains and talent will take you. You'll have a much better chance if you're competitive, aggressive, hard working, and mix well with all kinds of people, regardless of political persuasion. The world of advertising is one of *compromise.* Ad people are hard-headed realists.

Journalists tend to see themselves as working tirelessly for the public good. Advertising people know they are in business to help clients. Whether those clients are selling dog food, motorboats, or American flags makes little difference.

Advertising can be used effectively in "selling" many things that are not products in the

Advertisers remind readers that they sell education, health, and peace, as well as cookies and computers.

© Advertising Council. Used by permission.

traditional sense (see 12.1). It was the TV antismoking campaigns that helped lead to a total ban of cigarette commercials on the medium. Many of the top advertising agencies regularly contribute their time and energies to worthwhile causes and charities.

One tangible reward awaits those who do break into advertising—money. Even at the lowest levels, advertising positions tend to pay substantially more than comparable media jobs. A beginning agency copywriter can expect to earn 20 percent more than workers doing the same thing at radio or TV stations. This holds true for persons in production, art, and other areas as well.

Advertising/Case in Point: The Great Pet Food War

> I want tuna,
> I want liver,
> I want chicken,
> Please deliver.

The cat that sang this refrain for Meow Mix was supposed to convince us that our cats would never be happy until we delivered the product to them. This is one of the dozens of pet food commercials in recent years that have "humanized" pets in television, radio, and print. But when you stop and think about it, pets aren't human at all. Or are they?

Behind these commercials are thousands of hours of research designed to exploit our feelings about pets and to *sell us* one particular brand of pet food over another. Most veterinarians agree that pets are color blind and that even the taste of a particular food matters very little. Yet most of us are convinced about the virtues of the pet food we buy. Why?

Pet food commercials afford the perfect example of the victory of form over content in advertising. In France, most animals are happy getting along on table scraps, but the American pet must have pet food.

This phenomenon is a fairly recent one. Ac-

cording to an article in *The New Yorker*, until about 15 years ago there were only a few pet foods on the market. But by 1965, Americans were spending $700 million on their pets, and a scant ten years later, that figure had jumped to over $2.5 *billion*. Virtually all of this can be attributed to advertising. There is no evidence that our animals are any healthier or happier than before. Yet we believe our pets *have* to have these products.

The advertising agencies have us neatly divided into three camps. There's the "premium" buyer who buys only the best—brands advertised as "100 percent meat and meat by-products." Then there's the "practical" or "functional" consumer who buys whatever is cheapest—the cereal products. In the middle is the buyer of the "moist meal" pet foods, packaged in convenient foil pouches but supposedly tasting "like they just came out of the can"!

The most celebrated coup in the industry was the triumph of the Alpo campaign of the middle 1960s, which insisted that: "Your dog *needs* meat." There were endless variations. The goal was simple: to convince owners that their dogs *had* to have the premium-priced Alpo brand. In 1970, the Federal Trade Commission intervened. Their tests indicated that pets really didn't *need* meat at all. In fact, all pet foods—canned, moist, and cereal—had long been meeting government regulations requiring certain minimum nutritional content.

The new Alpo cry is: "Your dog *loves* meat"! Alpo, of course, was not the only pet food

Form or content? Purina contends that they put more "wow" in their cat food. What is wow?

manufacturer to use slogans. Gaines Burgers, a moist variety, boasted that its product was "like canned dog food, without the can." Ralston Purina asserted that its Chuck Wagon was "meaty, juicy, chunky." However, Chuck Wagon did not contain one speck of meat.

But the slogans of pet food manufacturers are not the real story. Of more interest is what

motivates us to spend all this money on our pets. The first response is obvious, we love them. We want them to have a "balanced diet," one that's good for them. We have emotional feelings about our pets that have been successfully exploited by sponsors and their agencies. Besides, who can resist a close-up of a little kitten or puppy (see 12.2), or the

Drawing by Koren; © 1976, The New Yorker Magazine, Inc.

antics of Morris the "finicky" cat? Pets are so . . . well . . . visual! That's why pet food commercials work so well on television. Despite healthy budgets for radio and print, TV remains king in the pet food ad business.

Television advertising has been the biggest single contributor to the rapid economic growth of many key industries like pet foods, which sell their products to a large number of consumers. Through heavy use of TV, today's unfamiliar brand name becomes tomorrow's institution.

Of course, the pet food war is but one example of thousands of wars being waged for our consumer dollars every day by advertisers. Vance Packard pointed out convincingly in *The Hidden Persuaders* that advertisers cash in on our fears, hopes, dreams, and anxieties by exploiting them to their own end. We must become more aware of this process if we are to make sensible choices about how we spend our money.

Packard feels that advertisers with their "depth manipulation" often make us do things that are irrational and illogical.

At times it is pleasanter or easier to be nonlogical. But I prefer being nonlogical by my own free will and impulse rather than to find myself manipulated into such acts.

The most serious offense many of the depth manipulators commit, it seems to me, is that they try to invade the privacy of our minds. It is this right to privacy in our minds—privacy to be either rational or irrational—that I believe we must strive to protect.

Media Mysteries: Advertising as Clue

The effectiveness of advertising is due to the considerable media skills of people in the in-

True beauty is timeless.

dustry. The most skilled copywriters, best artists, and most talented graphic design personnel labor over the national advertising campaigns that bombard us. This has led Marshall McLuhan to observe: "The ad is the meeting place for all the arts, skills, and all the media of the American environment."

The television scriptwriter has only 30 seconds to tell the story. Television advertising dispenses with plot line and brings us *action* and *vision*. We get action because television is motion—the scene may shift several dozen times in that 30 seconds. First a close-up of a hand holding a drink—suddenly a plane flies overhead—a calm stewardess pours a cup of coffee—a child laughs in glee while being served a hot dog as the clouds roll by outside the window.

We get vision because *form* is the important thing, *content* is secondary. The ad for a shirt company shows a field of daisies; there's no shirt and no people. The voice-over tells us: "This shirt makes you *feel* like a daisy." It's like Picasso's famous painting "Man in Chair." There is no man, no chair, only a collection of skewed lines that represent what it *feels like* to sit in a chair.

Print media, particularly magazines, are replete with examples. A full-page ad for silverware pictures a tree of four seasons (see 12.3). A Marlboro ad pictures a man herding horses down a hillside (see 12.4). The cigarette packages are almost hidden in the lower right-hand corner and the rest of the page is devoted to trees and a mountain stream. In another ad a tiny GM logo is in a lower left-hand corner

Chevrolet returns to Castle Rock.

and the Chevrolet is unrecognizably dwarfed by a huge canyon (see 12.5). In each case, visual space is given over to a scene that has, at best, a minimal "logical" connection with the product.

So motion and vision have become the tools of the advertising trade, shifting the emphasis from product to *environment*. The theory is that by surrounding the product with a pleasant environment, the medium can entice the consumer to give it a try.

But the consumer is also busy learning other things. Ads tell us a great deal about our society, and they help to influence and change that society. Although the first business of ads is to sell products, their influence doesn't stop there. In fact, that's where it begins. As McLuhan points out, "Advertising itself is an information commodity far greater than anything it advertises." In their rush to sell a product, advertisers sometimes don't even recognize the more important effects of their collective art—selling life-styles and social values to an entire generation of Americans.

Advertising acts as a DEW (distant early warning) line because it is first to reflect and encourage social trends. According to McLuhan, advertising "responds instantly to any social change, making ads in themselves invaluable means of knowing where it's at." For example, America's interest in ecology during the 1970s showed up often in advertising: ads featuring the "natural" environment to sell everything from cigarettes to silverware. The women's movement had barely gotten started when television ads began picturing women as mechanics and bank presidents. Ads are first used to reflect social trends because they *have* to be one step ahead. Competition in advertising is far more fierce than in programming, so advertising is often more interesting than the program itself.

Advertising also teaches us how to behave through little socialization lessons. Ads teach us that if we love our pets, we must feed them a special kind of food. And they teach us how and when to love *each other*. A wife makes her husband happy by straining his coffee through a special filter. Ads also provide a context and a meaning for all sorts of everyday experiences. A smelly house means social disapproval from important guests. Perhaps you feel you are immune from all of this—you

discount ads as "silly" and unrealistic. But if ads are unrealistic, it is because ad situations are *larger* then life—filled with attractive, interesting people and full of intrinsic meaning. We can't help being influenced by them.

Our new information environment is overflowing with print and electronic data. People who have developed the greatest skills in handling this environment are engaged in advertising. Their handiwork is the hundreds of advertising messages we receive and store daily. To deny that these messages are profoundly influencing us is to deny the influence of all mass communication.

Public Relations: The Subtle Semantic

Once upon a time there was a PR practitioner who approached a large corporation for a job and was interviewed by a hiring committee.

"What have you done?" they asked.

"Why, I'm responsible for the best PR campaign of all time. I was called in as a consultant by a young lady that was having terrible problems. She was living with seven strange men and people were beginning to talk."

"Oh, really—did you do her any good?"

"Oh, c'mon," he said impatiently. "Haven't you heard of Snow White and the Seven Dwarfs?"

Embodied in this story is the central function of public relations: to present the "image" of the client *in the best possible light.*

Many institutions and organizations, from university administrators to tavern owners, employ someone in a public relations capacity. The PR agent acts as a liaison between client and public. Sometimes the job is only a matter of answering the phone and giving information. More often it requires skills in journalism, broadcasting, advertising, and more. Like advertising, PR jobs are financially rewarding. Again, the job can be more demanding, more frustrating, and more rewarding than other media employment.

Press Agentry Pioneers: P. T. Barnum & Co.

PR is as old as media. As long as there have been public information channels, there have been people who would use them to influence public opinion. The acknowledged king of PR pioneers was Phineas Taylor Barnum. He was responsible for the success of midget Tom Thumb and Jenny Lind, the "Swedish Nightingale." Barnum made these people and many others into legends. Then of course there was the circus that bore his name. Barnum's favorite phrase, "There's a sucker born every minute," is still heard often. So effective was Barnum's PR that it remains a part of Americana almost 100 years after his death!

The term *public relations* did not come into being until the 20th century. Before that PR was known as press agentry. The press agents were masters at planting stories in newspapers. This kind of publicity was much more valuable than regular, paid-for display advertising, and it was free. There were many such campaigns during the late 19th century, but most notable, according to historian Marshall Fishwick, was the rise of Buffalo Bill.

Fishwick notes that a half dozen writers helped shape Buffalo Bill into the greatest American folk hero of all. "No one should underestimate their endeavors. More spectacular men had to be outdistanced. Mountains had to be made out of molehills." Almost all of the folk heroes from this era were virtually created through press agentry, among them Wyatt Earp, Calamity Jane, Wild Bill Hickok, Butch Cassidy, and the Sundance Kid. Some stories began with fact but all were eventually mostly fiction.

PR also moved into politics. The 1896 McKinley-Bryan presidential race was the beginning of modern political campaigning methods. There were posters, pamphlets, and publicity, much of it concocted by party press agents. The practice remains intact today. The information tools have changed a bit and candidates have moved to the electronic stage, but tactics remain essentially the same.

Most PR pioneers during the 1920s and 1930s were ex-newspapermen, who became famous for successful publicity campaigns for railroads, steel corporations, and others. PR text writers Scott M. Cutlip and Allen H. Center mention Ivy Lee, George Creel, Edward Bernays, and Carl Byoir, all of whom were responsible for a number of large-scale PR campaigns during this period.

Public Relations in the Global Village

There are well over 100,000 people actively engaged in public relations work today. PR people are information specialists who know how to sort through billions of bits of information and come up with "the pretty package" media consumers are looking for. PR textbooks stress brevity and simplicity. The public wants to *feel* informed without getting all the details. Television has become our primary source of news because we want instant information without the bothersome details in long columns of print.

The second reason for the PR boom is the increasing value—and the increasing cost—of access to media channels themselves. Sponsors pay more than $250,000 for one commercial minute during the Super Bowl. The average 30-second network prime-time TV spot costs $50,000. As media have become more powerful, obtaining *space* has become more desirable and more difficult. Many turn to the PR specialist whose prime function is obtaining that space free of charge. (An extreme example of free media coverage happens when fringe political groups kidnap or assassinate well-known people just to focus media attention on their concerns.)

Each of the 200 wealthiest corporations in America employs a public relations staff of at least 75 full-time persons. Large PR firms may have as many as 500 employees. Competent reporters who leave journalism for PR can expect an immediate salary increase of 25 percent or so. The chances are very good that they will return to the newsroom to see old friends ten years later and be earning double the salary of colleagues who stayed. Though writing is the skill most often mentioned as necessary for entry to PR, persons who specialize in public speaking, group communication skills, and electronic media production are finding PR positions, too.

In large corporations, the PR staff has monumental responsibilities. There are stockholders who want maximum return for their investment, employees who want higher wages, and a public convinced that all corporations are run by criminals. Out of this chaos, the PR department is expected to bring order. It does so by using the one tool of the trade: information. Stockholders' meetings are held, and quarterly reports are issued that speak in glowing terms of profits. Employee newsletters help create a sense of community and harmony. News releases tell of public services performed by corporation executives.

There are lots of PR people who work exclusively for nonprofit foundations and charities. The Camp Fire Girls, for example, maintains a full-time staff of public relations people who help plan national campaigns and the inevitable candy sales. PR staffs can also be found working for labor unions, government agencies, and churches. In each case, the job involves getting specific information to the public via the news media.

PR has formed a relationship with our mass communication system. Some feel it's a parasitic one, that PR feeds from the mass media and offers nothing in return. Others stress the symbiotic nature of the relationship, contending that PR people offer reporters new information and can be valuable news sources.

But it's the way PR practitioners use information that often lets the profession in for criticism. Some contend that those in PR are "hype artists" who will stop at nothing to get their clients favorable publicity. The most stinging indictments come from journalists, whose interests often conflict with the interests of PR practitioners. Idealistic journalists look down their noses at people who "prostitute" their media skills in the interests of a client, rather than use them for the public good. To make it worse, PR people are forced to deal with journalists on a regular basis, since newspaper reporters and editors act as gatekeepers in determining how much of the "news" supplied by PR people will get to the public.

Journalists call PR practitioners "flacks," and the Associated Press managing editor's guidelines define a "flack" as:

. . . a person who makes all or part of his income by obtaining space in newspapers without cost to himself or his clients. Usually a professional . . . they are known formally as public relations men.

A flack is a flack. His job is to say kind things about his client. He will not lie very often, but much of the time he tells less than the whole story. You do not owe the PR man anything. The owner of the newspaper, not the flack, pays your salary. Your immediate job is to serve the readers, not the man who would raid your columns.

The most common complaint against flacks concerns their attempts to "color" the news or grab free advertising for their clients. Reporters also resent that many of their own give up reporting for higher-paying PR positions.

PR practitioners have their own complaints against journalists. They often claim that their clients are victims of sensational reporting of news (usually to the detriment of the client). Quotes and other information from releases are taken out of context. Journalists fail to discriminate between "honest practitioners" and those who may be incompetent. How valid these claims are is a matter of debate.

Issues and Answers

The Selling of the President

In 1960, when the role of advertising and PR in politics was more apparent than ever before, *Life* magazine quoted one campaign strategist as saying, "I can elect any person to office

Television plays a major role in informing voters about current events as well as events of the past.

"The ignorance of one voter in a democracy impairs the security of all."

—John F. Kennedy

But how can we build a more informed electorate?

Some answers are clear: bring the candidates, their voices and views to every voter's home. Provide background and analysis. And television, most Americans agree, is a vital part of that process. A universal means for helping citizens relate their local problems to those of the country and the world.

In a Roper survey conducted after the last national election, a majority of those interviewed cited television by a two-to-one margin as the medium giving "the clearest understanding of the candidates and the issues." This year, television broadcasters are spending many hundreds of millions of dollars on news coverage that will help make this generation of voters the best informed in history.

Stay tuned as television continues to inform. And to entertain in many special ways, as the listing below attests.

Noah's Animals. Ark story from animals' point of view. Monday, April 5 (8-8:30 pm).

Dick Cavett's Backlot U.S.A. With Mae West, Gene Kelly, John Wayne, Mickey Rooney. Monday, April 5 (10-11 pm).

The Selfish Giant. Oscar Wilde tale, animated. Tuesday, April 6 (8-8:30 pm).

Santiago's America. ABC Afterschool Special— Youngster's odyssey to California. Wednesday, April 7 (4:30-5:30 pm).

Perry Como's Spring in New Orleans. Leslie Uggams, Dick Van Dyke at the Mardi Gras. Wednesday, April 7 (9-10 pm).

Truman at Potsdam. Hallmark Hall of Fame— Historic 1945 meeting of Truman, Stalin and Churchill. Thursday, April 8 (9-9:30 pm).

Women of the Year. Awards for outstanding contributions by women. Thursday, April 8 (9:30-11 pm).

The First Easter Rabbit. Animated, with voices of Burl Ives, Stan Freberg, Robert Morse. Friday, April 9 (8-8:30 pm).

The Story of David. ABC Theatre—Life of Biblical warrior-ruler with Timothy Bottoms, Anthony Quayle, Susan Hampshire, others. Friday, April 9; Sunday, April 11 (9-11 pm).

It's the Easter Beagle, Charlie Brown. Monday, April 12 (8-8:30 pm).

Rikki Tikki Tavi. Based on Kipling tale. Monday, April 12 (8:30-9 pm).

The Phantom Rebel. Special Treat—Drama set in Boston during Revolution. Tuesday, April 13 (4-5 pm).

The Original Rompin' Stompin' Hot and Heavy, Cool and Groovy All Star Jazz Show. CBS Festival of Lively Arts for Young People— With group of all-time jazz greats. Tuesday, April 13 (4-5 pm).

Last Days. Sandburg's Lincoln—Final segment, with Hal Holbrook, Sada Thompson. Wednesday, April 14 (10-11 pm).

The Waltons: The Easter Story. Thursday, April 15 (8-10 pm).

The Greatest Story Ever Told. Biblical film with Max Von Sydow, Sidney Poitier, Shelley Winters. Thursday, April 15; Saturday, April 17 (9-11 p.m.)

ABC News Closeup. Probes abuses of organized medicine. Thursday, April 15 (10-11 pm).

A Boy Named Charlie Brown. Feature film of "Peanuts" kids. Friday, April 16 (8-9:30 pm).

The Olympic Champions and Challengers. Personal stories of 24 American, Soviet athletes. Saturday, April 17 (8-9 pm).

The Right to Believe. Directions—History of religious freedom in America. Sunday, April 18 (12 noon-1 pm).

The Tony Awards. Broadway's annual tribute to stars, plays. Sunday, April 18 (9-11 pm).

Gun Control: Pro and Con. ABC News Closeup. Tuesday, April 20 (10-11 pm).

CBS Reports: Busing. Tuesday, April 20 (10-11 pm).

Blind Sunday. ABC Afterschool Special—A blind girl and athletic boy share each other's world. Wednesday, April 21 (4:30-5:30 pm).

Stop, Thief! The American Parade—Story of how Tweed Ring was exposed by free press. Thursday, April 22 (10-11 pm).

Mysteries of the Hidden Reefs. Undersea World of Jacques Cousteau—Explores reefs in Caribbean. Sunday, April 25 (7-8 pm).

Orangutans: Orphans of the Wild. Survival Anglia documentary. Wednesday, April 28 (8-9 pm).

Queen of the Stardust Ballroom. CBS Playhouse 90—Maureen Stapleton, Charles Durning in sensitive story of widow trying to start new life. Friday, May 7 (9-11 pm).

Eagle Come Home. Survival Anglia—Study of American Bald Eagle. Tuesday, May 11 (8-9 pm).

F. Scott Fitzgerald in Hollywood. ABC Theatre —With Jason Miller, Tuesday Weld, Julia Foster. Sunday, May 16 (9-11 pm).

The Emmy Awards. Outstanding television programs, stars. Monday, May 17 (9-11 pm).

Alan King Special. Four original plays by top playwrights. Tuesday, May 18 (10-11 pm).

The American Woman: Portraits of Courage. Celebrating the role of women from 1776 to 1976. Thursday, May 20 (1:30-3 pm).

The Pursuit of Happiness. Third in trilogy on the American experience. Thursday, May 27 (9:30-11 pm). Children's version—Saturday, May 29 (12:30-1 pm).

ABC News Closeup. Explores factors in crisis facing free public education. Thursday, May 27 (10-11 pm).

A Woman of Valor. True drama of Jessy Judah and family settling in New York at end of 18th century. Sunday, May 30 (5-6 pm).

Bolshoi Ballet. Hosted by Mary Tyler Moore from Russia. June TBA.

Fourth of July Celebrations. Networks plan all-day coverage of Americans celebrating the Bicentennial. Sunday, July 4.

The Olympic Games. From Montreal, Canada. July 16-August 3 on varied schedule.

REGULARLY SCHEDULED PROGRAMS

Monday through Friday: Sunrise Semester/ CBS Morning News/The Today Show/Good Morning America/Captain Kangaroo/Sesame Street/Mister Rogers/Electric Company/ Villa Alegre

Saturday: In the News/Schoolhouse Rock/ Emergency + 4/Land of the Lost/The Shazam!- Isis Hour/Westwind/The Lost Saucer/Fat Albert and the Cosby Kids /GO-USA/CBS Children's Film Festival/Weekend

Sunday: Vegetable Soup/In The News/ Schoolhouse Rock/Lamp Unto My Feet/Look Up and Live/Camera Three/These Are the Days/Make A Wish/Face the Nation/Meet the Press/Issues and Answers/Directions/60 Minutes/The Wonderful World of Disney/ Nova/Masterpiece Theatre

Note: This is, necessarily, a partial listing. Time (NYT), titles and casts of these national programs are subject to change. Please consult your station listings; check also for noteworthy local programs.

Television Information Office, 745 Fifth Avenue, New York 10022

if he has $60,000, an IQ of at least 120, and can keep his mouth shut.''

Since the 1896 campaign, the election of a President has been determined largely by the ability of information specialists to generate favorable publicity. In recent years that publicity has been supplanted by heavy spot buying on electronic media.

So many factors are involved in choosing a President that it is hard to say with any real empirical confidence how important any single medium is. The most talked-about medium in American politics is television (see 12.6). Highly publicized debates between candidates in 1960 and 1976 appear to have affected the outcomes. Richard Nixon (the early favorite)

The first televised presidential debates stirred controversy about TV's role in politics and helped establish the famous Kennedy image in the minds of the electorate.

would probably not have lost to Kennedy were it not for his poor showing on TV (see 12.7). Similarly the 1976 debates probably clinched Jimmy Carter's narrow victory over Gerald Ford.

Yet there were other elections where, according to political analyst Edward Chester, no amount of TV exposure could have changed the outcome: Goldwater versus Johnson in 1964 and Nixon versus McGovern in 1972. Television commercials seem to work best in close elections or in those where there is a large undecided vote. According to Associated Press, Gerald Ford's TV spots during the 1976 campaign probably swung over 100,000 undecided voters a day during the last few months of the campaign.

What effect does television have on the candidates themselves? It dictates priorities that are different from those of an earlier day. The physical appearance of the candidate is increasingly important. Does he or she look

"Well, at least we can say he's not a media candidate."

Drawing by Stevenson; © 1976, The New Yorker Magazine, Inc.

fit, well-rested, secure? Losing candidates like Adlai Stevenson, Hubert Humphrey, and Richard Nixon all seemed to look "bad" on TV. Nixon overcame this problem in 1972 with ads that featured longer shots of him being "presidential"—flying off to China. Close-ups were avoided.

Both John F. Kennedy and Jimmy Carter seemed more at home with the medium, perhaps because both were youthful, informal, and physically active outdoor types. Dwight Eisenhower and Lyndon Johnson seemed to have a paternal, fatherly image on the small screen. All of the recent Presidents have learned how to use the medium to their advantage, to "stage" events so as to receive maximum favorable coverage. This has added to the already awesome power of the incumbency.

Television has changed the importance of *issues.* It can be argued that since the 1960 presidential debates, we have elected people, not platforms. This is a major departure from earlier years. Franklin Roosevelt's radio charisma cannot be denied, but he was swept to power by one issue—the Great Depression.

All the print information we now receive is simpler and more condensed than ever before. Issues and print go together. Television is *images*, not issues. We develop a more personal, emotional feeling about the candidates. Jimmy Carter's spectacular rise to power was a testament to this new image orientation. No one really knew *what* he was going to do when he took office, since his entire campaign had been geared toward developing a relationship of trust with the electorate. "Trust me," he said, "I'll never lie to you."

My father, a long-time politician in southern California, has a favorite saying—"The worst thing a candidate can do is get bogged down in the issues." This trend has alarmed countless media critics. Politicians, newscasters, and others have stood in line to denounce it. They assert the important thing is *what candidates stand for*, not the candidates themselves. Everyone seems to agree that television has been detrimental to American politics; it has clouded the issues and confused the electorate. Media researchers Thomas E. Patterson and Robert D. McClure say: (1) "Viewers of the nightly network newscasts learn almost nothing of importance about a presidential election," and (2) "People are not taken in by advertising hyperbole and imagery . . . exposure to televised ads has *no effect on voters' images of the candidates.*" At the risk of bucking the trend, I disagree on both counts.

If the Watergate mess proved anything, it was that we need a President we are comfortable with, one we feel we *know* and can *trust*. Print afforded us no opportunity to get a "feel" for the person. We could study the issues, read the speeches, yes—but how would we "know" the candidate as we might a neighbor or casual acquaintance? Television (and television advertising) provides an audiovisual record of the candidate under all sorts of circumstances. It is with that knowledge that we can choose someone of integrity, at least someone with honorable intentions.

Of course, TV cannot guarantee honest candidates, but we rejected Richard Nixon in 1960 and we might have again had he not so successfully *avoided* any informal coverage. (Remember—he wouldn't let TV newscasters near him unless he had a suit on, for all we knew he wore a suit while walking on the beach.) Once he was President it was the intimate nature of the medium that brought him down. Even his well-rehearsed Watergate denials wouldn't work. He would sit there, surrounded by flags and piles of transcripts, and swear he was innocent. Yet the profuse sweat on his brow and the look in his eyes seemed to confirm his guilt.

Issues come and go, but we elect *people* to the presidency. In this fast-moving information environment, today's burning issue is tomorrow's historical footnote. It's far more important to develop a sense of what kind of person we are electing to the nation's highest office. Television affords us that opportunity in a way no other medium can.

Queries and Concepts

1. Design a print ad for your favorite product. Then follow up by writing copy for a 60-second television or radio ad. Which most effectively sells the product? Why?

2. Find three examples of magazine advertising you feel are in bad taste. How could they be changed so they still sell the product without what you consider offensive?

3. Think of the television commercial that

you hate more than any other. Write three paragraphs on what you find so objectionable about it. No fair using general words like "stupid" or "dumb"—be *specific*. Have you ever used the product?

4. Who feeds the pet in your house? Interview some pet owners about their pets' eating habits. What brand do they usually buy and why?

5. You are a public relations agent for a baseball player who has held out for a $1 million contract and has been booted off the team. In a fit of rage, he has beaten up the owner and his coach. The press is calling for a statement and you can't find your client anywhere. What do you do?

Readings and References

The Business of the Message

Philip Ward Burton and J. Robert Miller
Advertising Fundamentals. Columbus, Ohio: Grid, 1976.
This is a management-oriented text that discusses the business of advertising. Designed for the student who wants to become involved in the business. Sections include, "Structure of Advertising," "Promotional Aids," and

"Creative Advertising." A thorough job of assessing typical tasks in the field.

Scott M. Cutlip and Allen H. Center
Effective Public Relations, 5th ed. Englewood Cliffs, N.J.: Prentice-Hall, 1978.
First written in 1952, this text has become the standard in the field. It is written by two men heavily committed to the "positive" aspects of PR and it reflects that perspective. It is comprehensive and includes historical information on the pioneers of PR.

Doug Newsom and Alan Scott
This Is PR: The Realities of Public Relations. Belmont, Ca: Wadsworth, 1976.
This text is solid competition for Cutlip and Center. While covering most of PR's major areas, it is shorter than Cutlip and Center and, for the most part, successfully blends theory and practice with a less formal approach to the subject matter.

The Advertising Business Develops

Maurice Mandell
Advertising, 2d ed. Englewood Cliffs, N.J.: Prentice-Hall, 1974.
This is probably the most comprehensive and thorough textbook on advertising available today. It covers history, control, marketing, radio, TV, outdoor advertising, and much more.

A nice five-page mini-history of advertising is found in Agee, Ault, and Emery's *Introduc-*

tion to Mass Communications (New York: Dodd, Mead, 1970).

Radio Advertising; Television: The Ultimate Advertising Medium; Save Me a Spot

Elizabeth Heighton and Don R. Cunningham
Advertising in the Broadcast Media. Belmont, Ca.: Wadsworth, 1976.
A solid, up-to-date treatment of real-world advertising practices in the broadcast media. Well illustrated and very easy for the beginning student to read. Chapter 1 covers the development of radio advertising to 1946. There are also chapters on audience research and spot sales, and an entire section devoted to social responsibility. Highly recommended.

Advertising: Making a Living

All of the above sources devote some space to "breaking in" to the business. Your best bet is to talk with someone already at work in the industry. You'll find advertising and PR people who are happy to meet with eager students and discuss their fields.

Advertising/Case in Point: The Great Pet Food War

Thomas Whiteside
"Onward and Upward with the Arts (Pet Food)." *The New Yorker*, November 1, 1976, pp. 51–98.

Media Mysteries: Advertising as Clue

Marshall McLuhan
Culture Is Our Business. New York: Ballantine Books, 1972.
This is McLuhan on advertising and its social and cultural consequences. He juxtaposes full-page ads from magazines with a series of "probes," exploring the way advertising creates cultural norms and predicts future social trends. Fascinating stuff, but take it in small doses. The book is now out of print but is available in most libraries.

Public Relations: The Subtle Semantic; Press Agentry Pioneers: P. T. Barnum & Co.; Public Relations in the Global Village

Scott M. Cutlip and Allen H. Center's *Effective Public Relations*, 5th ed. (Englewood Cliffs, N.J.: Prentice-Hall, 1978) covers the basics on this as well as any of the other texts. For a more up-to-date discussion of current trends, see *Readers' Guide to Periodical Literature. U.S. News & World Report* is often a good source.

Issues and Answers: The Selling of the President

Edward W. Chester
Radio, Television and American Politics. New York: Sheed & Ward, 1969.

This serves as a good basic introduction to the field and covers developments through the 1960s.

For fascinating reading on the relationship between press and presidential candidates, read Timothy Crouse's *The Boys on the Bus* (Westminster, Md.: Random House, 1973).

Thomas E. Patterson and Robert D. McClure *The Unseeing Eye: The Myth of Television Power in National Politics.* New York: G. P. Putnam's, 1976.

The authors argue that the influence of TV has been far overrated by media analysts. The book is, in part, the results of a grant from the National Science Foundation. One problem: Much data for the empirical conclusions are taken from the 1972 Nixon-McGovern race, a very atypical election in a number of ways. Fascinating reading.

13

Popular Culture and Mass Communication

**Pop is an unflinching look at the real world today;
a fascination with and acceptance of our mechanized,
trivialized, urbanized environment; a mirror held up
to life, full of motion and madness.—Marshall Fishwick**

Defining Popular Culture

What is popular culture? Popular culture is something we all share—Johnny Carson, for example. Some of us may like Johnny Carson, some disdain him, some may not even watch him. But just about everyone knows who he is and what he does.

Popular culture is also the "things," the icons and artifacts of our society: McDonald's golden arches, the Kodak camera, the Coke bottle, and the T-shirt. These things are "of the masses," created by and/or for ordinary people. The terms *mass culture* and *popular culture* are really interchangeable, since it is appeal to the masses that makes popular culture popular.

Popular culture is so pervasive that it is almost invisible. McLuhan contends that all environments are invisible, and he uses the fairy tale of the emperor's new clothes to illustrate that we see only what we are conditioned to see. All the well-conditioned subjects saw the emperor's new clothes; it took the unconditioned child to exclaim, "But he has nothing on at all!" Popular culture is so much a part of our everyday life that we have to step back from doing it in order to see it.

One way to define popular culture is by what it *isn't*. It isn't *elite* culture. Our elite culture, which comes primarily from the European tradition, is anything deemed worthy of study and is included in the traditional curricula of colleges and universities: art, history, medicine, law, philosophy, and science. In contrast, popular culture is not what we study, but what we live with. Popular culture represents a common denominator, something that cuts across most economic, social, and educational barriers.

In America, Rembrandt represents elite culture, but Norman Rockwell is popular culture. Chamber music is elite, but rock is popular. Medicine is elite, but Marcus Welby is pop, and so on.

Some advocates of elite culture argue that the masses would be better off if they became "cultured." But the masses are already steeped in culture—mass culture. And much of the mass culture of today will be the elite culture of the future. For example, Shakespeare, whose plays are now considered the epitome of elite culture, supplied sex and violence to the masses of his day. Someday *Star Trek* may become elite culture; it can be argued that *Star Trek* provides much the same sort of material to the masses today that Shakespeare did 350 years ago.

Mass culture is largely uncharted as far as academic study is concerned. We have been studying elite things for so long that we have ignored the culture we all have in common. But this is changing, and popular culture is becoming at last an object of serious study at some universities. Bowling Green State University in Ohio, which boasts the nation's leading department of popular culture, has close to 1,000 students discovering the social significance of things like Volkswagens, comic books, science fiction, sports, film theory, women in literature, and more. According to department chairperson Ray Browne, "Popular culture is a very important segment of our society. The contemporary scene is holding us up to ourselves to see; it can tell us who we are, what we are, and why."

Of course, popular culture is an even newer academic discipline than communication. As a result, there is a great deal of debate about exactly what it is and whether it's an academic discipline at all. In this respect, it's developing like such disciplines as psychology, sociology, journalism, and business administration, all of which had to "earn their way" into acceptance during the first half of the 20th century.

In academe, the study of popular culture cuts across many disciplines, including American studies, sociology, psychology, anthropology, and communication. But it is with communication that it seems most at home, for mass culture has become the consequence of mass communication; print, radio, film, and television are today's channels of popular culture.

Popular Culture and Mass Communication

Before Gutenberg, the artist in society survived through subsidies from the wealthy classes. This is how we derived the term *patron of the arts*. Novelists, poets, and painters would dedicate and/or deliver their work to persons who could afford to support them.

With the rise of mass literacy came a new kind of patron and a change in the relationship between patron and artist. Artists were at the beck and call of not one patron, but thousands. The newly literate consumer had tastes that were noticeably different from those of the wealthy elite. If the artist were to profit, these tastes had to be placated. Hence, the arrival of the "commercial," or popular, artist and the popular arts.

Print was the first medium to offer a new palette for the commercial artist, and eventually came radio and television. These newer mass media have been almost exclusively given over to the popular arts. Electronic media are in the business of obtaining the largest possible audience; this means catering to public tastes. The popular artist, now as always, calculates the wants and needs of the mass audience, creates content in response to those needs, and delivers it to millions of patrons through mass media channels. What's more, it is done very quickly. The 15th-century writer may have taken years to complete a book. The modern mystery novelist may take only a few weeks. Some television scripts are written in even less time. Popular art is art in a hurry.

Researchers have long debated whether the mass media create popular culture or simply act as a mirror reflecting popular tastes and values. Actually TV and all mass media probably *refract* reality. The world we see on the TV screen, for example, is similar to REALIFE yet distorted. It is America as seen through the eyes and minds of producers, directors, and scriptwriters. It "imitates" life while creating a separate reality for the mass audience. Those who disdain popular culture feel this distortion may be harmful.

Yet it can be argued that the often simplistic world of mass media may offer consumers a buffer between themselves and modern REALIFE with all its complexity and technology. Further study could reveal that one function of mass media in our time has been to ease the transition from the relatively simple life-styles of a few decades ago to the accelerated and stress-filled life-styles of today and tomorrow. If TV is partly responsible for what author Alvin Toffler calls "future shock," it may also provide a temporary cure. To know for sure, we must put popular culture under the microscope of serious academic investigation.

Some research has been done and much remains to be done. But everyone agrees there is an important link between mass media and popular culture. If the mass media do not actually create popular art and popular culture, they certainly help make it conspicuous and abundant. People who favor elite art feel (with some justification) they are drowning in a sea of popular culture, promoted and perpetrated by the mass media. In any event, popular culture is so much a part of our mass communication system that distinctions between mass media and popular culture have become increasingly blurred.

Icons and Artifacts

To really understand the importance of icons we need to try to imagine a world without words. For the cave-dwelling family, communication was a system of grunts and gestures. Early cave dwellers drew pictures of animals and of themselves, leaving them for future generations. Early tribal civilizations lived in a world of symbols, just as we do today. But their symbols were *visual*, more direct than the written word. Of course, some of our words —*hiss*, for example—come close to duplicating the meaning they represent; but many more words—like *ambidextrous*—have no such obvious connection. It is only through rote learning that we come to know *ambidextrous* means the ability to use both right and left limbs with equal skill.

In a sense, words take us away from all that is direct and create a complex and confusing system of communication. Inside all of us, there is a cave dweller yearning to be free. So we develop a devotion to *things*, visual two- or three-dimensional objects. It is the degree of devotion that determines whether these things are icons or artifacts.

An artifact is an object, period. An icon is defined as "an object given uncritical devotion." Religion and politics have always made use of icons: the crucifix, the St. Christopher's medal, the Union Jack, the swastika. Icons are a necessary part of all cultures, and they pervade all our lives. They have become an especially visible

The ultimate icon: a Cadillac
Seville.

At home anywhere in the world.

International in size, Seville is responsive . . . maneuverable . . . easy to park. Smooth of ride.
Solid of feel. Altogether, a delight to drive. And efficient. In mileage tests conducted by
the Environmental Protection Agency, Seville got 13 miles per gallon in the city test. And
19 mpg in the highway test. Only your Cadillac dealer has it.

Seville
BY CADILLAC

part of our lives since our retribalization by television. The TV screen, which does not represent reality through words, has reintroduced us to thinking in pictures and sounds. So, like the cave dwellers, we are beginning to rely more heavily on visual and three-dimensional objects for communication and as symbols of worth. These objects, pictured daily on our mass media, are the icons of popular culture.

Among the more treasured icons is the automobile (13.1). Our cars have always been more than just a way to get from one place to another. They reflect and communicate our values, hopes, and dreams. Are you the practical, no-nonsense driver of an econ-

The stereo—whether it is a cabinet or a component system—how it looks is as important as how it sounds.

omy model? Or perhaps the proud owner of a luxurious, comfortable gas guzzler? Whatever the case, you have developed a personal and emotional commitment to your choice of automobile.

"Diamonds are a girl's best friend," while "clothes make the man." Even a book can be an icon, appreciated more for form than for content. Have you ever been to a house full of tastefully bound leather books that had never been opened? The television set is an icon of paramount importance. Likewise, the stereo can be a status symbol (see 13.2).

But one does not need to be wealthy to have a hoard of personal icons. Marshall Fishwick points out:

Even the poorest among us has his private icon bank. We make deposits there regularly, and withdraw more than we know. Just as we tuck away special treasures (notes, emblems, photos, medals) in the corners of drawers, so do we tuck away iconic images in the corners of our mind. We draw interest from our deposits. Icons have a way of funding us, sustaining whatever sense and form our lives assume. When we can no longer draw from an icon bank, we quickly go bankrupt.

So it would seem that we *need* our icons to survive. They are with us now more than ever, encouraged by mass advertising and electronic communication.

A thousand years from now, archaeologists will measure the worth of our culture from the objects we have left behind. As with the cultures of old, the objects most likely to remain are icons. Cultural artifacts disappear because they are thrown *away*. We may keep the wine bottle and throw away the cork. We keep our books but throw away our magazines. An icon is forever.

But what about our artifacts? Andy Warhol's Campbell tomato soup can painting and Oldenburg's pop depiction of the hamburger serve to remind us that it is the everyday things in our consumer society that make up our lives. It is as if the artists are saying, "Look (for better or worse), this *is* your art; these are the objects you have chosen." So in a sense, even our artifacts can be icons if they have a special symbolic meaning for us. The Coke bottle, for example, is perhaps the best-known American icon; its shape—and its meaning—are recognized in every corner of the globe. The Balinese have no word for *art;* they say they simply do everything as well as they can. For the Balinese there is little difference between popular and elite culture, icon and artifact.

The Events of Popular Culture

Each year during the third week of January, 70 million Americans sit down in front of their television sets and spend a few hours watching several dozen uniformed men carry a pigskin ball up and down a hundred yards of green grass. The game is the Super Bowl, and the teams are the winners of the National and American Conferences of the National Football League. To decide which team is "the best," there is a one-game playoff. The Super Bowl is the biggest event of popular culture.

Not all sports are part of popular culture, however. Squash, polo, and, until recently, tennis and golf were the property of the elite. Baseball, football, and basketball have long been the property of the masses, and with the arrival of electronic media, a permanent bond formed. People who could not attend the games followed them on radio and television.

The Super Bowl, the World Series, and other mass-communicated sports events are a vital part of our culture, reflecting its priorities and values. As with all popular culture, careful

Guest Essay by Marshall Fishwick

God and the Super Bowl

Dr. Fishwick is one of the best known of all scholars in the field of popular culture. He is a past president of the Popular Culture Association and has written more than a dozen books on American history and popular culture. He currently is Professor of Humanities at Virginia Polytechnic Institute in Blacksburg.

An Episcopal bishop recently commented that he was tiring of the NFL—it was too High Church. He gave this version of the Lord's Prayer:

Our football, which art on television
Hallowed be thy game.
Thy fullback run, thy pass be flung
In Miami as it is in Dallas.
Give us this day our four quarters
And forgive us our trips to the
    bathroom
As we forgive our fumblers.
And lead us not into conversation,
But deliver us from off-sides;
For this is the power and the
    popular culture
Forever and ever. Amen.

The Super Bowl provides the basis not only for recreation but for religion as well. This application of the word *religion* offends because our way of regarding religion as an *institution* prevents us from seeing the "sacred" or sacrosanct in everyday life. We *want* religion locked into a pietistic Sunday morning service, and we mold our language accordingly. Look at the faces of people listening to Easter sermons on the church's Super Sunday (Easter), and compare them with faces watching football's Super Sunday. Where is there more involvement?

Several years ago in Colorado (where the Denver Broncos roam), a fan attempted suicide by shooting himself in the head on the day after the Broncos fumbled seven times against the Chicago Bears.

"I have been a Broncos fan since they got organized," he wrote in his suicide note. "I can't stand their fumbling anymore."

He fumbled, too—the bullet did not reach a vital spot. Otherwise it would have been a splendid example of blood sacrifice demanded by a merciless God.

Traditional rituals were attuned to the seasons; throughout central North America, say anthropologists, they took the form of war games between tribes. How has this come down to our times? As "battles" between rival teams, with incantations, cheerleaders, and "fans" (short for *fanatic*) to urge armed (at least padded) warriors forward.

What is at stake in a "friendly game" is a minutely observed and monitored battle between aggressive male teams, who use cunning, deceit, and violence to attain their ends. Does this sound like a corporation or bureaucracy? Is the Bowl merely a mirror image of life out there?

And what about up there? Teams both play and pray to win. George Allen of the Washington Redskins insists on locker room prayers. The Miami Dolphins have a public pre-game prayer. "How touching a scene," reports Colman McCarthy of the *Washington Post;* "giant men, bruised and asweat, kneeling to acknowledge that however almighty their win may have been, there is still another Almighty, the

study yields clues about the sociological and psychological games we play in everyday life.

The Cult in Popular Culture

Webster's New World Dictionary defines *cult* as "devoted attachment to, or extravagant admiration for, a person, principle, etc., especially

when regarded as a fad." In most cases, mass media play an important role in bringing about popular cults.

Cults may form around political candidates who strike an emotionally responsive chord among a segment of the electorate. George Wallace is one recent example of a national candidate whose followers offered unquestioning loyalty and devotion.

When thousands of long-haired brightly clad "hippies" invaded San Francisco in the

Divine Coach . . . '' In such a scene the true meaning of popular culture can be found—if only we know how to find it.

Super Sunday dawns. Ten times ten thousand go to the Bowl itself. Millions more witness the events on television screens, ''against the beautiful skyline.'' The destiny-laden pregame coin flip (the coin, incidentally, is worth $4,000) sets the scene. Players come onto the field, amidst acclamations louder than any heard outside ancient Jerusalem's walls. They run, collide, bruise, bash. Now for the half-time festivities. Ten lines of young people march forth, precise as pistons in a well-tuned engine . . . females in yellow or orange, males in blue, white teeth shining as they sing, ''It's a Good Time to Know Your Neighbor.'' Four priest warriors dance on the drumhead/godhead. Now the hundred thousand worshippers are on their feet, tears in their eyes, singing:

America, America,
God sheds his grace on thee. . . .

Amen.

Marshall Fishwick

summer of 1967, they had a number of common political and social beliefs, many dealing with questions of religion. That movement, fanned by mass media coverage, can be justifiably labeled a cult.

Certainly the tribal ritualistic gatherings at rock concerts to see Bob Dylan, the Beatles, Elvis Presley, and others were and are cult-like. In the eyes of the devoted, these figures can do no wrong. In their presence, followers find a symbolic or mythic truth.

One of the most widespread cults to center around a television program is that of the Trekkies, fanatic devotees of the *Star Trek* series. Trekkies come in all ages, though most are 12–25 years old. Each year thousands of them gather at Star Trek conventions (cons) held in various major cities. Here they view *Star Trek* episodes they have seen countless times before. There are exhibitors selling everything from genuine plastic Spock ears to metal phaser guns.

"Of course, I didn't know George was a Trekkie when I married him."

Drawing by Ziegler; © 1976, The New Yorker Magazine, Inc.

The Trekkies do not sit passively and observe. Many dress up in the costumes of their favorite heroes and heroines: Captain Kirk, Mr. Spock, Klingons, robots, and even "Tribbles," the round, faceless, furry creatures featured in an early *Star Trek* episode.

Participants swap stories about their favorite episodes and trade trivia questions. Several years ago I participated in an academic panel at a Los Angeles con. There were half a dozen of us who had taught seminars on *Star Trek*, or used it as a jumping-off point for analyses of TV's influence in society.

I thought I was quite an expert, having read every available book and even talked with Gene Roddenberry (the creator and producer of the series). I quickly discovered I was among the most poorly informed at the con. These people had spent hours every day for years learning every detail. At a moment's notice they could tell you who starred in a given episode, what it was about, and even describe the scene before the first commercial!

Issues and Answers

The Dilemma of Popular Culture

One of the reasons for including a popular culture chapter in a book about mass media is to interest you in the consequences of mass communication at the earliest possible moment. I have found that my own students are willing to spend more time investigating history and current issues if they can link them up to the real world around them.

For too long we have ignored such things in favor of a more traditional historical approach. Mass media and popular culture are important because you *live* them every day. You wake up to popular culture in the morning and sleep with it each night, just as you wake to *Today* and go to sleep with *Tonight*.

You should also wake up to things around you. What you find in the textbooks (including this one) may not be much help. You need to examine your own life-style, icons, artifacts, television viewing habits, favorite singers, and favorite foods in order to understand yourself and your relationships with others.

The real problem is the invisible environment. Because you *live* popular culture, you may not think it is important. *Nothing could be further from the truth.* Yet, you will probably get little encouragement or support from your professors. This may indeed be something you need to do on your own, but it is critical. When Socrates said, "The unexamined life is not worth living," he could hardly have envisioned our vast electronic environment full of icons, artifacts, cults, sporting events, and instant information. If he were here today, he might add a second sentence, "The unexamined environment is not worth living *in.*"

actions. (If you can't justify them, throw them away!)

3. The Super Bowl is not the only event of popular culture that takes on overtly spiritual overtones. Can you think of others? What about television shows, are there any that involve religious values?

4. Can you think of several popular cults not mentioned in the text? Are you a member of any organization, formal or informal, that could be considered a popular cult?

5. Who is in the best position to investigate and evaluate popular culture: (1) those in elite culture who have risen above it, (2) those who experience it firsthand all the time, or (3) a Martian coming to Earth for the first time? Choose one and explain why.

Queries and Concepts

1. Make a list of your five favorite books. Which would be considered popular culture and which elite? Why?

2. Investigate your wallet and drawers to find your own icons. Why are you saving them? Write a paragraph on each, justifying your

Readings and References

Defining Popular Culture

Marshall Fishwick
Parameters of Popular Culture. Bowling Green, Ohio: Bowling Green University, Popular Press, 1974.
This is a collection of Fishwick's original essays, which probe into definitions of popular

culture and include pieces on "Fakelore," "Theology," "Mythology," and "Art."

The emperor's new clothes analogy is from Quentin Fiore and Marshall McLuhan's *The Medium Is the Massage* (Westminster, Md.: Random House, 1967).

Popular Culture and Mass Communication

Ray B. Browne and David Madden
The Popular Culture Explosion: Experiencing Mass Media. Dubuque, Iowa: Wm. C. Brown, 1972. Here is a magazine-style book that defines popular culture and answers the question, "Why study popular culture?" Hundreds of examples from newspapers and magazines are included.

Icons and Artifacts

Marshall Fishwick and Ray B. Browne
Icons of America. Bowling Green, Ohio: Bowling Green University, Popular Press, 1978.
Now in its third edition, this standard includes articles on the most talked-about icons of the 1970s. An anthology, highly recommended.

The Events of Popular Culture

For Michael Real's analysis of the Super Bowl as mythic spectacle, see the readings and references in Chapter 8.

The Cult in Popular Culture

The best coverage of the various movements in popular culture is in Russel Nye's *The Unembarrassed Muse: The Popular Arts in America* (New York: Dial Press, 1970).

Susan Sackett's *Letters to Star Trek* (New York: Ballantine Books, 1977) traces the Trekkie saga from beginning to present.

Issues and Answers: The Dilemma of Popular Culture

These issues are thoroughly covered in Herbert J. Gans's *Popular Culture and High Culture: An Analysis and Evaluation of Taste* (New York: Basic Books, 1977). The *Journal of Popular Culture* is available in many university libraries. It comes free with a membership in the Popular Culture Association. There are reduced rates for students. Those interested can write to the association at 101 University Hall, Bowling Green University, Bowling Green, Ohio, 43403.

14

Media, Message, and Social Change

Social scientists insist that any important conclusions about the effects of media be supported by solid evidence . . . most are quite wary of any simple answers or unverified conclusions concerning causal relations between media content and undesirable conduct. . . .—Melvin DeFleur

It is surely no wonder that a bewildered public should regard with cynicism a research tradition which supplies, instead of answers, a plethora of relevant, but inconclusive, and, at times, seemingly contradictory findings.—Joseph Klapper

Mass Communication Research

The study of mass media is relatively new. When compared with medicine, which is thousands of years old, or even with modern psychology, which is a product of this century, the formal study of communication is a babe. We have only begun to research the effects of mass media, a dynamic force that is reshaping our lives.

The direction of research in mass media is largely determined by the people who hold the purse strings. Much of the funding for large-scale studies comes from some level of government. These studies are often about violence, or involve the interests of minority or unfairly treated groups like blacks or women. They are prompted by the concern of the people (as expressed through their government) that certain media programs or practices may be harmful to society.

A second group of studies are done by students who write theses and dissertations in mass communication graduate schools. Usually these are directed by senior-level faculty members who either steer students to favorite research topics or let them make their own decisions. There are also studies funded by universities or private sources.

All these efforts contribute *something* to the accumulated knowledge that we have about issues in mass communication. But because research in mass media is so new, we have very few hard and fast conclusions. Not enough studies have been done in most areas to give us conclusive results.

Another reason we need more research in mass media is because the media themselves are constantly changing. They are not stable like a chemical formula; instead they are flexible and changing in both form and content. I spent three years working on a dissertation involving sex-role socialization on four very popular TV shows. Three of them are now off the air. This can be very frustrating. But it shows that we need more research in the field to help us keep current, cope with change, and better understand important media-related questions.

The study of mass media is so new that there is still some debate about whether it should be housed with art, humanities, or the social sciences. The creation of effective mass communication via print, radio, television, or film is an art. It involves the efforts of one or more artists. Each medium can point to its best and proudly proclaim it a unique art form. But mass communication is also a branch of human learning and belongs with other humanities, like English and foreign languages. Each medium has a "literature" all its own: in radio, it's sound; in television, pictures.

As far as research is concerned, mass communication is a social science. To understand its effects we borrow procedures from psychology and sociology. In fact, many of the most important communication researchers are psychologists and sociologists. They have developed methods for examining human attitudes, beliefs, and behaviors. They admit that the methods of the social scientist are not as exact or as pure as those of the physical scientist, since human behavior is simply not as predictable as a chemical solution or a physics experiment. But it *is* predictable to some degree. Social scientists adopt many of the statistical procedures used in the physical sciences in order to make more definite predictions about human behavior.

Procedures and Problems of Communication Research

We all have opinions about the influence of mass media, just as we have opinions about everything. These opinions are often based on information we have gathered and things we have been taught by our parents, teachers, and television sets. Occasionally, we engage in debate with others. We match our opinions against theirs and offer "facts" to back them.

But if that's all we do, then what we end up with is what we started with: *opinions.*

Of course it is possible to gather opinions in a systematic way. We might go to everyone in the country and ask what he or she thinks about TV and violence. We might find that 76.2 percent feel there is a relationship between TV viewing and violence. But this does not mean there *is* a relationship, only that more than three-quarters of the people *think there is.*

During recent years all social sciences have placed more and more emphasis on empirical research, which relies not on gathering opinions but on observing behaviors; not the behavior of one, but of many. The researcher gathers data systematically and makes conclusions based on the data. There are several steps involved in designing an empirical study, and each has its own pitfalls.

The first step is to identify an idea that is to be tested. The field is wide open, with an unlimited number of hypotheses—some far too general to be tested and some so small or obvious that they are not worth testing. The beginning research student often makes the mistake of asking too large a question. It might be impractical, for instance, to test whether TV violence causes violence in REALIFE, but we could design a nice study documenting the TV viewing habits among inmates of a juvenile detention school versus those of students in a public school. By obtaining this information we might contribute a small bit of data to help resolve the larger question.

A common way to test a hypothesis is to go at it backwards: to gather data in an attempt to disprove a null hypothesis. The null hypothesis claims there is no relationship between the elements in question. In this case our null hypothesis would be: There is no difference between the viewing habits and program preferences of the two groups being studied.

Then we must make a decision about research design. How can we gather data to test our null hypothesis? Are we going to ask these kids to report how many hours they watch TV per day? That's one simple way, but does it tell us what we want to know? And how do we know their answers will be accurate? Some subjects may report fewer hours than they actually watch, since there is a social stigma attached to spending too much time with the "boob tube." And, since TV watching is something we do on an irregular basis (some days we watch five hours, other days none), the chances are great that some error will be made. It would help if we could just station someone by the TV set both in private homes and in a detention home and see how many hours each kid watches it, but that's going to be difficult and time-consuming. Moreover, if we do manage to observe the subjects, are they going to watch what they normally would? These are just some of the problems of research design.

Once we have data, we have the job of analyzing and interpreting it. The first question is: Did we get enough data? Perhaps our N (number in the sample) was only 20. Does this really speak for the institution and the school? The community? Children in the United States? Children of the world? We must be careful when inferring that others behave like our test group.

The greatest pitfall in empirical research involves the problem of establishing causal inferences (see 14.1). It is all too easy to leap to conclusions. We may *infer*, for example, that since Lee Harvey Oswald was an ex-marine, and since he allegedly shot John F. Kennedy, all ex-marines are somewhat prone to violence, and therefore military training tends to make trainees more violent. But someone else might respond by saying an acquaintance was in the marines and now heads a committee for strict gun-control legislation, and therefore exposure in the marines makes someone realize how destructive guns can be. Who is right?

Most of what we hear and read about mass communication is the opinion of others. It is generally assumed that the more education or experience someone has in the field, the more valuable the opinion is. Still, even the most educated and experienced people can and do disagree.

That is why the social scientific methodology, which tries to go beyond gathering opinions, has become increasingly accepted among those who teach mass communication. Without it, there is really no way for us to go beyond the opinion stage. There are so many urgent social problems relating to mass media that we cannot ignore methods

The Kennedy assassination trig-
gered several empirical studies
measuring people's emotional response to the televised coverage of
the tragedy.

that provide us with new and more conclusive information. A theory that remains untested remains just a theory.

And so, should you go on to graduate school in mass communication, you will most likely need a passing knowledge of social scientific methods to conduct your own re-search.

Richard J. Hill, editor of *Sociometry* and a leading authority on statistical research, used to tell a story that illustrates the problem of establishing causality. He said that many years ago researchers discovered the water level of the Potomac River dropped in direct propor-tion to the number of peanuts consumed in Washington, D.C. The more peanuts con-sumed, the less water there was in the river. The obvious conclusion? People eating all those salted peanuts got thirsty and drank up all the water!

This makes sense, of a sort, but it doesn't have anything to do with reality. In the spring

ice melts and the river rises. In the summer water evaporates and the level goes down. Meanwhile baseball season goes into full swing (Washington had a team in those days), and the number of peanuts consumed rises, thanks to peanut-hungry fans. Baseball and melting ice were *intervening variables* that *ac-counted for* the peanut and water levels.

We must be careful not to establish cau-sality simply because the statistics (data) seem to support a certain theory. It is one thing to say that real-life crime rates and the number of crimes committed on TV have both risen in the last ten years. It is *quite another* to es-tablish a *causal relationship*, to say that one "causes" the other.

Causal ordering is another problem. It seemed to make sense that the peanut con-sumption caused the lower water levels, but the statistics offered equal support for the theory that lower water levels *caused* a higher consumption of peanuts. Of course, both hypotheses are nonsense, but causal *ordering* can be critical. If more real-life crimes encourage TV writers to think more about crime and put it into their scripts, that's one thing. If the true causal ordering is the reverse, we have an entirely different problem.

Finally, there is always a great temptation to yield to our own opinions and biases in such cases, or to design studies so that results will verify gut-level feelings. Yet it is the difference between gut-level feelings and empirical research that gives *credibility* to a point of view.

To avoid all these pitfalls we must choose the right statistical method to test our theories. There are a battery of tests available to help us decide if there is any significant difference between groups. There will always be differences between any two groups; but we want to know if there are any *statistically significant* differences that relate to our hypothesis. Choosing the appropriate statistical test helps us make that decision. All such tests have limitations. Some can be used only for certain kinds of data, others only when N is large.

TV Violence: The Medium in the Middle

In 1977 the then-popular Freddie Prinze of *Chico and the Man* was despondent over the breakup of his marriage. At age 22, he chose to end it all by putting a bullet through his head. The event received extensive media coverage. After several days in a hospital, he died. Thirteen-year-old Lynn Barrillier of Glendale, California, had worshiped Chico. Her parents found her hours after Prinze was pronounced dead. She had put a bullet through her own head and left a note instructing her parents to bury her as close to her hero as possible, and not to forget to bury a favorite picture of Prinze with her.

In 1977 *TV Guide* published a controversial story written by an inmate at Marquette Prison. He surveyed 200 of his fellow inmates and discovered that nine out of ten found television useful in planning future crimes. Four out of ten *took notes while watching their favorite crime shows*. During follow-up interviews they explained: "You can always learn a new twist to an old scam by watching TV, they have to pay those writers a helluva lot of money to keep coming up with different crimes . . . what's more, they lay it all out for you, so you know what to do to avoid getting caught by the cops like the criminals in the show."

Since media coverage of airline hijacking in the early 1960s fostered a whole series of airline crimes, many have wondered if both factual and fictional crime on TV may be a contributing factor to the real thing. The inmate's story offers strong evidence that it is doing just that.

In addition, radical political groups are finding media coverage a vital component in getting their message before the public. There seems to be an increasing amount of tailored-for-TV terrorism. (In the motion picture *Network*, a fictional group of radicals was given network resources to produce a television show. The resulting *Mao Tse Tung Hour* was a hit.)

It is easy to see why the question of violence and the media is the most urgent that faces communication researchers. There have always been people quick to blame the media for the social ills of the day. The story of the king who killed the messenger bringing news of his army's defeat comes to mind. (Come to think of it, that too is a pretty violent story.) TV violence has always been the subject of criticism, particularly for its effect on children.

But we musn't only blame the messenger for the message; we should also examine the *role* the messenger plays. And so, hundreds of millions of dollars have been spent to provide clues to the relationships among mass media, crime, and violence. Here are a few findings.

In a 1969 study, a task force on Mass Media and Violence for the National Commission on the Causes and Prevention of Violence warned that television often depicted violence as a way out of social problems. The hero or heroine often used violent means to resolve conflict. While calling for more research, the task force emphasized the dangers involved if TV violence does encourage viewers (especially small children) to commit acts of violence to solve their own problems.

A New York study released the same year put it even more strongly. The New York Department of Mental Hygiene had begun ten years earlier to investigate the TV viewing habits of 184 third-grade boys. In 1969 the group was interviewed as they graduated from high school. Most of the young men who had been exposed to high levels of TV violence ranked high in studies of aggression.

Congress also acted in 1969. A special committee headed by Senator John Pastore committed $1 million to answer the question: Is TV violence damaging the nation's children? The report, five volumes long and edited by 12 panel members, found that, while TV did not have an adverse effect on the majority of children, there was every indication that it may lead to increased aggressiveness in certain subgroups. These groups were those already prone to violent acts. The report concluded that TV viewing may be enough to "push them off the edge."

The National Association for Better Broadcasting estimates that the average child will see 13,000 violent TV deaths during his or her formative years. Networks have made an effort to cut back on violence during the family hours (before 9:00 P.M.), but there is still a steady diet of mayhem available every Saturday morning. A number of conflicting content analyses of cartoon violence have been done, but all agree that an average Saturday hour contains at least a dozen murders and as many as 50 serious injuries.

Children seem ready to accept the most outrageous behavior by TV characters and then try the stunts themselves. TV hosts for the old *Popeye* cartoon series quickly discovered they needed to instruct small viewers that Popeye didn't want them to hold a dozen nails in their mouths at once, or try to open sharp spinach cans with their teeth. During the height of the *Batman* craze in the late 1960s, and again with the coming of the *Six Million Dollar Man*, there was a rash of broken legs and arms as children tried to imitate the feats of their heroes.

It appears that children look for role models wherever they can find them. They want to be just like those they admire. They often cannot, or do not, distinguish between real-life models, like mom or dad, and those on TV. The most extensive research on violence and role modeling has been done by Albert Bandura, a psychologist at Stanford University. Bandura has reported dozens of laboratory studies in which children were shown violent films or TV programs and then released into a closely monitored play room. Often there are a number of toys available, including dominos, game boards, and "bobo dolls"—soft clown-like objects just the right size for punching. Invariably children who have seen the violent action seem more attracted to the bobo dolls, with which they try to "live out" experiences they saw on TV. Often they name the doll after the villain and feel they must punish it just as their TV hero or heroine did.

Bandura's experiments have been given special recognition because their findings have been consistent over many years. Much evidence has been compiled to support his position that children do indeed imitate TV violence by committing acts of violence on bobo dolls and, in some studies, on other children as well.

So much research has been done on the effects of TV violence on children that the adult audience has often been ignored. Adults too are learning from TV. Most adults are terrified by real-life violence, but why do they watch it night after night on television?

Perhaps the television world is a vicarious place where adults can watch behaviors they would never engage in themselves. But the steady diet of TV violence for adults may affect them in other ways. Some suggest that, like children, adults may become less sensitive to real-life violence. More research needs to be done before we will really know what effect TV violence has on adults. It would be good to know, for example, if it causes everyone to be a little more violent, or if it affects only those already prone to commit violent acts.

Not all reports have been entirely gloomy. Schramm, Lyle, and Parker concluded that for some children under some conditions TV may be harmful, for others it may be beneficial, and for *most* it makes little difference.

Networks, anxious to avoid public criticism, have released a barrage of studies that show little difference in aggression levels between

those who do and those who don't watch TV violence. Critics contend that networks release only those studies supporting that point of view in an effort to discourage public opinion that could force them to air less violent shows. Networks also point out that violence is natural in most children and was part of growing up long before television. They even say that TV enables children to gratify their need for violence in vicarious ways rather than in person.

Violence: The Silver Bullet

How can I summarize some 4,000 studies on TV violence that have been done since 1950?

Almost everyone who tries concludes that more research needs to be done, and of course it does. Yet there are some clear indications in what has been completed. If the purpose of social science research is to make it possible to prefer one course of social action to another, then surely 4,000 studies have given us something.

We can say, with data to back us up, that watching television violence has been proven harmful to small groups of children and adults. On the other hand, for the vast majority, it seems to make little difference in terms of *direct* violent real-life actions. Most of us *are* able to distinguish between TV and real-life violence.

The indirect effects are something else. TV _does_ influence the way we perceive the world around us. It pictures what is happening "out there" while we're safely tucked away in the comfort of our livingrooms. The picture is largely an ugly one, a world where crime and criminals abound, where violence is acceptable as a way to resolve conflict. It may not make us commit violent acts, but it probably colors the way we look at friends, neighbors, and strangers.

Professors George Gerbner and Larry Gross of the Annenberg School of Communications conducted research to find differences between people they identified as heavy (four or more hours per day) and light (two or fewer hours per day) TV viewers. Their sample included more than 300 teenagers in junior high school.

Heavy viewers thought there were more professional workers and law enforcement personnel than did light viewers. About 20 percent of TV characters are actively engaged in law enforcement, but less than 1 percent of the population are law enforcement people in real life. When asked, "Can most people be trusted?" heavy viewers were 35 percent more likely to check, "Can't be too careful." The evidence indicates that heavy viewers "see" their real world in terms of the one they find on TV.

TV violence is a silver bullet because it damages but seldom kills. It is well intentioned—TV programmers always make sure

the bad guy gets it in the end and the hero or heroine triumphs—yet it hurts just the same. For most of us, it's not a fatal blow but probably an unnecessary one.

Sex Roles in the Media

During the 1970s a new research area began to receive much attention. The rise in feminism prompted women to ask if mass media in general and television in particular were reinforcing outmoded and restrictive sex roles for women.

Linda Busby reviewed several dozen studies of the occupational roles of men and women in children's books, adult magazines, and television. She concluded that the media were not reflecting the diversity of occupations available for women. Women were most often pictured as housewives, mothers, or secretaries and were seldom shown as business executives, doctors, or blue-collar workers. Another study noted that the average age of TV women is 26 while the average TV man is 40. This is clearly not the case in real life. Other studies have shown that in print ads and on the screen, men are most often pictured as competent, aggressive, and in command of a situation, whereas women are inept, stupid, and dependent. A frequent type of television commercial pictures a woman in a domestic crisis that is resolved when the man enters the scene in the nick of time, product in hand.

Blended Scotch Whiskey · 86.8 Proof · © Schenley Imports Co., N.Y., N.Y.

The "voice-over" or voice of authority booms the virtues of the product. *It is a man's voice in almost nine out of ten commercials.*

Busby and others contend that children are taught a "sexist" view of life. Media emphasize women as "sex objects" while men solve the mysteries, arrest the criminals, and, in general, have all the fun.

What effect do stereotyped programs have on audience behavior, particularly that of chil-dren? As with violence, it is difficult to mea-sure the direct effects of media content. One study asked children to name characters they would like to be. Boys always chose male characters and girls often picked men as well. The same study offered evidence that children exposed to media content depicting women in stereotypical occupational roles were likely to find these roles appropriate for real-life women.

Mass media people responded by saying that they are showing "life as it is." "Most business executives *are* male and housewives *are* women," they say. They see no political point of view inherent in what they do.

One of the reasons media content may not accurately reflect changes in occupational status for women is that the gatekeepers and decision makers who control the media are men. Busby contends these men are simply not sensitive to changes that came in the wake of the new feminism of the 1970s.

Some changes are evident. STP ran a television commercial featuring a female mechanic. Dewar's Scotch ran a series of magazine ads featuring career women (see 14.2). Virginia Slims kept telling women: "You've come a long way, baby" (see 14.3). Clearly, this was a departure from traditional images of women in cigarette advertising. Virginia Slims models were assertive and independent, but some women wondered if they were really different. The Virginia Slims woman seemed to have traded her submissiveness to men for a submissiveness to cigarettes.

Ethnic Minorities in the Media

In 1971 Archie Bunker appeared in millions of American livingrooms and lamented the distribution of his hard-earned tax dollars to "all of them minorities—ya know, your coloreds—your Puerto Ricans—and all the rest of 'em that won't do an honest day's work." No one was sure if viewers would accept this kind of character. Of course, real-life counterparts existed, but on TV?

Producer Norman Lear predicted that "liberals" favorably predisposed toward minority groups would like the show. Archie's bigotry was usually exposed as shallow by his son-in-law "Meathead." What surprised Lear was Bunker's acceptance by millions of "rednecks." They took him for real! "Archie Bunker for President" signs began popping up on the bumpers of pickup trucks all over the country.

It is not always easy to predict how certain groups of media consumers will react to messages concerning ethnic minorities. In the early 1960s, virtually all the TV and magazine characters were white. Blacks seldom appeared on TV, and were seen in only those publications aimed at the black audience. Pressure was exerted to include blacks in all media. Slowly "tokens" began appearing in ads and as characters on regular TV series. Of these, Bill Cosby was most successful opposite Robert Culp in *I Spy*. Their warm relationship on and off the screen and the acceptance of Cosby by the mass audience encouraged TV producers to cast blacks in a greater number of starring roles. This move reflected growing government pressure to include blacks and other ethnic minorities in all levels of society.

By the late 1970s blacks occupied a large number of starring roles in television series. What's more, shows like *The Jeffersons*, *Good Times*, and *Sanford and Son* were near the top of the ratings. The success of *Roots* was another plus.

Television commercials and magazine ads featured blacks and other minorities. Films designed primarily for the black audience (*Shaft*, *Car Wash*) attracted a surprisingly large number of nonblacks during the 1970s. The arrival of disco music, initially sung and played by black groups, became the hottest trend in popular music.

Some of these changes may have been prompted by research done by social scientists during the 1950s and 1960s indicating that blacks were being shut out of America's cultural mainstream. These researchers contended that the tension that led to racial violence was part of the same problem.

Issues and Answers

Are Mass Media Equal Opportunity Employers?

Writer Dorothy Gilliam catalogs a list of grievances related to employment practices in mass media, particularly among newspapers. There, she says, blacks fill less than 2 percent of the editorial positions. Black reporters are assigned only to racially related stories and are systematically passed over for promotion. Even at the *Washington Post*, which employs more black reporters than any other major daily in the country, blacks are unhappy about promotion practices. Most white-owned dailies retain whites in all key decision-making roles.

This has discouraged blacks from joining the "white press" and has sent some veteran blacks back to black-owned and black-operated newspapers. Black newspapers usually cater exclusively to the black audience, leaving little room for dialogue and increased understanding between the races.

In radio and television newsrooms the story is much the same. Some blacks are beginning to find on-the-air positions and many stations employ at least one black reporter. But in key editorial positions, blacks are conspicuous by their absence.

Gilliam contends the FCC has been lax in forcing stations to hire or promote blacks. So far, the FCC has stayed out of the controversy, claiming that existing federal hiring laws already forbid such discrimination.

The fact is, we need blacks, women, and other minority representatives at every level of mass media employment. Unlike other industries, media owners cannot lament, "There are no qualified minority people to fill these positions." Competition is heated for media employment. Qualified minority applicants *can* be found to fill executive positions in journalism and broadcasting. Of course, it is not possible for every outlet to have an exact percentage of blacks, women, and other minorities among their executives. But *quotas within certain reasonable ratios* could be established.

The logical place to start is with broadcast stations. The FCC has already established its right to pass judgment on those who own and work in broadcasting. It is time they realized that existing government policies forbidding discrimination are not enough. Broadcasters must *seek out* qualified minority candidates for executive and other positions. If they don't, they are not living up to their commitment to operate in the public interest, convenience, and necessity.

Queries and Concepts

1. Give several examples of communication as art, language, and social science that are not mentioned in the text.

2. In a few paragraphs, describe a study you would like to do and how it would avoid the pitfalls described in the text (see pp. 286–289).

3. Make a list of ten statements that include causal inferences. How many of these could be tested empirically?

4. Interview a half dozen children about their favorite television characters. Have they ever tried to imitate those behaviors?

5. Collect a number of magazine advertisements that feature men and women. Analyze each in terms of the roles they are playing. Are these roles traditionally associated with masculinity or femininity?

Readings and References

Mass Communication Research

Hubert M. Blalock, Jr.
An Introduction to Social Research. Englewood Cliffs, N.J.: Prentice-Hall, 1970.
This is the easiest to understand introduction I know of for students who want to find out what research methodology is all about. Blalock is an acknowledged leader in the field and has written some texts that easily mystify the amateur; this one is brief, simple, and in paperback.

Hubert M. Blalock, Jr.
Causal Inferences in Nonexperimental Research. Chapel Hill: University of North Carolina Press, 1964.
The introductory chapter offers a simple introduction to causal thinking and theory, along with problems in the field and the causal model.

R. Gerald Kline and Phillip Tichenor, eds.
Current Perspectives in Mass Communication Research. Beverly Hills: Sage Publications, annual.
Each year Sage publishes an additional volume in this set, covering important issues in communication research. Extremely useful bibliographies and articles from top names in the field.

Wilbur Schramm and Donald F. Roberts, eds.
The Process and Effects of Mass Communications. Urbana: University of Illinois Press, 1971.
This anthology is the beginner's guide to communication research and includes articles from the last 40 years. Sections on the media and messages of communication, audiences, nature of effects, and social consequences. See especially Schramm's introduction, "The Nature of Communication Between Humans," for a theoretical overview. Highly recommended.

TV Violence: The Medium in the Middle

Albert Bandura, ed.
Psychological Modeling: Conflicting Theories. New York: Lieber-Atherton, 1971.
This is a useful overview into the whole question of modeling and the effects of television. Bandura describes a number of his own experiments and gives equal time to the opposition.

Grant Hendrick
"When Television Is a School for Criminals." *TV Guide,* January 29, 1977, p. 4.

Wilbur Schramm, et al.
Television in the Lives of Our Children. Stanford, Ca.: Stanford University Press, 1961.

Violence: The Silver Bullet

For summary reports on the effects of TV violence, see Ray Brown's *Children and Television* (Beverly Hills: Sage Publications, 1976) and Glucksmann's *Violence on the Screen* (London: British Film Institute Educational Dept., 1971). Most books on the effects of television devote some space to the question.

George Gerbner and Larry Gross
"The Scary World of TV's Heavy Viewer." *Psychology Today,* April 1976, pp. 41–45, 89.

Sex Roles in the Media

Linda J. Busby
"Sex-Role Research on the Mass Media." *Journal of Communication,* Autumn 1975, pp. 107–31.

"What Does 'She' Mean?" *Journal of Communication,* Winter 1978, pp. 130ff. This is a collection of updated articles on women and the media, with a special emphasis on the importance of language in mass communication.

Ethnic Minorities in the Media; Issues and Answers: Are Mass Media Equal Opportunity Employers?

An entire section of Alan Wells's anthology, *Mass Media and Society: Readings with Text* (Palo Alto, Ca.: National Press, 1972) is devoted to racism, sexism, and the mass media. Among the articles is Dorothy Gilliam's "What Do Black Journalists Want?"

15
The Future of Mass Communication

**It is the business of the future to
be dangerous.—Alfred North Whitehead**

Futurism and Me

Back during the bicentennial madness, I was invited to St. Louis to give a lecture on "The Future of America." I delivered the same presentation twice; during the day to a group of students and in the evening to their parents.

As usual, I accompanied the talk with a number of slides and some examples of rock music. The students seemed interested in my vision of the future of media and some possible consequences, though some said I didn't deal enough with social issues. Their parents reacted quite differently; they found me much too concerned with social issues. Some accused me of being pessimistic about the future, whereas their sons and daughters had seen me as a hopeless optimist.

Since the presentation was exactly the same for both audiences, I began to wonder what was happening. Perhaps the young are turning into grim realists, while the older generation slips into a fantasy utopia. That's a curious flip and it made me realize that it is dangerous to predict the future. Everyone has a personal vision and it's difficult to keep from stepping on toes. My own personal vision is formed largely from my knowledge of media and other things that intrigue me or (occasionally) irritate me.

The visions you will find in this chapter are not complete, and they could not be. Instead, I have chosen some fragments, probes if you will, that may provide clues to our future with media.

The full-page ads in this chapter provide a futuristic backdrop. It is the business of advertising to be one step ahead. The tremendous flexibility and creativity found in these ads stirs the imagination about what might happen in the next three or four decades.

Where does prediction leave off and futurism begin? Futurism is not prediction. Predictions are solid prognoses of coming events, whereas futurism is more subtle. It involves probing, asking, exploring. This chapter is designed to get you thinking about mass media and the future. I hope at least some of it will intrigue and/or irritate you. If it does, ask yourself why. That is where *your* exploration into the future begins.

Transportation: You Can't Get There from Here

When I first moved to Los Angeles, I climbed up to the top of a freeway overpass and looked at the sea of cars whizzing by below. On one side there were four lanes crammed with motorists going 65 miles per hour. On the other were four lanes of cars going the opposite way with equal tenacity. How absurd it all seemed! In a strange way they canceled each other out. Nobody was really going anywhere. The Beatles "Nowhere Man" would have made the perfect sound track.

The fact is that Americans have a tremendous preoccupation with their automobiles. Cars are much more than a means of getting

from here to there; *they are a way of life.* We are, as Marshall McLuhan has pointed out, a nation of "paraplegics in power armchairs."

Americans will continue to perceive their cars as part of their personal space. The auto is, in a sense, an extension of the house. For the young the van represents the merging of the home and automobile. This takes on extra significance since they often live with their parents and don't have a home of their own. For the older set there is the camper and the ultimate extension: a Rolls Royce, complete with phone, bar, and all the comforts of home. The Rolls is also a hedge against the future (see 15.1).

In a time when everything (including methods of transportation) is changing rapidly, the Rolls offers a security of sorts by assuring the prospective buyer that the Rolls Royce "will represent a worthy and almost timeless investment in the highest art of transportation." It is a valuable insulation against the ravages of time! People offering such product protection will find success among the confused victims of future shock.

The Rolls Royce chauffeur (optional) offers insulation against another part of the automobile phenomenon—our physical involvement with the open road. For a long time many car makers bragged about how their cars would make driving more comfortable, like not driving at all. We got softer tires, automatic transmissions, power steering, and power brakes. Then came the inevitable demise of the convertible.

But this trend will soon be reversed. Young people crave *multisensory involvement*, and driving is still of great social importance. Hence, they'll soon demand the return of the convertible just as they demanded the return of the four-speed transmission and a new smaller steering wheel to give them a "better sense of the road."

Is this part of the ecology movement—a return to the elements? "The quiet ride" meant driver removal from everything *outside* of the automobile, including fresh air and trees as well as smog and concrete. Paradoxically, the return of the convertible seems related to the recent proliferation of dirt bikes, power boats, and snowmobiles, all of which may be destroying the natural setting they are designed to explore (see 15.2).

A related ecological issue: How will we continue to come up with energy sources to support our mania for getting from here to there? In the future, solar energy will be harnessed to deliver cheap abundant energy to everyone. The idea of bringing power from a central source to us via wires or gas pumps will become outmoded. Exxon and your local electric company are already anticipating these changes (see 15.3). Major oil companies are diversifying by exploring the potential use of nonfossil fuels and home solar heating units. Their stockholders will not be left out in the cold.

It's a Clean Machine

In the future, waking, sleeping, and other functions will become increasingly systematized as machines take over the day-to-day chores that preoccupy so many of our waking hours. Already there are coffeepots set to perk when we arise—perhaps the smell of brewing coffee could combine with the pulsating electric light of modern alarm clocks.

There will be less to do, so "getting up and going to work" will become largely unnecessary. We will all have a lot of time on our hands, but even the hands of time are changing. As McLuhan said:

Ours is a brand new world of all-at-once-ness. Time has ceased . . . space has vanished.

Time has not really ceased but has become inaudible, thanks to the digital clock or watch with *no moving parts* (see 15.4).

When parts move, they wear out. The old watch with its thousands of parts provided the professional "tinkerer" with plenty of work—but the professional tinkerer, like so many others, is *out* in the new age. Quasar color TVs

with parts that "snap in" are only the beginning. Soon we will all become amateur tinkerers, doing our own repairs, easily snapping prepunched electric service modules in and out of our machine.

In the future, machines will control virtually every aspect of our environment. They will warm it in the winter and cool it in the summer. One interesting aspect of climate control is our need to hide it from everyone —the pool heater is in the shrubbery, the furnace in the basement. We try to make environmental control as invisible as the environment itself (see 15.5).

The next steps will involve complete time and space as well as environmental control. Buckminster Fuller's giant geodesic domes already provide this control for limited spaces. But machines will not only control *what we feel;* they will also tell us *how we feel* through biofeedback devices. Biofeedback means the ability to successfully monitor and record our own emotions. Many biofeedback machines are already in operation.

Enter BioQuest (see 15.6), the machine that will replace the doctor or medical researcher, the highest regarded specialist of 20th-century technology. Many computer companies have

tried to build a "human" element into their advertising to counteract growing suspicion that computers and machines are going to replace us all. However, the coming of the home computer and the proliferation of pocket calculators and other personal electronic devices should subdue this fear, particularly among the young.

The Media Machines: New Skin for the Old Ceremony

When McLuhan tells us, "the medium is the message," he is also reminding us that the content and consequence of mass media are sometimes by-products of their form. Hence, the technological evolution of radio, televi-

sion, print, and other current mass media forms will have far-reaching effects we cannot yet comprehend. Often media content is slow to change while media form changes drastically. For example, television is largely made up of content from radio. In the near future new media forms may still carry much of the content we know today.

New media forms will be constantly evolving. The newspaper will be replaced by a home teletype with self-recycling paper. Some of our trees are missing and we are running out of paper! Modern technology continues to make possible the production of more specialized newspapers and magazines. Soon we'll get only the 10 percent of the paper we might

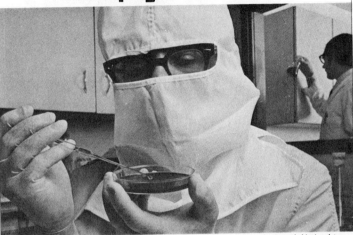

read, not the 90 percent we never read. Magazines will continue to cater more to *individual* work and leisure interests. The *mass* circulation (and paper-wasting) magazine will become a thing of the past.

Meanwhile audio recordings will probably displace radio as we know it. Individuals will record (and listen to) what they want to hear.

It will be harder for politicians to be on all sides of the issues when media consumers keep archives of audio and video information (see 15.7).

The "consumer revolution" in politics and social affairs is just getting under way. Ralph Nader has already realized that arming consumers with information is the first step. Con-

sumers will turn into reporters and archivists, storing enormous amounts of data for personal use. Electronic hand-held calculators and small "individual" TVs are only the beginning. Every person's private media mean big changes for politicians and voters alike.

With the introduction of relatively inexpensive home video recorders in the mid-1970s, Sony began a revolution in television. Betamax

permits instant retrieval of vital video information that has long been lost (see 15.8). Television is no longer here and gone, but here forever. Home video recorders will mean an end to networks as we know them. They give everyone his or her own network.

Coupled with CATV, program retrieval systems will provide a nonstop source of education and fantasy. Already on the market are

video-discs that work like records but can run up to 54,000 separate frames per half hour. With machines geared to select *individual* frames, storage and retrieval capacity boggles the imagination.

The addition of cameras to these units will completely change the nature of home movies.

Children and adults will be able to watch themselves on television and *become the program.*

But what of the telephone, the first personal electronic communication device? How long will we insist on making the new medium continue to do the work of the old? Patching

Today, just adding a few buttons
won't meet the telephone needs of small business.

The people of the Bell System wanted to give small businesses a phone system with big business service, without making the treasurer cry.

Which meant more than adding a button or two on a business phone. So the people of Western Electric got together with Bell Labs to build a new family of economical key telephone systems.

Western Electric engineers applied what they knew about modular design to these systems.

So adding a new feature is a simple matter of plugging in a new circuit board.

All of which resulted in some pretty useful features. For instance: now a person in a small business can set up conference calls at the touch of a button. Incoming calls can be announced through a speaker built into each desk phone, even when that phone's being used. If no one's there, a button stays lit to indicate a waiting message. Or someone can be paged through wall speakers around the office. And while that's being done, the caller on hold can be listening to music.

Built for your Bell Telephone Company by the people of Western Electric, these key telephone systems are already doing a lot to help small businesses manage their business better.

(🔔) Western Electric

We make things that bring people closer.

the existing phone isn't enough (see 15.9). We cannot continue to "add on" old features to every new medium.

In fact, technological media innovations like home video recorders are not really extensions of existing media at all. Each is an entirely new medium with form, content, and consequence yet to be discovered.

Commercial movies also provide us with clues toward future media phenomena. The success of the disaster films in the 1970s may give rise to a new interest in real-life disasters

in the 1980s. This means being "plugged in" to police and fire channels (see 15.10). For years newspapers have survived by reporting bad news; they'll be bypassed by participants who involve themselves directly in disaster via radio and TV. Disaster can be beautiful!

But for every beauty there is ugliness. The success of *Earthquake*, *Jaws*, *King Kong*, and other disaster movies points out that we are increasingly the emotional captives of the media manipulators. At any given moment we can be made to laugh, cry, or vomit. This is very reminiscent of Orwell's *1984*. In that novel, people are whipped into a frenzy against the "enemy" nation state. Later the same enemies are glorious "allies," while former friends are now the hated enemy. "Big Brother" may not be watching us in 1984, but are we watching it today?

I Like Your Style

The one unifying trend in all of this is the shift away from the importance of content to an increasing emphasis on form. It is *style*, not *substance*, that will be the wave of the future. Consider the accompanying table:

	Form	Content
A glass	Shape and feel	Function: holding liquid
Liquor	Shape of bottle Image of brand	Inebriation
Cigarettes	Package design Image of brand	The surgeon general has determined that smoking may be hazardous to your health.
Clothing	Social roles associated with specific types of clothing	Keeping you warm (and covered)

The glass of the future is here today (see 15.11) and with it a reminder that we are increasingly dependent on form over content in our material goods. Mass media have helped create this curious flip. Suddenly *how we look* is more important than *who we are.* "Style is everything." The question is not what's in the glass, but what the glass itself looks like, or even more importantly *how it feels.*

In 15.12 is it the liquor that has spilled out of the broken bottle or the broken bottle itself that makes a "grown man cry"? Many magazines are full of ads promoting one brand of alcohol over another. Yet is there really any difference between one bottle of vodka and another? The only differences may be the form of the bottle itself and the label.

Following the surgeon general's warning about smoking being hazardous to health, the first wave of "factual" cigarette brands may have emphasized content over form. But now, with so many competing brands, how are we to know what to believe? How about Decade, "the taste that took ten years to make"? (See 15.13.) No matter how long it took, or what the package says, smoking is still dangerous.

Smoking advertising made broadcast history when it followed hard liquor ads off the airwaves and onto the pages of newspapers and magazines. This meant far less fascination with cigarettes for a lot of heavy TV viewers.

One group that remained unaffected by the ban of TV cigarette commercials was teenagers. Teenagers are busy playing their music,

and still smoking up a storm. If the Rolling
Stones recorded an album devoted to the
stop-smoking movement, things might be different, but the Stones aren't involved in social
issues as cloudy as smoking. Besides, self-
destruction is very big among the young. The
older we get, the more valuable our time
becomes and the less we have of it.

Clothes were originally for keeping weather
out. Now they are designed to do much more
than that (see 15.14). Clothes are really more
"put on" than put on. We use them to explore

Have you ever seen a grown man cry?

roles that offer extensions of our beliefs and life-styles. This is equally true for the tattered pair of blue jeans and the mink coat.

As you think back over all you've read in *Mediamerica*, a second table might come to mind.

	Form	Content
Print media	Layout, headlines, photographs	Meaning of story
Radio music formats	Playlist, beat	Lyric or meaning

DECADE.
THE TASTE THAT TOOK TEN YEARS TO MAKE.

Originally, you couldn't get real cigarette taste without what has come to be known as tobacco 'tar.'

The problem of reducing this 'tar' to 5 mg. while maintaining taste is enormous. That's why when we set out to work, we didn't give ourselves a time limit.

The "Decade Total System."

How were we able to keep the taste in a low 'tar' when so many others have failed? Mainly by developing our unique "Total System" in which every part of a Decade cigarette is arranged in perfect balance with each other.

The tobacco, the filter, and even the paper.

Only by concentrating on these parts were we able to perfect the whole.

The Tobacco. "Flavor Packing"™ plus fifteen tobaccos boost taste.

Take the tobacco, for example. Its taste is boosted by a very unique method called "Flavor Packing" which allows us to concentrate a special patented tobacco flavorant in each Decade cigarette.

The Filter. Unique "Taste Channel" gives first puff impact.

Our filtration process is also unique. Simply, we've created a "Taste Channel" within the filter to give you that first puff impact you've come to expect from only the higher 'tar' cigarettes.

The Paper. High porosity paper controls burn rate.

Even our high porosity paper is specifically designed to give an efficient burn rate that delivers optimum taste with a minimum of 'tar.'

The result. A completely new kind of low 'tar' cigarette.

So try a pack of Decade for yourself. Regular or Menthol. And after one taste we think you'll agree that our last 10 years were well worth the effort.

Only 5 mg. 'tar.'

Regular and Menthol.

Warning: The Surgeon General Has Determined That Cigarette Smoking Is Dangerous to Your Health.

© Liggett Group Inc. 1977

5 mg. "tar", 0.5 mg. nicotine ave. per cigarette by FTC method.

	Form	Content
Television sitcoms	Set, character development	Plot
Television news	The human, "friendly" news format	The facts

The table gives a few examples of the mass media march away from content and toward form. Some feel that electronic media have always been more style than substance; the trends are clear today.

Formulas for choosing news have become

JAEGER. Here today and here tomorrow.

Our wool and camel's hair coat, skirt, multi-striped sweater and scarf are classic sport clothes from Britain. For they were created for today, tomorrow and all the seasons that follow.
JAEGER® London, Paris, Rome, New York.

Jewelry: Tiffany.

818 Madison Ave., New York, The Americana Shopping Center, Manhasset, N.Y., 272 Post Street, San Francisco, Cal., The Mall at Chestnut Hill, Newton, Mass., At Phipps Plaza, Atlanta, Ga., Water Tower Pl., Chicago, Ill.

so accepted that the three networks and the nation's major daily newspapers run virtually the same stories day after day. Now we are moving from global reporting to cracker-barrel consciousness. News is when someone makes no news. Charles Kuralt leads the way (see 15.15). When Kuralt gives us the "human side," he creates the non-newsmaker, and makes the average extraordinary.

We are entering an era when "human inter-est" stories will completely dominate the news landscape. As we become masters of our own

Charles Kuralt has pioneered a field of network television journalism in which he is still alone. His special kind of investigative reporting focuses on quality of life in the countryside, on creeds and customs, crafts and pastimes—and on places that produce much salt of the earth.

Kuralt brings a warm eye to the small event, and a good ear to the small talk of Main Street and country lanes. While earthquakes, bombings, and daily crises command the big headlines, Kuralt reports on sugaring-off time in the maple country, sponge-fishing in Florida, a ghost town in California, and a one-room schoolhouse in Louisiana. To prepare his report for the "CBS Evening News with Walter Cronkite," he leads a nomadic camera crew on an annual trek of some 40,000 miles.

Kuralt explores an integrity secured in lasting values. He finds half-full the glass that others find half-empty. Flag-waving is not his style; but his images of America may excite more good feeling about the country than a parade of fife and drum corps.

A national small-town paper...Mark Twain with a microphone...Currier and Ives with a camera—"On the Road with Charles Kuralt" is all of these—a unique institution.

HOW CAN HE BE SO FAMOUS WHEN HE NEVER MAKES THE FRONT PAGE?

⦿ CBS NEWS

media, we'll find that our own stories are as interesting as anyone else's. This will bring the end of the traditional newscast that concentrates on a few selected newsmakers.

We are moving away from the *what* and toward the *how*. The old expression, "What you see is what you get," is particularly apt here since what you see (at first glance or first listen) is often all there is. "I like your style" means I like you. Most media analysts find this revolting, perhaps even dangerous. But, as Wally might say, "That's the way it is!"

Are You an Orangutan?

Where do *you* fit in all this? Life in Mediamerica means taking part in the "games people play." Exploring and probing the consequences of mass communication need not be limited to a few unqualified specialists. *You* are the amateur about to embark on a lifetime journey of discovery through understanding media.

No medium can steal your soul, but it can change your vision of it. In your hands is the destiny of this incredible electronic village—a world far different from the one your parents were born into. Instant global communication has turned everything upside down, breaking old patterns, behaviors, and ideals.

The best you can hope for is a mosaic, a flexible pattern to help you comprehend what is happening. As you realize this, your special piece of the puzzle will become more meaningful. It may be helpful to listen to what Paul Simon says:

> Something tells me it's all happening at the zoo
> I do believe it
> I do believe it's true.*

He also says: "Orangutans are skeptical/Of changes in their cages." Are you an orangutan?

Queries and Concepts

1. There are dozens of specific predictions for the future in this chapter. Make a list of those you vehemently disagree with. Discuss with others.

*© 1967 Paul Simon. Used by permission.

2. Reread the section "Are You an Orangutan?" Write a one-page paper on its implications for you.

3. Make up your own table of media and related things, dividing them into form and content.

4. Does it seem to you that the overall future in our mass-mediated society is a positive one or a negative one? Why?

Readings and References

Alvin Toffler's *Future Shock* (New York: Bantam Books, 1971) still provides the best overview into the 21st century. A catalog of changes may be found in R. Buckminster Fuller's *I Seem to Be a Verb* (New York: Bantam Books, 1970). Quentin Fiore and Marshall McLuhan's *War and Peace in the Global Village* (New York: Bantam Books, 1971) and *Culture Is Our Business* (New York: Ballantine Books, 1972) explore the media's role in our changing environment. Ben H. Bagdikian's *The Information Machines: Their Impact on Men and the Media* (New York: Harper & Row, 1971) speculates on the future content of news and its consequence: the future society.

Name Index

Page numbers in italic indicate material in guest essays and numbered inserts.

Subject Index

Page numbers in italic indicate material in guest essays and numbered inserts.

BioQuest, 304–305
Birth of a Nation, 197, 201–202, 208
Blackboard Jungle, The, 125
Blacklisting, 213
Blacks in mass media
  jobs for, 296, 297
  stereotypes of, 285, 296
Blob, The, 214
"Blonde in the Bleachers," 132
Blondie, 65
"Blowin' in the Wind," 132
Bob Newhart, 147
Bonanza, 143, 154, 160, 169
Book clubs, 22
Book of World Records (Guinness), 15
Book reviews, 22
Books, 12, 15–29
  in American history, 19–22
  as arbiters of culture, 15, *16*, 24
  as business enterprise, 24–25
  censorship of, 26–29
  decline in reading of, 23–24
  early history of, 18–19
  films made from, 22
  instant, 22
  linear form of, 16–17
  paperback, 21–22
  and television, 10
"Born to Be Wild," 217
Boston Globe, 37
Bowling Green State University, 274–75
Brenda Starr, 65
Broadcasting, 110
Broadcasting Yearbook, 118
Broadcast Music, Incorporated (BMI), 124
Bronze Thrills, 87
Broom Hilda, 65
Buddy Holly Story, The, 197

California Split, 218
Calling All Cars, 98
Candy, 28
Cannon, 150
Canterbury Tales, 7, 19
Captain Kangaroo, 176, *177*
Captain Video, 176
Carefree, 205
Carnegie Commission on Educational Television, 191–92

Carol Burnett, 158
Cartoons on television, 176. *See also* Comic strips
Car Wash, 296
Casablanca, 212
Cashbox, 134
CBS Morning News, 170
Censorship
  of books, 26–29
  and film ratings, 222–23
  of newspapers, 50
  and radio, 114–16, 223
  selection vs. suppression of news, 234
  and television networks, 157–58, 159, 160, 163, 222–23
Channel capacity, 7
Charlie's Angels, 148, 149, 182
Chico and the Man, 289
Children and television
  sex role stereotypes, 294–95
  shows for, 176–77
  and violence, 6, 290–93
Children's Digest, 83
Citizen Kane, 44–45, 197, 208–12, 218, 220
Civilisation, 182
Cleopatra, 202
Close Encounters of the Third Kind, 22
Collier's, 75, 76
Columbia Broadcasting System, *96*, 98, 99–100, *142*, 143, 157–58, 252
Columbia Journalism Review, 56
Columbo, 149, 150, 162
"Come Monday," 132
Comic strips, 43, 64–67. *See also* Cartoons on television
Communication
  defined, 3–5
  form and content in, 4, 5, 6
  Shannon/Weaver model of, 4–6
  See also Mass communication
Communications Act of 1934, *96*, 115, 116, 242
Communicology, 11
Compressed Air, 87
Computers, 305
  use of, in printing, 19
Concentration, 173
"Convoy," *97*, 133

Cool Million, 155
Cosmopolitan, 74, 75, 76
Country and western music. *See* Music
Culture, popular, 13, 228
  academic study of, 274–75
  artifacts in, 274, 276, 279, 283
  cults in, 280–82
  defined, 274–75
  dilemma of, 282–83
  and elite culture, 25, 274, 276, 279
  icons in, 274, 276–79, 283
  as invisible environment, 274, 282–83
  and mass communication, 275–76, 282–83
  and sports, 279–80

"Dangling Conversation," 131
"Daniel and the Sacred Harp," 132
Decoding in communication, 5, 6
Deep Throat, 197
Department of Justice, 245
Dick Tracy, 65
Disc jockeys, 101–104, 231
Disco music. *See* Music
Dixie Dugan, 65
Donald Duck, 65
Don Kirshner's Rock Concert, 158
Donny and Marie, 158
"Don't Be Cruel," 125
Doonesbury, 55, 65, 66–67, 195
Dragnet, 149
Dr. Kildare, 155
Dr. Strangelove, 216

Earthquake, 197, 217, 311
East of Eden, 214
East Village Other, 46
Easy Rider, 197, 217
Ebony, 83
Ecology, 263, 302
Edge of Night, The, 170
Editor and Publisher, 52
Editorials, broadcast, 242–43
8½, 220
Electric Company, The, 183
Ellery Queen, 98
Employment, equal opportunity in, 297

Mass communication (continued)
  effects of, 180, 282–83, 289–96
  as field of study, 11–13, 228
  form and content in, 8–9, 47,
    312–17
  future of, 13, 300–19
  icons and artifacts in, 276
  media between receiver and
    source in, 5–6
  mediated experiences in,
    178–80
  personal awareness of, 282–83,
    318–19
  and popular culture, 275–76,
    282–83
  research
    causal inferences in, 287–89
    as human learning, 285–86
    procedures and problems in,
      286–89
    on sex role stereotypes,
      293–96
    and social sciences, 286
    on television violence,
      289–93
    types of, 285
  and society, 262–63
  See also Advertising; Culture,
    popular; Films; Mass media;
    Music; Newspapers; Radio;
    Television
Mass media
  cults in, 280–82
  defined, 5–6
  effects of, 282–83
  encoding and decoding in, 5–6
  form and content in, 4, 5, 6,
    8–9, 198, 253–54, 257,
    261–62, 312–17
  future technology of, 305–12
  McLuhan on, 8–9
  ownership consolidation of,
    243–45
  and politics, 266–70
  and popular culture, 275–83
  print vs. electronic, 10
  and public relations, 266
  as shaping and reflecting
    experience and values, 180,
    275–76
  and socialization, 263, 276
Match Game, 169
Maude, 146
Maverick, 140, 142, 154

"Maybe I'm Amazed," 131
"Mayflower" decision (FCC), 242
McCabe and Mrs. Miller, 218
McCall's, 76
McCloud, 98, 149, 162
McClure's, 73, 74, 75, 76, 78
McMillan and Wife, 162
Mercury Theatre of the Air, 99, 208
Merv Griffin, 175
Midnight, 61, 63
Midnight Special, The, 158
Miller v. California, 28–29
Minorities, ethnic, and mass
    media
  jobs for, 296, 297
  stereotypes about, 285, 296
Miss Peach, 65
Mod Squad, 149
Monty Python's Flying Circus,
    158–60
Moondog's Rock and Roll Party, 125
Motion Picture Association of
    America, 222–24
Motion Picture Patents
    Company, 197, 200
Motion pictures. See Films
Mr. Natural, 64
Ms., 73, 75, 77, 78
Muckrakers, new, 234
Munsey's, 73, 74, 75, 76, 78
Muzak, 108–109
Music, 12, 92, 97, 120–37
  classical, 110
  country and western, 108, 125,
    132, 133, 136
  disco, 128–29, 296
  45 rpm records, 125–26
  jazz, 109, 122–23
  making of "hits," 134–35
  in 1940s, 122–24
  radio formats for, 101, 105–10,
    314
  rhythm and blues, 125, 137
  rock
    British influence on, 126–27
    early years of, 124–26
    and "golden oldies," 129,
      131
    maturing of, 127–28
    new wave, 129
    in 1970s, 128–30
    and popular culture, 274
    punk, 129
    on television, 158

Music (continued)
  themes in lyrics of, 130–33
  78 rpm records, 125–26
  soul, 129, 137
Mutual Broadcasting System, 98
Mystery Movies, 162

Naked Ape, The, 28
Naked City, 149
Name That Tune, 173
Nashville, 133, 197, 218–19, 220
Nashville!, 83
Nashville Skyline, 128
Nation, The, 74
National Association for Better
    Broadcasting, 290
National Association of
    Broadcasters, 189, 252
National Broadcasting Company,
    96–97, 98, 99, 142, 143, 146,
    162, 163, 237, 252
National Commission on the
    Causes and Prevention of
    Violence, 290
National Enquirer, 2, 61–63, 64, 68,
    173, 235
National Geographic, 77
National Informer, 87
National Lampoon, 85
National Tattler, The, 61
Network, 218, 219, 290
New England Courant, 36
Newhouse group of newspapers,
    45–46
New nonfiction, 54, 56
News, 10, 13, 228
  as approximation of real
    events, 33–34
  audiences for, 31–33
  criteria for, 231–35
  delayed-reward, 232
  as entertainment, 64
  form and content in, 315–17
  "happy news," 241–42
  hard, 31, 231–32
  human interest stories as, 31,
    40, 61–62, 233, 316–17
  immediate-reward, 232
  and layout of newspaper,
    235–36
  media competition and
    symbiosis in presenting, 35,
    38

To the reader:

I'm sure you know by now that *Mediamerica* is somewhat different from most other textbooks you may have read. I have tried everything possible to make this text a positive communication experience for you. Yet communication cannot exist in a vacuum. It is only with the help of your input that I can make *Mediamerica* a better book for future readers. With that in mind, would you take a moment to fill out this postage-free questionnaire and mail it back to me? I'll look forward to hearing from you and to incorporating your suggestions into future editions of *Mediamerica*. Thank you!

School_____ Instructor's Name _____

Course Title and Number _____

1. What features did you like *most* about *Mediamerica?* _____

_____

2. What features did you like *least* about *Mediamerica?* _____

_____

3. What were the subjects you would like to have read more about? _____

_____

4. What were the subjects or sections, if any, you would like to see omitted? Why? _____

_____

5. Were there any portions of the book you found difficult to understand? If so, which ones? _____

_____

6. Were there any chapters or sections of the book you were not assigned to read? If so, which ones?____

_____

7. Were you able to use the recommended readings at the end of the chapter?_____

_____

8. How did you feel about the cartoons and graphics in the book? _____

_____

9. How does *Mediamerica* compare with other college textbooks you have read?_____

_____

10. Any other comments or suggestions?

CUT PAGE OUT

Optional:

Your name _____ Date _____

May Wadsworth quote you, whether in promotion for *Mediamerica* or in future publishing ventures?

Yes _____ No _____

Thanks again for taking the time to help.

FOLD HERE

_____

FOLD HERE

_____

**FIRST CLASS
PERMIT NO. 34
BELMONT, CA**

BUSINESS REPLY MAIL
No Postage Necessary if Mailed in United States

Dr. Edward Jay Whetmore

Wadsworth Publishing Co. Inc.
10 Davis Drive
Belmont, CA 94002

CUT PAGE OUT